Information Security: Principles and New Concepts
Volume I

Information Security:
Principles and New Concepts
Volume I

Edited by **Fiona Hobbs**

LANRYE
INTERNATIONAL

New Jersey

Published by Clanrye International,
55 Van Reypen Street,
Jersey City, NJ 07306, USA
www.clanryeinternational.com

Information Security: Principles and New Concepts
Volume I
Edited by Fiona Hobbs

International Standard Book Number: 978-1-63240-306-3 (Hardback)

Printed in the United States of America.

Contents

Preface

In contemporary times, there is no dearth of information. In fact, since the advent of technology and the World Wide Web, there has been an overload of information. All data needs to be recorded, saved and stored. However, some information is more crucial as compared to others. And this is where the concept of Information Security comes in. The origins of Information Security can be traced to the times of Julius Caesar in 50 B.C, when he invented the Caesar cipher. This mechanism was used to protect the confidentiality of correspondence and provided a means of detecting tampering, in case any. Regardless of the form that the data may take, electronic or physical, Information Security is a must in present times.

Information Security has grown and evolved significantly in recent years. Numerous occurrences of international terrorism, through disruption of data fuelled the need for better methods of Information Security. Today, it is an indispensable part of all the business operations across different domains. Protecting information has also become an ethical and legal requirement in many cases. Essentially, the practice of defending information from unauthorized access, use, disclosure and destruction is referred to as Information Security. The CIA triad of confidentiality, integrity and availability is one of the core principles of information security.

There are two important aspects to Information Security. These are Information Technology Security, which is concerned with technology security and Information Assurance, whose aim is to ensure that data is not lost during critical times.

I would like to thank all the contributors who have shared their knowledge in this book. I would also like to thank my family for their constant trust and support.

Editor

ISO/IEC 27000, 27001 and 27002 for Information Security Management

Georg Disterer

Department of Business Administration and Computer Science, University of Applied Sciences and Arts, Hannover, Germany

ABSTRACT

With the increasing significance of information technology, there is an urgent need for adequate measures of information security. Systematic information security management is one of most important initiatives for IT management. At least since reports about privacy and security breaches, fraudulent accounting practices, and attacks on IT systems appeared in public, organizations have recognized their responsibilities to safeguard physical and information assets. Security standards can be used as guideline or framework to develop and maintain an adequate information security management system (ISMS). The standards ISO/IEC 27000, 27001 and 27002 are international standards that are receiving growing recognition and adoption. They are referred to as "common language of organizations around the world" for information security [1]. With ISO/IEC 27001 companies can have their ISMS certified by a third-party organization and thus show their customers evidence of their security measures.

Keywords: Security; Standards; ISO/IEC 27000; ISO 27001; ISO 27002; ISO 27 K

1. Introduction

Information and information systems are an important foundation for companies. In particular more and more internal and inter-company data transfer and utilization of open networks increase the risks that information and information systems are exposed to. In order to reduce risks and avoid damages to companies care must be taken to assure adequate information security [2]. For the protection of the information and information systems the standards ISO 27000, ISO 27001 and ISO 27002 provide control objectives, specific controls, requirements and guidelines, with which the company can achieve adequate information security. In doing so ISO 27001 enables the company to be certified against the standard, whereby information security can be documented as being rigorously applied and managed in accordance with an internationally recognized organizational standard.

With a certification against ISO 27001 a company verifies the fulfillment of well-known and accepted security standards and thus promotes customers' trust. Likewise a verification of compliance with an international standard reduces the risk of fines or compensation payments as a result of legal disputes, since legal requirements such as provisioning according to "state-of-the-art" and with "due care and diligence" can be countered with standards compliance [3]. We present the ISO 27000 to ISO 27002 standards, their development and actual dissemination, and the ISO 27 K family of standards.

2. International Standards

Standards arise through the development of detailed descriptions of particular characteristics of a product or service by experts from companies and scientific institutions. They represent a consensus on characteristics such as quality, security and reliability that should remain applicable for an extended period of time and thus are documented and published. The objective of the development of standards is to support both individuals and companies when procuring products and services. Providers of products and services can boost their reputation by having certified their compliance with standards.

ISO is an organization founded in 1946 and supported by 159 countries; ISO is the leading issuing body for international standards. The standards ISO 27000 to ISO 27002 were developed in cooperation with the "International Electrotechnical Commission" (IEC), which is a leading global issuer of international standards in the electronics and electronic-related technologies sector.

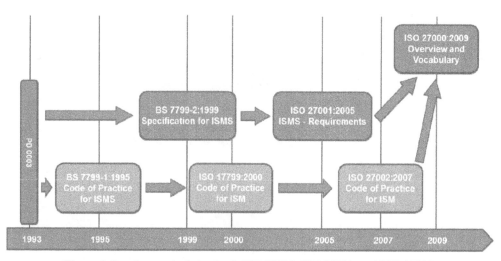

Figure 1. Development of standards ISO 27000, ISO 27001, and ISO 27002.

3. Development and Dissemination of ISO 27000 to ISO 27002 Standards

3.1. Development of Standards

The existence of the ISO 27000 to ISO 27002 standards can be traced back to 1993 (**Figure 1**), whereby a British professional association, the National Computing Centre (NCC), published a document titled "PD 0003 A Code of Practice for Information Security Management". The British Standards Institute (BSI) adopted this and issued "BS 7799-1 IT—Security techniques—Code of practice for information security management" as national standard in 1995.

The complementary part "BS 7799-2 Information security management systems—Specification with guidance for use" enables companies to certificate their processes. ISO harmonized this standard with others like ISO 9001 and developed the ISO 27001 in October 2005. Since then, companies can certify their processes according to this international standard.

ISO 27001 formed the foundation for the ISO 27 K family of standards, which encompass various standards for information security. In 2007 the old ISO 17799 standard was assigned to the ISO 27 K family as ISO 27002. In 2009 ISO 27000 was issued to provide an overview, introduction and explanation of terminology with the title "IT—Security techniques—Information security management systems—Overview and Vocabulary".

3.2. Current Dissemination of ISO 27001 Certification

At the end of year 2010 worldwide 15.625 certificates according to ISO 27001 are valid [4], more recent and reliable information do not exist. **Figure 2** shows the development from 2006 to 2010 and the large increase in the dissemination. With the high number of certificates in 2006 it should be noted that organizations that held certificates according to prior standards were able to convert these to ISO 27001 in a simplified process.

All our figures show the number of certificates according to ISO 27001, not the number of certified organizations. The number of organizations holding certificates cannot be given, because some organizations do have several certificates, e.g. for several sites or groups, other organizations do have one certificates for several sites.

The distribution of the certificates issued per region is shown in **Figure 3**. Alone 6.264 certificates were registered in Japan caused by local national legislations in Japan that often require the submission of proof or verification of security management conformance with standards. Furthermore, the surprisingly high number of certificates in Asia aside from Japan can be explained in part as follows: One objective of companies in Europe and North America is cost reduction through outsourcing of IT services. IT providers in Asia strive to achieve this objective primarily through the utilization of lower personnel costs. However, these providers are largely unknown in Europe and North America and have neither image nor reputation. Managers who are heading to outsource some of their IT activities need confidence in the reliability and professionalism of Asian IT providers. Normally they try to secure this by detailed and costly contracts and agreements, verifications, assessments, and reviews [5].

Independent attestations of the providers can be supportive and reinforcing. With a certificate according to ISO 27001 IT providers can thus document the conformity of their security processes with a recognized standard. The certificate serves as verification from an independent body and provides sureness about appropriate security measures; it serves as quality seal increasing the

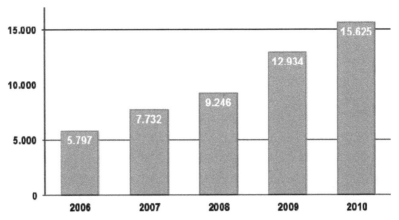

Figure 2. Number of certificates accord. ISO 27001 [4].

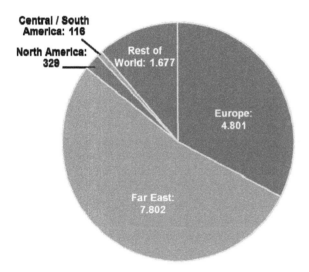

Figure 3. Number of certificates accord. ISO 27001 by regions [4].

Table 1. Number of certificates [4].

Top Countries in 2010	
Japan	6.264
India	1.281
United Kingdom	1.157
Taipei	1.028
China	957
Spain	711
Czech Republic	529
Italy	374
Germany	357
Romania	350

competitiveness of an IT provider [6].

The low number of 329 certificates registered in North America confirms the common assumption that international IT standards do not currently draw much attention there [7]. In Europe ISO 27001 has been widely disseminated, many European countries are in the list given in **Table 1**. The high number of certificates in the UK can also be explained by the fact that a British standard was the basis for the international ISO 27001 standard and so there is a longer tradition of certification according to security standards.

4. ISO 27000

The ISO 27000 standard was issued in 2009 to provide an overview for the ISO 27 K family of standards and a common conceptual foundation [8]. 46 basic information security terms are defined and differentiated in the "Terms and conditions" section. The meaning of information security and systematic engagement with security

aspects is derived from the risk for companies whose business processes are increasingly dependent on information processing and whose complex and interlinked IT infrastructures are vulnerable to failures and disruptions. As with other IT standards, the ISO 27 K family of standards refer directly to the "Plan-Do-Check-Act" (PDCA cycle) cycle—well known from Deming's classic quality management (**Figure 4**), which emphasizes the necessity of process orientation as well as integration of the planning of operations and the constant checking of planing-compliant implementation [6].

In the planning phase for an ISMS the requirements for protection of the information and the information systems will be defined, risks identified and evaluated, and suitable procedures and measures for reducing risks developed. These procedures and measures will be implemented during implementation and operations. The reports generated through continuous monitoring of operations will be used to derive improvements and for further development of the ISMS.

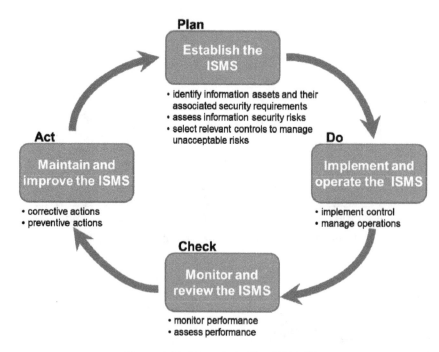

Figure 4. PDCA cycle in ISO 27000 [9].

5. ISO 27001

5.1. Content

The ISO 27001 standard was published in 2005 under the title "Information technology—Security techniques—Information security management systems—Requirements". In 42 pages it describes the requirements that an ISMS must fulfill in order to achieve certification. As a framework, the standard is aimed at companies from all sectors and of all sizes. However, there is some doubt over the suitability for SMEs [10]. Concrete measures for the fulfillment of requirements are not be stipulated by the standard but rather must be developed and implemented on a company-specific basis. Certification requirements of ISO 27001 are elucidated through the elaboration of terms and concepts and supplemented with a implementation guideline within ISO 27002.

The focal point of ISO 27001 is the requirement for planning, implementation, operation and continuous monitoring and improving of a process-oriented ISMS. The approach should be aligned with the PDCA cycle (**Figure 4**). The coverage and scope of an ISMS should be defined for planning and implementation. Risks should be identified and assessed [8] and control objectives should be defined for the information and information systems. Suitable measures for protecting operations should be derived from these. In annex A of the standard a total of 39 control objectives and 134 measures for security management are listed and thus expressly stipulated. The control objectives are listed in **Table 2**, subdivided by domains. These are described further and de-

tailed in the ISO 27002 standard [11].

Adequate training should be developed for the implementation in order to push though the stipulated procedures and to establish them, and to generate awareness of their necessity [8]. The compliance with the procedures must be continuously monitored. The measures should be checked and improved in the course of continuous improvement and security risks should be identified and assessed in order to continuously increase the effectiveness and efficiency of the ISMS [8].

Requirements, which are to be applied to the ISMS documentation, are described in the standard through the stipulation of essential content, necessary documents as well as specifications and monitoring structures for document management, such as:

- Change and approvals processes
- Version control
- Rules for access rights and access protection
- Specifications for filing systems [8]

Responsibilities of top management in all phases of the PDCA cycle are listed [8]. They encompass determination and implementation of a security policy, the definition of roles and responsibilities, the recruitment and preparation of necessary personnel and material resources as well as decisions on risks management.

The improvement and further development of the ISMS is to be implemented continuously, based on the security policy, the logging and evaluation of operations, the results of testing as well as the results from improvement measures. In addition the improvement and further development should be pushed forward through

Table 2. ISO 27001 control objectives [8].

Domain	Control objectives
Security policy	To provide management direction and support for information security in accordance with business requirements and relevant laws and regulations.
Organization of information security	To manage information security within the organization.
	To maintain the security of the organization's information and information processing facilities that are accessed, processed, communicated to, or managed by external parties.
Asset management	To achieve and maintain appropriate protection of organizational assets.
	To ensure that information receives an appropriate level of protection.
Human resources security	To ensure that employees, contractors and third party users understand their responsibilities, and are suitable for the roles they are considered for, and to reduce the risk of theft, fraud or misuse of facilities.
	To ensure that all employees, contractors and third party users are aware of information security threats and concerns, their responsibilities and liabilities, and are equipped to support organizational security policy in the course of their normal work, and to reduce the risk of human error.
	To ensure that employees, contractors and third party users exit an organization or change employment in an orderly manner.
Physical and environmental security	To prevent unauthorized physical access, damage and interference to organization's premises and information.
	To prevent loss, damage, theft or compromise of assets and interruption to the organization's activities.
Communications and operations management	To ensure the correct and secure operation of information processing facilities.
	To implement and maintain the appropriate level of information security and service delivery in line with third party service delivery agreements.
	To minimize the risk of systems failures.
	To protect the integrity of software and information.
	To maintain the integrity and availability of information and information processing facilities.
	To ensure the protection of information in networks and the protection of the supporting infrastructure.
	To prevent unauthorized disclosure, modification, removal or destruction of assets, and interruption to business activities.
	To maintain security of information and software exchanged within an organization and with external entities.
	To ensure the security of electronic commerce services, and their secure use.
	To detect unauthorized information processing activities.
Access control	To control access to information.
	To ensure authorized user access and to prevent unauthorized access to information systems.
	To prevent unauthorized user access, compromise or theft of information and information processing facilities.
	To prevent unauthorized access to networked services.
	To prevent unauthorized access to operating systems.
	To prevent unauthorized access to information held in application systems.
	To ensure information security when using mobile computing and teleworking facilities.
Information systems acquisition, development and maintenance	To ensure that security is an integral part of information systems.
	To prevent errors, loss, unauthorized modification or misuse of information in applications.
	To protect the confidentiality, authenticity or integrity of information by cryptographic means.
	To ensure the security of system files.
	To maintain the security of application system software and information.
	To reduce risks resulting from exploitation of published technical vulnerabilities.
Information security incident management	To ensure information security events and weaknesses associated with information systems are communicated in a manner allowing timely corrective action to be taken.
	To ensure a consistent and effective approach is applied to the management of information security incidents.
Business continuity management	To counteract interruptions to business activities and to protect critical business processes from the effects of major failures of information systems or disasters and to ensure their timely resumption.
Compliance	To avoid breaches of any law, statutory, regulatory or contractual obligations, and of any security requirements.
	To ensure compliance of systems with organizational security policies and standards.
	To maximize the effectiveness of and to minimize interference to/from the information systems audit process.

regular internal audits. Adequate implementation of the security policy as well as its suitability and completeness [8] are to be assured through annually management reviews.

5.2. Certification Process

To verify the compliance of the ISMS with ISO 27001 a company has to pass a certification procedure steered by an authorized certification organization (Registered Certification Bodies RCB), ISO provides a list of RCBs. The company initiates the procedure by selecting an RCB. In a preliminary examination with the support of the RCS a determination can be made to ascertain the extent to which there already is conformity according the standard and which needs for actions still exist for successful certification. Correspondingly, the measures necessary for ISMS conformity should be carried out in a preparation project. Appropriate knowledge and experience with certification processes as well as special expertise in information security is necessary for this and should be obtained by calling in external experts if required.

In the first instance the examination for certification (audit) comprises of a check of all documents (security policy, process descriptions, etc.) by the RCB, therefor the documents are to be sent to the certificating organization. Checking the documentation serves as a preparation for the main audit, where representatives of the certification organization carry out a detailed examination during an on-site visit lasting several days. This will include interviews being conducted with all responsible persons whereby they will explain their understanding of the security policy, describe processes, present details and features on a random basis, explain process documentation as well as discuss known weaknesses and improvement measures initiated.

Then the certification organization will generate a report in which the audit results are explained and improvement measures to be implemented necessarily before the next audit are listed. In case of a positive overall result the company receives the official certificate to attest the ISMS conformity with the requirements of ISO 27001.

The implementation of an appropriate ISMS can take a few months to some years, depending largely on the maturity of IT security management within an organization. When processes according framework like COBIT, ISO 20000, or ITIL are already established, time and costs of implementation will be lower. The process of certification will take a few months additionally [12].

The certificate has validity for 3 years; after this a re-certification can be applied for generally requiring less effort than the initial certification. The continuous observance of the requirements of standard ISO 27001 and continuous improvement of the ISMS is assured through annual monitoring audits. These audits are carried out by auditors from the RCB, whereby the first monitoring audit must take place before 12 months have passed since issuing the certificate. If serious deviations from the requirements of the standard should be discovered during a monitoring audit then the RCB can suspend or even withdraw the certificate until the deviations are rectified.

Some national alternatives exist. For German companies the federal office for information security (BSI) offers since 1994 a procedural guideline—so-called "IT-Grundschutz"—to support authorities and companies regarding security. In 2006 this specifications were been revised based on ISO 27001 and the concordance between "IT-Grundschutz" of BSI and the ISO 27001 standard was verified officially. Since 2006 BSI assigns this "ISO 27001 certification based on IT-Grundschutz" with which both the conformity with ISO 27001 and an assessment of the IT security measures against IT-Grundschutz catalogues are certified.

6. ISO 27002

The codified requirements in ISO 27001 are expanded and explained in ISO 27002 in the form of a guideline. The manual was first issued in the year 2000—at that time with the designation "ISO 17799", under the title "Information technology—Security techniques—Code of practice for information security management". In 2007 this was revised and aligned to the 27 K family of standards and the designation was changed to ISO 27002. With the development of ISO 27002 common practices—often also known as best practices—were offered as procedures and methods proven in practice, which could be adapted to the specific requirements within companies. In order to explain the importance of information security for companies, risks for the information security of a company and the necessity to have targeted and agreed measures ("controls") within the framework of an ISMS [11] are set out. Necessary steps for identification and evaluation of security risks are described in order to ascertain the requirement to protect information and information systems [11]. The continuing development of ISO 27002 is based on the presentation of ISO 27001, whereby the 39 control objectives listed in the annex to ISO 27001 (**Table 2**) are explained in more detail. A total of 134 measures, which are justified and described in detail, are assigned to these objectives [11].

The fundamental guidelines for ensure information security are to be defined and specified in the form of security policies by the management of the company. The distribution and enforcement of these policies within the company also serves to emphasize the importance of information security and the management attention for this topics. The information security must be organizationally anchored in the company so that the measures for information security can be efficiently promoted and established. So roles and responsibilities are to be defined and in particular duties for maintaining confidentiality and rules for the communications with external parties (customer, suppliers, authorities etc.) are to be specified. All tangible and intangible assets that are to be protected by the measures for information security are to be identified and classified in order to draw up specific responsibilities and handling rules.

Security risks are also caused by vulnerabilities of the IT systems. Here it must be assumed that more than half of all attacks are initiated by internal personnel—however a large proportion will also be initiated by joint actions from internal and external personnel [13]. Because internal personnel can use insider knowledge (on internal processes, habits, weak points, social relations etc.) for attacks they should be considered to have a higher potential for success and damage [14]. Corresponding risks must be taken into account with personnel measures such as recruiting, decruiting and allocating. So, for example, the access rights for a user must be restricted to the extent necessary to carry out the work that the user is assigned to. With changes in responsibilities, duties or jobs the access rights should be adapted accordingly and if personnel are laid off then the access rights should be revoked promptly.

Physical security measures should be provided to protect the infrastructure from unauthorized entry, access, theft, damage and destruction. To ensure proper and correct operation of the IT systems the ideal routine operations should be documented in a manual (standard operating procedures). Likewise, processes and procedures for exceptional circumstances, delays, outages, faults or catastrophic events should be specified and documented. Technical or organizational changes should be checked for potential effects on the operations of the IT systems before being implemented. Likewise security incidents should be documented, analyzed and evaluated for possible or essential improvements to the security system. Lastly, suitable measures must be implemented to fulfill compliance requirements. In particular copyrights and exploitation rights, requirements for data security and data protection are cited in the standard—these must be regulated and assured in a verifiable manner.

7. Further Standards in the ISO 27 K Family

The 27 K family of standards (also designated as "ISO 27 K" or "ISO 27000 series") is managed under the title: "Information technology—Security techniques" and describes the requirements for an information security management system (ISMS) as well as for certifications

in a comprehensive and detailed manner [9]. The family of standards represents a collection of both new and already well-known standards, which have been reworked and revised to bring them up to date and also to harmonize their content and format. With this collection ISO follows the objective of having cohesive standards in the area of information security as well as a compatibility with the various standards. This achieves the goal of offering comprehensive support to companies of all sizes, sector and types in ensuring information security [9]. The publishing of the 27 K family of standards is not completed or closed at this point in time—many standards are in the drafting or development stage, further supplements will follow. **Table 3** shows the current status as well as the immediate planning.

Figure 5 shows the interrelations of the standards in the 27 K family, separated into requirements and guidelines. ISO 27001 contains requirements that must be verified for certification according to this standard. ISO 27006 contains the requirements that must be fulfilled in order to be accredited as a certification organization. All further standards can be considered as guidelines for different domains to ensure information security.

8. Summary

Information and information systems are exposed to risks more and more through the increasing support to business processes provided by information technology as well as the increased level of networking within companies and with external parties. An effective ISMS helps to reduce risks and to prevent security breaches.

The ISO 27000, 27001 and 27002 standards form a framework to design and operate an ISMS, based on long lasting experiences of development. With this companies are offered the opportunity to align their IT procedures and methods for ensuring an adequate level of information security with an international standard.

Certification of an ISMS according to ISO 27001 also projects a positive image through the verification of a systematic management of information security. This standard is also called upon in legal rulings as a yardstick and a basis for assessment on the subject of information security—here a certificate according to ISO 27001 proves a "provision of state-of the-art services" regarding information security. Organizations can demonstrate that they are "fit-enough" to provide IT services in a secure way [1]. With the certificate a verification of compliance with respect to information security can be rendered.

The ISO 27000, 27001 and 27002 standards have been widely disseminated in Europe and Asia. The significance of a certification of compliant information security with procurement decisions for IT services will increase and so a further increase in the number of certifications

Table 3. The ISO 27 K family of standards [15].

ISO-Norm	Title	Status
ISO 27000	Information security management systems—Overview and vocabulary	published 2009
ISO 27001	Information security management systems—Requirements	published 2005
ISO 27002	Code of practice for information security management	published 2007
ISO 27003	Information security management system implementation guidance	published 2010
ISO 27004	Information security management—Measurement	published 2009
ISO 27005	Information security risk management	published 2011
ISO 27006	Requirements for bodies providing audit and certification of ISMSs	published 2011
ISO 27007	Guidelines for ISMS auditing	published 2011
ISO 27008	Guidelines for auditors on ISMS controls	published 2011
ISO 27010	ISMSs for inter-sector and inter-organizational communications	published 2012
ISO 27011	Information security management guidelines for telecommunications organizations based on ISO/IEC 27002	published 2008
ISO 27013	Guidance on the integrated implementation of ISO/IEC 20000-1 and ISO/IEC 27001	under development
ISO 27014	Proposal on an information security governance (ISG) framework	under development
ISO 27016	Information security management—Organizational economics	under development
ISO 27017	Guidelines on information security controls for use of cloud computing	under development
ISO 27018	Code of practice for data protection controls for public cloud computing	under development
ISO 27031	Guidelines for ICT readiness for business continuity	under development
ISO 27032	Guidelines for cyber security	under development
ISO 27033-1	Network security—Part 1: Overview and concepts	published 2009
ISO 27033-2	Network security—Part 2: Guidelines for the design and implementation	published 2012
ISO 27033-3	Network security—Part 3: Reference networking scenarios	published 2010
ISO 27033-4	Network security—Part 4: Securing communications between networks	under development
ISO 27033-5	Network security—Part 5: Securing communications across networks using VPNs	under development
ISO 27033-6	Network security—Part 6: Securing IP network access using wireless	under development
ISO 27034-1	Application security—Part 1: Overview and concepts	published 2011
ISO 27034-2	Application security—Part 2: Organization normative framework	under development
ISO 27034-3	Application security—Part 3: Application security management process	under development
ISO 27034-4	Application security—Part 4: Application security validation	under development
ISO 27034-5	Application security—Part 5: Application security controls data structure	under development
ISO 27035	Information security incident management	under development
ISO 27036	Information security for supplier relationships	under development
ISO 27037	Guidelines for identification, collection and/or acquisition and preservation of digital evidence	under development
ISO 27038	Specification for digital redaction	under development
ISO 27039	Selection, deployment and operations of intrusion detection systems	under development
ISO 27040	Storage security	under development
ISO 27041	Guidance on assuring suitability and adequacy of investigation methods	under development
ISO 27042	Guidelines for the analysis and interpretation of digital evidence	under development
ISO 27043	Investigation principles and processes	under development

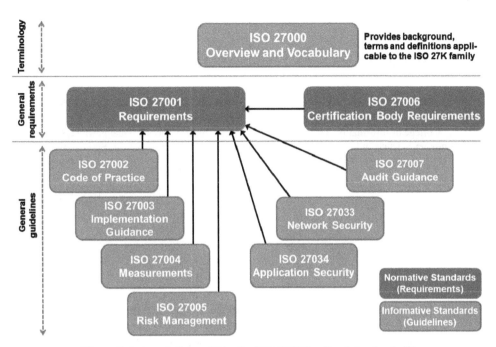

Figure 5. Interrelations within the ISO 27 K family of standards [9].

according to ISO 27001 is also to be expected.

REFERENCES

[1] E. Humphreys, "Information Security Management System Standards," *Datenschutz und Datensicherheit*, Vol. 35, No. 1, 2011, pp. 7-11.

[2] BSI, "IT-Sicherheitsmanagement und IT-Grundschutz, BSI-Standards zur IT-Sicherheit," Köln, 2005.

[3] C. Pelnekar, "Planning for and Implementing ISO 27001," *ISACA Journal*, Vol. 4, No. 4, 2011, pp. 1-8.

[4] ISO/Nielsen, "The ISO Survey of Certifications," International Organization for Standardization ISO, Geneve, 2011.

[5] Deloitte, "Financial Services Global Security Study," Deloitte, London, 2010.

[6] G. Disterer, "Zertifizierung der IT Nach ISO 20000," *Wirtschaftsinformatik*, Vol. 51, No. 6, 2009, pp. 530-534.

[7] M. Winniford, S. Conger and L. Erickson-Harris, "Confusion in the Ranks," *Information Systems Management*, Vol. 26, No. 2, 2009, pp. 153-163.

[8] ISO 27001, "Information Technology, Security Techniques, Information Security Management Systems, Requirements," International Organization for Standardization ISO, Geneve, 2005.

[9] ISO 27000, "Information Technology, Security Techniques, Information Security Management Systems, Overview and Vocabulary," International Organization for Standardization ISO, Geneve, 2009.

[10] Y. Barlette and V. Fomin, "Exploring the suitability of IS Security Management Standards for SMEs," In: R. H. Sprague, Ed., *Proceeding of 41st Hawaii International Conference on System Sciences (HICSS)*, Los Alamitos, 2008, pp. 308- 317.

[11] ISO 27002, "Information Technology, Security Techniques, Code of Practice for Information Security Management," International Organization for Standardization ISO, Geneve, 2005.

[12] A. Teubner and T. Feller, "Informationstechnologie, Governance und Compliance," *Wirtschaftsinformatik*, Vol. 50, No. 5, 2008, pp. 400-407.

[13] R. Richardson, "CSI Computer Crime and Security Survey," Computer Security Institute and Federal Bureau of Investigation, Washington, 2008.

[14] J. D'Arcy and A. Hovav, "Deterring internal information systems misuse," *Communications of the ACM*, Vol. 50, No. 10, 2007, pp. 113-117.

[15] "ISO IT Security Techniques," 8 August 2012. www.iso.org

Diffusion Analysis of Message Expansion in STITCH-256

Norziana Jamil[1,2], Ramlan Mahmod[2], Muhammad Reza Z'aba[3], Nur Izura Udzir[2], Zuriati Ahmad Zukarnain[2]

[1]College of Information Technology, Universiti Tenaga Nasional, Kajang, Malaysia
[2]Faculty of Computer Science and Information Technology, Universiti Putra Malaysia, Seri Kembangan, Malaysia
[3]Cryptography Lab, MIMOS Berhad, Technology Park Malaysia, Bukit Jalil, Malaysia

ABSTRACT

Cryptographic hash functions are built up from individual components, namely pre-processing, step transformation, and final processing. Some of the hash functions, such as SHA-256 and STITCH-256, employ non-linear message expansion in their pre-processing stage. However, STITCH-256 was claimed to produce high diffusion in its message expansion. In a cryptographic algorithm, high diffusion is desirable as it helps prevent an attacker finding collision-producing differences, which would allow one to find collisions of the whole function without resorting to a brute force search. In this paper, we analyzed the diffusion property of message expansion of STITCH-256 by observing the effect of a single bit difference over the output bits, and compare the result with that of SHA-256. We repeated the same procedure in 3 experiments of different round. The results from the experiments showed that the minimal weight in the message expansion of STITCH-256 is very much lower than that in the message expansion of SHA-256, *i.e.* message expansion of STITCH-256 produce high diffusion. Significantly, we showed that the probability to construct differential characteristic in the message expansion of STITCH-256 is reduced.

Keywords: STITCH-256; Message Expansion; Diffusion; Hash Function

1. Introduction

Recent advances in the cryptanalysis of hash functions [1-12], to name a few, have led to the unexpected failure of some popular algorithms, such as MD4, MD5, SHA-0, SHA-1, HAVAL-128, and RIPEMD. From this cryptanalysis, we understand that these broken hash functions can have two distinct messages yielding the same hash value, known as a collision. The new cryptanalysis techniques introduced by Wang *et al.* [13-16] provided this breakthrough in cryptography, finding collisions for MD4, MD5, SHA-0, SHA-1, HAVAL-128, and RIPEMD. It was found that the most successful attack on these hash functions is a differential attack, whereby a difference in the messages leads to zero difference in the output of the hash function. In other words, the collision is obtained by constructing a collision path, or characteristic, that fulfills certain conditions with respect to the message differences. In SHA-0, SHA-1, and the MD-family of hash functions, a message with a small difference in the expanded keys is first obtained. This is then used to construct a collision path in the step transformation. This paper focuses only on the first part, which is the message expansion.

Briefly, message expansion in the SHA-family is performed by recursive expansion. In SHA-1, for example, the message expansion accepts a 512-bit input that is divided into sixteen 32-bit words $W_0, \cdots, W_{15}$. Sixty-four additional expanded message words are generated as follows:

$$W_i = \left(W_{i-3} \oplus W_{i-8} \oplus W_{i-14} \oplus W_{i-16}\right) ROTL^1$$

for $i = 16, \cdots, 79$.

Message expansion in SHA-1 differs from that of SHA-0 only in the rotation of one bit to the left. The 80 words can be considered to constitute a linear code over F_2. Due to the quasi-cyclic nature of message expansion in SHA-0 and SHA-1, the full collision path can easily be constructed, as in the attack by Wang *et al.* This can be seen, for example, in SHA-0 message expansion, where differential characteristics with a probability of 1 can easily be constructed in the first 16 steps, as a single bit difference affects fewer than 28 bits in the output. In SHA-1, the code gives a minimum weight of no more than 44 for the full rounds. These traits were exploited by Wang *et al.* in order to find a collision path for the whole hash function with a complexity of 2^{69} hash operations [14].

As a consequence of the work by Wang *et al.*, the MD-family and SHA-0/1 hash functions are no longer suitable for secure communications. SHA-256 has now become the recommended hash function for many applications that require secure communication. The message expansion in SHA-256 is slightly different from its predecessors. It is the first hash function to use nonlinear modular addition in its message expansion, and successfully increases the minimum Hamming weight of the output bits from 44 (in a full round of SHA-1 message expansion) to 507 for a single-bit difference over a full round. To the best of our knowledge, no optimal lower bound on the minimum weight of the output bits has yet been found by the cryptographic community. However, it is important to have a high minimum weight for a single-bit difference over a full round of message expansion to prevent an attacker from constructing a collision path. This is because of a useful heuristic, often used in the analysis of SHA-0 and SHA-1, suggests that each weight of the output bits lowers the probability of successful collision characteristics by, on average, a factor of $2^{-2.5}$ [6].

STITCH-256 [17] is a dedicated cryptographic hash function that also employs message expansion as a source of diffusion. In this paper, we describe the message expansion process in STITCH-256 and compare it with that in SHA-256. This paper is organized as follows: In Sections 2 and 3, we briefly describe the message expansion methods of SHA-256 and STITCH-256, respectively. We then analyze the diffusion property of the two message expansion procedures in Section 4, and show that the minimum weight of the STITCH-256 output bits is higher than the minimum weight of the SHA-256 output bits. Finally, we offer some concluding remarks in Section 5.

2. Message Expansion of SHA-256

In this section, we briefly describe the message expansion process of SHA-256. We use the notation shown in **Table 1** throughout this paper.

In SHA-256, the pre-processing involves padding followed by message expansion. A message of arbitrary length is first padded to form multiple 512-bit message blocks. Each of the message blocks is denoted by a row vector m represented by sixteen 32-bit words, $M_0, \cdots, M_{15}$. The input message is then expanded to sixty four 32-bit words by the message expansion process, and this can be considered as a 2048-bit expanded message row vector w. The message words W_t are defined as follows:

$$W_i = \begin{cases} M_i & \text{for } 0 \leq i \leq 15 \\ \sigma_1(W_{t-2}) + W_{t-7} + \sigma_0(W_{t-15}) + W_{t-16} & \text{for } 16 \leq i \leq 63 \end{cases}$$

Table 1. Notation.

Notation	Description
$A \oplus B$	XOR operation of A and B.
$A + B$	Addition of A and B modulo 232.
M_i	The i-th block of the 32-bit input message M.
W_i	The i-th block of the 32-bit input message word W.
$ROTR/L^n(A)$	Bit rotation of A by n position/s to the right/left respectively.
$SHFR/L^n(A)$	Bit shift of A by n position/s to the right/left respectively.
N	Number of rounds in the message expansion.

where $\sigma_0(x) = ROT^7(x) \oplus ROT^{18}(x) \oplus ROT^3(x)$ and $\sigma_1(x) = SHF^{17}(x) \oplus SHF^{19}(x) \oplus SHF^{10}(x)$.

In total, there are 144 addition (modulo 32) operations and 192 XOR, rotation, and shift operations used in the message expansion of SHA-256.

3. Message Expansion of STITCH-256

In this section, we describe the message expansion procedure of STITCH-256. We use the notation in **Table 1**. In STITCH-256, the pre-processing again involves padding, whereby the arbitrary length message is extended to an exact multiple of 512-bits. This is followed by the message expansion, which works as follows:

$$W_i = M_i \quad \text{for } 0 \leq i \leq 15$$

$$ROT W_i = {}^{11}\left(s_0\left(W_{i-16}, W_{i-15}, W_{i-14}, W_{i-13}\right) \right.$$
$$+ s_1\left(W_{i-12}, W_{i-11}, W_{i-10}, W_{i-9}\right) \oplus SV_0 \Big)$$
$$+ ROT^{13}\left(s_0\left(W_{i-8}, W_{i-7}, W_{i-6}, W_{i-5}\right) \right.$$
$$+ s_1\left(W_{i-4}, W_{i-3}, W_{i-2}, W_{i-1}\right) \oplus SV_1 \Big)$$

for $16 \leq t \leq 63$

where

$$\sigma_0(w, x, y, z) = w \oplus x \oplus y \oplus z$$

and $\sigma_1(w, x, y, z) = w + x + y + z$

We use two salt values to support the message expansion of STITCH-256, where $SV_0 = 67452301$ and $SV_1 = 41083726$. In the message expansion of STITCH-256, every sixteen message words are taken into account to form the $(i-16)$-th message word. This is to maximize the bit propagation in the message expansion of STITCH-256. The bit rotations in the message expansion of STITCH-256 are carefully selected to increase the diffusion to the whole message expansion. The message expansion of STITCH-256 is illustrated as in **Figure 1**.

In STITCH-256, the 512-bit message input is expanded to thirty-two 32-bit message words. This gives the output of message expansion as 1024 bits. All the message words $W1, \cdots, W_{31}$ are then reordered to cater to

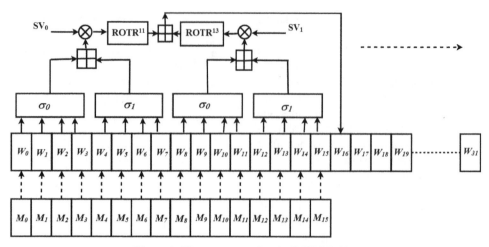

Figure 1. Message expansion in STITCH-256.

different message ordering in each line. The compression function of STITCH-256 requires eight $\sum j(M)$ for the whole function as described earlier and the orderings are depicted in **Figure 2**.

Figure 2 shows the input order of message words $M_0, \cdots, M_{15}$ applied to $B_j (1 \leq j \leq 4)$ branches. The number with an asterisk denotes the message words W_i for $16 \leq i \leq 31$. This means 1' refers to message words W_{16}, 2' refers to message word W_{17}, so on and so forth.

4. Finding Lowest Weight in the Message Expansion of SHA-256 and STITCH-256

In this analysis, we want to find the low weight in the message expansion of STITCH-256 and compare it with that of SHA-256. We compare with SHA-256 as both formulas used in the message expansion of STITCH-256 and SHA-256 are non-linear recursive functions, in which the formula used in the message expansion of STITCH-256 is inspired from the formula used in the

message expansion of SHA-256. To do this, we investigate the effect of a single bit difference at j-th bit of a message word to the whole message words. We consider variants of SHA-256 and STITCH-256 message expan0 sions from a reduction to 32, 64 and 80 steps. We used all-zero vector as the sample data. Then, a single bit is flipped and we record the Hamming weight in the output bit. We repeat this procedure until all the individual input bits are flipped. The results of the experiments are shown in the following sections.

4.1. Experiment 1:32 Rounds of Message Expansion

We show the results of the number of affected bits for a single bit difference in both STITCH-256 and SHA-256 algorithms, running in 32 rounds each. The results are depicted in two types of reading, *i.e.* at bit level as in **Figure 3** and **Figure 5**, and at byte level as in **Figure 4**

Branch	Msg Ord	0	1	2	3	4	5	6	7	8	9	10	11	12	13	14	15
1	1	0	1	2	3	4	5	6	7	8	9	10	11	12	13	14	15
	2	15'	0'	1'	2'	3'	4'	5'	6'	7'	8'	9'	10'	3'	12'	13'	14'
2	3	14	15	0	1	10	11	4	5	6	7	8	9	2	3	12	13
	4	13'	14'	15'	0'	9'	10'	11'	4'	5'	6'	7'	8'	1'	2'	3'	12'
3	5	12	13	14	15	8	9	10	11	4	5	6	7	0	1	2	3
	6	3'	12'	13'	14'	7'	8'	9'	10'	11'	4'	5'	6'	15'	0'	1'	2'
4	7	2	3	12	13	6	7	8	9	10	11	4	5	14	15	0	1
	8	1'	2'	3'	12'	5'	6'	7'	8'	9'	10'	11'	4'	13'	14'	15'	0'

Figure 2. Message orderings for four branches in STITCH-256.

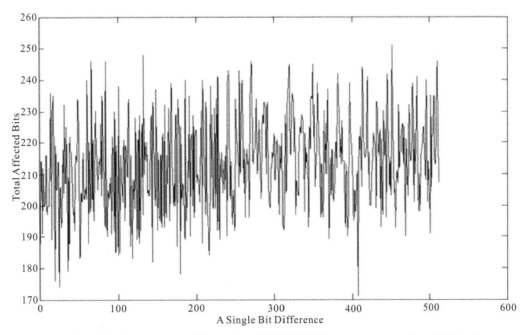

Figure 3. Diffusion property of 32 rounds of STITCH-256 message expansion at bit level.

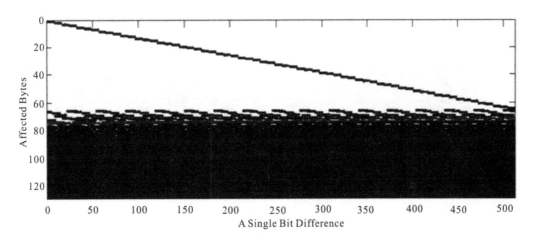

Figure 4. Diffusion property of 32 rounds of STITCH-256 message expansion at byte level.

and **Figure 6**.

4.2. Experiment 2:64 Rounds of Message Expansion

We show the results of the number of affected bits for a single bit difference in both STITCH-256 and SHA-256 algorithms, running in 64 rounds each. The results are depicted in two types of reading, *i.e.* at bit level as in **Figure 7** and **Figure 9**, and at byte level as in **Figure 8** and **Figure 10**.

4.3. Experiment 3:80 Rounds of Message Expansion

We show the results of the number of affected bits for a

single bit difference in both STITCH-256 and SHA-256 algorithms, running at 80 rounds each. The results are depicted in two types of reading, *i.e.* at bit level as in **Figure 11** and **Figure 13**, and at byte level as in **Figure 12** and **Figure 14**.

For a particular round of message expansions for both algorithms, two types of graph reading are shown as above; the first figure (or upper figure, for e.g. in **Figure 3**) in each of the algorithm shows a single-bit difference versus the total number of affected bits, while the second figure (or lower figure, for e.g. in **Figure 4**) shows a single bit difference versus the affected bytes. Note, that in the first graph of all the variants of SHA-256, there is a pattern to the total number of affected bits that decreases as the position of single-bit difference increase. This is in

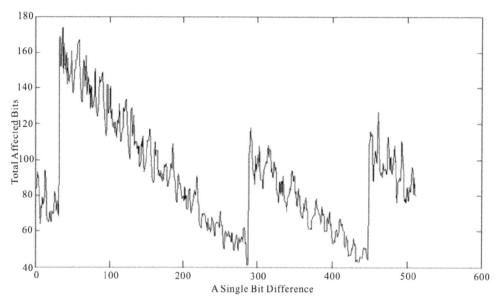

Figure 5. Diffusion property of 32 rounds of SHA-256 message expansion at bit level.

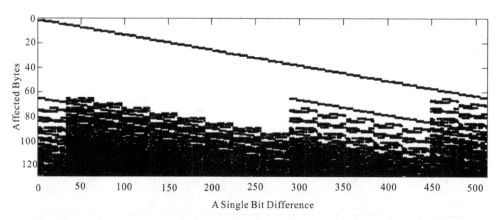

Figure 6. Diffusion property of 32 rounds of SHA-256 message expansion at byte level.

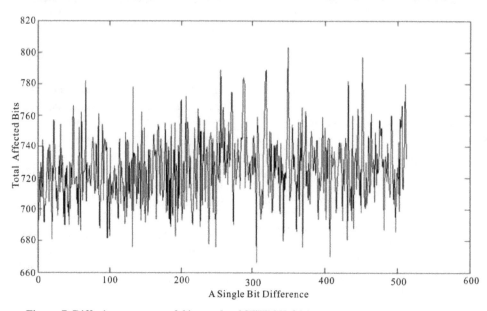

Figure 7. Diffusion property of 64 rounds of STITCH-256 message expansion at bit level.

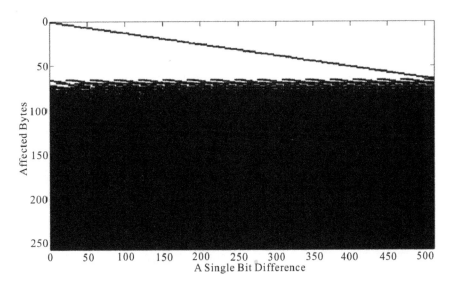

Figure 8. Diffusion property of 64 rounds of STITCH-256 message expansion at byte level.

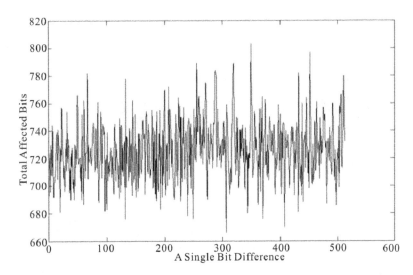

Figure 9. Diffusion property of 64 rounds of SHA-256 message expansion at bit level.

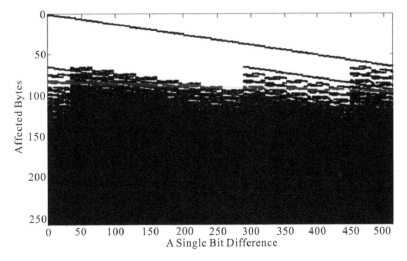

Figure 10. Diffusion property of 64 rounds of SHA-256 message expansion at byte level.

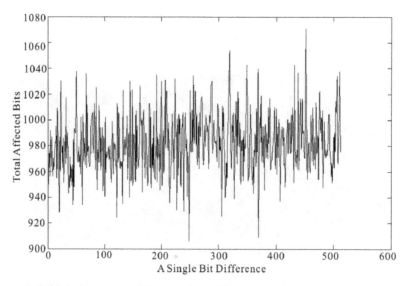

Figure 11. Diffusion property of 80 rounds of STITCH-256 message expansion at bit level.

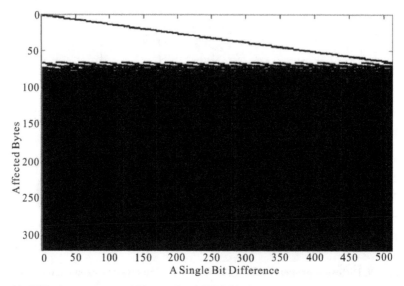

Figure 12. Diffusion property of 80 rounds of STITCH-256 message expansion at byte level.

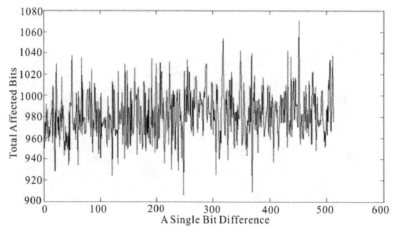

Figure 13. Diffusion property of 80 rounds of SHA-256 message expansion at bit level.

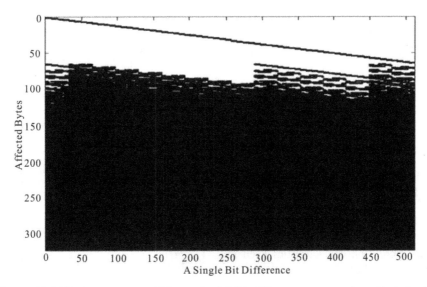

Figure 14. Diffusion property of 80 rounds of SHA-256 message expansion at byte level.

contrast to the message expansion of STITCH-256 which does not show any predictable pattern as the single-bit difference changes. This randomness presents some difficulties to an attacker seeking to fulfill the condition of chaining variables in the first step of the compression, as the distribution of bit propagation seems to be unpredictable and more bits are affected by a single-bit difference.

Table 2 shows the average number of affected bits for a single bit difference in the message expansion of both STITCH-256 and SHA-256. As shown in **Table 2**, the average number of affected bits for a single bit difference in the message expansion of STITCH-256 is higher than that of SHA-256. It can be seen that the message expansion of STITCH-256 produces, on average, more than 100 bits in the output get affected for a single bit flipping in input. We then find the lowest minimum weight in the output of message expansion for both algorithms when a single bit in input is flipped. **Table 3** shows the result of lowest minimum weight from the message expansion formula in STITCH-256 and SHA-256 algorithms. The lowest minimum weight for both algorithms is increasing and different for different rounds.

From the result shown in **Table 3**, it can be seen that the formula used in the message expansion of STITCH-256 produces larger lowest minimum weight in the

output than that of SHA-256 for different rounds. In principle, a larger minimum weight implies that the differential cryptanalysis of the compression function will be more complex [18]. Finally, we derive lower and upper bounds for the probability of a successful differential collision characteristic in STITCH-256. These are shown in **Table 4**. To the best of our knowledge, no optimal lower bound on the minimum weight of the output bits has yet been found by the cryptographic community. However, it is important to have a large minimum weight for a single-bit difference over a full round of message expansion to prevent an attacker from constructing a collision path. This is because useful heuristic, often used in the analysis of SHA-0 and SHA-1, suggests that each weight of the output bits lowers the probability of successful collision characteristics by, on average, a factor of $2^{-2.5}$ [16].

5. Conclusion

In this paper, we analyzed the effect of a single-bit difference (or the diffusion property) of the message expansion process of STITCH-256, and compared it with that of SHA-256. It is shown that the number of affected bits in output is higher in the message expansion of STITCH-256 than that of SHA-256, thus telling us that the diffusion of the message expansion of STITCH-256 is

Table 2. An average number of affected bits for a single bit difference in the message expansion of STITCH-256 and SHA-256.

No of rounds	STITCH-256	SHA-256
32	215	90
64	716	598
20	1024	852

Table 3. Minimum weight of message expansion in STITCH-256 and SHA-256.

Num of round	SHA-256	STITCH-256
32	41	171
64	507	666
80	765	906

Table 4. Lower and upper bound for probability of successful differential collision attack in STITCH-256.

Num of round	Lower bound	Upper bound
32	$2^{-171 \times 2.5}$	$2^{-251 \times 2.5}$
64	$2^{-666 \times 2.5}$	$2^{-803 \times 2.5}$
80	$2^{-906 \times 2.5}$	$2^{-1071 \times 2.5}$

better than the message expansion of SHA-256. Both message expansions of STITCH-256 and SHA-256 employ addition modulo 232, which means no linear code can be constructed for them. The high diffusion in the message expansion of STITCH-256 as shown in the lower bound derived for the probability of successful differential collision characteristics tells that it is infeasible to construct such a collision characteristics even in the message expansion of STITCH-256.

REFERENCES

[1] K. Aoki, J. Guo, K. Matusiewicz, Y. Sasaki and L. Wang, "Preimages for Step-Reduced SHA-2," In: M. Mitsuri, Ed., *Advances in Cryptology—ASIACRYPT* 2009, Springer, Berlin, 2009, pp. 578-597.

[2] E. Biham and R. Chen, "Near-Collisions of SHA-0," In: M. Franklin, Ed., *Advances in Cryptology—Crypto* 2004, Springer, Berlin, 2004, pp. 290-305.

[3] E. Biham and R. Chen, "New Results on SHA-0 and SHA-1," 2004.

[4] A. Biryukov, M. Lamberger, F. Mendel and I. Nikolic, "Second-Order Differential Collisions for Reduced SHA-256," In: D. H. Lee and X. Y. Wang, Eds., *Advances in Cryptology—ASIACRYPT* 2011, Springer, Berlin, 2011, pp. 270-287.

[5] F. Chabaud and A. Joux, "Differential Collisions in SHA-0," In: H. Krawczyk, *Advances in Cryptology—Crypto'* 98, Springer, Berlin, 1998, pp. 56-71.

[6] E. Grechnikov, "Collisions for 72-Step and 73-Step SHA-1: Improvements in the Method of Characteristics," 2010.

http://eprint. iacr.org.

[7] V. Rijmen and E. Oswald, "Update on SHA-1," In: A. J. Menezes, Ed., *Topics in Cryptology—CTRSA* 2005, Springer, Berlin, 2005, pp. 58-71.

[8] K. Matusiewicz and J. Pieprzyk, "Finding Good Differential Patterns for Attacks on SHA-1," In: Ø. Ytrehus, Ed., *Coding and Cryptography*, Springer, Berlin, 2006, pp. 164-177.

[9] S. Manuel and T. Peyrin, "Collisions on SHA-0 in one Hour," In: K. Nyberg, Ed., *Fast Software Encryption*, Springer, Berlin, 2008, pp. 16-35.

[10] Y. Sasaki, L. Wang and K. Aoki, "Preimage Attacks on 41-Step SHA-256 and 46-Step SHA-512," 2009. http://eprint.iacr.org/2009/479.pdf

[11] M. Stevens, "Single-Block Collision Attack on MD5," 2012. http://eprint.iacr.org/2012/040.pdf

[12] T. Xie and D. Feng, "Construct MD5 Collisions Using Just a Single Block of Message," 2010. http://eprint.iacr.org/2010/643.pdf

[13] X. Wang, D. Feng, X. Lai and H. Yu, "Collisions for Hash Functions MD4, MD5, HAVAL-128 and RIPEMD,' 2004.

[14] X. Wang, Y. Yin and H. Yu, "Finding Collisions in the Full SHA-1," In: V. Shoup, Ed., *Advances in Cryptology—Crypto* 2005, Springer, Berlin, 2005, pp. 17-36.

[15] X. Wang, H. Yu and Y. Yin, "Efficient Collision Search Attacks on SHA-0," In: V. Shoup, Ed., *Advances in Cryptology—Crypto* 2005, Springer, Berlin, 2005, pp. 1-16.

[16] C. Jutla and A. Patthak, "A Simple and Provably Good Code for SHA Message Expansion," 2005.

[17] N. Jamil, R. Mahmod, M. Zaba, N. Udzir and Z. Zukarnain, "STITCH-256: A Dedicated Cryptographic Hash Function," *Journal of Applied Sciences*, Vol. 12, 2012, pp. 1526-1536.

[18] J. Liu, H. Jiang and S. Huang, "Nonlinear Message Expansion for Hash Function," *Computer Science and Information Technology*, 2008, pp. 779-784.

3

On the Security of Anonymous Authentication Protocol for Mobile Pay-TV

Walid I. Khedr

Faculty of Computers and Informatics, Zagazig University, Zagazig, Egypt

ABSTRACT

One of the promising multimedia services is the mobile pay-TV service. Due to its wireless nature, mobile pay-TV is vulnerable to attacks especially during hand-off. In 2011, an efficient anonymous authentication protocol for mobile pay-TV is proposed. The authors claim that their scheme provides an anonymous authentication to users by preventing intruders from obtaining users' IDs during the mutual authentication between mobile subscribers and head end systems. However, after analysis, it was found that the scheme does not provide anonymous authentication and users can be easily tracked while using their anonymous identity. The scheme is also subject to denial of service attack. In this paper the deficiencies of the original scheme are demonstrated, and then a proposed improved scheme that eliminates these deficiencies is presented.

Keywords: Authentication; Conditional Access Systems; Mobile Pay-TV Services; Privacy

1. Introduction

With the increased integration of pay-TV and wireless communication, multimedia pay service plays an important role in mobile broadcast TV services [1]. As these services are usually delay-sensitive due to high mobility feature and frequent handoffs, a fast and secure authentication scheme for such mobile broadcast TV services should be developed.

In order to reduce the delay introduced by the high mobility features and frequent handoffs and guarantee a secure and convenient access of services by authorized subscribers, a secure access management mechanism is required. This access management is provided by a conditional access system (CAS). A typical model of CAS consists of two parts, a head end system and numerous receivers, and the model is comprised of several important components [2], which include:

- Subscriber Authorization/Management System (SAS/SMS): subsystems responsible for subscriber authorization and management; its works including key management, user authentication, entitlement messages delivery, subscriber information management and rights management.
- Encrypter: a component for enciphering Control Word (CW), keys, or sensitive information.
- Multiplexer (MUX): a component for multiplexing A/V, data or IP into MPEG-2 transport stream.
- Scrambler: a component for signal scrambling.
- Transmitter: a subsystem for signal transmission.
- Receiver: a subscriber device with a CAS module used for access control.

Several CASs have been proposed to guarantee a secure and convenient access of services by authorized subscribers. Many studies have classified these schemes into symmetrical key-based schemes and public key-based schemes.

Public key-based conditional access system [3-5] may realize privacy preservation and avoid communicating with a third party during the handoff process. These methods suffer the heavy computation burden. In [6], a subscriber first has to register his subscriber information with a signature to a provider by applying public key cryptosystem. When a subscriber wants to subscribe to any programs, he uses his device to send a subscription message to the provider. The provider then sends a receipt with a signature for confirming this subscription to the subscriber. However, the scheme [6] only protects the customers' privacy, but not the provider's [2]. In [7], an "e-ticket" scheme for the authentication of pay-TV system is proposed. The scheme employed an encrypted authentication message with a blind and anonymous signature based on RSA public key cryptosystem to do the mutual-authentication to protect the privacy for both customers and service provider. The schemes proposed in [8] and [9] are based on a public-key cryptosystem employing the technique of the multi-key RSA. While transmitting a requested TV program, the multimedia server and proxy server cooperatively encrypt the requested program without collusion attacks. In public-key cryptosystem each user possess a unique public/private key pair, so a multimedia server has to encrypt services with each user's specific public key which makes them inefficient and not suitable for mobile pay-TV systems.

Symmetrical key-based conditional access system [10-14] suffers from its troublesome key distribution and the involvement of a third party. In [14], an efficient anonymous authentication protocol for mobile pay-TV is proposed. The authors claim that their scheme provides an anonymous authentication to users by preventing intruders from obtaining users IDs during the mutual authentication between mobile subscribers and head end systems. However, after analysis, it was found that the scheme does not provide anonymous authentication and users can be easily tracked while using their anonymous identity. The scheme also is subject to DoS attack.

In this paper an improved scheme that enhances the Chen's scheme [14] is proposed. The deficiencies of the original scheme are demonstrated, and then a proposed improved scheme that eliminates these deficiencies is presented. The proposed scheme ensures the anonymity of the subscribers during handoffs operations, and ensures the anonymous mutual authentication between subscribers and head end systems with low computation and communication costs. Finally a mechanism that prevents denial of service attack is proposed.

The rest of this paper is organized as follows: Section 2 briefly reviews the Chen's scheme. Section 3 presents the security analysis of Chen's scheme. Section 4 presents the improved scheme. The security analysis and performance evaluation of the improved scheme are presented in Section 5. Finally, Section 6 concludes the paper.

2. Review of the Chen's Scheme

The scheme proposed in [14] introduced an efficient and anonymous mutual authentication protocol that eliminates the high computational cost and prevents security attacks introduced in a previous related protocol [15]. There are four phases in Chen's scheme, which includes initialization, issue, subscription and hand-off Phase.

2.1. Initialization Phase

This phase is invoked whenever user U_i registers to the subscribers' database server (DBS) of HES via Subscriber Authorization System and Subscriber Management System (SAS/SMS) and the DBS saves U_i's identity ID. Both U_i and HES uses a set-top-box (STB) as a secure channel during this phase. The following steps are performed to complete this phase [14]:

1) U_i chooses his ID_i and pw_i and generates a random number b for calculating $PWB = h(pw_i, b)$. Then, U_i submits ID_i and PWB to the pay-TV system server S.

2) S checks the database whether his ID_i is already in the database or not. If ID_i is already in the database, S checks whether U_i performs a re-registration or not. If U_i performs a re-registration then S sets ID_i's registration number $N = N + 1$ and updates ID_i and N in the database otherwise S suggests U_i to choose another ID_i. If ID_i is not in the database then S sets $N = 0$ and stores values of ID_i and N in the database.

3) S calculates K, UD, Q and K, UD, Q and R, where:
$$K = h(ID_i \oplus PWD),$$
$$UD = h(ID_i \| N),$$
$$Q = h(UD \| x) \oplus PWB,$$
$$R = h(PWB \| ID)_i \oplus h(y),$$ where y is the secret key of the remote server stored in the hash function and x is the secret key of S.

4) S issues a smart card containing $[K, R, Q]$ to U_i over a secure channel.

5) U_i stores the random number b on the smart card. Such that the smart card contains $[K, R, Q, b]$.

2.2. Issue Phase

Assume that U_i's mobile subscriber device (MS_i) asks a service R_t and the HES performs this authentication process of issue phase for U_i to obtain a right code θ_i. The statements are described as follows:

1) U_i enters his ID_i and PW_i in order to login for obtaining the service, MS_i performs the following computations.

- Calculates PWB and $h(ID_i \oplus PWD)$ to verify whether $K = h(ID_i \oplus PWD)$. If it does not hold, MS_i terminates the request.

- Calculates $P = Q \oplus PWB = h(UD \| x)$ and
$$h(y) = h(PWB \| ID_i) \oplus R$$

- Generates a random number n_i and calculates:
$$R_i = R_t \oplus h(y \| n_i), \quad CID_i = ID_i \oplus h(y \| T_i \| n_i)$$
$$C_i = h(P \| CID_i \| T_i \| n_i).$$

Here T_1 is the current timestamp

- Sends the message $m = [R_i, C_i, CID_i, T_1, n_i]$ to HES.

2) HES receives the message at the timestamp T_2 and performs the following computations:

- Checks the validity of $(T_2 - T)_1 \le \Delta T$. If it does not hold, HES terminates the request.

- Calculates $ID_i = CID_i \oplus h(y\|T_1\|n_i)$ and verifies if ID_i is a valid user's identity. If it does not hold, *HES* terminates the login request, otherwise *HES* checks the value of N in the database and calculates $P' = h(UD\|x)$, where $UD = h(ID_i\|N)$.

- Calculates $C_i' = h(P'\|CID_i\|T_1\|n_i)$ and checks whether $C_i' = C_i$. If they are equal, *HES* accepts U_i's request of authentication.

- Calculates $R_t = R_i \oplus h(y\|n_i)$

- Then, HES chooses a token θ_i for U_i and stores it into DBS, and calculates:
  $D_i = h(P'\|CID_i\|T_2\|n_i)$ $E_i = \theta_i \oplus h(P'\|T_2\|n_i)$.

- Broadcasts the mutual authentication message
  $m_2 = [D_i, E_i, T_2]$.

  3) After receiving message m_2 at the time T_3, U_i checks the validity of $(T_3 - T_2) \leq \Delta T$. If it does not hold, U_i terminates the request. Otherwise, U_i executes the following operations to authenticate *HES*.

- Calculates $D_i' = h(P\|CID_i\|T_2\|n_i)$ and checks whether $D_i' = D_i$. If they are equal, U_i accepts HES's request of mutual authentication.

- U_i calculates the certified token
  $\theta_i = E_i \oplus h(P\|T_2\|n_i)$ as the authentication session key to get service of the pay-TV system.

2.3. Subscription Phase

After obtaining a right code θ_i, U_i's MS_i asks a service R_t using θ_i and the *HES* performs this authentication process. The statements are described as follows:

1) U_i entries his ID_i and PW_i in order to login for obtaining the service, MS_i performs the following computations.

- Calculates PWB and $h(ID_i \oplus PWD)$ to verify whether $K = h(ID_i \oplus PWD)$. If it does not hold, MS_i terminates the request.

- Calculates $P = Q \oplus PWB = h(UD\|x)$ and
  $h(y) = h(PWB\|ID)_i \oplus R$.

- Generates a random number n_i and calculates:
  $R_i = \theta_i \oplus h(y\|n_i)$, $CID_i = ID_i \oplus h(y\|T_1\|n_i)$
  $C_i = h(P\|CID_i\|T_i\|n_i)$.
  Here T_1 is the current timestamp

- Sends the message $m = [R_i, C_i, CID_i, T_1, n_i]$ to HES.

  2) *HES* receives the message at the timestamp T_2 and performs the following computations:

- Checks the validity of $(T_2 - T_1) \leq \Delta T$. If it does not hold, HES terminates the request.

- Calculates $ID_i = CID_i \oplus h(y\|T_1\|n_i)$ and verifies if ID_i is a valid user's identity. If it does not hold, *HES* terminates the login request, otherwise *HES* checks

the value of N in the database and calculates
$P' = h(UD\|x)$, where $UD = h(ID_i\|N)$.

- Calculates $C_i' = h(P'\|CID_i\|T_1\|n_i)$ and checks whether $C_i' = C_i$. If they are equal, *HES* accepts U_i's request of authentication.

- Calculates $\theta_i = R_i \oplus h(y\|n_i)$.

- Then, HES chooses a token γ_i for U_i and calculates
  $D_i = h(P'\|CID_i\|T_2\|n_i)$ and $E_i = \gamma_i \oplus h(P'\|T_2\|n_i)$.

- Broadcasts the mutual authentication message
  $m_2 = [D_i, E_i, T_2]$.

  3) After receiving message m_2 at the time T_3, U_i checks the validity of $(T_3 - T_2) \leq \Delta T$. If it does not hold, U_i terminates the request. Otherwise, U_i executes the following operations to authenticate *HES*.

- Calculates $D_i' = h(P\|CID_i\|T_2\|n_i)$ and checks whether $D_i' = D_i$. If they are equal, U_i accepts HES's request of mutual authentication.

- U_i calculates the certified token
  $\gamma_i = E_i \oplus h(P\|T_2\|n_i)$ as the authentication session key to get service of the pay-TV system.

2.4. Hand-Off Phase

When MS_i moves to a new coverage area that older HES cannot support such that a hand-off occurs, MS_i needs to performer-authentication without re-login. The statements are described as follows:

1) MS_i performs the following computations:

- Generates a random number n_i and calculates:
  $Z_i = \theta_i \oplus h(y\|n_i)$, $CID_i = ID_i \oplus h(y\|T_1\|n_i)$
  $C_i = h(P\|CID_i\|T_i\|n_i)$.
  Here T_1 is the current timestamp

- Sends the message $m = [Z_i, C_i, CID_i, T_1, n_i]$ to HES.

  2) *HES* receives the message at the timestamp T_2 and performs the following computations:

- Checks the validity of $(T_2 - T_1) \leq \Delta T$. If it does not hold, HES terminates the request.

- Calculates $ID_i = CID_i \oplus h(y\|T_1\|n_i)$ and verifies if ID_i is a valid user's identity. If it does not hold, *HES* terminates the login request, otherwise *HES* checks the value of N in the database and calculates
  $P' = h(UD\|x)$, where $UD = h(ID_i\|N)$.

- Calculates $C_i' = h(P'\|CID_i\|T_1\|n_i)$ and checks whether $C_i' = C_i$. If they are equal, *HES* accepts U_i's request of authentication.

- Calculates $\theta_i = Z_i \oplus h(y\|n_i)$

- Then, HES chooses a token γ_i for U_i and calculates
  $D_i = h(P'\|CID_i\|T_2\|n_i)$ and $F_i = \gamma_i \oplus h(P'\|T_2\|n_i)$

- Broadcasts the mutual authentication message
  $$m_2 = [D_i, F_i, T_2]$$

3) After receiving message m_2 at the time T_3, U_i checks the validity of $(T_3 - T_2) \leq \Delta T$. If it does not hold, U_i terminates the request. Otherwise, U_i executes the following operations to authenticate *HES*.

- Calculates $D_i' = h(P \| CID_i \| T_2 \| n_i)$ and checks whether $D_i' = D_i$. If they are equal, U_i accepts HES's request of mutual authentication.
- U_i calculates the certified token
  $$\gamma_i = F_i \oplus h(P \| T_2 \| n_i)$$ to obtain new HES's service.

3. Security Analysis of Chen's Scheme

In [14] the authors claim several security properties such as anonymous service, mutual authentication, resisting replay attacks, resisting man-in-the-middle-attack, and forgery difficulty. However, in this section, it is shown that Chen's scheme vulnerable to man-in-the-middle-attack which leads to DoS attack. It is also found that the scheme does not provide anonymous service. The aforementioned weaknesses are presented in detail as follows.

3.1. Corrections to Chen's Scheme

Before we present the weakness of Chen's scheme, there are some mistakes in the scheme that should be corrected. In step 3 of the initialization phase (Section 2.1), the system server S calculates R using the following equation:

$$R = h(PWB \| ID_i) \oplus h(y) \qquad (1)$$

Here, y is a secret key of the remote server S which is stored in the hash function and known only to S.

In step 1 of the issue phase (Section 2.2), the mobile subscriber MS extracts $h(y)$ from R by computing $h(y) = h(PWB \| ID_i) \oplus R$ and use it to compute R_i and CID_i as follows:

$$R_i = R_t \oplus h(y \| n_i) \qquad (2)$$

$$CID_i = ID_i \oplus h(y \| T_1 \| n_i) \qquad (3)$$

As shown in Equations (2) and (3), the authors use $h(y \| n_i)$ and $h(y \| T_1 \| n_i)$ to compute R_i and CID_i respectively, which is not possible; since the MS_i does not know the secret key y to be able to compute $h(y \| n_i)$ and $h(y \| T_1 \| n_i)$. So, the MS could not compute R_i and CID_i as $h(y \| n_i)$ and $h(y \| T_1 \| n_i)$ are one way hash functions *i.e.* it is not possible to extract y from both $h(y \| n_i)$ and $h(y \| T_1 \| n_i)$. The same mistake is found in step 1 of the subscription phase (Section 2.3) and step 1 of the hand-off phase (Section 2.4) when

computing (R_i, CID_i) and (Z_i, CID_i) respectively. To correct this mistake, the MS should replace y by $h(y)$ in Equations (2) and (3). This mistake can also be corrected by just replacing $h(y)$ by y in Equation (1) in the initialization phase *i.e.* $R = h(PWB \| ID_i) \oplus y$. We chose the second option.

3.2. Attack on Anonymous Service

The Chen's scheme is subject to MS tracking attack. This attack can be performed as follows:

1) An attacker A registers to the subscribers' database server (DBS) like any other user and chooses his ID_A and pw_A and generates a random number b for calculating $PWB = h(pw_A, b)$. Then, A submits ID_A and PWB to the pay-TV system server S.

2) S calculates:

$$K = h(ID_A \oplus PWD)$$

$$UD = h(ID_A \| N)$$

$$Q = h(UD \| x) \oplus PWB$$

$$R = h(PWB \| ID_i) \oplus y.$$

S issues a smart card containing $[K, R, Q]$ to A over a secure channel.

3) The attacker A reads R from its smart card and compute $y = h(PWB \| ID_A) \oplus R$.

Note that based on the corrections presented in section 3.1, $h(y)$ is replaced by y in the step 2. Using the computed y the attacker A can perform MS tracing attack during issue phase, subscription or hand-off phases as follows:

1) The attacker A intercept message m during any of the three phases and extracts CID_i, T_1 and n_i from m. Using these three values and the computed y, the attacker can compute the MS' ID (ID_i) as follows:

$$ID_i = CID_i \oplus h(y \| T_1 \| n_i) \qquad (4)$$

This allows the attacker to track MS_i; since ID_i is a fixed value for each user U_i.

2) The attacker A can also know the service R_t that the MS_i asked from HES by intercepting message m during the issue phase and extracting R_i and n_i from m. Using these two values and the computed y, the attacker can compute R_t as follows:

$$R_t = R_i \oplus h(y \| n_i) \qquad (5)$$

3) The attacker A can also know the right code θ_i that used by MS_i to access service R_t by intercepting message m during the subscription or the hand-off phases and extracting (R_i, n_i) or (Z_i, n_i) respectively from m. Using either of these two values and the computed y, the attacker can compute θ_i as follows:

$$\theta_i = R_i \oplus h\left(y \| n_i\right) \qquad (6)$$

$$\theta_i = Z_i \oplus h\left(y \| n_i\right) \qquad (7)$$

3.3. Denial of Service Attack

The scheme is subject to denial of service attack. This attack can be performed through two methods. The first method can be performed during the subscription and hand-off phases by applying man-in-the-middle attack as follows:

1) The attacker A intercept message m_2 during any of the two phases and extract:

$E_i = \gamma_i \oplus h\left(P' \| T_2 \| n_i\right)$ or

$F_i = \gamma_i \oplus h\left(P' \| T_2 \| n_i\right)$ respectively.

2) The attacker generates a random session key γ_A and computes:

- $E_i' = \gamma_A \oplus E_i = \gamma_A \oplus \gamma_i \oplus h\left(P' \| T_2 \| n_i\right)$
  $= \gamma_i' \oplus h\left(P' \| T_2 \| n_i\right)$ or
- $F_i' = \gamma_A \oplus F_i = \gamma_A \oplus \gamma_i \oplus h\left(P' \| T_2 \| n_i\right)$
  $= \gamma_i' \oplus h\left(P' \| T_2 \| n_i\right)$

3) After receiving message m_2, U_i calculates the session key:

- $\gamma_i' = E_i \oplus h\left(P \| T_2 \| n_i\right)$ or
- $\gamma_i' = F_i \oplus h\left(P \| T_2 \| n_i\right)$

This results in U_i and *HES* using different session keys (γ', γ respectively) which prevent U_i from getting the service of the pay-TV system.

The second method can be performed during the hand-off phase as follows:

1) The attacker uses a rogue HES to transmit messages using a high signal strength in order to force MS_i to discard the signal sent by the legitimate HES and roam with the rogue HES.

2) When MS_i roam with the rogue HES, it needs to perform re-authentication without re-login by sending $m : Z_i, C_i, CID_i, T_1, n_i$, where:

$Z_i = \theta_i \oplus h\left(y \| n_i\right)$

$CID_i = ID_i \oplus h\left(y \| T_1 \| n_i\right)$

$C_i = h\left(P \| CID_i \| T_1 \| n_i\right).$

3) The rogue HES receives the message and immediately reply with message $m_2 : D_i, F_i', T_1$, where

$D_i = C_i = h\left(P \| CID_i \| T_1 \| n_i\right)$ and F_i' is a random value generated by the rogue HES.

4) After receiving message m_2 at the time T_3, U_i checks the validity of $\left(T_3 - T_1\right) \leq \Delta T$ which should hold; since $\left(T_3 - T_1\right)$ should equal to the round trip time (RTT) between U_i and the rogue HES. Note that ΔT should be less than or equal to 200 milliseconds as stated in [16]. It

is clear that the RTT between U_i and the rogue HES is less than 200 milliseconds; since they are within the transmission range of each other.

5) U_i calculates $D_i' = h\left(P \| CID_i \| T_1 \| n_i\right)$ and checks whether $D_i' = D_i$ and accepts the rogue HES's request of mutual authentication.

6) U_i calculates the false authentication session key $\gamma_i' = F_i' \oplus h\left(P \| T_1 \| n_i\right)$, which prevents U_i from getting the service of the pay-TV system.

4. The Improved Scheme

To withstand the above attacks, we propose an improved scheme based on the original Chen's scheme [14] with lightweight modifications. The improved scheme introduces few modifications to the four phases as follows.

4.1. Initialization Phase

As assumed in [14], both S and its HESs share a secret key x. Both U_i and HES use a set-top-box (STB) as a secure channel during this phase. The following steps are performed to complete this phase:

1) U_i chooses his ID_i and pw_i and generates a random number b for calculating $PWB = h\left(pw_i, b\right)$. Then, U_i submits ID_i and PWB to the pay-TV system server S.

2) S checks the database whether his ID_i is already in the database or not. If ID_i is already in the database, S checks whether U_i performs a re-registration or not. If U_i performs a re-registration then S sets ID_i's registration number $N = N + 1$ and updates ID_i and N in the database otherwise S suggests U_i to choose another ID_i. If ID_i is not in the database then S sets $N = 0$ and stores values of ID_i and N in the database.

3) S calculates the following values:

- $K = h\left(ID_i \oplus PWD\right)$
- A user authentication key for each user
  $y_i = h\left(x \| ID_i\right)$, where x is the secret key of S.
- A new permutation of the MS_i's ID
  ($CID_i^1 = h\left(y_i, ID_i\right)$) to be used by MS_i's as a new ID during the next communication with the HES.
- $UD = h\left(CID_i^1 \| N\right)$, $P_i^1 = h\left(UD \| x\right)$ and
  $Q = E_{y_i}\left(P_i^1\right)$
- $k_i^1 = h\left(x \| CID_i^1\right)$, $z_i^1 = E_{k_i^1}\left(CID_i^1, y_i\right)$ and
  $R = h\left(PWB \| ID_i\right) \oplus y_i$

4) S sends $\left[K, R, Q, z_i^1\right]$ to U_i over the secure channel.

5) U_i computes $y_i = h\left(PWB \| ID_i\right) \oplus R$ and stores $\left[K, R, Q, z_i^1, b, y_i\right]$.

The user U_i uses CID_i^1 to identify itself to the next HES during the issue phase, the subscription phase or the hand-off phase. This new ID should be known to the next HES to be able to authenticate U_i. So, the current HES encrypt the new ID (CID_i^1) along with user authentication key y_i and send it to U_i which sends it to the next HES in the next phase. Note that only HESs can decrypt z_i^1; since the decryption key k_i^1 is generated using the secret key x which is only known to the server S and its HESs.

4.2. Issue Phase

Assume that U_i's mobile subscriber device (MS_i) asks a service R_t and the HES performs this authentication process of issue phase for U_i to obtain a right code θ_i. The statements are described as follows:

1) U_i enters his ID_i and PW_i in order to login for obtaining the service, MS_i performs the following computations.

- Calculates PWB and $h(ID_i \oplus PWD)$ to verify whether $K = h(ID_i \oplus PWD)$. If it does not hold, MS_i terminates the request.
- Calculates $P_i^1 = D_{y_i}(Q)$
- Generates a random number n_i and calculates:

$$R_i = R_t \oplus h(y_i \| n_i)$$

$$CID_i^1 = h(y_i, ID_i)$$

$$C_i = h(P_i^1 \| CID_i^1 \| T_i \| n_i).$$

Here T_1 is the current timestamp

- Sends the message m to HES:

$$(m : R_i, C_i, CID_i^1, T_1, z_i^1, n_i) \| HMAC(y_i, m)$$

Here $HMAC(y_i, m)$ is the HMAC of the message m using the key y_i

2) HES receives the message at the timestamp T_2 and performs the following computations:

- Checks the validity of $(T_2 - T_1) \le \Delta T$. If it does not hold, HES terminates the request.
- To validate the $HMAC$ and the new ID (CID_i^1),

  HES calculates $k_i^1 = h(x \| CID_i^1)$ and

  $D_{k_i^1}(z_i^1) = (CID_i^{'1}, y_i)$ to get the user authentication key y_i.

- Uses y_i to validate $HMAC(y_i, m)$ then checks whether the computed $CID_i^{'1}$ equal to CID_i^1. If it does not hold, HES terminates the login request, otherwise HES checks the value of N in the database and calculates $P_i^{'1} = h(UD \| x) = h(h(CID_i^1 \| N) \| x)$.

- Calculates $C_i' = h(P_i^{'1} \| CID_i^1 \| T_1 \| n_i)$ and checks whether $C_i' = C_i$. If they are equal, HES accepts U_i's request of authentication.

- Calculates $R_t = R_i \oplus h(y_i \| n_i)$

- Then, HES chooses a token θ_i for U_i and stores it

into DBS, and calculates:

$$D_i = h(P_i^{'1} \| CID_i^1 \| T_2 \| n_i) \quad E_i = \theta_i \oplus h(P_i^{'1} \| T_2 \| n_i)$$

- Computes a new permutation of the MS_i's ID ($CID_i^2 = h(y_i, CID_i^1)$) to be used by MS_i's as a new ID during the next communication with the HES.

- Compute $UD = h(CID_i^2 \| N)$, $P_i^2 = h(UD \| x)$ and

  $Q = E_{y_i}(P_i^2)$.

- $k_i^2 = h(x \| CID_i^2)$, $z_i^2 = E_{k_i^2}(CID_i^2, y_i)$.

- Broadcasts the mutual authentication message

  $(m_2 : D_i, E_i, T_2, Q, z_i^2) \| HMAC(y_i, m_2)$.

3) After receiving message m_2 at the time T_3, U_i checks the validity of $(T_3 - T_2) \le \Delta T$ and uses y_i to validate the HMAC. If they do not hold, U_i terminates the request. Otherwise, U_i executes the following operations to authenticate HES.

- Calculates $D_i' = h(P_i^1 \| CID_i^1 \| T_2 \| n_i)$ and checks whether $D_i' = D_i$. If they are equal, U_i accepts HES's request of mutual authentication.

- U_i calculates the certified token $\theta_i = E_i \oplus h(P_i^1 \| T_2 \| n_i)$ as the authentication session key to get service of the pay-TV system.

- U_i stores $Q = E_{y_i}(P_i^2)$, θ_i, CID_i^1 and z_i^2.

4.3. Subscription Phase

After obtaining a right code θ_i, U_i's MS_i asks a service R_t using θ_i and the HES performs this authentication process. The statements are described as follows:

1) U_i entries his ID_i and PW_i in order to login for obtaining the service, MS_i performs the following computations.

- Calculates PWB and $h(ID_i \oplus PWD)$ to verify whether $K = h(ID_i \oplus PWD)$. If it does not hold, MS_i terminates the request.

- Calculates $D_{y_i}(Q) = P_i^2$.

- Generates a random number n_i and calculates

  $R_i = \theta_i \oplus h(y_i \| n_i)$, $CID_i^2 = h(y_i, CID_i^1)$ and

  $C_i = h(P_i^2 \| CID_i^2 \| T_1 \| n_i)$. Here T_1 is the current timestamp.

- Sends the message m to HES:

  $(m : R_i, C_i, CID_i^2, T_1, z_i^2, n_i) \| HMAC(y_i, m)$.

2) HES receives the message at the timestamp T_2 and performs the following computations:

- Checks the validity of $(T_2 - T)_1 \le \Delta T$. If it does not hold, HES terminates the request.

- To validate the $HMAC$ and the new ID (CID_i^2), HES calculates $k_i^2 = h(x \| CID_i^2)$ and

  $D_{k_i^2}(z_i^2) = (CID_i^{'2}, y_i)$ to get the user authentication key y_i.

- Uses y_i to validate $HMAC(y_i, m)$ then checks whether the computed $CID_i'^2$ equal to CID_i^2. If it does not hold, HES terminates the login request, otherwise HES checks the value of N in the database and calculates $P_i'^2 = h(UD \| x) = h(h(CID_i^2 \| N) \| x)$.

- Calculates $C_i' = h(P_i'^2 \| CID_i^2 \| T_1 \| n_i)$ and checks whether $C_i' = C_i$. If they are equal, HES accepts U_i's request of authentication.

- Calculates $\theta_i = R_i \oplus h(y_i \| n_i)$.

- Then, HES chooses a token γ_i for U_i and calculates $D_i = h(P_i'^2 \| CID_i^2 \| T_2 \| n_i)$ and $E_i = \gamma_i \oplus h(P_i'^2 \| T_2 \| n_i)$.

- Computes a new permutation of the MS_i's ID ($CID_i^3 = h(y_i, CID_i^2)$) to be used by MS_i's as a new ID during the next communication with the HES.

- Computes $UD = h(CID_i^3 \| N)$, $P_i^3 = h(UD \| x)$ and $Q = E_{y_i}(P_i^3)$.

- $k_i^3 = h(x \| CID_i^3)$, $z_i^3 = E_{k_i^3}(CID_i^3, y_i)$.

- Broadcasts the mutual authentication message $(m_2 : D_i, E_i, T_2, Q, z_i^3) \| HMAC(y_i, m2)$.

3) After receiving message m_2 at the time T_3, U_i checks the validity of $(T_3 - T_2) \leq \Delta T$ and uses y_i to validate the HMAC. If they do not hold, U_i terminates the request. Otherwise, U_i executes the following operations to authenticate HES.

- Calculates $D_i' = h(P_i^2 \| CID_i^2 \| T_2 \| n_i)$ and checks whether $D_i' = D_i$. If they are equal, U_i accepts HES's request of mutual authentication.

- U_i calculates the certified token $\gamma_i = E_i \oplus h(P_i^2 \| T_2 \| n_i)$ as the authentication session key to get service of the pay-TV system.

- U_i stores $Q = E_{y_i}(P_i^3)$, γ_i, CID_i^2 and z_i^3.

4.4. Hand-off Phase

When MS_i moves to a new coverage area that older HES cannot support such that a hand-off occurs, MS_i needs to performer-authentication without re-login. The statements are described as follows:

1) MS_i performs the following computations:

- Calculates $D_{y_i}(Q) = P_i^3$.

- Generates a random number n_i and calculates $Z_i = \theta_i \oplus h(y_i \| n_i)$, $CID_i^3 = h(y_i, CID_i^2)$ and $C_i = h(P_i^3 \| CID_i^3 \| T_1 \| n_i)$. Here T_1 is the current timestamp.

- Sends the message m to HES: $(m : Z_i, C_i, CID_i^3, T_1, z_i^3, n_i) \| HMAC(y_i, m)$.

2) HES receives the message at the timestamp T_2 and performs the following computations:

- Checks the validity of $(T_2 - T)_1 \leq \Delta T$. If it does not hold, HES terminates the request.

- To validate the HMAC and the new ID (CID_i^3), HES calculates $k_i^3 = h(x \| CID_i^3)$ and $D_{k_i^3}(z_i^3) = (CID_i'^3, y_i)$ to get the user authentication key y_i.

- Uses y_i to validate $HMAC(y_i, m)$ then checks whether the computed $CID_i'^3$ equal to CID_i^3. If it does not hold, HES terminates the login request, otherwise HES checks the value of N in the database and calculates $P_i'^3 = h(UD \| x) = h(h(CID_i^3 \| N) \| x)$.

- Calculates $C_i' = h(P_i'^3 \| CID_i^3 \| T_1 \| n_i)$ and checks whether $C_i' = C_i$. If they are equal, HES accepts U_i's request of authentication.

- Calculates $\theta_i = Z_i \oplus h(y_i \| n_i)$

- Then, HES chooses a token γ_i for U_i and calculates $D_i = h(P_i'^3 \| CID_i^3 \| T_2 \| n_i)$ and $F_i = \gamma_i \oplus h(P_i'^3 \| T_2 \| n_i)$

- Computes a new permutation of the MS_i's ID ($CID_i^4 = h(y_i, CID_i^3)$) to be used by MS_i's as a new ID during the next communication with the HES.

- Computes $UD = h(CID_i^4 \| N)$, $P_i^4 = h(UD \| x)$ and $Q = E_{y_i}(P_i^4)$

- $k_i^4 = h(x \| CID_i^4)$, $z_i^4 = E_{k_i^4}(CID_i^4, y_i)$.

- Broadcasts the mutual authentication message $(m_2 : D_i, F_i, T_2, Q, z_i^4) \| HMAC(y_i, m2)$.

3) After receiving message m_2 at the time T_3, U_i checks the validity of $(T_3 - T_2) \leq \Delta T$ and uses y_i to validate the HMAC. If they do not hold, U_i terminates the request. Otherwise, U_i executes the following operations to authenticate HES.

- Calculates $D_i' = h(P_i^3 \| CID_i^3 \| T_2 \| n_i)$ and checks whether $D_i' = D_i$. If they are equal, U_i accepts HES's request of mutual authentication.

- U_i calculates the certified token $\gamma_i = F_i \oplus h(P_i^3 \| T_2 \| n_i)$ as the authentication session key to get service of the pay-TV system.

- U_i stores $Q = E_{y_i}(P_i^4)$, γ_i, CID_i^3 and z_i^4.

5. Security and Performance Analysis

In this section, the security of the proposed improved scheme with respect to the resistance to user tracking and denial of service attack is analyzed. This section also evaluates the performance of the proposed scheme.

5.1. Resistance to User Tracking

The proposed improved scheme prevents user tracking by ensuring the anonymity feature of users. As discussed in Section 3.2, an attacker can track a legitimate user by registering himself to the subscribers' database server (DBS) like any other user, then receives $R = h\left(PWB\|ID_i\right) \oplus y$ which is used by the attacker to compute $y = h\left(PWB\|ID_A\right) \oplus R$. Using the computed y the attacker A can perform MS tracing attack as described in Section 3.2. The attacker is able to perform this attack; because the server S uses the same secret y to compute the R values for all users. So, if the attacker extracts y from his R value, he can use the same y to extract the IDs of other uses.

In the proposed scheme, the server S generate a unique user authentication key $y_i = h\left(x\|ID_i\right)$ for each user using the hash of the user ID and the server's own secret key x. This prevent an attacker A form using his user authentication key (y_A) to extract the IDs of other uses. The proposed scheme also preserves users' privacy by using pseudo identity, CID_i^j to identify users. This pseudo identity generated using a one-way function combined with the user authentication key, y_i, and the user's previous CID_i^{j-1}: $CID_i^j = h\left(y_i, CID_i^{j-1}\right)$ and is updated in each phase. So, it is impossible to anticipate the messages of the user each phase which guarantees indistinguishability. Also the integrity of messages exchanged between users and HES is guaranteed due to the use of timestamps and the HMAC of each message which is included with the message. The HMAC value is computed using the user authentication key (y_i) which is only known to U_i and HES.

5.2. Resistance to Denial of Service Attack

As discussed in Section 3.3, Chen's scheme is subject to denial of service attack. The attacker can perform this attack because the integrity of message m_2 of the subscription and hand-off phases is not guaranteed. So, an attacker can easily modify E_i or F_i during the subscription or hand-off phases without being detected by U_i which prevents him from getting the service of the pay-TV system.

In the proposed scheme, the integrity of messages exchanged between users and HES is guaranteed due to the use of timestamps and the HMAC of each message which is included with the message. The HMAC value is computed using the user authentication key, (y_i) which is only known to U_i and HES. This prevents the DoS attack that can be launched against the Chen's scheme as described in Section 3.3. This also prevents the attacker from making an impersonation attack and replay attacks using the open values and some modified values.

5.3. Performance Analysis

This section evaluates the performance of the proposed scheme. To analyze the efficiency of the proposed scheme, the proposed scheme is compared with the Chen's scheme [14]. The efficiency of the proposed scheme is analyzed with the same metrics used in Chen's scheme analysis. We define the notation t_H as the hash computation time and t_E as the symmetric encryption/decryption time. The four phases of both the Chen's scheme and the proposed scheme are simulated and implemented using OpenSSL library [17] on an Intel Dual- Core CPU at 2.30 GHz. **Table 1** shows a comparison between the Chen's scheme and the proposed scheme with respect to the hash computation time and the symmetric encryption/decryption time. Note that we neglect the XOR operation since it is an extremely light-weight one. As shown in **Table 1**, the proposed scheme takes the following extra operation for each phase:

- It takes extra 3 hash operations and more two symmetric encryption/decryption about extra 62 μs for the initialization phase.
- It takes extra 6 hash operations and more four symmetric encryption/decryption about extra 81 μs for the issue phase.
- It takes extra 6 hash operations and more four symmetric encryption/decryption about extra 81 μs for the subscription phase.
- It takes extra 8 hash operations and more four symmetric encryption/decryption about extra 89 μs for the hand-off phase.

This indicates that the proposed scheme introduces a minor increase in computation overhead, which is the cost to enhance the security of the original scheme.

6. Conclusion

Recently, an efficient anonymous authentication protocol for mobile pay-TV is proposed [14]. However, the scheme is vulnerable to user tracking attack and denial of service attack. An improved scheme is proposed to prevent these two attacks by lightweight modifications and, thus, can be applied in environments requiring a high level of security. The improved scheme introduces a minor increase in computation overhead and maintains the

Table 1. Performance comparison.

Phase	Chen's Scheme	Proposed Scheme
Initialization	$6t_H = 30\mu s$	$9t_H + 2t_E = 92\mu s$
Issue	$16t_H = 67\mu s$	$22t_H + 4t_E = 148\mu s$
Subscription	$16t_H = 67\mu s$	$22t_H + 4t_E = 148\mu s$
Hand-off	$12t_H = 52\mu s$	$20t_H + 4t_E = 141\mu s$

same number of messages of the original scheme.

REFERENCES

[1] H. S. L. Pequeno, G. A. M. Gomes, R. M. C. Andrade, J. N. de Souza and M. F. de Castro, "FrameIDTV: A Framework for Developing Interactive Applications on Digital Television Environments," *Journal of Network and Computer Applications*, Vol. 33, No. 4, 2010, pp. 503-511.

[2] H.-M. Sun and M.-C. Leu, "An Efficient Authentication Scheme for Access Control in Mobile Pay-TV Systems," *IEEE Transactions on Multimedia*, Vol. 11, No. 5, 2009, pp. 947-959.

[3] X. Li, J. Niu, M. Khurram Khan and J. Liao, "An Enhanced Smart Card Based Remote User Password Authentication Scheme," *Journal of Network and Computer Applications*, Vol. 36, No. 5, 2013, pp. 1365-1371.

[4] X. Li, Y. Xiong, J. Ma and W. Wang, "An Efficient and Security Dynamic Identity Based Authentication Protocol for Multi-Server Architecture Using Smart Cards," *Journal of Network and Computer Applications*, Vol. 35, No. 2, 2012, pp. 763-769.

[5] Z. Tan, "A Lightweight Conditional Privacy-Preserving Authentication and Access Control Scheme for Pervasive Computing Environments," *Journal of Network and Computer Applications*, Vol. 35, No. 6, 2012, pp. 1839-1846.

[6] N.-Y. Lee, C.-C. Chang, C.-L. Lin and T. Hwang, "Privacy and Non-Repudiation on Pay-TV Systems," *IEEE Transactions on Consumer Electronics*, Vol. 46, No. 1, 2000, pp. 20-27.

[7] R. Song and L. Korba, "Pay-TV System with Strong Privacy and Non-Repudiation Protection," *IEEE Transactions on Consumer Electronics*, Vol. 49, No. 2, 2003, pp. 408-413.

[8] S. F. Yeung, J. C. Lui and D. K. Yau, "A Multikey Secure Multimedia Proxy Using Asymmetric Reversible Parametric Sequences: Theory, Design and Implementa-tion," *IEEE Transactions on Multimedia*, Vol. 7, No. 2, 2005, pp. 330-338.

[9] H. Roh and S. Jung, "An Authentication Scheme for Consumer Electronic Devices Accessing Mobile IPTV Service From Home Networks," 2011 *IEEE International Conference on Consumer Electronics* (*ICCE*), Las Vegas, 9-12 January 2011, pp. 717-718.

[10] Y.-L. Huang, S. Shieh, F.-S. Ho and J.-C. Wang, "Efficient Key Distribution Schemes for Secure Media Delivery in Pay-TV Systems," *IEEE Transactions on Multimedia*, Vol. 6, No. 5, 2004, pp. 760-769.

[11] H.-M. Sun, C.-M. Chen and C.-Z. Shieh, "Flexible-Pay-per-Channel: A New Model for Content Access Control in Pay-TV Broadcasting Systems," *IEEE Transactions on Multimedia*, Vol. 10, No. 5, 2008, pp. 1109-1120.

[12] R. Di Pietro and R. Molva, "An Optimal Probabilistic Solution for Information Confinement, Privacy, and Security in RFID Systems," *Journal of Network and Computer Applications*, Vol. 34, No. 3, 2011, pp. 853-863.

[13] W. I. Khedr, "SRFID: A Hash-Based Security Scheme for Low Cost RFID Systems," *Egyptian Informatics Journal*, Vol. 14, No. 1, 2013, pp. 89-98.

[14] T.-H. Chen, Y.-C. Chen, W.-K. Shih and H.-W. Wei, "An Efficient Anonymous Authentication Protocol for Mobile Pay-TV," *Journal of Network and Computer Applications*, Vol. 34, No. 4, 2011, pp. 1131-1137.

[15] J.-H. Yang and C.-C. Chang, "An ID-Based Remote Mutual Authentication with Key Agreement Scheme for Mobile Devices on Elliptic Curve Cryptosystem," *Computers & Security*, Vol. 28, No. 3-4, 2009, pp. 138-143.

[16] WMF-T33-107-R020v02, "Architecture, detailed Protocols and Procedures," 2012.

[17] OpenSSL, "OpenSSL 1.0.1e," 2013.

4

A Socio-Technical Approach to Cyber Risk Management and Impact Assessment

Konstantinia Charitoudi, Andrew Blyth
Information Security Research Group, University of Glamorgan, Trefforest, UK

ABSTRACT

Technology is increasingly being used by organisations to mediate social/business relationships and social/business transactions. While traditional models of impact assessment have focused on the loss of confidentiality, integrity and availability, we propose a new model based upon socio-technical systems thinking that places the people and the technology within an organisation's business/functional context. Thus in performing risk management in a cyber security and safety context, a detailed picture of the impact that a security/safety incident can have on an organisation is developed. This in turn stimulates a more holistic view of the effectiveness, and appropriateness, of a counter measure.

Keywords: Impact Assessment; Risk Management; Socio-Technical Systems

1. Introduction

It is clear that, given the level of complexity of Information Systems Security (ISS) risk management's simple linear models as proposed in most of the existing approaches will not be able to capture such complexities [1]. To achieve a more complete picture of the risks that cyber attacks pose to safety and security a more social oriented model must be developed that views an organisation as a holistic construct comprising of people and technology; and allow for the relationships and interactions between them to be better modelled and understood.

The term socio-technical system is used to describe the function and form that people (individuals, groups, roles and organisations), physical equipment (buildings, surroundings, etc.), hardware and software, laws and regulations that accompany the organisations (e.g. laws for the protection of privacy), data (what data are kept, in which formats, who has access to them, where they are kept) and procedures (official and unofficial processes, data flows, relationships play in comprising an organisation [2]. From a risk assessment perspective the challenge is to understand that impact that a potential loss of cyber safety and security can have on the organisation.

Thus our target is to construct a framework that will allow us to reason about risk and impact assessment as a stateful model on a socio-technical systems level so as to better capture the dynamics of a cybernetic organisation and its state of affairs. It is in the cybernetic organisations' nature that we can find the arguments for the need of a more social approach to cyber security and safety. The socio-technical systems (STS) have as a main target to blend both the technical and the social systems in an organization. This can be viewed as a necessary condition within a risk management framework as both aspects are of equal importance [3]. We will use stateful models to express the status quo of an organization, *i.e.* the current state of the systems, personnel and processes at each discrete moment before and after an event have occurred. This is going to give us a better perspective of the dependencies, responsibilities and finally reliabilities that run through the entire hierarchical chain of an organisation. Thus it will allow us to be able to run different threat scenarios and detect the potential vulnerabilities in a corporate network through forward and backward chaining.

2. What Is a Socio-Technical System

The socio-technical systems (STS) concept first appeared in the 1950s, as a project for the Tavistock Institute in London, in an attempt to focus on the group relations at all levels in an organization and come up with innovative practices in organizational development to increase productivity without the need for a major capital [3,4]. By socio-technical systems we mean people (individuals, groups, roles and organizations), physical equipment (buildings, surroundings, etc.), hardware and software, laws and regulations that accompany the organizations (e.g. laws for the protection of privacy), data (what data are kept, in which formats, who has access to them, where they are kept) and procedures (official and unofficial processes, data flows, relationships, in general anything that describes how things work, or better should work in an organization) [5].

Socio-technical systems are focusing on the groups as working units of interaction that are capable of either linear "cause-effect" relationships, or non-linear ones more complex and unpredictable [4]. They are adaptable to the constantly changing environment and the complexity that lies in the heart of most organizations.

The concept of tasks, their owners, their meaningfulness and the entire responsibility modelling as well as the dependencies are also a big part of this theory. In this study we treat people and systems as actors of certain tasks over a state of affairs. They are agents that comply with the same rules and norms, when it comes to the way they operate and interact with other agents for the accomplishment of states of affairs, with a model we are introducing in another section below. By agents, we mean individuals, groups of people or systems that hold roles and thus responsibilities for the execution or maintenance of certain tasks with certain objectives; we expanded the classic definition used in Artificial Intelligence [5].

Along with the socio-technical systems approach we will use Role Theory on the agents as each one of them in an organization fulfils some roles in association with certain states of affairs. Role Theory emphasizes on the fact that roles are basically sets of rights and responsibilities, expectations, behaviours or expected behaviours and norms. People's behaviour in organizations is bounded by specific context subject to both social and legal compliance, depending on their position in the hierarchy.

The objective of this is to be able to assist the performance of Responsibility Modelling on the socio-technical systems [5] to analyse their internal structure, the responsibility flows and the dependencies. This will provide us with the necessary information and structure upon which we can apply scenarios that simulate behaveiours deviating from the expected (e.g. attack scenarios) [6], along with logical rules that best describe the organization at hand, its expected behaviour and targets, that will allow us to locate vulnerabilities in the supply chain and express cause and effect, in case anything changes to the environment beyond expectation.

Different types of threats and countermeasures, different exposures, the variety of information and the heterogeneous data make it hard to manage risk. "Thus, it is clear that, given the level of complexity of Information Systems Security (ISS) risk management, simple linear models as proposed in most of the existing approaches will not be able to capture such complexities [1]." For this reason, we suggest the socio-technical systems approach combined with Role Theory and eventually Responsibility and Dependencies Modelling, as we think it works much better than linear models and is far more capable to map down the complex relationships, that more realistically represent organizations of any size and it is the nature of the information they provide that makes them appropriate for impact assessment and vulnerability analysis.

3. Impact Assessment

More and more security breaches are taking place the last few years, with a major pick on the attacks in 2011. DoS attacks, Botnets, Ghostnet, Operation Aurora, Flame, Stuxnet, Duqu and the very recent Gauss virus are only some of the major attacks that took place since 2009 onwards. No matter what the measures and the controls though, the assets or the information an organization is managing are never fully secure.

Thus businesses and organizations are utilising in Risk Assessment and Risk Management methods as a tool to mitigate this threat. The reason being, they are trying to prevent those breaches and consequently damage or loss of assets and information. Impact assessment is a critical tool in understanding how a Computer network Attack can impact on an organisation and can this be used as both a planning tool to allow for structured arguments and business investment to be considered and as a post-incident mitigation tool. Key to this decision process is situational awareness.

ISO 27005 is an Information Security Risk Management guideline applicable to organizations of all types that is why we are going to follow its definitions for Risk Assessment (RA). It provides a Risk Assessment Framework without providing specific methodologies and within this framework, Risk Assessment is recognized as the overall process of Risk Analysis and Risk Evaluation. Risk Analysis itself, is further divided in Risk Identification and Risk Estimation [7], i.e. any systematic use of information to identify sources and estimate the risk.

Risk estimation is the process used to assign values to the probability and consequence of risk and usually that is where the results of the overall process come from. In the process of Risk Identification we can place the identification of assets, threats, existing controls, vulnerabilities and impact. In essence, it is the finding, listing and characterizing elements of risk.

According to the same standards, the definition to threat is a potential cause of an incident that may result in an adverse change to an asset, a group of assets or an organization. Vulnerabilities are weaknesses in an information system, system security procedures, internal controls, or implementation that could be exploited or triggered by a threat source. Impact Assessment is defined as adverse change to the level of business objectives achieved, *i.e.* the loss of productivity and market share, or brand deterioration, penalties etc. It is used as a factor, along with the likelihood of occurrence of an event, the vulnerabilities and threats, to calculate and evaluate the risk.

Over the past years, a lot of methodologies have been developed in order to manage Information Systems Security (ISS) and Information Assurance (IA) [7,8]. Usually in the literature review Risk Assessment methods are divided into three categories, the qualitative ones, the quantitative ones and those that are a combination of both. The quantitative ones provide probabilistic results as to what is the percentage of running the risk, while the qualitative ones present results in predetermined scales of High-Medium-Low levels of risk. All the methods that appear in the literature have certain limitations so far, according to our opinion, and very few focus on the impact assessment side to properly estimate the impact itself and not to use impact to estimate the risk. Our approach is not focusing on the risk and threats side like the current methodologies and frameworks; we focus on impact and the propagation of it in the entire supply chain. Trying to calculate the probability of an event happening and predict it might be one perspective.

There is great difficulty in estimating the probability of loss occurrence as most methods suggest that such information is obtained by discussions with the users in order to understand the threat propagation. The problem with this approach is that these discussions are limited and they rarely help the analysts to get complete awareness and estimate the risk correctly [1]. Even when there is a proper understanding of the risk propagation it is extremely hard to quantify this even in a probabilistic way. So we suggest that a more automated method is necessary without excluding the human factor out of the equation. This can be achieved via the utilisation of a socio-technical approach that maps down business processes and roles, responsibilities and dependencies of tasks and considering impact as failure in states of affairs.

The problem with using stochastic probabilistic approaches is the "correct" metrics and the probabilities to estimate the magnitude and the probability of loss. By the term "correct", we mean metrics accurate and descriptive enough to capture the organization's pulse and priorities, in order to take the right threats into consideration and calculate the appropriate risks that actually make sense for the particular organization. In addition to that, as stated by the Risk Assessment Review Group Report of the NRC in 1978, for methods like these it is conceptually impossible to be mathematically complete [9]. It is an inherent limitation due to Gödel's theorem and thus they will always be subject to review and doubt as to

their completeness. Whilst the problem with the qualitative approaches is that they are not specific enough with the results they provide and not customized enough to make sense. So we think an approach using a stateful model and reasoning is needed, to be able to make forward and backward inferences about scenarios that have either happened or are trying to construct them.

Furthermore, most approaches do not capture the complex interrelationships of the corporations with very few exceptions. It is in those internal relationships and structures, that most of the uncertainty and risk is lying and not in the environmental uncertainty [10]. MIT argued that the chain-of-events concept that most current risk assessment methods use couldn't account for nonlinear and indirect relationships that describe most accidents in complex systems. For this reason, our approach as stated before is that of socio-technical systems and role theory with main focus on the responsibility and dependencies modelling part, along with a rule based framework capable of forward and backward inferences, to provide impact assessment. Socio-technical systems are scalable and adaptable, capable of mapping those complex nonlinear relationships in the organizations and thus we claim that they are capable of providing better incident and impact analysis.

4. The Framework

To perform risk management in a cyber security and safety context we must understand that relationship and interactions that technical and people have within an organisation. We have defined a responsibility with reference to a state of affairs and the ability of an agent to fulfil, or maintain, it. This definition gives rise to the question of how a given agent can achieve this within the context of a socio-technical system. **Figure 1** defines a framework within which responsibilities are mapped down into tasks that are executed by agents. A task is the primary vehicle through which the state of a sociotechnical system is changed and manipulated.

Within **Figure 2** we can see that a process of mapping responsibilities into set of tasks is achieved via the performance of a set of roles. The function of a role is to define the behaviour in terms of interactions that an agent engages in when executing a task. From a formal perspective we can define the following basic sets that will be used to model and express a socio-technical system.

The mapping from a responsibility to a role is achieved via obligations. Each responsibility will give rise to a requirement for a set of behaviours that maintain, and/ or achieve a state of affairs. The requirement is termed as an obligation and hence an obligation may be said to be a relationship between a given single responsibility and a set of roles. The concept behind these functions is to al-

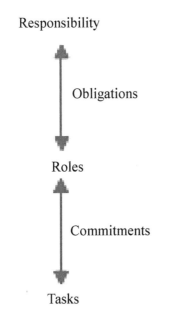

Responsibility

Obligations

Roles

Commitments

Tasks

Figure 1. The framework.

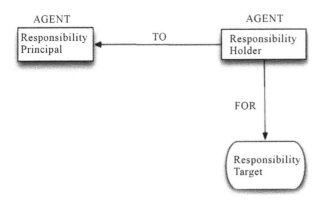

Figure 2. The responsibility relationship.

low us to express a set of necessary and sufficient conditions that must be achieved in order for a responsibility to be fulfilled.

These conditions take the form of requirements for the performance of a set of roles via a set of agents.Thus an obligation can be formally defined as a function that takes a responsibility as input and maps that responsibility to the set of roles that must be performed in-order for the responsibility to be fulfilled. For example, the doctor agent may be said to be responsible for the delivery of healthcare. This responsibility gives rise to a set of obligations for the doctor to perform a set of roles such as diagnoses illness and prescribe treatment.

The mapping from a role to a set of tasks, or actions is achieved via a series of commitments. From a philosophical perspective a commitment is to define those tasks that must be executed in order to the performance of the role to be true. Formally a commitment functions to define a mapping from a role to a set of tasks. The role of a task is to define a series of interactions that function to manipulate the state of the socio-technical system.

For example when a doctor performs the function of prescribe-treatment the doctor must first authenticate themselves to the medical patient information system, then select the patient, and finally select an treatment plan from a set of predefined intervention plans.

Within the specification of a responsibility, role and task is the concept of sequentiality. This can be used to express and represent the concept of dependability. Dependability is defined as the necessary conditions that must be achieved in order for a statement to be true. For example, in order for a doctor to perform the role prescribe-treatment, the doctor must first have made a diagnosis. In order for the action select intervention plan to be performed the action of selecting a patient must first be performed.

5. Responsibility Modelling

Responsibility modelling is the analysis and design technique of the responsibilities within an organization with purpose to explore the internal structure and the dependencies in the socio-technical systems [5,11]. It is one way of exploring the relationships amongst personnel, technical infrastructure, resources and business processes. What is interesting is that the risk associated with any deviation from the expected behaviour can be explored. In the event of an unanticipated change, a before and after analysis can determine what effect the event could have or had on the socio-technical system.

According to dictionary definitions, responsibility has two meanings:

1) The state of having a duty to deal with a certain state of affairs.

2) The state of being accountable or to blame for a certain state of affairs.

The first case has a causal connotation meaning the agent has the responsibility for doing something-making an event happen. The second case has a connotation of blame between the actual action and the results of it, but does not necessarily imply causality for the agent held accountable. For example, the parents are held responseble for the actions of their children. As a result, two types of responsibilities can be distinguished, a causal responsibility and a consequential responsibility [5,11]. For instance, each member of a crew of a ship or a plane is causally responsible for the performance of certain tasks but the captain or the pilot is always consequently responsible for the state of the ship or plane.

Responsibility is associated with agents, resources and tasks [11] as defined in the ART model later on and it is defined as the duty from one agent (the responsible) to another (the authority or principal) for the accomplishment of a state of affairs, whether this is the execution, maintenance or avoidance of certain tasks, subject to conformance with the organizational culture (**Figure 1**: The Responsibility Relationship). Thus the characteristics of a responsibility consist of: who is responsible to whom, for what state of affairs, which are the obligations of the responsibility holder in order to fulfil his/her responsibility and what type of responsibility it is [5].

Causal responsibility lies effectively between one agent and a state of affairs, while the consequential responsibility is a three-way relationship between two agents and a state of affairs. In this case the agent who holds the responsibility can be held accountable, culpable or liable to the "authority" agent as seen in **Figure 1**. Apparently, the most important part of the diagram for the consequential responsibility is the relationship between two agents as the most important question to be answered is "who is responsible to whom and in what respect?". On the other hand, for the causal responsibility the most important part is the relationship between the agent and the task as the most important question to be answered is "who is responsible for this action?".

Causal responsibility is a dynamic functional relationship between an agent and a state of affairs, while consequential responsibility indicates the structural relationships within organisations and their objectives. Due to its nature, more than one agent may hold consequential responsibility; it could rest upon an entire organisation, whereas the causal usually lies upon one agent. However, the latest can also be delegated from one agent to another, while the first one is normally not capable of that although it can be transferred.

6. The Concept of Role

6.1. On the Nature of Roles

At its simplest level the concept of a role is used to define behaviour in terms of is a set of rights, duties, expectations, norms and behaviours that a person has to face and fulfil. When modelling a socio-technical system we distinguish between two major, and distinct, concepts of a role [8]. A structural role, which is a relation between agents, corresponds to the consequential responsebility aspect of role and functions to define the context of the behaviour. Examples of structural roles are supervisor-subordinate, supplier-customer, provider-consumer, and so on. This is in contrast to a functional role, which is a relation between agents, and corresponds to the behavioural and interactional aspect of role. The functions roles function to define the tasks that an agent must execute in collaboration with other agents in order to fulfil a responsibility. Hence our concept of role allows us to distinguish the following:

• Agencies and agents with associated responsibilities

to other agencies and agents.
• Tasks that interact through the utilisation of resources and are structured into actions and operations.

This distinction between functional and structural roles enables us to represent and analyse the relations between functional and structural concepts and to express the way in which they operate in real organisations. A marked advantage of our socio-technical modelling technique is the way in which we can compose and decompose our models for the purposes of ascertaining requirements at various levels of agency (individual, group or organisation). Our use of the abstract term 'agency', for example, is deliberate so that we can discuss who or what corresponds to the agency.

While agents act as the primary manipulators of the systems state, agencies act as repositories for responsebilities, and structural roles act as their binding points [5]. A structural relationship serves as a means for the responsibilities to flow from one agency to another and thus responsibilities flow through an organisation.

6.2. Structural Role and Relationships

A structural role is defined by the set of responsibilities that bind to it. Each responsibility in the set in turn defines a set of roles. Each role in turn defines a set of tasks that the role holder is engaged in performing. The key to understanding the nature of structural roles and their relationships with each other is in understanding the primary purpose of the socio-technical model and the uses to which it will be put. The socio-technical model facilitates a problem solver to model, and to comprehend, how organisational attributes like responsibilities are established, flow through an organisation and are then fulfilled.

Structural relationships of the particular types and under a particular set of circumstances may be transitive in nature [5]. A requirement on the notation is that it allows us to express and describe the types of relationships and circumstances under which they are transitive. The set of structural roles that an agent can hold is divided into three types, a power relationship, a peer relationship and a service relationship. These relationships are described as follows:
• The Peer Relationships—The peer relationship is a far more subtle relationship than the power relationship, as this appears to be more social in nature than the power relationship. In a peer relationship two or more agents share a common power relationship with a third agent. It is important to note however that this power relationship should be of the same type. In a peer relationship there is no implication of enforcement, in fact, it is exactly the lack of this attribute that is characteristic of peer relationships and makes them

special. Consequently when two agents are in this relationship they may request that each other perform various services, but they lack the facility or the power to enforce execution. As a result agreement to perform a service is achieved by means of negotiation. An example of a peer relationship is that of the colleague relationship.

- The Service Relationships—In a service relationship one or both of the agents have the power to invoke the execution of a pre-defined and agreed task by another agent. This task will in some way relate to both the invoking and executing agents. An example of a service relationship is the consumer-supplier relationship, an example of which is the relationship that most people can be said to hold with an electricity board. In this relationship, one agent acts as the consumer of a service while another agent acts as the supplier of that service. The difference between a service relationship and a power relationship is that when the consuming agent is dissatisfied with the service provided by the supplying agent then the consuming agent may appeal to a third agent. It is this third agent that has the ability to enforce its judgements on both the supplying and consuming agents. A service relationship is in essence one agent invoking the performance of a predefined activity by another agent with predefined rules for the enforcement of the correct execution of that task.

- The Power Relationships—The essence of a power relationship is that one agency has the power to make and enforce demands on another agency. It is important to note however that the enforcement of these demands may be made via a third agency. An example of a power relationship is the supervisor-subordinate relationship that can exist in most organisations. There are however many different types of this relationship, for example master-slave. In this relationship the supervisor has the power to define the responsibilities and obligations that a subordinate is required to fulfil, and to judge whether or not the responsibilities were correctly discharged. The subordinate is not totally subservient to the supervisor in that the responsibilities and obligations that the subordinate is required to fulfil are defined by means of interaction between the two agencies.

6.3. Functional Roles and Interactions

Interactions link together two functional roles in different agents or agencies where each agent or agency is called a role holder. One of the purposes of Interactions is to define the behaviour that a role holder may engage in with another role holder within the context of a structural relationship. We may say that one of the purposes of a structural relationship is to define the context for a functional relationship. In defining and modelling the behaviour of a role holder, the problem solvers are in fact defining and modelling the set of allowable Interactions that can exist for that particular role holder.

Interactions aid in the identification of the organisational objects that are required to give meaning to the behaviour associated with a responsibility [12,13]. The purpose of an interaction from the perspective of its role holders is to facilitate the correct discharge of their responsibilities. The behaviour that one role holder may engage in with another takes the form of interactions. The context of these interactions is defined by the structural roles within which they are said to take place.

In the socio-technical systems model the interaction between two role holders defines how, when, where and under what circumstances responsibilities are established, flow through the organisation and are finally discharged or fulfilled. By modelling the life cycle of responsibilities we may attempt to answer a number of types of questions:

- The first type of question allows for the examination of the possible conflicts that could arise for any given role holder. The term conflict is used to denote a situation where a role holder is either obliged or responsible to perform an action, or bring about some state of affairs, whilst at the same time being obliged or responsible either not to perform the action, or not to bring about some state of affairs.

- The second type of question is concerned with the elucidation of the conditions under which an agent cannotfulfil a responsibility.

- The third type of question is concerned with the elucidation of what objects act as tokens of responsibilities.

- The fourth type of question is concerned with the delineation of the valid accesses to objects that act as tokens of either responsibility.

- The fifth type of question is concerned with the examination and comprehension of the correct creation and deletion of the objects that act as tokens of either responsibility.

7. The ART Model of Socio-Technical Systems

The core idea is to develop a rule [13]-based reasoning framework that will be able to identify the incoming threats viewing the organization from a cybernetic systems organism perspective.

The goal to be achieved is to use reasoning to bridge both the ICT infrastructure and the business processes, as a socio-technical approach, to assure that the business services are safely delivered as scheduled and the organization meets its objectives. This means that all resources/assets are available to all eligible agents, *i.e.* agents with the appropriate access rights on those resources/assets and all agents are able to execute all actions that have been assigned to them in order to fulfil their responsibilities.

In order to have a full perspective of the supply chain *i.e.* both the human factor and the complex ICT systems, we need taxonomic and ontological structures that are able to express the enterprise view in a socio-technical way, such as the one in **Figure 3**. The socio-technical model presented in **Figure 3** is comprised of a basic taxonomy and ontology of agents-resources-tasks.

The agents are the holders of responsibilities, they can be viewed as primary manipulators of the state or structure of the system and they are the only objects that can create, modify or destroy other objects, through the responsibilities that are associated with them. Actions are the operations that change the state of the system, and they are performed by agencies. All actions must induce state changes in the system that is visible to one or more agencies. The resources can be of two types: physical or logical, where physical resource are tangible objects such as servers, planes, tankers, and logical resources include information, time etc. When modelling organizations as a socio-technical system resources act either as tokens of responsibility signifying that an agency has a binding responsibility upon them, or as objects for which some agency is responsible.

The basic components of this architecture, like mentioned before, are three, Agents, Resources and Tasks:

- Agent: This is a name attached to a set of consequential responsibilities such as accountability, liability and culpability. It also allows for the expression of legal obligation.
- Resource: A Resource is an answer to "with", or "by-means-of-what" questions. For example, when a doctor makes a diagnosis they may do so by looking at an x-ray of a broken leg. Thus the x-ray functions as a resource over which the doctor has access rights.
- Task: A Task is to be distinguished from the doer of the task. Thus a task is a functional answer to "a what" question, and takes a verbal form of the specification of a functional role. For example, a doctor may perform the function role "Diagnosing Illness" when performing the task Delivery of Heath Care.

On those basic components, relationships are formed in order to describe the interactions between them:

- Task-Task: tasks interact with each other via interacttions. Such interactions are usually mediated by the exchange of resources; through direct interactions, such as interrupts, can also occur.
- Task-Resource: The relation between an task and an resource is an access mode, such as reads or writes (for information assets) or provides or consumes (for commodity assets).
- Resource-Resource: The relation between resource is what in information technology terms is called, the conceptual schema.
- Agent-Resource: The relation between an agent and an resource is an access right, such as the right: to-create, to-destroy, to-allocate, to-take-ownership-of.
- Agent-Task: The set of tasks with which an agent has some relation constitute the functional relationships of that agent and relates to the behaviour associated with that agent. For example, we can make some elementary distinctions between the functional relationships as follows:
  ○ The **Observer** of a task knows that it is taking place and may, or may not, know of any of the relationships which now follow.
  ○ The **Owner** of a task has the ability to destroy it; (the owner of an action may differ from the creator of an action, since ownership can be transferred).
  ○ The **Customer** of a task has the ability to change its specification.
  ○ The **Performer** of a task is the agent responsible for executing the tasks and performing the interactions.

By the *functional relationship* we mean two related things: a capability exists to perform the action and this capability by virtue of some legal instrument can be enforced by recourse to something outside the system (e.g. judicial)

- Agent-Agent: The set of agents with which an agent has some relation constitute the structural roles of that agent and relates to the responsibilities that bind agents together in webs that form structural schema.

The structural relationship diagrams that will be introduced in this section are normative. That is they attempt to explain what is required for a particular structural relationship in order for it to be such a relationship. Therefore we term such a diagram an explication of

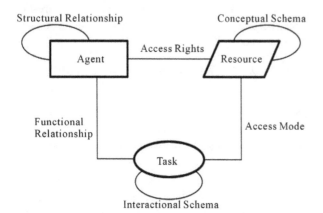

Figure 3. A socio-technical cybernetic enterprise model.

the structural relationship that it represents. When modelling the structural relationships that can exist within a socio-technical system there are two questions that the model should be able to answer. The first question is "what responsibilities are allowed to exist within the relationship?" The second question is what "socio-technical objects, *i.e.* resources etc., must exist in order to support and give meaning to the responsibilities?" It is important to note that these objects can act in several ways.

A structural relationship diagram is depicted in **Figure 3** and in this diagram there are a few things that should be pointed out. The first is that each object type is represented as a distinct shape, *i.e.* the agents are drawn as rectangles, the tasks as ovals and the resources as rhomboids. The arcs also have a condition associated with them. The task that is shown at the centre of **Figure 3** is derived from the responsibilities and obligations that a particular agency may hold. Responsibility is a three-place relationship between two agencies and a state of affairs. For this relationship we say that the agency A is responsible (in some way) to the agency B for bringing about or maintaining a state of affairs.

It is from this that the task definition is derived. A structural relationship diagram can be used in one of two ways by the problem owners. The first is to help them in their task of requirement elicitation by prompting them to ask certain questions.

For example "when and under what conditions is this relationship between two objects meaningful?" The second is in allowing them to explore the ramifications, implications and possible contradictions of policy statements.

The role and function of the responsibility dependency tree is to define the logical structures through which a responsibility is fulfilled within a socio-technical system. This graph/tree-based structure is represented in **Figure 4**. The responsibility dependency tree is a directed graph in which any two vertices are connected by exactly one simple path. In order words any connected graph without cycles is a free [14,15].

In addition, an undirected tree has the property that the path from any leaf node in the graph to the any other node in the graph is unique. This structure is a graph based formal semantic representation of dependence logic.

For the purpose of syntactic and semantic interoperability the following is a formal representation of the functional dependency between a responsibility depicted in **Figure 3** and its associated structural roles. Dependence logic is a logic of imperfect information and its semantics can be obtained from first order logic.

8. Summary and Conclusions

The methods and methodologies that have been deve-

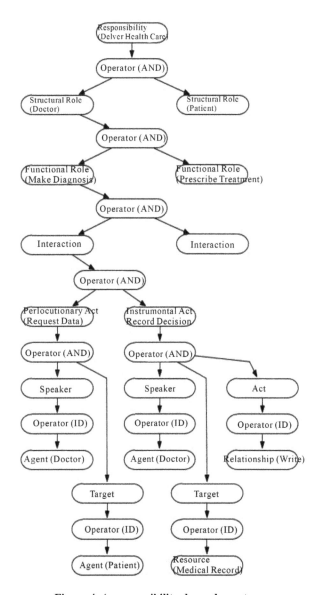

Figure 4. A responsibility dependency tree.

loped in order to manage Information Systems Security and Information Assurance have certain limitations so far, according to our opinion. They don't incorporate technology fully, but at the same time they don't include properly the human factor either [6]. They are focusing too much on probabilistic models with metrics that don't provide much help. The main target is risk analysis and predictions of events leaving out other equally important factors like impact and situational awareness. They are not complex enough or adaptable enough models to map all aspects of organisations not even the most important one the human personnel. They cannot reflect the interdependencies of assets or the correlations of data.

The RA methods were used in the past to evaluate situations or estimate the probability of an incident to occur and maybe disrupt the business processes or interfere with the business objectives. The same methods are now used to evaluate the risk of security events to happen [16,17]. Those processes were designed to handle natural disaster events, accidents and anything that could make an organisation not to meet its objectives. We believe that more is needed than just an expansion of those frameworks to include security incidents and technology that was incorporated the past decades.

Our model focuses on impact; on the implications events can have on the supply chain and business processes and not on risk estimation and the prediction of events. The main objective is to be able to perform impact assessment, to provide situational awareness and feed in mitigation strategies. It provides a socio-technical stateful ontology capable to represent the complex models of organisations where humans and technology interact to achieve common objectives and it is adaptable and scalable enough to follow unpredictable evolvement. As a stateful model, it allows us to find a path between states so that we can make forward or backward inferences that will allow us to understand how to transit from a state to another and thus better analyse events, the impact, the dependencies and how to mitigate risk. The model will be executable since the engine will be running in real-time after bounding the search space with certain criteria and it supports some kind of temporality.

REFERENCES

[1] Lili Sun, R. P. Srivastava and T. J. Mock, "An Information Systems Security Risk Assessment Model under Dempster-Shafer Theory of Belief Functions," *Journal of Management Information Systems*, Vol. 22, No. 4, 2006, pp. 109-142.

[2] Collaboration, "Socio-technical Systems Engineering Handbook," St. Andrews University, St Andrews, 2011.

[3] W. M. Fox, "Sociotechnical System Principles and Guidelines: Past and Present," *Journal of Applied Behavioral Science*, Vol. 31, No. 1, 1995, pp. 91-105.

[4] E. Trist and K. Bamforth "Some Social and Psychological Consequences of the Longwall Method of Coal Getting," *Human Relations*, Vol. 4, No. 1, 1951, pp. 3-38.

[5] G. Dewsbury and J. Dobson, "Responsibility and Dependable Systems," Springer, Berlin, 2007.

[6] P. Periorellis and J. E. Dobson, "Organisational Failures in Dependable Collaborative Enterprise Systems," *Journal of Object Technology*, Vol. 1, No. 3, 2002, pp. 107-117.

[7] B. Aubert, M. Patry and A. Rivard, "A Framework for Information Technology Outsourcing Risk Management," ACM SIGMIS Database, New York, 2005.

[8] K. Padayschee, "An Interpretive Study of Software Risk Management Perspectives, SAICSIT'02," *Proceedings of the 2002 Annual Research Conference of the South African Institute of Computer Scientists and Information Technologists on Enablement Through Technology*, 2002, Port Elizabeth, pp. 118-127

[9] H. W. Lewis, *et al.*, "Risk Assessment Review Group Report to the U.S. Nuclear Regulatory Commission," National Technical Information Service, Technical Report, Alexandria, 1978.

[10] R. Carvajal, "Systemic Netfields: The Systems' Paradigm Crises. Part I," *Human Relations*, Vol. 36, No. 3, 1983, pp. 227-246.

[11] A. J. C. Blyth, "Enterprise Modelling and Its Application to Organisational Requirements, Capture and Definition," Ph.D. Thesis, University of Newcastle, Newcastle, 1995.

[12] J.R. Searle, "Speech Acts: An Essay in the Philosophy of Languages," Cambridge University Press, Cambridge, 1984.

[13] J. J. Thomson, "Acts and Other Events (Contemporary Philosophy Series), Cornell University Press, New York, 1977.

[14] R. Nederpelt and F. Kamareddine, "Logical Reasoning: A First Course," College Publications, London, 2004.

[15] M. Blowfield and A. Murray, "Corporate Responsibility," Oxford University Press, Oxford, 2011.

[16] K. Brand and H. Boonen, "IT Governance CobiT 4.1—A Management Guide," 3rd Edition, Van Haren Publishing, Zaltbommel, 2008

[17] C Feltus, "Strengthening Employee's Responsibility to Enhance Governance of IT: COBIT RACI Chart Case Study," *Proceedings of the First ACM Workshop on Information Security Governance*, New York, 9-13 November 2009, pp. 23- 32.

5

Frequency Hopping Spread Spectrum Security Improvement with Encrypted Spreading Codes in a Partial Band Noise Jamming Environment

Amirhossein Ebrahimzadeh, Abolfazl Falahati

Digital Cryptography and Coding Laboratory (DCCS Lab), Department of Electrical Engineering,
Iran University of Science and Technology, Tehran, Iran

ABSTRACT

Frequency Hopping Spread Spectrum (FHSS) system is often deployed to protect wireless communication from jamming or to preclude undesired reception of the signal. Such themes can only be achieved if the jammer or undesired receiver does not have the knowledge of the spreading code. For this reason, unencrypted M-sequences are a deficient choice for the spreading code when a high level of security is required. The primary objective of this paper is to analyze vulnerability of linear feedback shift register (LFSRs) codes. Then, a new method based on encryption algorithm applied over spreading codes, named hidden frequency hopping is proposed to improve the security of FHSS. The proposed encryption security algorithm is highly reliable, and can be applied to all existing data communication systems based on spread spectrum techniques. Since the multi-user detection is an inherent characteristic for FHSS, the multi-user interference must be studied carefully. Hence, a new method called optimum pair "key-input" selection is proposed which reduces interference below the desired constant threshold.

Keywords: Frequency Hopping Spread Spectrum; Key Distribution Centre; Key Encryption Key; Linear Feedback Shift Register; Frequency Hopping Code Division Multiple Access; Direct Sequence Spread Spectrum

1. Introduction

Further employment of wireless communication system to exchange vital and critical electronic information requires an urgent attention to design reliable secure systems. This requirement is further strengthen for military communication systems where information transmission heavily relies upon wireless networks [1].

In fact the major advantage of a mobile set narrowband signal transmission is its efficient use of available frequency due to only a fraction of signal transmission frequency being used for a single subscriber. Indeed, a drawback is obvious, as it requires a well coordinated frequency allocation for different subscribers' signal which are now quiet vulnerable to signal jamming and interception.

In [2,3], the fundamental goal of spread spectrum system is considered as; to increase the dimensional characteristic of the signal, hence, to make eavesdropping and/or jamming more difficult since there are more dimensions of the signal to consider. In fact, the main method of increasing the dimensionality of the signal is to widen the signal's spectral occupancy [2,3].

In spread spectrum techniques, security against tapping and jamming is greater compared with narrowband spectrum techniques. Signals of spread spectrum are indistinguishable from background noise to anyone who does not know the coding scheme. The disadvantage of spread spectrum is its relatively high complexity of the coding mechanism which results in complex radio hardware designs and higher costs. Nonetheless, because of its remarkable advantages, spread spectrum has been adopted by many wireless technologies. For example, the IEEE 802.11b standard for wireless LAN employs DSSS over the 2.4-GHz free spectrum, whereas the Bluetooth standard uses frequency hopping spread spectrum (FHSS) for simplicity [1-3].

Furthermore, the main weakness of the wireless communication security system is the simplicity of accessing the communicating signal through the channel. Eavesdroppers can easily place an antenna in the desired field and after demodulation, the message bits can be obtained in the base-band form. If the messages are encrypted, after storing the encrypted messages with some crypto-analysis methods, the original message can be smeared out. Now, if the received radio signals from the wireless channel is spread in a form that the intruder cannot access the despread spectrum and receives only a signal similar to noise, a perfectly secure radio transmission channel is achieved [3-5].

Moreover, specifically the security of the frequency hopping code division multiple access (FH-CDMA) system mainly relies on the long-code generator that consists of a 42-bit long-code mask generated by a 42-bit LFSRs. However, if eavesdroppers can obtain 42 bits of plaintext-cipher-text pairs, the long-code mask can be recovered after dropping the transmission on the traffic channel for about one second [3,6,7].

The fast correlation attack method based on a recently established linear statistical weakness of decimated LFSR sequences for reconstruction of LFSR code is described in [8]. With this method eavesdropper can recover LFSR sequence that he knows the LFSR feedback polynomial. A method of blind estimation of PN code in multipath fading direct sequence spread spectrum systems is proposed in [9]. In this article a combed method is presented to estimate the unknown PN spreading sequence for direct sequence spread spectrum (DS-SS) signals in frequency selective fading channel. It is proven that LFSR codes are vulnerable to cipher-text-only attacks [10] and security weakness of white Gaussian sequence is investigated in [11].

This preface and further studies show that LFSR codes, white Gaussian sequences and other unencrypted codes have security weaknesses and can be recovered by eavesdroppers. So a method which can guarantee systems against the probable attacks is urgently required.

In this manuscript, a new method called hidden frequency hopping spread spectrum is proposed to augment the built-in security of FH-CDMA systems by applying cryptographic algorithm in the channelization code sequence.

2. Security Enhancement in FHSS System with Encryption Hidden within SS

In FHSS technique, several users spread their signal spectrum through available wideband frequency spectrum as narrowband sections with a special code which is called frequency hopping. These codes must have a low cross-correlation since other signals have little interference over the desired signal. On the other hand, although M-sequences which are generated by LFSR have fair cross-correlation properties but they produce a weak security system for eavesdroppers to track the transmitted spread signals. Therefore, FH-CDMA uses a long-code to scramble the signal in wireless channels, thus the security is set up in the physical layer. The available security which is produced by this method is very low and not suitable for data communication considered. In this article, for security enhancement, a model is proposed that every user encrypts a special spreading code (e.g. a code

that is made by the M-sequence generators) with his private key. The model is shown in **Figure 1**. Encrypted codes are then used as the spreading code in the channelization section. At destination, the receiver who knows his private key is able to regenerate the spreading code to de-spread the transmitted signal [3].

On the other hand, the security by the proposed method is related to the encryption algorithm, not to the LFSR complexity. If a suitable algorithm such as RC5, IDEA or any block cipher algorithm is chosen, then a desired high privacy can be obtained [12,13].

3. The Proposed System Model

Although spread spectrum systems are used for narrowband interference mitigation and have good efficiency in preventing intentional and unintentional channel interference, if jammer uses similar spreading codes method, it can be successful in deteriorating such techniques. The level of signal destruction depends on similarity between jammer and transceiver PN codes. This mechanism is different for FHSS and DSSS systems but FH systems are desired. In this method, jammer operates intelligently, after accessing the channel and receive spread signals, it finds spreading technique and PN sequence pattern. Then it generates similar PN pattern and can synchronize itself with the transceiver system to track the modulation type. It should be mentioned that jammer can be located between transmitter and receiver so to provide the man in the middle attack. So jammer can interfere with data signal or change receiver to a useless one and mask itself as an allowable user.

A proposed hidden frequency hopping method can be used to prevent sequence pattern disclosure. Therefore, complexity in this process solely depends upon encryption complexity. Let's consider MFSK transceiver which employs FHSS with encrypted PN sequences, Gaussian noise power and partial band noise jamming function j(t). Suppose that jammer can access channel and obtain desired information from this system.

First a Key Distribution Centre (KDC) generates and transmits agreeable session key to receiver by secure procedure. Session key is a symmetrical key that BTS and SS know and its transmission would be performed by asymmetric pair public-privet key encryption. In this manner symmetric key encrypts SS public key and only SS can decrypt it. Then desired key is transmitted trough unsecure channel by secure process. Public asymmetric key is called Key Encryption Key (KEK). After key exchange, transmitter and receiver have the same encryption key to be able to encrypt PN codes that generate hidden narrow band frequencies. The transceiver system can now be synchronized, track encrypted PN codes, access hidden hopped frequencies and finally obtains

Frequency Hopping Spread Spectrum Security Improvement with Encrypted Spreading Codes in a
Partial Band Noise Jamming Environment

39

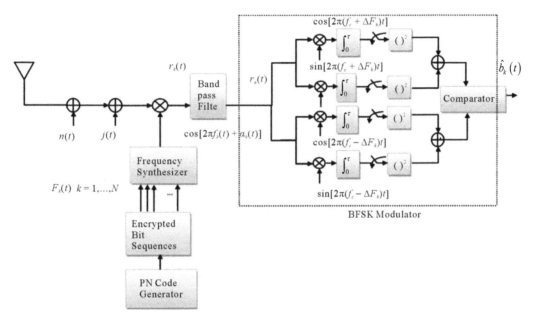

Figure 1. Proposed FHSS with hidden PN sequences for MFSK receiver (M = 2).

original data signals.

Therefore, the jammer applies interference power on narrow band hopped channels randomly and so the bit error rate can be computed as

$$
\begin{aligned}
&P_{\text{s-encrypted}} \\
&= P_S\left(\text{error}|\text{hit}\right) \times P_{\text{hit}} + P_S\left(\text{error}|\text{no-hit}\right) \times P_{\text{no-hit}}
\end{aligned}
\tag{1}
$$

where P_S presents symbol error probability and P_{hit} is the probability of signal hitting the jammer.

Suppose that the transceiver and jammer have the same hop period T_H, the number of hoped channel N_H with different start signaling. Because jammer doesn't have session key, it can't obtain spreading codes, synchronize with transceiver and to know start transceiver signaling. Thus, the time of transceiver signaling is given by

$$
T_{\text{sent-signal}} = T_H - t_{s_0}
\tag{2}
$$

where t_{s0} is the transceiver signalling start time. The jammer signalling time is

$$
T_{\text{sent-signal}} = T_H - t_{s_0}
\tag{3}
$$

where t_{j0} is start time of jammer signaling, and $0 \le t_{s_0}$ & $t_{j_0} \le T_H$. So jammer and transceiver signal hit occurs in joint time hop period. This value can be expressed as

$$
\alpha = \min\left\{T_{\text{sent-signal}}, T_{\text{sent-jammer}}\right\}
\tag{4}
$$

Figure 2 describes the transceiver signal and jammer signal collision behaviour. So within this behaviour, the probability of jammer and transceiver signal hit in k-th hop is

$$
P_{\text{hit}} = \frac{\alpha}{T_H}
\tag{5}
$$

and

$$
P_{\text{no-hit}} = 1 - P_{\text{hit}}
\tag{6}
$$

If jammer uses partial band noise jammer, with standard M-ary FSK modulation that uses one out of M frequencies each second, the bit error probability can be obtained as

$$
\begin{aligned}
&P_{\text{s-encrypted}} \\
&= \left(1 - \frac{\alpha}{T_H}\right) \frac{1}{2(M-1)} e^{\frac{E_b}{2N_0}} \sum_{q=2}^{M} \binom{M}{q} (-1)^q e^{\frac{E_b(2-q)}{2qN_0}} \\
&+ \frac{\alpha}{T_H} \frac{1}{2(M-1)} e^{-\frac{E_b}{2N_T}} \sum_{q=2}^{M} \binom{M}{q} (-1)^q e^{\frac{E_b(2-q)}{2qN_T}}
\end{aligned}
\tag{7}
$$

where E_b is bit energy, N_0 is the one-sided noise spectral density, and N_T is the total AWGN and jammer noise.

Considering α is maximized by $t_{s_0} = t_{j_0} = t$ as

$$
\alpha_{\max} = \min\left\{T_{\text{sent-signal}}, T_{\text{sent-jammer}}\right\}_{t_{s_0} = t_{j_0} = t}
\tag{8}
$$

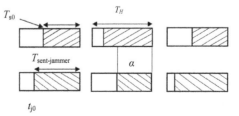

Figure 2. Collision of jammer and transceiver signals.

And maximum term for synchronization α_{Sync} can be given by

$$\alpha_{Sync} = \alpha_{max} = T_H - t \qquad (9)$$

In fact, this is obtained when jammer can synchronize itself with victim transceiver system. If jammer doesn't have session key, it can't access α_{max}.

The cross-correlation of some codes such as Gold and Kassami is lower than the encrypted codes, so a method must be used to optimize the input interference of the system to an acceptable extent. For this reason, an interference threshold is selected for the channel according to the channel interference average for 100 or 1000 times tests. In these tests the channel minimum value interference are calculated and a constant threshold is selected for a channel with a number of users, then the multi-user interference is estimated for each user who enters the network and this value is compared with the threshold level. If the result is less than threshold level, the optimum pair "key-input" is saved for new user and the data is sent confidently such that the interference do not exceed the threshold level. If the interference value is more than the threshold level, the user has to generate another PN and give it to the cryptographer for generating a frequency whose interference is not more than the threshold level. If p is probability of failure and $(1 - p)$ is the probability of success, the probability of achieving the desired code after k-tries is

$$P(A) = p^k \times (1-p) \qquad (10)$$

4. Simulation Results

To perform simulation purposes, an averaging over different keys is employed to mitigate the dependency of BER results on the chosen keys. The simulation results given in **Figure 3** show that the mean value of interference among the encryption algorithm outputs is higher than the M-sequence codes. These values are estimated for 256 channel hops and 1000 iterations. It is dependent upon the selected keys and the encryption algorithm inputs. **Figure 4** represents the number of users trying to find optimum pair "key-input" for 32, 64, 128, 256 and 512 channel hops.

Figure 5 indicates the BER performance when the number of users is increased. This means that the interference is directly proportional to number of users. **Figure 6** represents the effect of FHSS system to mitigate the interference in multi-user channel for 64, 128, 256 and 512 channel hops. **Figure 7** compares m-sequence codes with encrypted codes considering both optimum and non-optimum key method in order to select pair input-key for 256 channel hop. This performance shows that the interference value for encrypted codes is higher

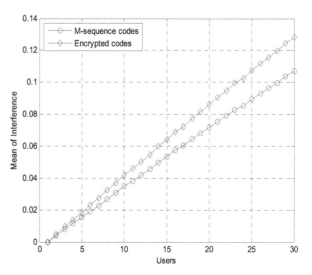

Figure 3. Comparing mean of interference M-sequence and encrypted codes in channel with 256 hop.

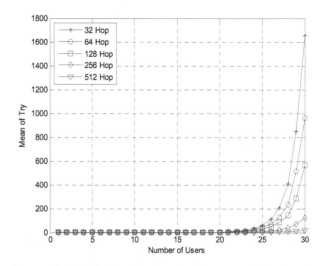

Figure 4. Calculation of mean try to access desired pair input-key with optimum interference.

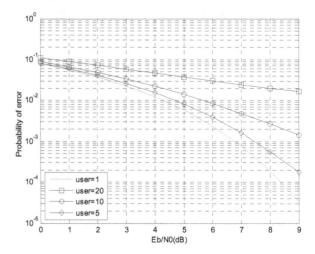

Figure 5. Probability of error for various number of users with 256 channel hop.

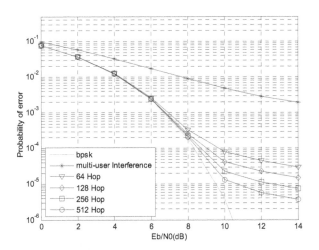

Figure 6. Probability of error for different channel hops in AWGN channel.

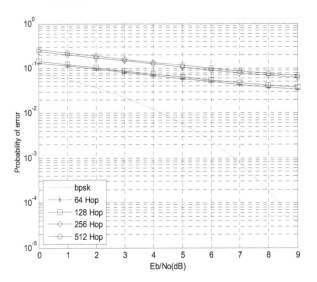

Figure 7. Comparing probability of error for M-sequence, encrypted and optimum encrypted code in 256 channel hop.

than unencrypted m-sequence codes and employing optimum method improves this value further.

Figure 8 represents the probability of decoding when wrong code is used. By comparing **Figure 6** with **Figure 8**, it's clear that if wrong codes are used, bit error rate becomes very high. In other words, if eavesdropper uses wrong code or key, it receives partial error frequency. To receive hidden frequencies, it must have access to a session key that victim transceiver employs.

5. Conclusions

A thorough investigation revealed security weaknesses of PN sequences. These drawbacks are challenged deploying a new method called hidden frequency hopping to augment the built-in security of FHSS systems. It is named hidden frequency hopping method since a known cryptographic algorithm is hidden within the PN codes.

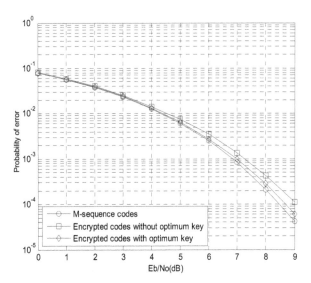

Figure 8. Uncertainty performance when a wrong key is inserted.

The jammer and transceiver signal hit occurrence in joint time hop period, the parameter α, is determined by analysis through the jammer and transceiver signalling start times. This value allows determination of the probability of the jamming signal colliding with the desired signal. It is found that, maximum value of α is reached when the jammer can determine the signalling start time to synchronize itself with the victim (a common un-encrypted method) and it is observed that with the proposed technique, the jammer can never reach maximum value to synchronize itself with the victim.

Simulation results show that when the proposed encrypted codes are utilized, the received channel interference increases. Naturally, this phenomenon makes the signal detection procedure more complex. Therefore, an optimum pair "key-input" algorithm is proposed to reduce the associated interference to the desired level. For instance, by employing codes with a good orthogonal behaviour, indeed, still algorithm can provide small amount of error but it also reduce the data transmission speed.

Furthermore, the performance of the encrypted FH/SS code is as good as unencrypted sequences when correct key is applied. When a wrong key is employed, system security is guaranteed.

6. Acknowledgements

Authors would like to thank the financial support of ITRC (Iran Telecommunication Research Company) for this project.

REFERENCES

[1]   P. Zheng, L. Peterson, B. Davie and A. Farrel, "Wireless

Network Complete," Elsevier publisher, Amsterdam, 2009.

[2]   Telecommunications Industry Association, "Mobile Station-Base Station Compatibility Standard for Dual-Mode Wideband Spread Spectrum Cellular System," Telecommunications Industry Association, Arlington, 1998.

[3]   M. Tafaroji and A. Falahati, "Improving Code Division Multiple Access Security by Applying Encryption Methods over the Spreading Codes," *IET Communication*, Vol. 1, No. 3, 2007, pp. 398-404.

[4]   J. L. Massey, "Shift-Register Synthesis and BCH Decoding," *IEEE Transactions on Information Theory*, Vol. 15, No. 1, 1969, pp. 122-127.

[5]   I. Mansour, G. Ghalhoub and A. Quilliot, "Security Architecture for Wireless Sensor Networks Using Frequency Hopping and Public Key Management," *IEEE International Conference on Networking, Sensing and Control* (ICNSC), Delft,11-13 April 2011, pp. 526-531.

[6]   V. K. Gray, "IS-95 CDMA and CDMA2000," Prentice-Hall, Upper Saddle River, 2000.

[7]   J. K. Tugnait and T. Li, "Blind Detection of Asynchronous CDMA Signals in Multipath Channels Using Code-Constrained Inverse Filter Criteria," *IEEE Transactions on Signal Process*, Vol. 49, No. 7, 2001, pp. 1300-1309.

[8]   J. Colic, "Towards Fast Correlation Attacks on Irregularly Clocked Shift Registers, Information Security Research Centre," *EUROCRYPT'95 Proceedings of the 14th Annual International Conference on Theory and Application of Cryptographic Techniques*, Louvain-la-Neuve, pp. 248-262.

[9]   X. Xu, "Blind Estimation of PN Code in Multipath Fading Direct Sequence Spread Spectrum Systems," *11th IEEE International Conference on Communication Technology Proceeding*, Hangzhou, 10-12 November 2008, pp. 213-216.

[10]   Q. Ling, T. Li and J. Ren, "Physical Layer Built-in Security Enhancement of DS-CDMA Systems Using Secure Block Interleaving," *Conference Record of the Thirty-Eighth Asilomar Conference on Signals, Systems and Computers*, Pacific Grove, 7-10 November 2004, pp. 1105-1109.

[11]   L. Gang and A. Nakansu and M. Ramkumar, "Security and Synchronization in Watermark Sequences," *2002 IEEE International Conference on Acoustics, Speech, and Signal Processing* (*ICASSP*), Orlando, 13-17 May 2002, pp. IV-3736-IV-3739.

[12]   B. Schneier, "Applied Cryptography: Protocols, Algorithms and Source Code in C," 2nd Edition, John Wiley & Sons, Hoboken, 1996.

[13]   B. S. Kaliski, and L. Y. Yiqun, "On the Security of the RC5 Encryption Algorithm," RSA Laboratories Technical Report, Cambridge, 1998.

6

The Package Concept for Enforcing Usage Control

Patricia Ghann, Changda Wang, Conghua Zhou

School of Computer Science and Telecommunication Engineering, Jiangsu University, Jiangsu, China

ABSTRACT

Access and usage control is a major challenge in information and computer security in a distributed network connected environment. Many models have been proposed such as traditional access control and UCONABC. Though these models have achieved their objectives in some areas, there are some issues both have not dealt with. The issue of what happens to a resource once it has been accessed rightfully. In view of this, this paper comes out with how to control resource usage by a concept known as the package concept. This concept can be implemented both with internet connection and without the internet connection to ensure continual control of resource. It packages the various types of resources with the required policies and obligations that pertain to the use of these different resources. The package concept of ensuring usage control focuses on resource by classifying them into three: Intellectual, sensitive and non-sensitive resources. Also this concept classifies access or right into three as: access to purchase, access to use temporally online and access to modify. The concept also uses biometric mechanism such as fingerprints for authentication to check redistribution of resource and a logic bomb to help ensure the fulfillment of obligations.

Keywords: Access Control; Usage Control; Policies; Obligation; User or Subject; Biometric Finger Print; Logic Bomb; Remote Client

1. Introduction

Computers and computer systems play a vital role in the lives of the individual. The use of computer systems is seen almost everywhere. For example, insurance companies, healthcare services, banking, education and many more. The advancement in computer and information technology has increased the amount of data collected, whereas the improvement in network infrastructure has resulted in the uncontrolled distribution of information. Although the impact of these technologies cannot be over emphasized, a critical issue in computer security concerns how data and resources can be protected. Access control and usage control are challenging issues that face information security currently. Access control has been given adequate attention by researchers in the past. Usage control on the other hand is a new concept proposed by Park and Sandhu (2000) that seeks to enhance on access control. By controlling who has access to which data, traditional access control mechanisms such as DAC, MAC and RBAC, dealt with just an aspect of the problem. Usage control has been proposed to argument access control by controlling what happens to data after access has been granted. UCON introduces authorization, obligation and condition for decision making as well as continuity of decision and mutability of attributes [1]. However it does not go beyond what happens to a particular resource once it has been "rightfully" accessed using UCON. For an example, imagine a subject is able to purchase an eBook online using UCON implementation system where the right to access is influenced by authorization, obligation and condition. After successfully paying for the eBook, it becomes his property however the subject has no right to redistribution since the subject is not the original owner and hence redistribution would result in loss of profit by the provider. This is also similar to the purchase of movie or music CDs online. That is, what measures should be implemented to ensure that, obligations and policies such as non-redistribution of resources are adhered to. In view of this, the paper explores the idea of obligation and proposes a method of ensuring the fulfillment of obligation on a remote client server which is one of the pressing issues facing information security. The rest of the paper is organized as follows; Sections 2.0 and 2.1 is about traditional access control and prior work respectively, Section 2.2 is about the limitations of traditional access control while Section 2.3 is about usage control. In Section 3 we introduce our method of ensuring the enforcement of obligation on a remote client server. Section 3.1 is about biometric fingerprint authorization, 3.2 is about logic bomb. Sections 4 and the last part are conclusion and references accordingly.

2. Traditional Access Control

Access control determines which subjects can access which resources under which circumstances. In the history of computer and information security, various attempts have been made to ensure trusted control in terms of information or digital resource usage. The earliest approach has been traditional access controls such as mandatory access control (MAC), discretionary access control (DAC) and role-based access control (RBAC). In a distributed networking environment recently, access control still remains a major challenge for computer and information security. Providers of services, resources and digital content need to selectively determine who can access these and exactly what access is provided [2]. Hence the objective of access controls. There has been much research with progress in access control for the past thirty years with prominence centered on access control matrix. With access matrix, a right is unambiguously granted to a subject to access an object in a specific mode for example, read or write mode. This right exists whether or not the subject is currently accessing the object. It is also a presumed that, the right enables repeated access until it is finally revoked. According to research, access matrix is not explicitly represented in practical terms. Instead access control lists (ACLs), capabilities or access relations are often used [3]. A variety of DAC, MAC and RBAC models have emerged to accommodate a diverse range of real-world access control policies. However, the practice of access control has grown very far away from the access matrix abstraction; nonetheless the core idea that, access is driven by rights granted to a subject to access an object had still remained. Traditionally, access control has focused on the protection of computer and information resources in a closed system environment. The enforcement of control has been primarily based on identities and attributes of known users by using a reference monitor and specified authorization rules [4]. In today's network-connected, highly dynamic and distributed computing environments, digital information is likely to be used and stored at various locations, hence has to be protected regardless of user location and information location.

2.1. Prior Work

Trust management emerged as an enhancement on traditional access control by giving consideration to unknown users and utilizing their credentials in an open environment. However it focused on static entities with charac-

teristics that do not change with time [5]. Recent research came out with digital right management which uses a client-side reference monitor to control usage of already disseminated digital objects. This model has brought out a significant new perspective on access control problems. Various efforts have been made by researchers to ensure trusted client-side computing. For example Microsoft's Palladium and Intel-driven trusted computing platform alliance (TCPA) [TCPA 2002] originating from AEGIS [6]. These have gained serious attention and concern because of their potential impacts on security and privacy issues. Because of DRM's potential opportunity for commercial sector; current DRM solutions have been largely driven by commercial entities and are mainly focused on intellectual property rights protection which is based on payment functions [7-9]. All these models discussed above have tried to protected information or digital resources in one way or another. The fact however remains, in a modernized and computerized era currently, where digital resource are available and can be shared and stored in various devices, these models are inadequate in ensuring access control and hence achieving confidentiality, integrity and availability [10,11].

2.2. Limitations of Traditional Access Control

Traditional access control models are not adequate for today's distributed, network-connected digital environment [12].

- Authorization only—No obligation or condition based control
- Decision is made before access—No ongoing control
- No consumable rights—No mutable attributes
- Rights are pre-defined and granted to subjects

In view of the above enlisted problems of traditional access control, the need to have a flexible access control in a highly dynamic and distributed environment such as currently seems laudable. This is because information or digital resources can be located in various places and thus the need for a general client-side platform [13]. The multi aspect nature of access control decisions in terms of subject and object attributes, obligations, conditions and the dynamism of subject and object attributes has necessitated the need for a more comprehensive model such as usage control by Sandhu and Park.

2.3. Usage Control (UCON)

This is a model that addresses information security challenges faced in a modern application and computer environment by providing richer, finer and persistent controls on information or digital resources as compared to traditional access control policies and models. In contrast to traditional access control or trust management, it covers both centrally environment and an environment where central control authority is not available. UCON also deals with privacy issues in both commercial and non-commercial environments. The main advantage of UCON lies in its strength to express diverse access cases [1]. The concept of usage control encompasses traditional access control, trust management and digital right management in a single framework. As a result of this, UCON's objectives include privacy protection, intellectual right protection and sensitive information protection. In terms of domain control and reference monitor, UCON authorization system can be situated either on server-side reference monitor or a client-side reference monitor or on both. This architecture provides a two-tier usage control over digital resources.

A usage decision in UCON is made by policies of authorizations, obligations, and conditions (also referred as UCONABC core models). In terms of continuity of decision, usage control can be enforced before or during an access process. The distinguishing properties of UCON, beyond traditional access control models are the continuity of access decisions and the mutability of subject and object attributes [14]. In UCON as compared to traditional access control, authorization decisions are not only checked and made before an access, but may be repeatedly checked during the access and may revoke the access if some policies are not satisfied, according to changes of the subject or object attributes, or environmental conditions. The concept of UCON fails to consider what happens to data or information after it has been granted in the absence of internet connection; in other words, the concept of mutability and continuity, only is achieved once a subject is using the internet. In light of this, we propose a means of ensuring the fulfillment of obligations a on a remote client server. We do this by a concept we have termed the "package concept". Much attention and research have focused on the architectural aspect of enforcing obligations without any attention on the information itself. As mentioned previously, Usage control does not answer the question of what happens to resource after it has been rightfully accessed and has now become the subject's property literally. Thus if a subject uses usage controls decision factors, authorization, obligation and conditions with mutability and continuity to rightfully access a music file, movie or a white paper, he can redistribute these resources since he has paid for it. This however would affect the provider or owner of such resource in terms of revenue generation. In the next section we introduce the package concept of enforcing obligation to ensure usage control.

3. The Package Concept of Enforcing Obligation and Ensuring Control of Resource on a Remote Client

We propose a system that would use the various archi-

tectural designs that has already been proposed so far to help ensure control of resource. A method that would help enforce obligation in remote client server by focusing on the resource itself. Firstly, we classify objects or digital resources as follows:

- Intellectual resource (INTELL)
- Sensitive resource (SEN)
- Non-sensitive resource (NSEN)

We make this division as most of the resources available on the internet basically fall within this classification. This classification is in line with the coverage of UCON, except that we have captured privacy protection under sensitive resources and other resources that do not belong to intellectual or sensitive resources as non-sensitive resources. This is to ensure that policies and obligations required for the accessibility of resources are formulated appropriately and attached to these resources; thus help a subjects to know what exactly they are going in for and what is required from them.

Based on the above classification, we formulate the appropriate obligations and encapsulated them with each group of resource. Thus instead of stating obligation and policies separately from a resource, obligation and policies covering these groups of objects or resource are stated and attached to each group by the service provider. Secondly, access to a particular resource must be through authorization using a biometric mechanism such as fingerprints. The subjects would have to input three different fingerprints from among ten fingers. This would ensure that resource is not given to an unauthorized person as the requested resource, would have subject's fingerprints embedded into it. Obligations consist of actions and time within which they are supposed to be fulfilled. This is to ensure that when access is granted, to a particular group of resource, the subject cannot give resource to any other person. For example if a subject want to purchase an eBook, movie or music CD, he is suppose to register, if the registration is by finger prints, the service provider accepts the finger prints and encrypt it into these resource before it access to purchase is granted. This is done so that subject cannot redistribute resources.

3.1. Biometric Authorization by Fingerprints

Biometrics is a general term used to describe characteristics or processes. As a characteristic, it is the measurable biological (anatomical and physiological) and behavioral characteristics that can be used for automated recognition. As a process it encompasses the automated methods of recognizing an individual based on measurable biological (anatomical and physiological) as well as behavioral characteristics. The above definition basically classifies biometrics into two main types as behavioral and physical biometrics. Behavioral biometrics basically measures the characteristics which are acquired naturally over a time and is mostly used for verification. For instance speaker recognition for analyzing vocal behavior, signature for analyzing signature dynamics and keystroke for measuring the time spacing of two typed words.

Physical biometrics on the other hand, measures the inherent physical characteristics on the individual and as such can be used for either identification or verification. Examples of physical biometric include; fingerprint for analyzing fingertip patterns, facial recognition for measuring facial characteristics, iris scan for analyzing features of colored ring of the eye and many more.

We propose a biometric authorization by fingerprints for analyzing fingertip patterns to help ensure usage control. This is because most sites require attributes of subject such as password and user name for authorization. This however can be stolen or verbally transferred to other people. However a random selection of three fingerprints from among ten fingers is difficult to steal or be verbally transferred to other people. A subject who wants to have access to a particular type of resource would have to provide a random sample of his or her three fingerprints. Once the fingerprints are collected, the type of access and the type of resources are selected by the subject.

Resources or digital information are accessed on online in three main ways. These include the following:

- Access to purchase
- Access to read, listen or watch or download online
- Access to modify or use online

Access to Purchase: This type of access employs UCON pre-authorization by fingerprints as the decision factor. In this type of access, a subject may want to purchase an eBook, music or movie online. These types of resources are classified as intellectual resources. As a result, the main policy may be non-redistribution by subjects. To enforce this policy, the fingerprints of the subject are encrypted into the resource. Thus limiting redistribution by location; in other words, the subject would have to move from place to place in order to redistribute this resource.

Access to Read, Listen or Watch Online: Resources involved in this type of access include intellectual, sensitive and non-sensitive. Intellectual resource may include access to read a book, journal and articles. Sensitive resource can include access to read a bank statement or a medical report. Non-sensitive resource can include intellectual resource such as music, movie or wiki document. With this type of access, UCONABC model is very effective in ensuring usage control. With sensitive information like, bank statement and medical report, fingerprint of identifee subject is required in the form of pre-authorization and this is encrypted into the said resource before access is granted.

Access to Modify or Use: This type of access is mostly required in the health services; for instance, a doctor requiring patient's record for treatment, on the patient's day of appointment. Since the resource involve is sensitive, the doctor is requested for his fingerprint as a pre-authorization. There can also be ongoing check to ensure that the doctor is indeed authorized. Furthermore, since sensitive information is been handled, a logic bomb can be implement in the resource with an obligation that specifies the duration of access to such a record or resource. For example, a logic bomb can be implemented so that, the doctor is allowed a maximum of one hour on a patient, after which the record is temporary destroyed. When this happens, the doctor would be asked for his or her fingerprints again but this time around with a "mark" which would enable management to request for some explanations as well as investigations.

3.2. A Logic Bomb Mechanism

In order to ensure that obligations that are encapsulated with resources are fulfilled, we proposed a logic bomb to help accomplish this task. A logic bomb or slag code is a program, or portion of a program, which lies dormant until a specific piece of program logic is activated. The common activator for a logic bomb is a date. The logic bomb checks the system date and does nothing until a pre-programmed date and time is reached. At that point, the logic bomb activates and executes its code. The logic bomb can also be programmed so as to wait for a certain message from the subject. When the logic bomb sees that message, or when the logic bomb stops seeing that message, it activates and executes its code. The most dangerous form of the logic bomb is a logic bomb that activates when something doesn't happen. We therefore use a logic bomb programmed along these two dimensions; date and message from subject. With date, obligations that need to be fulfilled with certain durations can be implemented. For example delete within 90 days. This is however similar to the classic use for a logic bomb to ensure payment for software. If payment is not made by a certain date, the logic bomb activates and the software automatically deletes itself. With the message, the logic bomb would be programmed to receive fingerprints of user at certain random interval for verification especially in the case of access to purchase or modify. This would ensure that only authorized subjects have access to resource and minimized redistribution of resources. **Figure 1** is an illustration of how a particular resource can be accessed in the package.

How to Access a Particular Resource
1) Input three finger prints
2) Upon acceptance of fingerprints

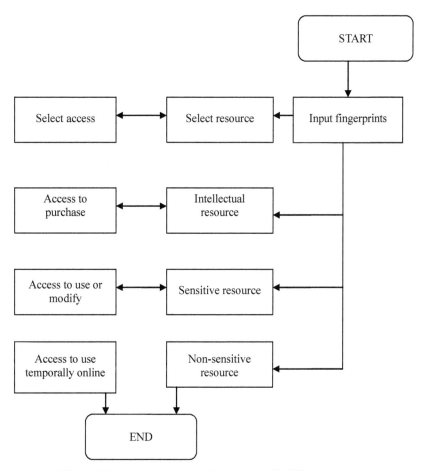

Figure 1. Packaged concept of resources with different access.

3) Select type of resource
- If access is to purchase an intellectual or sensitive resource, fingerprints are encrypted into resource before resource is accessed for purchase.
- If access is to modify, fingerprints are obtained for authorization and encrypted into modified section for accountability.
- If access is to use online, fingerprints is obtained for authorization and access is permitted based on UCONABC.

With usage control, actions are classified into two. Actions performed by a subject and actions performed by the system. These actions are as follows:

1) Tryaccess(s, o, r): generating a new access request (s, o, r), performed by subjects.

2) Permitaccess(s, o, r): granting the access request of (s, o, r), performed by the system.

3) Denyaccess(s, o, r): rejecting the access request of (s, o, r), performed by the system.

4) Revokeaccess(s, o, r): revoking an ongoing access (s, o, r), performed by the system.

5) Endaccess(s, o, r): ending an access(s, o, r), performed by a subjects.

6) Preupdate(attribute): updating a subject or an object attribute before granting access or after denying an access, performed by the system.

7) On update (attribute): updating a subject or an object attribute during the usage phase, performed by the system.

It should be emphasized that onupdate actions may be performed repeatedly by a system in order to continuously update an attribute and s, o, r refers to subject, object and right respectively.

A logical model of UCON consist of a 5-tuple; M = (S, PA, PC, AA, AB) where

S is a set of sequences of system states

PA is a finite set of authorization predicates built from the attributes of subjects and objects

PC is a finite set of usage control predicates built from the system attributes

AA is a finite set of usage control actions

AB is a finite set of obligation actions

A logical Formula is also defined in UCON by the following in BNF grammar:

$$\text{ø::= a}|p(t1, \cdots , tn)|(\neg\text{ø})|(\text{ø}\wedge\text{ø})|(\text{ø} \rightarrow \text{ø})|\square\text{ø}|\Diamond\text{ø}|O\text{ø}|\text{ø}U\text{ø}|\blacksquare\text{ø}|\blacklozenge\text{ø}|O\text{ø}|\text{ø}S\text{ø}|,$$

where a is an action, p is a predicate of arity n, and t1, ...

tn are terms.

If in a state sequence sq of a model M, a state s satisfies a formula ø, we write M, sq, s| = ø. The satisfaction relation |− is defined by induction on the structure of ø and only for s0 ∈ sq. specifically, M,sq,s0|= p if f s0 [[p]], where $p \in PA \cup PC$.

Access to Purchase: an e-book online the following rules are applied

1) Permitacess(s, o, purchase) → ♦tryaccess(s, o, purchase) ∧ (s. fingerprints ≥ 3) ∧ (encrypt.o.intell)

2) Permitaccess(s, o, purchase) → ◊onupdate(s. fingerprints ≥ 3) ∧ ◊(endaccess(s, o, purchase) ∨ revokeaccess(s, o. purchase))

The first policy says permit access once a subject tries access and has input his fingerprints to be encrypted into the resource to be purchased. The second policy says although the subject has purchased the resource, he is expected eventually to provide his fingerprints at some point when accessing. Otherwise access is ended or revoked indicating that he is not the rightful owner of the resource.

Access to Modify: (Doctor-patient relationship) the following rules can be applied

1) Permitacess(s, osen, modify) → ♦tryaccess(s, osen, modify) ∧ (s. fingerprints ≥ 3) ∧ (encrypt. osen)

2) Permitaccess(s, osen, modify) → ◊onupdate(s. fingerprints ≥ 3) ∧ ◊(endaccess(s, osen, modify) ∨ revokeaccess(s, osen, modify))

3) Endaccess(s, osen, modify) → ◊postupdate(records. fingerprints)

4) Revokeaccess(s, osen, modify) → postupdate(records. fingerprints)

Access to Use Temporary: e.g. watch, listen and read the following rules can be applied

1) Permitacess(s, o, watch) → ♦tryaccess(s, o, watch) ∧ (♦ob1 ∧ ♦ob2 ∧ ⋯ ∧ ♦obi)

2) Permitaccess(s, o, watch) → ◊onupdate(s. fingerprints ≥ 3) ∧ ◊(endaccess(s, o, watch) ∨ revokeaccess(s, o. watch))

The first policy regarding this type of access is, permitaccess to watch once there is a tryaccess and the necessary obligations is fulfilled like click and advertisement every 30 minutes. The second policy states that in the event that the resource is downloaded and used off-line, the subject needs to fulfill some obligations. For example delete movie or music within 90 days. To ensure that is obligation is adhere to; we use a logic bomb and program it to explode within the stipulated time. This will limit unauthorized redistribution of resource to some extent and hence protect resources.

4. Conclusion

To ensure that control is still exerted on resources no matter the location, the package concept is proposed to be used with UCONABC to enforce usage control. With the implementation of biometric fingerprints and logic bomb in a particular resource, the unauthorized dissemination or redistribution of resources can be minimized and obligations would be enforced through the package concept.

REFERENCES

[1] A. Lazouski, F. Martinelli and P. Mori, "Usage Control in Computer Security, a Survey," *Computer Science Review*, Vol. 4, No. 2, 2010, pp. 81-99.

[2] J. Park and R. Sandhu, "A Usage Control (UCON) Model for Social Network Privacy," 2010.

[3] J. Park, X. Zhang and R. S. Sandhu, "Attribute Mutability in Usage Control," *Proceedings of IFIP TC*11/*WG, Eighteen Annual Conferences on Data and Application Security*, Kluwer, Vol. 144, 2004, pp.15-29.

[4] J. Wu and S. Shimatoto, "Usage Control Based Security Access Scheme for Wireless Sensor Network," *Proceedings of IEEE International Conference on Communication (ICC 2010)*, Cape Town, 23-27 May 2010, pp. 1-5.

[5] M. Sastry, R. Krishnan and R. Sandhu, "A New Modeling Paradigm for Dynamic Authorization in Multi-Domain Systems," In: *Communications in Computer and Information Science*, Springer, Berlin, 2007, pp. 153-158.

[6] R. Alnemr, *et al.*, "Enabling Usage Control Reputation Objects, A Discussion on e-Commerce and Internet of Services Environments," *Journal of Theoretical and Applied Electronic Commerce Research Electronic Version*, Vol. 5, No. 2, 2010, pp. 59-79.

[7] W. Shin and S. B. Yoo, "Secured Web Services Based on Extended Usage Control," In: *PAKDD Workshops, Lecture Notes in Computer Science*, Springer, Berlin, 2007, pp. 656-663.

[8] B. X. Zhao, *et al.*, "Towards a Time—Based Usage Control Model," W3C Privacy and Data Usage Control Workshop, Cambridge, 2010.

[9] C. Moucha, E. Lovat and A. Pretschner, "A Virtual Usage Control Bus System," *Journal of Wireless Mobile Networks, Ubiquitous Computing and Dependable*, Vol. 2 No. 4, 2010, pp. 84-101.

[10] C. Bettini, S. Jajodia, X. S. Wang and D. Wijesekera, "Obligation Monitoring in Policy Management," *Proceedings of 3rd IEEE International Workshop for Distributed Systems and Networks Policy*, Monterey, 2002, pp. 2-12.

[11] D. Basin, *et al.*, "Monitoring Usage Control Policies in Distributed Systems," *IEEE*, 2011, pp. 88-95.

[12] D. Basin, *et al.*, "MONPOLY: Monitoring Usage Control Policies," *Lecture Notes in Computer Science*, Vol. 7186, 2012, pp. 360-364.

[13] E. Maler, "Controlling Data Usage with User—Managed Access (UMA)," W3C Privacy and Data Usage Control Workshop, Cambridge, 2010.

[14] G. D. Bai, *et al.*, "Context-Aware Usage Control for Android," *6th international ICST Conference on Security and Privacy in Communication*, Singapore, 7-9 September, 2010, pp. 326-343.

7

Peak-Shaped-Based Steganographic Technique for MP3 Audio

Raffaele Pinardi[1], Fabio Garzia[1,2], Roberto Cusani[1]

[1]Department of Information, Electronics and Telecommunications Engineering Sapienza University of Rome, Rome, Italy
[2]Wessex Institute of Technology, Southampton, UK

ABSTRACT

The aim of this work is the development of a steganographic technique for the MP3 audio format, which is based on the Peak Shaped Model algorithm used for JPEG images. The proposed method relies on the statistical properties of MP3 samples, which are compressed by a Modified Discrete Cosine Transform (MDCT). After the conversion of MP3, it's possible to hide some secret information by replacing the least significant bit of the MDCT coefficients. Those coefficients are chosen according to the statistical relevance of each coefficient within the distribution. The performance analysis has been made by calculating three steganographic parameters: the Embedding Capacity, the Embedding Efficiency and the PSNR. It has been also simulated an attack with the Chi-Square test and the results have been used to plot the ROC curve, in order to calculate the error probability. Performances have been compared with performances of other existing techniques, showing interesting results.

Keywords: Peak-Shaped Steganography; MP3 Steganography

1. Introduction

Steganography techniques are used to hide secret information in the most common audio/video formats. There are three main different kinds of audio/video steganography [1]:

1) insertion steganography, where the secret message is inserted in the cover object;

2) substitution steganography, where some bits of the cover object are substituted with the bits of the secret message;

3) constructing steganography, where an ad hoc cover object is generated to contain the secret message.

The developed technique is based on LSB steganography, a substitution steganography, that replaces the least significant bit of the audio/video file with the secret message bit. This method is very simple to implement and does not allow the human eye/hear to perceive significant changes in the stego object. In **Figure 1** an example is shown: the letter "A" is embedded in the audio samples replacing the least significative bit.

However, this technique has lower resistance to the statistical attacks since with a proper steganalysis it is possible to detect the secret information. To solve this problem, Model Based Steganography can be used [2]. The cover object is divided into two parts, x_a and x_β, to embed the secret information. The first part is the most relevant, and it will not be modified. The second one is less relevant with respect the other and it will contain the secret message. The division is based on the statistical model of the cover object.

After the embedding process, x_β contains the secret information, called x_β. The union between this part and x_a is the stego object.

The purpose of this paper is to present a new steganographic algorithm for the MP3 [3-5] format based on the change, in the Peak Shaped Based for the JPEG [6], of the discrepancy equation, adapting it to vectors and studying the statistical distribution of the MDCT [3-5] coefficients. In the following the analysis of the performance of the proposed algorithm is shown and it is demonstrated that this method does not introduce audible distortion when the signal audio is reproduced. Further, it is demonstrated that this method does not create relevant statistical differences in the samples distribution, showing its suitability for steganographic applications and its robustness to steganographic attacks.

2. The MP3 Format and Compression

The MP3 format was born to have good audio quality and low file size [3,4]. An audio file is first converted into a digital format, with a sampling, and then it is processed with the human psychoacoustic model [3-5].

Sampled Audio Stream (16 bit)	A in binary	Audio stream with encoded message
1001 1000 0011 1100	0	1001 1000 0011 1100
1101 1011 0011 1100	1	1101 1011 0011 1001
1011 1100 0011 1101	1	1011 1100 0011 1101
1011 1111 0011 1100	0	1011 1111 0011 1100
1011 1010 0111 1111	0	1011 1010 0111 1110
1111 1000 0011 1100	1	1111 1000 0011 1101
1101 1100 0111 1000	0	1101 1100 0111 1000
1000 1000 0001 1111	1	1000 1000 0001 1111

Figure 1. LSB example: the letter "A" is inserted into an audio file by replacing the least significant bit.

With this model it is possible to delete the frequency that the human ear can't hear; an algorithm characterized by this properties is called "lossy" because it deletes some information. This happens with a compression, that uses the MDCT [3,5], the Modified Discrete Cosine Transform, described in the following equation:

$$X_k = \sum_{n=0}^{2M-1} x(n) h_k(n) \qquad (1)$$

that is another version of the DCT-II used in the JPEG format, where:

$$h_k(n) = w(n) \sqrt{\frac{2}{M}} \cos\left[\frac{(2n+M+1)\cdot(2k+1)\cdot\pi}{4M}\right] \qquad (2)$$

and $w(n)$ is a window (it is possible to choose different kinds of windows).

The audio samples are processed in a MDCT filterbank. The audio sequence is divided in "frame", each frame contains M samples and is processed as in **Figure 2**.

3. Peak Shaped Based Steganography and MP3

3.1. Peak Shaped Based Steganography

The Peak Shaped Based (PSB) [6] steganography has been used for the JPEG format. This is a method based on:
- LSB steganography;
- Least significant bit;
- Model Based steganography [2].

The JPEG coefficient are, for first, divided by group, indicated with $g(b)$ [6]:

$$g(b) = \text{sign}(b) \cdot \left\lfloor \frac{b}{2} \right\rfloor \qquad (3)$$

and by offset, indicated with $O(b)$ [6]:

$$O(b) = |b - 2 \cdot g(b)| + 1 \qquad (4)$$

where b is the JPEG coefficient and $|b| > 1$.

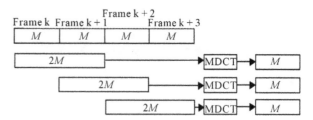

Figure 2. MDCT filterbank.

The PSB algorithm is based on an assumption, from the properties of the JPEG coefficients statistical distribution processed by the algorithm F5, which is [6]:

$$h(b) > h(b+1) \qquad (5)$$

$$h(b) + h(b+1) > h(b+1) - h(b+2) \qquad (6)$$

where $h(b)$ indicates the histogram of the coefficient b. With this assumption is possible to calculate a probability, called "offset probability".

Subsequently the coefficients are processed with the "discrepancy", an operator that allows to calculate the statistical dependence between two closer coefficients. This is defined as follows:

$$S_0 = \frac{\sum_{j=1}^{4} \sum_{i=1}^{64} q^i \cdot \left| \hat{b}_0^j - \hat{b}_i^j \right|}{4} \qquad (7)$$

where [6]:

$$\hat{b}_i^j = \begin{cases} b_i^j, b_i^j \in x_\alpha \\ 2 \cdot g(b_i^j), b_i^j \in x_\beta \end{cases} \qquad (8)$$

where, as shown in **Figure 3**, the blocks from 1 to 4 are the neighbors of the 0th. Each block contains 64 DCT-II coefficient, 8*8, and their sequences composing the JPEG image.

3.2. Differences between JPEG and MP3

To apply the PSB algorithm to the MP3 format it is necessary to study the differences between this format and the JPEG standard, in order to identify possible changes. These differences are:
- the JPEG uses the DCT-II while the MP3 uses the MDCT;
- the JPEG works on blocks; each blocks, or matrix, size is 8*8. Instead, the MP3 works on frame; each frame has dimension equal to 1*1152, that are vectors;
- the PSB is based on an assumption from the F5 algorithm, that is used for the JPEG format.

Concerning the first point, it is possible to notice that the PSB works on the coefficients. It is therefore necessary to demonstrate that the DCT-II and the MDCT statistical distributions have the same properties.

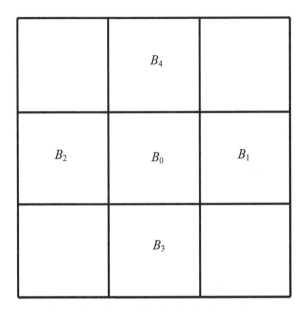

Figure 3. Adjacent blocks to the block B_0.

Concerning the second point, it is necessary to detect the operations that in the PSB works on matrix and, to apply it on the MP3 format, transforming them in operations that works on vectors.

Concerning the third point, it should be studied the statistical distribution of the MP3 coefficients after the F5-algorithm in order to identify if this distribution has the same properties than the JPEG distribution processed by F5.

3.2.1. MP3 Discrepancy

The JPEG discrepancy works on matrix, as described in paragraph 3.1. It is necessary to modify this operation to enable it to operate on vectors. Considering the MP3 format, and the MP3 frames, it is possible to call one of them as k_0. The discrepancy works on the previous frame and the subsequent. The frames are showed in **Figure 4**. The mean is done only for 2 frames because 2 frames are taken and each frame contains 576 coefficients.

$$S_0 = \frac{\sum_{j=1}^{2}\sum_{i=1}^{576} q^i \left| \hat{b}_0^j - \hat{b}_i^j \right|}{2} \quad (9)$$

where $\hat{b}_i^j$ is the same as in the JPEG discrepancy.

3.2.2. Statistical Distribution of the MP3 Coefficients

The statistical distribution of the MP3 coefficients, after the compression, is Peak Shaped [7]. This trend can be modeled by the Generalized Gaussian (GG). The GG varies with a parameter, called r, and it is possible to choose different values of r, *i.e.* $r = 2$ is a Gaussian, $r = 1$ is a Laplacian etc. A good approximation for the distribution of the MP3 coefficient has the value r set to 0 or 1,

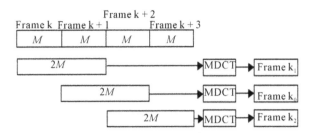

Figure 4. The frames on which works the MP3 discrepancy.

as shown in **Figure 5**.

With the parameter r set to 0.5, it is possible to have the best approximation of the statistical distribution. It is possible to choose the value $r = 1$, the Laplacian distribution, to have a good approximation with low complexity.

The Laplacian distribution is used to approximate the statistical distribution of the JPEG coefficients, as well [8-10].

3.3. The PSB over MP3

Using the previous considerations, it is possible to apply the Peak Shaped Based steganography to the MP3 format. In fact it is possible to utilize the assumption used by this algorithm from the F5 [11] steganography because the MP3 coefficients and the JPEG coefficients have the same statistical distribution. F5 modifies the coefficients, without considering their source.

Having both formats, namely both transformed, the same statistical distribution of the coefficients, the use of different transformed becomes irrelevant to the development of the algorithm.

3.4. The Embedding Process

In the following, the list of steps of the embedding process is reported:

- the first step is represented by the analysis of the MP3 statistical distribution;
- successively the value of Hg vector that contains the histograms of the MP3 is calculated;
- with the Hg values it is possible to exclude the samples that are statistical most significant;
- the Hg values allow the calculus, with the algorithm shown in **Figure 6**, of the offset probability vector, called P;
- each frame of the MP3 file, that contains 576 coefficients, is taken and analyzed;
- the coefficients b are divided by group, with the $g(b)$ (4), and by offset, with the $O(b)$ (5);
- the discrepancy is calculated by means of Equation (9);
- with the discrepancy, the vector P and a PRNG, according with the secret key, it is possible to determi-

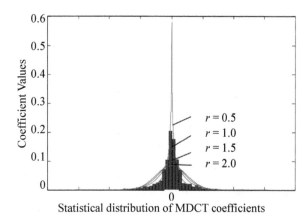

Statistical distribution of MDCT coefficients

Figure 5. Statistical distribution of the MP3 coefficients approximated with the GG [7].

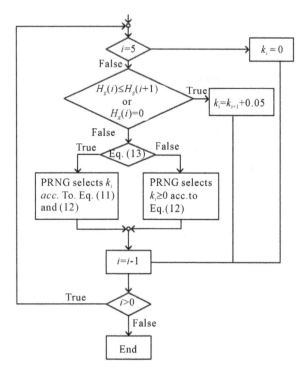

Figure 6. Block diagram of the calculus of the offset probability vector _P_.

nate the coefficients that contain the stego message;
- the offset of each coefficient that is possible to modify is changed according to the value of the bit of the secret message, as showed in **Table 1**.

To extract the secret message the embedding process must be repeated to determinate the coefficients that were modified. The analysis of each offset allows the reconstruction of the secret message.

4. Results

4.1. Performance Parameters

To analyze the performance of a steganographic techni-

Table 1. Offset of each coefficient that is changed.

	Even	Odd
0	No change	Decrease
1	Increase	No change

que three parameters are used:
- Embedding capacity;
- PSNR;
- Embedding efficiency.

4.1.1. Embedding Capacity
The embedding capacity (EC) [7,10] indicates the maximum data size that it is possible to hide in the cover object. It is defined as follows:

$$EC = \frac{\langle \text{secret message size} \rangle}{\langle \text{cover object size} \rangle} \qquad (10)$$

4.1.2. PSNR
The Peak to Noise Ratio [10] provides the similarity between the cover object, the original file, and the stego object, the file where the secret message has been hidden. It is defined through the Mean Square Error (MSE):

$$MSE = \left[\frac{1}{M \cdot N} \right]^2 \sum_{i=0}^{M-1} \sum_{j=0}^{N-1} \left(I(i,j) - I^i(i,j) \right)^2 \qquad (11)$$

$$PSNR = 10 \cdot \log_{10} \left(\frac{255^2}{MSE} \right) \qquad (12)$$

4.1.3. Embedding Efficiency
Through the Embedding Efficiency (EE) [2,12] it is indicated the average number of bits inserted for each change. It is defined as follows:

$$EE = \frac{\langle \text{secret message size} \rangle}{\langle \text{number of changes} \rangle} \qquad (13)$$

4.2. Peak Shaped Based for MP3 Performance

To evaluate the PSB for MP3 performance it is necessary to compare the Efficiency, the Capacity and the PSNR with different kinds of steganographyc algorithms and with the original PSB, that it was implemented for the JPEG format.

4.2.1. JPEG Performance
The embedding capacity and efficiency for the Model Based Steganography for the JPEG format are shown in **Table 2**.

The PSNR is evaluated for the PSB algorithm for the JPEG format, as shown in **Table 3**. MB1 and MB2 are two model based techniques used in [2], PSB is the Peak

Table 2. Model based steganography performance [2].

Image Name	File Size	Message Size	Capacity	Efficiency
Barb	48,459	6573	13.56%	2.06
Boat	41,192	5185	12.59%	2.94
Bridge	55,689	7022	12.61%	2.07
Goldhill	48,169	6607	13.72%	2.11
Lena	37,678	4707	12.49%	2.16
Mandrill	78,316	10,902	13.92%	2.07

Table 3. PSNR for the JPEG-PSB algorithm [6].

PSNR	Min	Mean	Max
MB1	34.2 dB	40 dB	43.6 dB
MB2	35.2 dB	39.9 dB	44.3 dB
PSB	34.2 dB	40.4 dB	46.6 dB

Shaped Steganography used for the JPEG format.

4.2.2. PSB for MP3

To calculate the Embedding Capacity for the MP3-PSB steganography it is necessary to calculate the file size as follows:

$$L = \frac{\text{bitrate} \cdot M}{\langle \text{sampling frequency} \rangle} \qquad (14)$$

A new variable is defined and it is called L_s that is the secret message length. Then the Capacity is:

$$C = \frac{L_s \cdot 100}{L} \qquad (15)$$

and the results are shown in **Table 4**.

The PSNR is evaluated as described in Equation (11) and the results are showed in **Table 5**.

The Efficiency is calculated by analyzing the number of changes to insert the secret message in the cover object. It is possible to see the performance in **Table 6**.

4.2.3. MP3 Steganography Comparison

In **Tables 7** and **8** the PSNR and the Capacity are illustrated for different kinds of steganographyc algorithms for MP3 format.

4.3. Steganalysys

With the steganalysis [9] it is possible to have a better analysis of the PSB-MP3 performance. This method calculated two probabilities, the False Alarm probability, when a cover object is classified as stego, and the Missed Detection probability, when a stego object is classified as cover. The first one is indicated with the symbol P_{fa}

Table 4. PSB-MP3 capacity.

Capacity	Min	Mean	Max
PSB-MP3	4.45%	12.75%	22.05%

Table 5. PSNR for PSB-MP3.

PSNR	Min	Mean	Max
PSB-MP3	55.67 dB	58.21 dB	62.90 B

Table 6. Efficiency for the PSB-MP3.

Efficiency	Min	Mean	Max
PSB-MP3	1.9969	1.9995	2.0012

Table 7. Capacity for different algorithm.

Steganographyc Technique	Embedding Capacity
Peak Shaped for MP3	12.75%
Generic LSB	34%
Tone Insertion	0.006%
Phase Coding	0.02%
Spread Spectrum	0.003%
Echo Data Hiding	0.012%
SVD	0.08%
VAS	10%

Table 8. PSNR for different algorithms.

Steganographyc Technique	PSNR
Peak shaped for MP3	58.21 dB
Phase Coding	69.5 dB
Spread Spectrum	44 dB
SVD	41 dB

and the second one with the symbol P_{md}. The values of these probabilities depend on a threshold, called τ, that modify the steganalysis system accuracy.

With these probabilities it is possible to calculate other parameters, like the detection probability, $P_{det} = 1 - P_{md}$, and the error probability P_{err}:

$$P_{err} = \frac{1}{2} \cdot \left(P_{fa} + P_{md} \right) \qquad (16)$$

4.3.1. Chi-Square Test

A steganalytic technique that is possible to use for the PSB-MP3 is the Chi-Square test [12]. Some parameters are calculated with the histograms of the MDCT coefficients probability distribution and the results of the

Chi-Square test are compared with the threshold.

One method to calculated the chi-square test is the Zhang-Ping attack [13] that evaluates two variables:

$$f_0 = \sum_{i>0} h_{2i} + \sum_{i<0} h_{2i+1} \qquad (17)$$

$$f_1 = \sum_{i<0} h_{2i} + \sum_{i>0} h_{2i+1} \qquad (18)$$

and if $f_1 > f_0$ it will calculate the chi-square values:

$$\text{chi}^2 = \frac{(f_0 - f_1)^2}{f_0 + f_1} \qquad (19)$$

to compare with the threshold.

4.3.2. ROC Curve

This analysis to evaluate the PSB performances is done on a random set of MP3 files. With the comparison with the threshold and the Chi-Square value it is possible to calculate the two probabilities of false alarm and missed detection, shown in **Table 9**.

With these two probabilities it is possible to graph the ROC curve. This curve indicates the efficiency of the steganalytic method. If the curve is near the first quadrant bisector the steganographyc algorithm is very strong, otherwise the steganalytic method is efficient.

In **Figure 7** it is possible to see the ROC curves (solid line) of the PSB algorithm for the MP3. This curve is very smash on the first quadrant bisector (dashed line). This indicates that the steganographyc method is very robust when this steganalytic algorithm is used. When the ROC curve is far from the bisector the steganographic algorithm isn't very robust or else the steganalytic technique is very efficacious. Instead when this curve is very close to the bisector the technique is very secure, since there is perfect security when the ROC curve is exactly equal to the bisector.

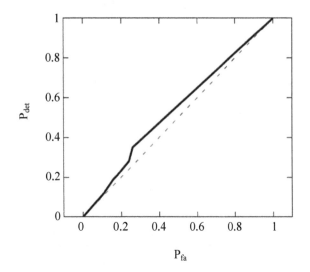

Figure 7. ROC curve for the PSB-MP3.

Table 9. False alarm, missed detection and detection probabilities when the threshold takes different values.

Tau	P_{fa}	P_{md}	$P_d = 1 - P_{md}$
0.01	0.26	0.65	0.35
0.1	0.24	0.72	0.28
0.5	0.18	0.79	0.21
1	0.16	0.81	0.19
10	0.11	0.88	0.12

5. Conclusions

A new steganographic algorithm for the MP3 format has been developed by changing, in the Peak Shaped Based for the JPEG, the discrepancy equation, adapting it to vectors and studying the statistical distribution of the MDCT coefficients. The analysis of the performance of this algorithm showed that this method does not introduce audible distortion when the signal audio is reproduced. Further, this method does not create relevant statistical differences in the samples distribution.

The Peak Shaped Based for the MP3 has an high capacity compared to the other algorithms and a good PSNR. In fact the mean Embedding Capacity is equal to 12.75%, higher than the most relevant techniques used for MP3 steganography; the PSNR is equal to 58.21 dB, higher than the PSB for the JPEG.

A steganalytic attack has been simulated to evaluate the robustness of the algorithm. This attack is implemented on the Zhang Ping analysis and on the Chi-Square test. This attack has been adapted to the PSB-MP3 since it was created for the JSteg steganography. By calculating the false alarm probability and the missed detection probability it is possible to draw the ROC curve. The analysis of this curve shows that this attack is not suitable for this steganographic method because the ROC is crushed on the bisector. The error probability, calculated with the ROC curve, tends to 0.5 when the threshold increases; when it takes this values the choice is completely random.

The steganographyc algorithm implemented, as assumed, is resistant to the statistical attacks.

REFERENCES

[1] G. Kipper, "Investigator's Guide to Steganography," Auerbach Publications, Boca Raton, 2003.

[2] P. Sallee, "Model-based Steganography," Springer Verlang, Berlin, 2004.

[3] A. Spanias, T. Painter and V. Atti, "Audio Signal Process And Coding," John Wiley and Sons, Hoboken, 2007.

[4] U. Zolzer, "Digital Audio Signal Processing," John Wiley and Sons, Hoboken, 2008.

[5] J. S. Jacaba, "Audio Compression Using Modified Discrete Cosine Transform: The MP3 Coding Standard," University of the Philippines, Manila, 2001.

[6] L. Rossi, F. Garzia and R. Cusani, "Peak-Shaped-Based Steganographic Technique for JPEG Images," *EURASIP Journal on Information Security*, 2009, Article ID: 382310.

[7] R. Yu, X. Lin, S. Rahardja and C. C. Ko, "A Statistic Study of the MDCT Coefficient Distribution for Audio," *IEEE International Conference on Multimedia and Expo*, Taipei, 30-30 June 2004, pp. 1483-1486.

[8] D. Liu, H. Zhang, M. Polycaropou, C. Alippi and H. He, "Advances in Neural Networks," Springer Verlag, Berlin, 2011.

[9] R. Bohme, "Advanced Statistical Steganalysis," Springer, Berlin, 2010.

[10] K. B. Shiva Kumar, K. B. Raja and R. K. Chhotaray, "Sabyasachi Pattanaik, Bit Length Replacement Steganography Based on DCT Coefficients," *International Journal of Engineering Science and Technology*, Vol. 2, No. 8, 2010, pp. 3561-3570.

[11] A. Westfeld, "F5-A Steganographic Algorithm," Springer Verlang, Berlin, 2001.

[12] K. Lee, A. Westfeld and S. Lee, "Category Attack for LSB Steganalysis of JPEG Images," Springer Verlang, Berlin, 2006.

[13] T. Zhang and X. Ping, "A Fast and Effective Steganalytic Technique against Jsteg-Like Algorithms," *Proceedings of the* 2003 *ACM Symposium on Applied Computing* (*SAC*), Melbourne, 9-12 March 2003, pp. 307-311.

8

Watermarking Images in the Frequency Domain by Exploiting Self-Inverting Permutations

Maria Chroni, Angelos Fylakis, Stavros D. Nikolopoulos
Department of Computer Science, University of Ioannina, Ioannina, Greece

ABSTRACT

In this work we propose efficient codec algorithms for watermarking images that are intended for uploading on the web under intellectual property protection. Headed to this direction, we recently suggested a way in which an integer number w which being transformed into a self-inverting permutation, can be represented in a two dimensional (2D) object and thus, since images are 2D structures, we have proposed a watermarking algorithm that embeds marks on them using the 2D representation of w in the spatial domain. Based on the idea behind this technique, we now expand the usage of this concept by marking the image in the frequency domain. In particular, we propose a watermarking technique that also uses the 2D representation of self-inverting permutations and utilizes marking at specific areas thanks to partial modifications of the image's Discrete Fourier Transform (DFT). Those modifications are made on the magnitude of specific frequency bands and they are the least possible additive information ensuring robustness and imperceptiveness. We have experimentally evaluated our algorithms using various images of different characteristics under JPEG compression. The experimental results show an improvement in comparison to the previously obtained results and they also depict the validity of our proposed codec algorithms.

Keywords: Watermarking Techniques; Image Watermarking Algorithms; Self-Inverting Permutations; 2D Representations of Permutations; Encoding; Decoding; Frequency Domain; Experimental Evaluation

1. Introduction

Internet technology, in modern communities, becomes day by day an indispensable tool for everyday life since most people use it on a regular basis and do many daily activities online [1]. This frequent use of the internet means that measures taken for internet security are indispensable since the web is not risk-free [2,3]. One of those risks is the fact that the web is an environment where intellectual property is under threat since a huge amount of public personal data is continuously transferred, and thus such data may end up on a user who falsely claims ownership.

It is without any doubt that images, apart from text, are the most frequent type of data that can be found on the internet. As digital images are a characteristic kind of intellectual material, people hesitate to upload and transfer them via the internet because of the ease of intercepting, copying and redistributing in their exact original form [4]. Encryption is not the problem's solution in most cases, as most people that upload images in a website want them to be visible by everyone, but safe and

theft protected as well. Watermarks are a solution to this problem as they enable someone to claim an image's ownership if he previously embedded one in it. Image watermarks can be visible or not, but if we don't want any cosmetic changes in an image then an invisible watermark should be used. That's what our work suggests a technique according to which invisible watermarks are embedded into images using features of the image's frequency domain and graph theory as well.

We next briefly describe the main idea behind the watermarking technique, the motivation of our work, and our contribution.

1.1. Watermarking

In general, watermarks are symbols which are placed into physical objects such as documents, photos, etc. and their purpose is to carry information about objects' authenticity [5].

A digital watermark is a kind of marker embedded in a digital object such as image, audio, video, or software and, like a typical watermark, it is used to identify ownership of the copyright of such an object. Digital watermarking (or, hereafter, watermarking) is a technique for protecting the intellectual property of a digital object; the idea is simple: a unique marker, which is called watermark, is embedded into a digital object which may be used to verify its authenticity or the identity of its owners [6,7]. More precisely, watermarking can be described as the problem of embedding a watermark w into an object I and, thus, producing a new object I_w, such that w can be reliably located and extracted from I_w even after I_w has been subjected to transformations [7]; for example, compression, scaling or rotation in case where the object is an image.

In the image watermarking process the digital information, *i.e.*, the watermark, is hidden in image data. The watermark is embedded into image's data through the introduction of errors not detectable by human perception [8]; note that, if the image is copied or transferred through the internet then the watermark is also carried with the copy into the image's new location.

1.2. Motivation

Intellectual property protection is one of the greatest concerns of internet users today. Digital images are considered a representative part of such properties so we consider important, the development of methods that deter malicious users from claiming others' ownership, motivating internet users to feel safer to publish their work online.

Image Watermarking, is a technique that serves the purpose of image intellectual property protection ideally as in contrast with other techniques it allows images to be available to third internet users but simultaneously carry an "identity" that is actually the proof of ownership with them. This way image watermarking achieves its target of deterring copy and usage without permission of the owner. What is more by saying watermarking we don't necessarily mean that we put a logo or a sign on the image as research is also done towards watermarks that are both invisible and robust.

Our work suggests a method of embedding a numerical watermark into the image's structure in an invisible and robust way to specific transformations, such as JPEG compression.

1.3. Contribution

In this work we present an efficient and easily implemented technique for watermarking images that we are interested in uploading in the web and making them public online; this way web users are enabled to claim the ownership of their images.

What is important for our idea is the fact that it suggests a way in which an integer number can be represented with a two dimensional representation (or, for short, 2D representation). Thus, since images are two dimensional objects that representation can be efficiently marked on them resulting the watermarked images. In a similar way, such a 2D representation can be extracted for a watermarked image and converted back to the integer w.

Having designed an efficient method for encoding integers as self-inverting permutations, we propose an efficient algorithm for encoding a self-inverting permutation π^* into an image I by first mapping the elements of π^* into an $n^* \times n^*$ matrix A^* and then using the information stored in A^* to mark specific areas of image I in the frequency domain resulting the watermarked image I_w. We also propose an efficient algorithm for extracting the embedded self-inverting permutation π^* from the watermarked image I_w by locating the positions of the marks in I_w; it enables us to recontract the 2D representation of the self-inverting permutation π^*.

It is worth noting that although digital watermarking has made considerable progress and became a popular technique for copyright protection of multimedia information [8], our work proposes something new. We first point out that our watermarking method incorporates such properties which allow us to successfully extract the watermark w from the image I_w even if the input image has been compressed with a lossy method. In addition, our embedding method can transform a watermark from a numerical form into a two dimensional (2D) representation and, since images are 2D structures, it can efficiently embed the 2D representation of the watermark by marking the high frequency bands of specific areas of an image. The key idea behind our extracting method is that it does not actually extract the embedded information instead it locates the marked areas reconstructing the watermark's numerical value.

We have evaluated the embedding and extracting algorithms by testing them on various and different in characteristics images that were initially in JPEG format and we had positive results as the watermark was successfully extracted even if the image was converted back into JPEG format with various compression ratios. What is more, the method is open to extensions as the same method might be used with a different marking procedure such as the one we used in our previous work. Note that, all the algorithms have been developed and tested in MATLAB [9].

1.4. Road Map

The paper is organized as follows. In Section 2 we present an efficient transformation of a watermark from an integer form to a two dimensional (2D) representation through the exploitation of self-inverting permutation properties. In Section 3 we briefly describe the main idea behind our recently proposed image watermarking algorithm, while in Section 4 we present our contribution with this paper. In Section 5 we show properties of our image watermarking technique and evaluate the performance of the corresponding watermarking algorithms. Section 6 concludes the paper and discusses possible future extensions.

2. Theoretical Framework

In this section we first describe discrete structures, namely, permutations and self-inverting permutations, and briefly discuss a codec system which encodes an integer number w into a self-inverting permutation π. Then, we present a transformation of a watermark from a numerical form to a 2D form (*i.e.*, 2D representation) through the exploitation of self-inverting permutation properties.

2.1. Self-Inverting Permutations

Informally, a permutation of a set of objects S is an arrangement of those objects into a particular order, while in a formal (mathematical) way a permutation of a set of objects S is defined as a bijection from S to itself (*i.e.*, a map $S \rightarrow S$ for which every element of S occurs exactly once as image value).

Permutations may be represented in many ways. The most straightforward is simply a rearrangement of the elements of the set $N_n = \{1, 2, \cdots, n\}$; in this way we think of the permutation $\pi = (5, 6, 9, 8, 1, 2, 7, 4, 3)$ as a rearrangement of the elements of the set N_9 such that "1 goes to 5", "2 goes to 6", "3 goes to 9", "4 goes to 8", and so on [10,11]. Hereafter, we shall say that π is a permutation over the set N_9.

Definition: Let $\pi = (\pi_1, \pi_2, \cdots, \pi_n)$ be a permutation over the set N_n, where $n > 1$. The inverse of the permutation π is the permutation $q = (q_1, q_2, \cdots, q_n)$ with $q_{\pi_i} = \pi_{q_i} = i$. A self-inverting permutation (or, for short, SiP) is a permutation that is its own inverse: $\pi_{\pi_i} = i$.

By definition, a permutation is a SiP (self-inverting permutation) if and only if all its cycles are of length 1 or 2; for example, the permutation $\pi = (5, 6, 9, 8, 1, 2, 7, 4, 3)$ is a SiP with cycles: (1,5), (2,6), (3,9), (4,8), and (7).

2.2. Encoding Numbers as SiPs

There are several systems that correspond integer numbers into permutations or self-inverting permutation [10]. Recently, we have proposed algorithms for such a system which efficiently encodes an integer w into a self-inverting permutations π and efficiently decodes it. The algorithms of our codec system run in $O(n)$ time,

where n is the length of the binary representation of the integer w, while the key-idea behind its algorithms is mainly based on mathematical objects, namely, bitonic permutations [12].

We briefly describe below our codec algorithms which in fact correspond integer numbers into self-inverting permutations; we show the correspondence between the integer $w = 12$ and the self-inverting permutation $\pi = (5, 6, 9, 8, 1, 2, 7, 4, 3)$ by the help of an example.

Example W-to-SiP: Let $w = 12$ be the given watermark integer. We first compute the binary representation $B = 1100$ of the number 12; then we construct the binary number $B' = 0000 \parallel 1100 \parallel 1$ and the binary sequence $B^* = (1, 1, 1, 1, 0, 0, 1, 1, 0)$ by flipping the elements of B'; we compute the sequences $X = (5, 6, 9)$ and $Y = (1, 2, 3, 4, 7, 8)$ by taking into account the indices of 0s and 1s in B^*, and then the bitonic permutation $\pi = (5, 6, 9, 8, 7, 4, 3, 2, 1)$ on $n' = 9$ numbers by taking the sequence $X \parallel Y^R$; since n' is odd, we select 4 cycles $(5, 1)$, $(6, 2)$, $(9, 3)$, $(8, 4)$ of lengths 2 and one cycle (7) of length 1, and then based on the selected cycles construct the self-inverting permutation $\pi = (5, 6, 9, 8, 1, 2, 7, 4, 3)$.

Example SiP-to-W: Let $\pi = (5, 6, 9, 8, 1, 2, 7, 4, 3)$ be the given self-inverting permutation produced by our method. The cycle representation of π is the following: (1,5), (2.6), (3,9), (4,8), (7); from the cycles we construct the permutation $\pi = (5, 6, 9, 8, 7, 4, 3, 2, 1)$; then, we compute the first increasing subsequence $X = (5, 6, 9)$ and the first decreasing subsequence $Y = (8, 7, 4, 3, 2, 1)$; we then construct the binary sequence $B^* = (1, 1, 1, 1, 0, 0, 1, 1, 0)$ of length 9; we flip the elements of B^* and construct the sequence $B' = (0, 0, 0, 0, 1, 1, 0, 0, 1)$; the binary number 1100 is the integer $w = 12$.

2.3. 2D Representations

We first define the two-dimensional representation (2D representation) of a permutation π over the set $N_n = \{1, 2, \cdots, n\}$, and then its 2DM representation which is more suitable for efficient use in our codec system.

In the 2D representation, the elements of the permutation $\pi = (\pi_1, \pi_2, \cdots, \pi_n)$ are mapped in specific cells of an $n \times n$ matrix A as follows:

$$\text{number } \pi_i \rightarrow \text{entry } A\left(\pi_i^{-1}, \pi_i\right)$$

or, equivalently, the cell at row i and column π_i is labeled by the number π_i, for each $i = 1, 2, \cdots, n$.

Figure 1(a) shows the 2D representation of the self-inverting permutation $\pi = (6, 3, 2, 4, 5, 1)$.

Note that, there is one label in each row and in each column, so each cell in the matrix A corresponds to a unique pair of labels; see, [10] for a long bibliography on permutation representations and also in [13] for a DAG representation.

Based on the previously defined 2D representation of a permutation π, we next propose a two-dimensional marked representation (2DM representation) of π which is an efficient tool for watermarking images.

In our 2DM representation, a permutation π over the set N_n is represented by an $n \times n$ matrix A^* as follows:

- the cell at row i and column π_i is marked by a specific symbol, for each $i = 1, 2, \cdots, n$;
- in our implementation, the used symbol is the asterisk, i.e., the character "*".

Figure 1(b) shows the 2DM representation of the permutation π. It is easy to see that, since the 2DM representation of π is constructed from the corresponding 2D representation, there is also one symbol in each row and in each column of the matrix A^*.

We next present an algorithm which extracts the permutation π from its 2DM representation matrix. More precisely, let π be a permutation over N_n and let A^* be the 2DM representation matrix of π (see, **Figure 1(b)**); given the matrix A^*, we can easily extract π from A^* in linear time (i.e., linear in the size of matrix A^*) by the following algorithm:

Algorithm Extract_π_from_2DM

Input: the 2DM representation matrix A^* of π;

Output: the permutation π;

Step 1: For each row i of matrix A^*, $1 \le i \le n$, and for each column j of matrix A^*, $1 \le j \le n$, if the cell (i, j) is marked then $\pi_i \leftarrow j$;

Step 2: Return the permutation π;

Remark 1. It is easy to see that the resulting permutation π, after the execution of Step 1, can be taken by reading the matrix A^* from top row to bottom row and write down the positions of its marked cells. Since the permutation π is a self-inverting permutation, its 2D matrix A has the following property:

- $A(i, j) = j$ if $\pi_i = j$, and
- $A(i, j) = 0$ otherwise, $1 \le i, j \le n$.

Thus, the corresponding matrix A^* is symmetric:

- $A^*(i, j) = A^*(j, i) = \text{"mark"}$ if $\pi_i = j$, and

- $A^*(i, j) = A^*(j, i) = 0$ otherwise, $1 \le i, j \le n$.

Based on this property, it is also easy to see that the resulting permutation π can be also taken by reading the matrix A^* from left column to right column and write down the positions of its marked cells.

Hereafter, we shall denote by π^* a SiP and by n^* the number of elements of π^*.

2.4. The Discrete Fourier Transform

The Discrete Fourier Transform (DFT) is used to decompose an image into its sine and cosine components. The output of the transformation represents the image in the frequency domain, while the input image is the spatial domain equivalent. In the image's fourier representation, each point represents a particular frequency contained in the image's spatial domain.

If $f(x, y)$ is an image of size $N \times M$ we use the following formula for the Discrete Fourier Transform:

$$F(u, v) = \sum_{x=0}^{N-1} \sum_{y=0}^{M-1} f(x, y) e^{-j2\pi\left(\frac{ux}{N} + \frac{vy}{M}\right)} \quad (1)$$

for values of the discrete variables u and v in the ranges $u = 0, 1, \cdots, N-1$ and $v = 0, 1, \cdots, M-1$.

In a similar manner, if we have the transform $F(u, v)$ i.e the image's fourier representation we can use the Inverse Fourier Transform to get back the image $f(x, y)$ using the following formula:

$$f(x, y) = \frac{1}{NM} \sum_{u=0}^{N-1} \sum_{v=0}^{M-1} F(u, v) e^{j2\pi\left(\frac{ux}{N} + \frac{vy}{M}\right)} \quad (2)$$

for $x = 0, 1, \cdots, N-1$ and $y = 0, 1, \cdots, M-1$.

Typically, in our method, we are interested in the magnitudes of DFT coefficients. The magnitude $|F(u, v)|$ of the Fourier transform at a point is how much frequency content there is and is calculated by Equation (1) [14].

3. Previous Results

Recently, we proposed a watermarking technique based on the idea of interfering with the image's pixel values in the spatial domain. In this section, we briefly describe the main idea of the proposed technique and state main points regarding some of its advantages and disadvantages. Recall that, in the current work we suggest an expansion to this idea by moving from the spatial domain to the image's frequency domain.

3.1. Method Description

The algorithms behind the previously proposed technique were briefly based on the following idea.

The embedding algorithm first computes the 2DM representation of the permutation π^*, that is, the $n^* \times n^*$ array A^* (see, Subsection 2.3); the entry (i, π_i^*) of the

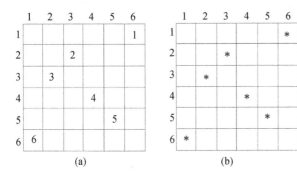

(a)   (b)

Figure 1. The 2D and 2DM representations of the self-inverting permutation $\pi = (6, 3, 2, 4, 5, 1)$.

array A^* contains the symbol "$*$", $1 \le i \le n^*$.

Next, the algorithm computes the size $N \times M$ of the input image I and according to its size, covers it with an $n^* \times n^*$ imaginary grid C, which divides the image into $n^* \times n^*$ grid-cells C_{ij} of size $\left\lfloor \dfrac{N}{n^*} \right\rfloor \times \left\lfloor \dfrac{M}{n^*} \right\rfloor$, $1 \le i, j \le n^*$.

Then the algorithm goes first to each grid-cell C_{ij}, locates its central pixel p_{ij}^0 and also the four pixels p_{ij}^1, p_{ij}^2, p_{ij}^3, p_{ij}^4 around it, $1 \le i, j \le n^*$ (these five pixels are called *cross* pixels), and then computes the difference between the brightness of the central pixel p_{ij}^0 and the average brightness of twelve neighboring pixels around the cross pixels, and stores the resulting value in the variable dif $\left(p_{ij}^0 \right)$. Finally, it computes the maximum absolute value of all $n^* \times n^*$ differences dif $\left(p_{ij}^0 \right)$, $1 \le i, j \le n^*$, and stores it in the variable Maxdif(I).

The embedding algorithm goes again to each central pixel p_{ij}^0 of each grid-cell C_{ij}, $1 \le i, j \le n^*$, and if the corresponding entry $A^*(i, j)$ contains the symbol "$*$", then it increases the value of each one of the five cross pixels by Maxdif(I) $-$ dif $\left(p_{ij}^0 \right)$ $+$ c, where c is a positive number used to make marks robust to transformations.

In a similar manner, the extracting algorithm is searching each line i of the imaginary grid C to find among the n^* grid-cells $C_{i1}, C_{i2}, \cdots, C_{in^*}$ the column j of the one that has the greatest difference between the twelve neighboring and the five cross pixels, $1 \le i, j \le n^*$; then, the element π_i^* is set equal to j.

3.2. Main Points

First we should mention that for images with general characteristics and relatively large size this method delivers optically good results. By saying "good results" we mean that the modifications made are quite invisible. Also the method's algorithms run really fast as they simply access a finite number of pixels. Furthermore, both the embedding and extracting algorithms are easy to modify and adjust for various scenarios.

On the other hand, the method fails to deliver good results either for relatively small images or for images that depict something smooth which allows the eye to distinct the modifications on the image. Also we decided to move to a new method as there were also problems due to the fact that the positions of the crosses are centered at strictly specific positions causing difficulties in the extracting algorithm even for the smallest geometric changes such as scaling or cropping where we may lose the marked positions.

4. The Frequency Domain Approach

Having described an efficient method for encoding inte-

gers as self-inverting permutations using the 2DM representation of self-inverting permutations, we next describe codec algorithms that efficiently encode and decode a watermark into the image's frequency domain [14-17].

4.1. Embed Watermark into Image

We next describe the embedding algorithm of our proposed technique which encodes a self-inverting permutation (SiP) π^* into a digital image I. Recall that, the permutation π^* is obtained over the set N_{n^*}, where $n^* = 2n + 1$ and n is the length of the binary representation of an integer w which actually is the image's watermark [12]; see, Subsection 2.2.

The watermark w, or equivalently the self-inverting permutation π^*, is invisible and it is inserted in the frequency domain of specific areas of the image I. More precisely, we mark the DFT's magnitude of an image's area using two ellipsoidal annuli, denoted hereafter as "Red" and "Blue" (see, **Figure 2**). The ellipsoidal annuli are specified by the following parameters:

- P_r, the width of the "Red" ellipsoidal annulus,
- P_b, the width of the "Blue" ellipsoidal annulus,
- R_1 and R_2, the radiuses of the "Red" ellipsoidal annulus on *y*-axis and *x*-axis, respectively.

The algorithm takes as input a SiP π^* and a digital image I, in which the user embeds the watermark, and returns the watermarked image I_w; it consists of the following steps.

Algorithm Embed_SiP-to-Image

Input: the watermark $\pi^* \equiv w$ and the host image I;

Output: the watermarked image I_w;

Step 1: Compute first the 2DM representation of the permutation π^*, *i.e.*, construct an array A^* of size $n^* \times n^*$ such that the entry $A^*\left(i, \pi_i^* \right)$ contains the symbol "$*$", $1 \le i \le n^*$.

Step 2: Next, calculate the size $N \times M$ of the input image I and cover it with an imaginary grid C with $n^* \times n^*$ grid-cells C_{ij} of size $\left\lfloor \dfrac{N}{n^*} \right\rfloor \times \left\lfloor \dfrac{M}{n^*} \right\rfloor$, $1 \le i, j \le n^*$.

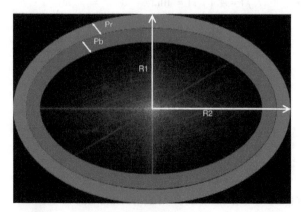

Figure 2. The "Red" and "Blue" ellipsoidal annuli.

Step 3: For each grid-cell C_{ij}, compute the Discrete Fourier Transform (DFT) using the Fast Fourier Transform (FFT) algorithm, resulting in a $n^* \times n^*$ grid of DFT cells F_{ij}, $1 \le i, j \le n^*$.

Step 4: For each DFT cell F_{ij}, compute its magnitude M_{ij} and phase P_{ij} matrices which are both of size $\left\lfloor \dfrac{N}{n^*} \right\rfloor \times \left\lfloor \dfrac{M}{n^*} \right\rfloor$, $1 \le i, j \le n^*$.

Step 5: Then, the algorithm takes each of the $n^* \times n^*$ magnitude matrices M_{ij}, $1 \le i, j \le n^*$, and places two imaginary ellipsoidal annuli, denoted as "Red" and "Blue", in the matrix M_{ij} (see, **Figure 2**). In our implementation,

- the "Red" is the outer ellipsoidal annulus while the "Blue" is the inner one. Both are concentric at the center of the M_{ij} magnitude matrix and have widths P_r and P_b, respectively;
- the radiuses of the "Red" ellipsoidal annulus are R_1 (on the y-axis) and R_2 (on the x-axis), while the "Blue" ellipsoidal annulus radiuses are computed in accordance to the "Red" ellipsoidal annulus and have values $\left(R_1 - P_r\right)$ and $\left(R_2 - P_r\right)$, respectively;
- the inner perimeter of the "Red" ellipsoidal annulus coincides to the outer perimeter of the "Blue" ellipsoidal annulus;
- the values of the widths of the two ellipsoidal annuli are $P_r = 2$ and $P_b = 2$, while the values of their radiuses are $R_1 = \left\lfloor \dfrac{N}{2n^*} \right\rfloor$ and $R_2 = \left\lfloor \dfrac{M}{2n^*} \right\rfloor$.

The areas covered by the "Red" and the "Blue" ellipsoidal annuli determine two groups of magnitude values on M_{ij} (see, **Figure 2**).

Step 6: For each magnitude matrix M_{ij}, $1 \le i, j \le n^*$, compute the average of the values that are in the areas covered by the "Red" and the "Blue" ellipsoidal annuli; let $AvgR_{ij}$ be the average of the magnitude values belonging to the "Red" ellipsoidal annulus and $AvgB_{ij}$ be the one of the "Blue" ellipsoidal annulus.

Step 7: For each magnitude matrix M_{ij}, $1 \le i, j \le n^*$, compute first the variable D_{ij} as follows:

$$D_{ij} = \begin{cases} \left| AvgB_{ij} - AvgR_{ij} \right|, & \text{if } AvgB_{ij} \le AvgR_{ij} \\ 0, & \text{otherwise} \end{cases}.$$

Then, for each row i of the magnitude matrix M_{ij}, $1 \le i, j \le n^*$, compute the maximum value of the variables $D_{i1}, D_{i2}, \cdots, D_{in^*}$ in row i; let $\mathrm{Max}D_i$ be the max value.

Step 8: For each cell (i, j) of the 2DM representation matrix A^* of the permutation π^* such that $A_{ij}^* = $ "*" (i.e., marked cell), mark the corresponding grid-cell C_{ij}, $1 \le i, j \le n^*$; the marking is performed by increasing all the values in magnitude matrix M_{ij} covered by the "Red" ellipsoidal annulus by

the value

$$AvgB_{ij} - AvgR_{ij} + \mathrm{Max}D_i + c, \qquad (3)$$

where $c = c_{opt}$. The additive value of c_{opt} is calculated by the function $f(\ )$ (see, Subsection 4.3) which returns the minimum possible value of c that enables successful extracting.

Step 9: Reconstruct the DFT of the corresponding modified magnitude matrices M_{ij}, using the trigonometric form formula [14], and then perform the Inverse Fast Fourier Transform (IFFT) for each marked cell C_{ij}, $1 \le i, j \le n^*$, in order to obtain the image I_w.

Step 10: Return the watermarked image I_w.

In **Figure 3**, we demonstrate the main operations performed by our embedding algorithm. In particular, we show the marking process of the grid-cell C_{44} of the Lena image; in this example, we embed in the Lena image the watermark number w which corresponds to SiP $(6, 3, 2, 4, 5, 1)$.

4.2. Extract Watermark from Image

In this section we describe the decoding algorithm of our proposed technique. The algorithm extracts a self-

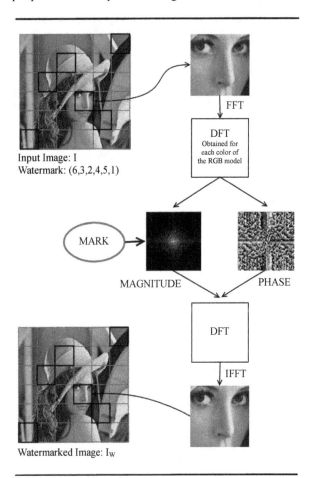

Figure 3. A flow of the embedding process.

inverting permutation (SiP) π^* from a watermarked digital image I_w, which can be later represented as an integer w.

The self-inverting permutation π^* is obtained from the frequency domain of specific areas of the watermarked image I_w. More precisely, using the same two "Red" and "Blue" ellipsoidal annuli, we detect certain areas of the watermarked image I_w that are marked by our embedding algorithm and these marked areas enable us to obtain the 2D representation of the permutation π^*. The extracting algorithm works as follows:

Algorithm Extract_SiP-from-Image

Input: the watermarked image I_w marked with π^*;

Output: the watermark $\pi^* = w$;

Step 1: Take the input watermarked image I_w and calculate its $N \times M$ size. Then, cover it with the same imaginary grid C, as described in the embedding method, having $n^* \times n^*$ grid-cells C_{ij} of size $\left\lfloor \dfrac{N}{n^*} \right\rfloor \times \left\lfloor \dfrac{M}{n^*} \right\rfloor$.

Step 2: Then, again for each grid-cell C_{ij}, $1 \le i, j \le n^*$, using the Fast Fourier Transform (FFT) get the Discrete Fourier Transform (DFT) resulting a $n^* \times n^*$ grid of DFT cells.

Step 3: For each DFT cell, compute its magnitude matrix M_{ij} and phase matrix P_{ij} which are both of size $\left\lfloor \dfrac{N}{n^*} \right\rfloor \times \left\lfloor \dfrac{M}{n^*} \right\rfloor$.

Step 4: For each magnitude matrix M_{ij}, place the same imaginary "Red" and "Blue" ellipsoidal annuli, as described in the embedding method, and compute as before the average values that coincide in the area covered by the "Red" and the "Blue" ellipsoidal annuli; let $AvgR_{ij}$ and $AvgB_{ij}$ be these values.

Step 5: For each row i of M_{ij}, $1 \le i \le n^*$, search for the j_{th} column where $AvgB_{ij} - AvgR_{ij}$ is minimized and set $\pi^*_i = j$, $1 \le j \le n^*$.

Step 6: Return the self-inverting permutation π^*.

Having presented the embedding and extracting algorithms, let us next describe the function f which returns the additive value $c = c_{opt}$ (see, Step 8 of the embedding algorithm Embed_SiP-to-Image).

4.3. Function f

Based on our marking model, the embedding algorithm amplifies the marks in the "Red" ellipsoidal annulus by adding the output of the function f. What exactly f does is returning the optimal value that allows the extracting algorithm under the current requirements, such as JPEG compression, to still be able to extract the watermark from the image.

The function f takes as an input the characteristics of the image and the parameters R_1, R_2, P_b, and P_r of our proposed marking model (see, Step 5 of em-

bedding algorithm and **Figure 2**), and returns the minimum possible value c_{opt} that added as c to the values of the "Red" ellipsoidal annulus enables extracting (see, Step 8 of the embedding algorithm). More precisely, the function f initially takes the interval $[0, c_{max}]$, where c_{max} is a relatively great value such that if c_{max} is taken as c for marking the "Red" ellipsoidal annulus it allows extracting, and computes the c_{opt} in $[0, c_{max}]$.

Note that, c_{max} allows extracting but because of being great damages the quality of the image (see, **Figure 4**). We mentioned relatively great because it depends on the characteristics of each image. For a specific image it is useless to use a c_{max} greater than a specific value, we only need a value that definitely enables the extracting algorithm to successfully extract the watermark.

We next describe the computation of the value c_{opt} returned by the function f; note that, the parameters P_b and P_r of our implementation are fixed with the values 2 and 2, respectively. The main steps of this computation are the following:

(1) Check if the extracting algorithm for $c = 0$ validly obtains the watermark $\pi^* = w$ from the image I_w; if yes, then the function f returns $c_{opt} = 0$;

(2) If not, that means, $c = 0$ doesn't allow extracting; then, the function f uses binary search on $[0, c_{max}]$ and computes the interval $[c_1, c_2]$ such that:

- $c = c_1$ doesn't allow extracting,
- $c = c_2$ does allow extracting, and
- $|c_1 - c_2| < 0.2$;

(3) The function f returns $c_{opt} = c_2$;

As mentioned before, the function f returns the optimal value c_{opt}. Recall that, optimal means that it is the smallest possible value which enables extracting $\pi^* = w$

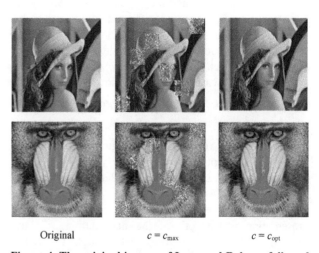

Original $c = c_{max}$ $c = c_{opt}$

Figure 4. The original images of Lena and Baboon followed by their watermarked images with different additive values c, i.e., the optimal value and a relatively large value c; both images are marked with the same watermark (6,3,2,4,5,1).

from the image I_w. It is important to be the smallest one as that minimizes the additive information to the image and, thus, assures minimum drop to the image quality.

5. Experimental Evaluation

In this section we present the experimental results of the proposed watermarking method which we have implemented using the general-purpose mathematical software package Matlab (version 7.7.0) [9].

We experimentally evaluated our codec algorithms on digital color images of various sizes and quality characteristics. Many of the images in our image repository where taken from a web image gallery [18] and enriched by some other images different in sizes and characteristics. Our experimental evaluation is based on two objective image quality assessment metrics namely Peak Signal to Noise Ratio (PSNR) and Structural Similarity Index Metric (SSIM) [19].

There are three main requirements of digital watermarking: fidelity, robustness, and capacity [5]. Our watermarking method appears to have high fidelity and robustness against JPEG compression.

5.1. Design Issues

We tested our codec algorithms on various 24-bit digital color images of various sizes (from 200×130 up to 4600×3700) and various quality characteristics.

In our implementation we set both of the parameters P_r and P_b equal to 2; see, Subsection 4.1. Recall that, the value 2 is a relatively small value which allows us to modify a satisfactory number of values in order to embed the watermark and successfully extract it without affecting images' quality. There isn't a distance between the two ellipsoidal annuli as that enables the algorithm to apply a small additive information to the values of the "Red" annulus. The two ellipsoidal annuli are inscribed to the rectangle magnitude matrix, as we want to mark images' cells on the high frequency bands.

We mark the high frequencies by increasing their values using mainly the additive parameter $c = c_{opt}$ because alterations in the high frequencies are less detectable by human eye [20]. Moreover, in high frequencies most images contain less information.

In this work we used JPEG images due to their great importance on the web. In addition, they are small in size, while storing full color information (24 bit/pixel), and can be easily and efficiently transmitted. Moreover, robustness to lossy compression is an important issue when dealing with image authentication. Notice that the design goal of lossy compression systems is opposed to that of watermark embedding systems. The Human Visual System model (HVS) of the compression system attempts to identify and discard perceptually insignificant information of the image, whereas the goal of the watermarking system is to embed the watermark information without altering the visual perception of the image [21].

The quality factor (or, for short, Q factor) is a number that determines the degree of loss in the compression process when saving an image. In general, JPEG recommends a quality factor of 75 - 95 for visually indistinguishable quality loss, and a quality factor of 50 - 75 for merely acceptable quality. We compressed the images with Matlab JPEG compressor from imwrite with different quality factors; we present results for $Q = 90$, $Q = 75$ and $Q = 60$.

The quality function f returns the factor c, which has the minimum value c_{opt} that allows the extracting algorithm to successfully extract the watermark. In fact, this value c_{opt} is the main additive information embedded into the image; see, formula (3). Depending on the images and the amount of compression, we need to increase the watermark strength by increasing the factor c. Thus, for the tested images we compute the appropriate values for the parameters of the quality function f; this computation can be efficiently done by using the algorithm described in Subsection 4.3.

To demonstrate the differences on watermarked image human visual quality, with respect to the values of the additive factor c, we watermarked the original images Lena and Baboon and we embedded in each image the same watermark with $c = c_{max}$ and $c = c_{opt}$, where $c_{max} \gg c_{opt}$; the results are demonstrated in **Figure 4**.

5.2. Image Quality Assessment

In order to evaluate the watermarked image quality obtained from our proposed watermarking method we used two objective image quality assessment metrics, that is, the Peak Signal to Noise Ratio (PSNR) and the Structural Similarity Index Metric (SSIM). Our aim was to prove that the watermarked image is closely related to the original (image fidelity), because watermarking should not introduce visible distortions in the original image as that would reduce images' commercial value.

The PSNR metric is the ratio of the reference signal and the distortion signal (*i.e.*, the watermark) in an image given in decibels (dB); PSNR is most commonly used as a measure of quality of reconstruction of lossy compression codecs (e.g., for image compression). The higher the PSNR value the closer the distorted image is to the original or the better the watermark conceals. It is a popular metric due to its simplicity, although it is well known that this distortion metric is not absolutely correlated with human vision.

For an initial image I of size $N \times M$ and its watermarked image I_w, PSNR is defined by the formula:

$$\text{PSNR}\left(I, I_w\right) = 10\log_{10}\frac{N_{\max}^2}{\text{MSE}}, \qquad (4)$$

where $N_{\max}$ is the maximum signal value that exists in the original image and MSE is the Mean Square Error given by

$$\text{MSE}\left(I, I_w\right) = \frac{1}{N \times M}\sum_{i=0}^{N-1}\sum_{j=0}^{M-1}\left(I(i,j) - I_w(i,j)\right)^2. \quad (5)$$

The SSIM image quality metric [19] is considered to be correlated with the quality perception of the HVS [22]. The SSIM metric is defined as follows:

$$\text{SSIM}\left(I, I_w\right)$$
$$= \frac{\left(2\mu\mu_w + C_1\right)\left(2\sigma\left(I, I_w\right) + C_2\right)}{\left(\mu^2 + \mu_w^2 + C_1\right)\left(\sigma(I)^2 + \sigma(I_w)^2 + C_2\right)}, \qquad (6)$$

where μ and μ_w are the mean luminances of the original and watermarked image I respectively, $\sigma(I)$ is the standard deviation of I, $\sigma(I_w)$ is the standard deviation of I_w, whereas C_1 and C_2 are constants to avoid null denominator. We use a mean SSIM (MSSIM) index to evaluate the overall image quality over the M sliding windows; it is given by the following formula:

$$\text{MSSIM}\left(I, I_w\right) = \frac{1}{M}\sum_{i=0}^{M}\text{SSIM}\left(I, I_w\right). \qquad (7)$$

The highest value of SSIM is 1, and it is achieved when the original and watermarked images, that is, I and I_w, are identical.

Our watermarked images have excellent PSNR and SSIM values. In **Figure 5**, we present three images of different sizes, along with their corresponding PSNR and SSIM values. Typical values for the PSNR in lossy image compression are between 40 and 70 dB, where higher is better. In our experiments, the PSNR values of 90% of the watermarked images were greater than 40 dB. The SSIM values are almost equal to 1, which means that the watermarked image is quite similar to the original one, which proves the method's high fidelity.

In **Tables 1** and **2**, we demonstrate the PSNR and SSIM values of some selected images of various sizes used in our experiments. We observe that both values, PSNR and SSIM, decrease as the quality factor of the images becomes smaller. Moreover, the additive value c that enables robust marking under qualities $Q = 90, 75$ and 60 does not result in a significant image distortion as **Tables 1** and **2** suggest; see also the watermarked images on **Figure 5**.

In closing, we mention that Lena and Baboon images of **Figure 4** are both of size 200×200. Lena image has PSNR values 55.4, 50.1, 46.2 and SSIM values 0.9980, 0.9934, 0.9854 for $Q = 90, 75$ and 60, respectively, while Baboon image has PSNR values 52.7, 46.2, 42.5

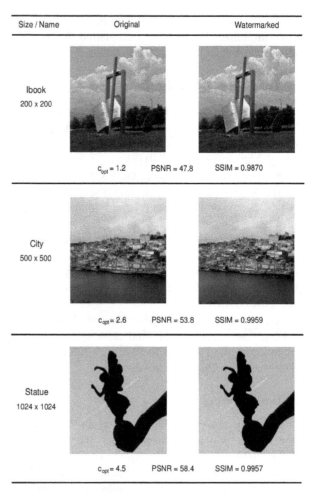

Figure 5. Sample images of three size groups for JPEG quality factor $Q = 75$ and their corresponding watermarked ones; for each image, the c, PSNR and SSIM values are also shown.

Table 1. The PSNR values of watermarked images of different sizes under JPEG qualities $Q = 90, 75$ and 60.

Image	Size	Qual. 90	Qual. 75	Qual. 60
Ibook		54.7	47.8	42.9
City	200	52.6	47.3	43.6
Statue		52.3	46.2	42.6
Ibook		58.3	54.5	46.5
City	500	58.7	53.8	44.7
Statue		60.7	51.5	49.6
Ibook		65.6	57.9	52.0
City	1024	64.4	56.7	49.6
Statue		67.5	58.4	51.4

Table 2. The SSIM values of watermarked images of different sizes under JPEG qualities $Q = 90, 75$ and 60.

Image	Size	Qual. 90	Qual. 75	Qual. 60
Ibook City Statue	200	0.9972	0.9870	0.9670
		0.9959	0.9860	0.9705
		0.9898	0.9664	0.9419
Ibook City Statue	500	0.9981	0.9957	0.9782
		0.9985	0.9959	0.9743
		0.9978	0.9838	0.9767
Ibook City Statue	1024	0.9995	0.9975	0.9913
		0.9995	0.9974	0.9884
		0.9995	0.9957	0.9813

and SSIM values 0.9978, 0.9908, 0.9807 for the same quality factors.

5.3. Other Experimental Outcomes

In the following, based on our experimental results, we discuss several impacts concerning characteristics of the host images and our embedding algorithm, and also we justify them by providing explanations on the observed outcomes.

5.3.1. The Additive Value Influences

As the experimental results show the PSNR and SSIM values decrease after embedding the watermark in images with lower quality index in its JPEG compression; see, **Tables 1** and **2**. That happens since our embedding algorithm adds more information in the frequency of marked image parts. By more information we mean a greater additive factor c; see, Equation (3).

We next discuss an important issue concerning the additive value $c = c_{opt}$ returned by function f; see, Subsection 4.3. In **Table 3**, we show a sample of our results demonstrating for each JPEG quality the respective values of the additive factor c_{opt}. The figures show that the c_{opt} value increases as the quality factor of JPEG compression decreases. It is obvious that the embedding algorithm is image dependent. It is worth noting that c_{opt} values are small for images of relatively small size while they increase as we move to images of greater size.

Moving beyond the sample images in order to show the behaviour of additive value c_{opt} under different image sizes, we demonstrate in **Figure 6** the average c_{opt} values of all the tested images grouped in three different sizes. We decided to select three representative groups for small, medium, and large image sizes, that is, 200×200, 500×500 and 1024×1024, respectively. For

each size group we computed the average c_{opt} under the JPEG quality factors $Q = 90, 75$ and 60.

As the experimental results suggest the embedding process requires greater optimal values c_{opt} for the additive variable c as we get to JPEG compressions with lower qualities. The reason for that can be found looking at the three main steps of JPEG compression:

1) In the first step, the image is separated into 8×8 blocks and converted to a frequency-domain representation, using a normalized, two-dimensional discrete cosine transform (DCT) [23].

2) Then, quantization of the DCT coefficients takes place. This is done by simply dividing each component of the DCT coefficients matrix by the corresponding constant from the same sized Quantization matrix, and then rounding to the nearest integer.

3) In the third step, it's entropy coding which involves arranging the image components in a "zigzag" order employing run-length encoding (RLE) algorithm that groups

Table 3. The optimal c values for watermarking image samples with respect to JPEG qualities $Q = 90, 75$ and 60.

Image	Size	Qual. 90	Qual. 75	Qual. 60
Ibook City Statue	200	0.4	1.2	2.3
		0.5	1.2	2.0
		0.6	1.5	2.4
Ibook City Statue	500	1.4	2.3	6.1
		1.4	2.6	7.6
		1.1	3.5	4.4
Ibook City Statue	1024	1.7	4.7	9.5
		1.9	5.3	12.5
		1.4	4.5	10.5

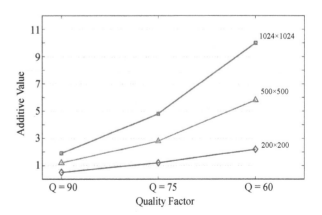

Figure 6. The average optimal c values for the tested images grouped in three deferent sizes under the JPEG quality factors $Q = 90, 75$ and 60.

similar frequencies together, inserting length coding zeros, and then using Huffman coding on what is left.

Focusing on the second step, we should point out that images with higher compression (lower quality) make use of a Quantization matrix which typically has greater values corresponding to higher frequencies meaning that information for high frequency is greatly reduced as it is less perceivable by human eye.

As we mentioned our method marks images in the higher frequency domain which means that as the compression ratio increases marks gradually become weaker and thus c_{opt} increases to strengthen the marks.

Furthermore, someone may notice that c_{opt} also increases for larger images. That is because regardless of the image size the widths of the ellipsoidal annuli remain the same meaning that the larger the image the less frequency amplitude is covered by the constant sized annuli. That makes marks less robust and require a greater c_{opt} to strengthen them.

5.3.2. Frequency Domain Imperceptiveness

It is worth noting that the marks made to embed the watermark in the image are not just invisible in the image itself but they are also invisible in the image's overall Discrete Fourier Transform (DFT). More precisely, if someone suspects the existence of the watermark in the frequency domain and gets the image's DFT, it is impossible to detect something unusual. This is also demonstrated in **Figure 7**, which shows that in contrast with using the ellipsoidal marks in the whole image, using them in specific areas makes the overall DFT seem normal.

6. Concluding Remarks

In this paper we propose a method for embedding invisible watermarks into images and their intention is to prove the authenticity of an image. The watermarks are given

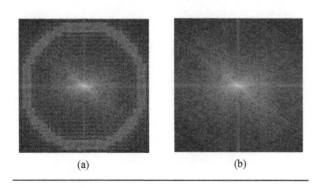

(a)   (b)

Figure 7. (a) The DFT of a watermarked image marked on the full image's frequency domain. (b) The DFT of a watermarked image marked partially with our technique.

in numerical form, transformed into self-inverting permutations, and embedded into an image by partially marking the image in the frequency domain; more precisely, thanks to 2D representation of self-inverting permutations, we locate specific areas of the image and modify their magnitude of high frequency bands by adding the least possible information ensuring robustness and imperceptiveness.

We experimentally tested our embedding and extracting algorithms on color JPEG images with various and different characteristics; we obtained positive results as the watermarks were invisible, they didn't affect the images' quality and they were extractable despite the JPEG compression. In addition, the experimental results show an improvement in comparison to the previously obtained results and they also depict the validity of our proposed codec algorithms.

It is worth noting that the proposed algorithms are robust against cropping or rotation attacks since the watermarks are in SiP form, meaning that they determine the embedding positions in specific image areas. Thus, if a part is being cropped or the image is rotated, SiP's symmetry property may allow us to reconstruct the watermark. Furthermore, our codec algorithms can also be modified in the future to get robust against scaling attacks. That can be achieved by selecting multiple widths concerning the ellipsoidal annuli depending on the size of the input image.

Finally, we should point out that the study of our quality function f remains a problem for further investigation; indeed, f could incorporate learning algorithms [24] so that to be able to return the c_{opt} accurately and in a very short computational time.

REFERENCES

[1] S. Garfinkel, "Web Security, Privacy and Commerce," 2nd Edition, O'Reilly, Sebastopol, 2001.

[2] L. Chun-Shien, H. Shih-Kun, S. Chwen-Jye and M. L. Hong-Yuan, "Cocktail Watermarking for Digital Image Protection," *IEEE Transactions on Multimedia*, Vol. 2, No. 4, 2000, pp. 209-224.

[3] J. C. Davis, "Intellectual Property in Cyberspace—What Technological/Legislative Tools are Necessary for Building a Sturdy Global Information Infrastructure?" *Proceedings of the IEEE International Symposium on Technology and Society*, Glasgow, 20-21 June 1997, pp. 66-74.

[4] J. J. K. O'Ruanaidh, W. J. Dowling and F. M. Boland, "Watermarking Digital Images for Copyright Protection," *Proceedings of the IEE Vision, Image and Signal Processing*, Vol. 143, No. 4, 1996, pp. 250-256.

[5] I. J. Cox, M. L. Miller, J. A. Bloom, J. Fridrich and T. Kalker, "Digital Watermarking and Steganography," 2nd

Edition, Morgan Kaufmann, Burlington, 2008.

[6]   D. Grover, "The Protection of Computer Software—Its Technology and Applications," Cambridge University Press, New York, 1997.

[7]   C. Collberg and J. Nagra, "Surreptitious Software," Addison-Wesley, Boston, 2010.

[8]   I. Cox, J. Kilian, T. Leighton and T. Shamoon, "A Secure, Robust Watermark for Multimedia," *Proccedings of the 1st International Workshop on Information Hiding*, Vol. 1174, 1996, pp. 317-333.

[9]   R. C. Gonzalez, R. E. Woods and S. L. Eddins, "Digital Image Processing Using Matlab," Prentice-Hall, Upper Saddle River, 2003.

[10] R. Sedgewick and P. Flajolet, "An Introduction to the Analysis of Algorithms," Addison-Wesley, Boston, 1996.

[11] M. C. Golumbic, "Algorithmic Graph Theory and Perfect Graphs," Academic Press Inc., New York, 1980.

[12] M. Chroni and S. D. Nikolopoulos, "Encoding Watermark Integers as Self-Inverting Permutations," *Proccedings of the 11th International Conference on Computer Systems and Technologies*, ACM ICPS 471, 2010, pp. 125-130.

[13] M. Chroni and S. D. Nikolopoulos, "An Efficient Graph Codec System for Software Watermarking," *Proceedings of the 36th International Conference on Computers, Software, and Applications, Workshop STPSA'12*, 2012, pp. 595-600.

[14] R. C. Gonzalez and R. E. Woods, "Digital Image Processing," 3rd Edition, Prentice-Hall, Upper Saddle River, 2007.

[15] V. Solachidis and I. Pitas, "Circularly Symmetric Watermark Embedding in 2D DFT Domain," *IEEE Transactions on Image Processing*, Vol. 10, No. 11, 2001, pp. 1741-1753.

[16] V. Licks and R. Hordan, "On Digital Image Watermarking Robust to Geometric Transformations," *Proceedings of the IEEE International Conference on Image Proceesing*, Vol. 3, 2000, pp. 690-693.

[17] E. Ganic, S. D. Dexter and A. M. Eskicioglu, "Embedding Multiple Watermarks in the DFT Domain Using Low and High Frequency Bands," *Proceedings of Security, Steganography, and Watermarking of Multimedia Contents VII*, Jan Jose, 17 January 2005, pp. 175-184.

[18] F. Petitcolas, "Image Database for Watermarking," September 2012. http://www.petitcolas.net/fabien/watermarking/

[19] Z. Wang, A. C. Bovic, H. R. Sheikh and E. P. Simoncelli, "Image Quaity Assessment: From Error Visibility to Structural Similarity," *IEEE Transactions on Image Processing*, Vol. 13, No. 4, 2004, pp. 600-612.

[20] M. Kaur, S. Jindal and S. Behal, "A Study of Digital Image Watermarking," *Journal of Research in Engineering and Applied Sciences*, Vol. 2, No. 2, 2012, pp. 126-136.

[21] J. M. Zain, "Strict Authentication Watermarking with JPEG Compression (SAW-JPEG) for Medical Images for Medical Images," *European Journal of Scientific Research*, Vol. 42, No. 2, 2010, pp. 250-256.

[22] A. Hore and D. Ziou, "Image Quality Metrics: PSNR vs. SSIM," *Proceedings of the 20th International Conference on Pattern Recognition*, Istanbul, 2010, pp. 2366-2369.

[23] N. Ahmed, T. Natarajan and K. R. Rao, "Discrete Cosine Transform," *IEEE Transactions on Computers*, Vol. 23, No. 1, 1974, pp. 90-93.

[24] S. Russell and P. Norvig, "Artificial Intelligence: A Modern Approach," 3rd Edition, Prentice-Hall, Upper Saddle River, 2010.

9

Diminution in Error Approximation by Identity Authentication with IPAS for FTLSP to Enhance Network Security

Kuljeet Kaur, Geetha Ganesan

School of Computer Applications, Lovely Professional University, Phagwara, India

ABSTRACT

In this paper, we have proved the diminution in error approximation when identity authentication is done with Ideal Password Authentication Scheme (IPAS) for Network Security. Effectiveness of identity authentication parameters for various attacks and security requirements is verified in the paper. Result of analysis proves that IPAS would enhance the transport layer security. Proof of efficiency of result is generated with drastic diminution in error approximation. IPAS would have advanced security parameters with implemented RNA-FINNT which would result in fortification of the transport layer security protocol for enhancement of Network Security.

Keywords: Fingerprint; Error Approximation; Network Security; Fortification; Transport Layer

1. Introduction

Identity Authentication could be done with Password, Smart Cards and Fingerprints. As the Smart card loss is very common attack on the network so this identity authentication parameter is not completely reliable. Password faces the dictionary attacks, stolen verifier attack, and man in the middle attack etc in common. So it states that there should be an Ideal Password Authentication Scheme which should have an assimilation of most effective identity authentication parameters. Survey on user's choice was done and it concluded that fingerprint would be the most acceptable identity authentication parameter in future along with password [1]. So assimilation of password and fingerprint would generate an ideal password authentication scheme [2].

Fingerprint could be extracted on the basis of template, texture and minutiae points. Amongst the three minutiae points, it is the most effective as no one has the same number of points on the same place. Minutiae points give uniqueness to the fingerprint. There are various algorithms for extracting minutiae points like grid hash, angle hash and minimum distance hash. But we derived a new algorithm RNA-FINNT for extracting the minutiae point's values of the fingerprint [3]. This paper has validation of diminution in error approximation in terms of percentage. IPAS which is generated with assimilation of

password and fingerprint is used to validate the results. RNA-FINNT is used to extract values of minutiae points [3]. Calculations with respect to various fingerprint extraction algorithms are done by assimilating them with Password. Comparative analysis of all these calculations validates that the percentage of error would reduce when password is assimilated with fingerprint in which extraction of minutiae points is performed by RNA-FINNT.

Remainder sections of the paper prove this validation. Section 2 proposes methodology for proving the diminution in error approximation, Section 3 states the effectiveness of Identity Authentication Parameters for various Attacks and Security Requirements, Section 4 generates a proof of Diminution in Error Approximation and Section 5 suggests the advanced security parameters of ideal password authentication scheme which results in fortification of transport layer security protocol for enhancement of network security.

2. Proposed Methodology for Proving the Diminution in Error Approximation

To prove diminution in error approximation we have used a comparative study in which assimilation of existing fingerprint extraction algorithms is dome with password. Our new algorithm RNA-FINNT is also assimilated with password which generates an ideal password authentication scheme. Multi server environment is required for implementation of IPAS [4]. Methodology proves that IPAS results in diminution in error approximation. Flowchart defines the proposed methodology (**Figure 1**).

2.1. Mentioned below Is the Stepwise Process for Proving Diminution in Error Approximation

Step 1: Calculate the total number of Attacks and Security Requirements possible on each Identity Authentication Parameter. This implies for password, fingerprint (extraction with Grid Hash Algorithm) [5], fingerprint (extraction with Angle Hash Algorithm) [5], fingerprint (extraction with Minimum Distance Hash Algorithm) [5]

and fingerprint (extraction with RNA-FINNT Hash Algorithm) [3].

Step 2: Calculate the total number of Attacks and Security Requirements possible if password is assimilated with on each Identity Authentication Parameter. This implies for password assimilation with fingerprint (extraction with Grid Hash Algorithm), fingerprint (extraction with Angle Hash Algorithm), fingerprint (extraction with Minimum Distance Hash Algorithm) and fingerprint (extraction with RNA-FINNT Hash Algorithm) respectively.

Step 3: Proof would be derived from the result of Step 2 that less number of attacks are possible if password is assimilated with fingerprint (extraction with RNA-FIN-

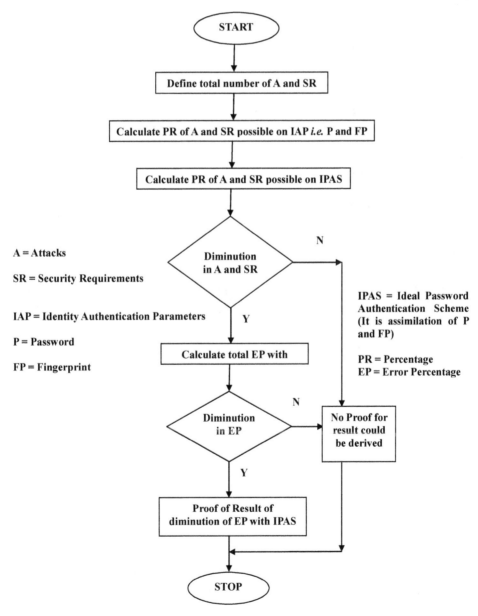

Figure 1. Proposed methodology for proving diminution in error approximation.

NT Hash Algorithm) which is an Ideal Password Authentication Scheme.

Step 4: Calculate the total error percentage if password is assimilated with on each Identity Authentication Parameter. This implies for password assimilation with fingerprint (extraction with Grid Hash Algorithm), fingerprint (extraction with Angle Hash Algorithm), fingerprint (extraction with Minimum Distance Hash Algorithm) and fingerprint (extraction with RNA-FINNT Hash Algorithm) respectively.

Step 5: Proof would be derived from the result of Step 4 that less number of error would be there if password is assimilated with fingerprint (extraction with RNA-FINNT Hash Algorithm) which is an Ideal Password Authentication Scheme.

Error Approximation = e
Password = p
Total Number of defined Attacks and Security Requirements = n
Number of Attacks on p = t (p)
Error Approximation in p = p (e)
Fingerprint Extracted Value through Grid Hash Algorithm = f (g)
Number of Attacks on f (g) = t (f (g))
Error Approximation in f (g) = f (g) (e)
Fingerprint Extracted Value through Angle Hash Algorithm = f (a)
Number of Attacks on f (a) = t (f (a))
Error Approximation in f (a) = f (a) (e)
Fingerprint Extracted Value through Minimum Distance Hash Algorithm = f (m)
Number of Attacks on f (m) = t (f (m))
Error Approximation in f (m) = f (m) (e)
Fingerprint Extracted Value through RNA-FINNT Hash Algorithm = f (r)
Number of Attacks on f (r) = t (f (r))
Error Approximation in f (r) = f (r) (e)
Total Number of Attacks and Security Requirements possible if:
1) p is assimilated with f (g) = p (f (g))
2) p is assimilated with f (a) = p (f (a))
3) p is assimilated with f (m) = p (f (m))
4) p is assimilated with f (r) = p (f (r))
Total Error Percentage when p is assimilated with f (g) = te (pg)
Total Error Percentage when p is assimilated with f (a) = te (pa)
Total Error Percentage when p is assimilated with f (m) = te (pm)
Total Error Percentage when p is assimilated with f (r) = te (pr)
Total Number of defined Attacks and Security Requirements are n but if:
1) p is assimilated with f (g) = n (p (f (g)))

2) p is assimilated with f (a) = n (p (f (a)))
3) p is assimilated with f (m) = n (p (f (m)))
4) p is assimilated with f (r) = n (p (f (r)))

2.2. Proposed Methodology for Validating Results

Step 1: Calculate the total number of Attacks and Security requirements possible on each Identity Authentication Parameter.

$$p(e) = (t(p) \div n \times 100)$$

$$f(g)(e) = (t(f(g)) \div n \times 100)$$

$$f(a)(e) = (t(f(a)) \div n \times 100)$$

$$f(m)(e) = (t(f(m)) \div n \times 100)$$

$$f(r)(e) = (t(f(r)) \div n \times 100)$$

Step 2: Calculate the total number of Attacks and Security requirements possible if p is assimilated with each Identity Authentication Parameter.

$$p(f(g)) = t(p) + t(f(g)) - (t(p) \cup t(f(g)))$$

$$p(f(a)) = t(p) + t(f(a)) - (t(p) \cup t(f(a)))$$

$$p(f(m)) = t(p) + t(f(m)) - (t(p) \cup t(f(m)))$$

$$p(f(r)) = t(p) + t(f(r)) - (t(p) \cup t(f(r)))$$

Step 3: Proof is derived from Step 2 that less number of attacks are possible if p is assimilated with f (r) *i.e.* an Ideal Password Authentication Scheme.

Proof: $p(f(r))$ is best for Identity Authentication.

Step 4: Calculate the Total Error Percentage if p is assimilated with each Identity Authentication Parameter.

$$te(pg) = p(e) + f(g)(e) - n(p(f(g)))$$

$$te(pa) = p(e) + f(a)(e) - n(p(f(a)))$$

$$te(pm) = p(e) + f(m)(e) - n(p(f(m)))$$

$$te(pr) = p(e) + f(r)(e) - n(p(f(r)))$$

Step 5: Proof is derived from Step 4 that less number of error would be there if assimilation of p with f(r) is implemented *i.e.* Ideal Password Authentication Scheme.

When the above mentioned steps are executed in the sequential order then the resulted output shows the error diminution. This process is implemented through the framework specifically designed to prove the result [6]. Through the framework fingerprint extraction is done through RNA-FINNT and is assimilated with the Password. This assimilation is IPAS which is an Ideal Password Authentication Scheme and results in the diminution of error percentage while matching the fingerprint. Section 4 validates the result with exact data for proving the diminution in the error approximation.

3. Effectiveness of Identity Authentication Parameters for Various Attacks and Security Requirements

As mentioned in Section 2 flowchart (**Figure 1** and **Table 1**) comparative study of the attacks and security requirements in context to the existing and new fingerprint algorithms is to be done for proving diminution in error approximation. Standard attacks and security requirements are denial of service [7], DNS poisoning [8], forgery attack [9], man in the middle attack [10], forward secrecy [11], ping of death [12], mutual authentication [13], IP spoofing [14], parallel session [15], ping broadcast [16], password guessing [17], server spoofing [18], replay [15], session hijacking [19,20], mutual authentication [13], smart card loss [21], smurf [22], stolen verifier

Table 1. Comparative study of attacks and security requirements on identity authentication parameters.

S. No	Security Requirements and Attacks	p	$f(g)$	$f(a)$	$f(m)$	$f(r)$
1	Denial of Service Attack [7]	Y	Y	Y	Y	Y
2	DNS Poisoning [8]	Y	N	N	N	N
3	Forgery Attack [9]	Y	Y	Y	Y	Y
4	Man in the Middle Attack [10]	Y	Y	Y	Y	N
5	Forward Secrecy [11]	Y	Y	N	Y	N
6	Ping of Death [12]	Y	Y	Y	Y	Y
7	Mutual Authentication [13]	N	Y	Y	Y	Y
8	IP Spoofing [14]	Y	Y	Y	Y	N
9	Parallel Session Attack [15]	Y	Y	Y	Y	Y
10	Ping Broadcast [16]	Y	Y	Y	Y	Y
11	Password Guessing Attack [17]	Y	N	N	N	N
12	Server Spoofing [18]	Y	Y	Y	Y	N
13	Replay Attack [15]	Y	Y	Y	Y	N
14	Session Hijacking [19,20]	Y	Y	Y	Y	Y
15	Smart Card Loss Attack [21]	N	N	N	N	N
16	Smurf Attack [22]	Y	Y	Y	Y	N
17	Stolen Verifier Attack [21]	Y	Y	Y	Y	N
18	Teardrop Attack [23]	Y	Y	Y	Y	Y
	Total Number of Attacks	16	15	14	15	8

[21] and tear drop [23].

Password = p

Fingerprint Extracted Value through Grid Hash Algorithm = $f(g)$

Fingerprint Extracted Value through Angle Hash Algorithm = $f(a)$

Fingerprint Extracted Value through Minimum Distance Hash Algorithm = $f(m)$

Fingerprint Extracted Value through RNA-FINNT Hash Algorithm = $f(r)$

Proof of Validation

Total Attacks = 18

$p = 16, f(g) = 15, f(a) = 14,$

$f(m) = 15, f(r) = 8$

Out of total 18, number of attacks possible on password is 16, fingerprint (extraction with Grid Hash Algorithm) is 15, fingerprint (extraction with Angle Hash Algorithm) is 14, fingerprint (extraction with Minimum Distance Hash Algorithm) is 15 and fingerprint (extraction with RNA-FINNT (Reduced Number of Angles Fingerprint) Hash Algorithm) is 8. This implies that only 8 attacks or security requirements are possible on IPAS (Ideal Password Authentication Scheme).

4. Proof of Diminution in Error Approximation

While validating the diminution in error approximation, RNA-FINNT is implemented in IPAS [24]. In RNA-FINNT number of minutiae points extracted is more than 12 so the overall reduction of error while extracting fingerprint is 4 [25]. On the basis of result of Section 3 (number of attacks) the steps of Section 2 are followed and below mentioned is the validation of the result. Below mentioned steps proved that as only 8 attacks are possible on RNA-FINNT so it result in diminution of error approximation.

Proposed Methodology for Validating Results

Step 1: Calculate the total number of Attacks and Security requirements possible on each Identity Authentication Parameter

$$p(e) = (t(p) \div n \times 100) = 16 \div 18 \times 100 = 88.8 = 89$$

$$f(g)(e) = (t(f(g)) \div n \times 100) = 15 \div 18 \times 100 = 83.3 = 83$$

$$f(a)(e) = (t(f(a)) \div n \times 100) = 14 \div 18 \times 100 = 77.7 = 78$$

$$f(m)(e) = (t(f(m)) \div n \times 100) = 15 \div 18 \times 100 = 83.3 = 83$$

$$f(r)(e) = (t(f(r)) \div n \times 100) = 8 \div 18 \times 100 = 44.4 = 44$$

Step 2: Calculate the total number of Attacks and Security requirements possible if p is assimilated with each Identity Authentication Parameter.

$$p\big(f(g)\big)=t(p)+t\big(f(g)\big)-\big(t(p)\cup t\big(f(g)\big)\big)=16+15-18=13$$

$$p\big(f(a)\big)=t(p)+t\big(f(a)\big)-\big(t(p)\cup t\big(f(a)\big)\big)=16+14-18=12$$

$$p\big(f(m)\big)=t(p)+t\big(f(m)\big)-\big(t(p)\cup t\big(f(m)\big)\big)=16+15-18=13$$

$$p\big(f(r)\big)=t(p)+t\big(f(r)\big)-\big(t(p)\cup t\big(f(r)\big)\big)=16+8-18=6$$

Step 3: Proof is derived from Step 2 that only 6 numbers of attacks are possible if p is assimilated with f (r) *i.e.* an Ideal Password Authentication Scheme.

Proof: p $(f(r))$ is best for Identity Authentication.

Step 4: Calculate the Total Error Percentage if p is assimilated with each Identity Authentication Parameter.

$$te(pg)=p(e)+f(g)(e)-n\big(p\big(f(g)\big)\big)=89+83-100=72$$

$$te(pa)=p(e)+f(a)(e)-n\big(p\big(f(a)\big)\big)=89+78-100=67$$

$$te(pm)=p(e)+f(m)(e)-n\big(p\big(f(m)\big)\big)=89+83-100=72$$

$$te(pr)=p(e)+f(r)(e)-n\big(p\big(f(r)\big)\big)=89+44-100=33$$

Step 5: Proof is derived from Step 4 that only 33% of error would be there if assimilation of p with $f(r)$ is implemented *i.e.* Ideal Password Authentication Scheme.

When password is assimilated with fingerprint (extraction with Grid Hash Algorithm) or fingerprints (extraction with Angle Hash Algorithm) or fingerprints (extraction with Minimum Distance Hash Algorithm) or fingerprint (extraction with RNA-FINNT Hash Algorithm) the error approximation is 72, 67, 73 and 33 respectively. Result derived is that in IPAS number of minutiae points extracted are more than12 so the error percentage drastically gets reduced to 4 [25] and IPAS error approximation on the basis of attacks and security requirements over the transport layer is just 33.

5. Advanced Security Parameters of IPAS Results in FTLSP for Enhancement of Network Security

When only limited attacks or security requirements could be practiced by intruders over the network then data would remain more secure. These attacks hinder the data communication on the transport layer. RNA-FINNT resulted to generate an ideal password authentication scheme which has password assimilated with fingerprint. Extraction process with the help of RNA-FINNT has improved and this would enhance the security at the network layer. With IPAS intruder cannot impersonate a legal user by stealing the user's ID and PW from the password table whenever user accesses data from remote server because storage at the server is done with hash code values. Along with this mutual authentication is implemented in the multi server environment so that IP or Server Spoofing could be eliminated. The organization

which would be using this IPAS should have Secured Socket Layer implemented in the Virtual Private Network because it enhances the security of a message transmission on the internet.

6. Conclusion

Conclusion is that implementation of ideal password authentication scheme results in the diminution of error approximation, fortifies the transport layer (Secured Socket Layer implemented in the Virtual Private Network of an organization) and enhances the network security.

REFERENCES

[1] K. Kaur and G. Geetha, "Survey for Generating an Ideal Password Authentication Scheme Which Results in Fortification of Transport Layer Security Protocol," *International Journal of Computer Science and Information Technologies*, Vol. 3, No. 2, 2012, pp. 3608-3614. http://www.ijcsit.com/ijcsit-v3issue2.php

[2] K. Kaur and G. Geetha, "Fortification of Transport Layer Security Protocol by Using Password and Fingerprint as Identity Authentication Parameters," *International Journal of Computer Applications*, Vol. 42, No. 6, 2012, pp. 36-42.

[3] K. Kaur and G. Geetha, "Fortification of Transport Layer Security Protocol with Hashed Fingerprint Identity Parameter," *International Journal of Computer Science Issues*, Vol. 9, No. 2, 2012, pp. 188-193.

[4] K. Kaur and G. Geetha, "Generating Multi Server Environment for implementation of Ideal Password Authentication Scheme," *International Journal of Advances in Computer Networks and Its Security*, Vol. 2, No. 3, 2012, pp. 2250-3757.

[5] S. Goyal and M. Goyal, "Generation of Hash Functions

from Fingerprint Scans," 2011.

[6] K. Kaur and G. Geetha, "Framework for Proving Fortification of TLSP with IPAS," *International Journal of Computer Engineering and Technology*, Vol. 3, No. 2, 2012, pp. 499-505.

[7] C. A. Huegen, "Network-Based Denial of Service Attacks". www.pentics.net/ denial-of-service/presentations/.../1998-0209_dos.pp...

[8] K. Davis," DNS Cache Poisoning Vulnerability Explanation and Remedies," Viareggio, 2008. www.iana.org/about/.../davies-viareggio-entropyvuln-081002.pdf

[9] D. A. McGrew and S. R. Fluhrer, "Multiple Forgery Attacks against Message Authentication Codes," Cisco Systems, Inc., San Jose, 2005. eprint.iacr.org/2005/161.pdf

[10] A. Ornaghi and M. Valleri, "Man in the Middle Attacks Demos," BlackHat Conference, USA, 2003.

[11] D. G. Park, C. Boyd and S.-J. Moon, "Forward Secrecy and Its Application to Future Mobile Communications Security". www.dgpark6.com/ Down/pkc2000_FwdSec.pdf

[12] R. Bidou, "Ping of Death". www.iv2-technologies.com/ DOSAttacks.pdf

[13] "Mutual Authentication". en.wikipedia.org/wiki/Mutual_authentication

[14] C. Hofer and R. Wampfler, "IP Spoofing". rvs.unibe.ch/teaching /cn%20applets/IP_Spoofing/IP%20Spoofing.pdf

[15] A. Yasinsac and S. Goregaoker, "An Intrusion Detection System for Security Protocol Traffic," Department of Computer Science, Florida State University, Tallahassee, 1996, p. 12.

16] "Ping Broadcast".

en.wikipedia.org/wiki/Broadcast_radiation

[17] V. Goyal, V. Kumar, M. Singh, A. Abraham and S. Sanyal, "CompChall: Addressing Password Guessing Attacks," 2003. http://eprint.iacr.org /2004/136.pdf

[18] L. Seltzer, "Spoofing Server-Server Communication: How You Can Prevent It," 2009. www.verisign.com/ssl/ssl.../ssl.../whitepaper-ev-prevent-spoofing.pdf

[19] S. Kapoor, "Session Hijacking Exploiting TCP, UDP and HTTP Sessions". infosecwriters.com/text_resources/.../SKapoor_SessionHijacking.pdf

[20] R. Ramasamy and A. P. Muniyandi, "New Remote Mutual Authentication Scheme Using Smart Cards," *Transactions on Data Privacy*, Vol. 2, No. 2, 2009, pp. 141-152.

[21] H. Jeong, D. H. Won and S. Kim, "Weaknesses and Improvement of Secure Hash-Based Strong-Password Authentication Protocol," *Journal of Information Science and Engineering*, Vol. 26, No. 5, 2010, pp. 1845-1858.

[22] "Smurf Attack". http://en.wikipedia.org/wiki/Smurf_attack

[23] "Teardrop Attack Detection". https://www.daxnetworks.com/Dax/Products/Switch/DTS_T5C_24G_24GT.htm

[24] K. Kaur and G. Geetha, "Implementing RNA-FINNT in Ideal Password Authentication Scheme Results in Fortification of Transport Layer Security Protocol," *International Journal of Advances in Computer Science and Its Application*, Vol. 2, No. 3, 2012, pp. 201-205.

[25] K. Kaur and G. Geetha, "Validation of RNA-FINNT for Reduction in Error Percentage," *International Journal of Advances in Computer Science and Its Application*, Vol. 3, No. 1, 2013, pp. 22-26.

10

Personality Traits and Cognitive Determinants—An Empirical Investigation of the Use of Smartphone Security Measures

Jörg Uffen, Nico Kaemmerer, Michael H. Breitner
Information Systems Institute, Leibniz Universität, Hannover, Germany

ABSTRACT

In the last years, increasing smartphones' capabilities have caused a paradigm shift in the way of users' view and using mobile devices. Although researchers have started to focus on behavioral models to explain and predict human behavior, there is limited empirical research about the influence of smartphone users' individual differences on the usage of security measures. The aim of this study is to examine the influence of individual differences on cognitive determinants of behavioral intention to use security measures. Individual differences are measured by the Five-Factor Model; cognitive determinants of behavioral intention are adapted from the validated behavioral models theory of planned behavior and technology acceptance model. An explorative, quantitative survey of 435 smartphone users is served as data basis. The results suggest that multiple facets of smartphone user's personalities significantly affect the cognitive determinants, which indicate the behavioral intention to use security measures. From these findings, practical and theoretical implications for companies, organizations, and researchers are derived and discussed.

Keywords: Security Measures; Personality Traits; Behavioral Models; Mobile Security; Smartphones

1. Introduction

In the last years, mobile devices have introduced a new dimension into life and work. Increasing capabilities have caused a paradigm shift in the way users view and use mobile devices [1]. Smartphones and other mobile devices, such as tablet PCs, are small, easy to carry and powerful in computational and storage capabilities. Particularly smartphones and tablet PCs are being used in a business context and replacing classic business mobile phones and to some extent, notebook PCs. Organizational decision-makers have increasingly come to accept the use of mobile and private devices and applications in the organizational IS environment [2]. Hence, research studies emphasize management's concerns about the protection of organizational information asset [1,3]. Smartphone users' behavior in different situations and how they cope with security measures become important in the organizational information security context. While researchers focus on technical issues or on organizational perspectives of mobile security (e.g. [1]), behavioral research is very limited up to now [3].

The attempt of this study is to examine how behavioral cognitive determinants affect the behavioral intention to use smartphone security measures. In information security research, the adoption of behavioral models, such as theory of planned behavior (TPB) and core constructs of the technology acceptance model (TAM), is well established to explain and predict user behavior (for a list see, for example [4,5]. Only a few studies have investigated the rooting behavioral determinants that lead to different attitudes and behavioral intentions. Fishbein and Ajzen [6] recognized the potential importance of additional external behavioral influence factors that are outside the TPB. The authors explicitly stated that individual differences in personality are external variables that influence a specific behavior indirectly through mediating cognitive constructs contained within the TPB [6,7]. Therefore, this study investigates the relationship between personality traits and cognitive behavioral models. Other research studies, for example Devaraj *et al.* [8] and Nov and Ye [9], investigated the relationship between personality traits and TAM in a different IS context. The authors found that personality traits are useful predictors of attitudes and beliefs. Wang [2] incorporated personality traits into the IS continuance model to examine the influence of personality traits on an individual's IS continuance intention. The author suggested that personality traits and cognitive determinants on behavior, as provided by the TPB and the TAM constructs of attitude and behavioral intention, might be integrated into a single model. We make a theoretical contribution by conceptualizing that smartphone users' actions and decisions are significantly driven by their personalities. Personality is measured using the five-factor model (FFM) [10]. We explore the following research question by testing an integrated personality model:

How do smartphone users' personality traits influence the cognitive determinants of their usage of security measures?

This paper is structured as follows: first, we provide a theoretical basis and outline the identified research gap. After presenting the model development and analysis, we report and discuss the results of our empirical investigation. Finally, we conclude with a discussion of implications for practice and research, limitations, and an outlook for future research.

2. Theoretical Background

2.1. Key Areas Comprising Mobile Security

Rapid changes in the use of mobile devices have caused a paradigm shift in the information security context. The definition of mobile devices includes portable electronic devices that store potentially critical information and data [11]. Although this broad definition includes laptops and notebooks or personal digital assistants (PDA), the focus of this paper lies on multi-function pocket and handheld devices such as smartphones or tablet PCs (in the following, referred to as smartphones) that use touch-sensitive screens. Due to increasing mobility, easier communication, and processing ability, individuals carry smartphones with critical information and data with them [12], which results in an even larger user base [13]. Besides the ability to run many applications, individuals can access, store, and manipulate private data, as well as critical information from organizational networks such as emails, contact details of clients and suppliers, and calendar items [11,12]. To prevent data loss, smartphones typically include security measures, also referred to as countermeasures or security mechanisms [4,14], such as password protection, backup and restore, and remote device wipe [12]. Organizations integrate security aspects of employee-owned and organizational mobile devices into their information security strategies and policies. Therefore, national and international organizations issued fundamental best-practices, guidelines and standards, such as the International Standards Organization's (ISO) Code of Practice (ISO/IEC 27001; ISO/IEC 27002) or National Institute of Standards and Technology (NIST)

special publications such as SP 800 - 124, which provide recommendations regarding the implementation and management of security measures for smartphones. But these standards or guidelines are generic in scope and do not focus on the different security requirements within organizations.

Even if challenges for securing smartphones are very similar to those encountered with personal computers or laptops and notebooks, often smartphone users themselves are the private owner and and in some cases responsible for the device's configuration and use of security measures [11]. For example, optionally activated security measures bear the risk that users are not willing to actively enable them [12]. For this reason, it is essential to understand the cognitive processes of smartphone users that lead to the actual usage of security measures for smartphones. Currently, only few research studies have started to incorporate cognitive variables into behavioral models that consider the use of different security measures for smartphones [12]. For example, in their research study, Clarke and Furnell [15] elaborated that a significant proportion of smartphone users do not enable PIN-based authentication. The authors examined the attitudes of smartphone users towards PIN- and biometric based security measures. Ben-Asher *et al.* [16] surveyed smartphone users' security needs and concerns, as well as their awareness of security measures. Results suggest that the needs of smartphone users are diverse and increasing awareness encourages users to activate simple security measures. Using protection motivation theory, Tu and Yuan [12] conceptualized a research model that provides an understanding on how smartphone users behave in coping with security threats of loss and theft. These studies and concepts emphasize that smartphone users' cognitive factors are diverse and depend on the influence of other external variables such as individual differences. Prior literature did not reveal an accepted and integrated model that investigates the influence of personality traits on security-related behavior in a smartphone user context.

2.2. Personality Traits and Behavioral Cognition Models in IS Research

The investigation of individual differences has become omnipresent in IS research. Researchers have incorporated related cognitive and personality-related variables into various IS success outcome models in order to predict and explain actual behavior. The integration of personality traits in behavioral cognition models is a relatively young research area in the IS domain. Personality researchers use classification systems that summarize individual differences in personality into fundamental facets of each individual. These traits determine cognitive and behavioral patterns that remain more or less stable across different situations [17]. Personality traits are commonly referred to as the agile organization within the human being "of those psycho physiological systems that determine his characteristic behavior and thought" ([18], p. 28). The most frequently used taxonomy in personality research is the FFM [19]. The FFM, a parsimonious and comprehensive model of personality, became widely accepted in personality research because its validity was verified by multiple empirical studies [19,20]. Despite criticism of the number and labels of FFM factors (e.g. [19]), a number of beneficial properties are associated with the use of the FFM: stability, presence, and collective appreciation [17]. Its five broad traits are generally characterized as follows (e.g. [10,17,19]):

1) Extraversion is the degree to which an individual is cheerful, assertive, ambitious, and social;

2) Agreeableness is the tendency to be trustful, straightforward, helpful, and willing to cooperate;

3) Persistence, self-control, self-discipline, and dutifulness represent conscientiousness;

4) Openness to experience indicates an appreciation for variety of creativity, flexibility, adventurousness, and imagination; and finally,

5) Anxiety, pessimism, impulsiveness and personal insecurity are related to neuroticism.

To understand the link between a smartphone user's personality and his or her influence factors of actual behavior towards the use of security measures, cognitive processes must be taken into account. As proposed by Devaraj *et al.* [8], the influence of personality traits on behavior is mediated by cognitions, as implied by the TPB or the TAM. TPB and TAM are the most widely applied models of goal-specific cognition and are widely supported by research studies for their predictive power [4,8]. Both models are an adaptation of the theory of reasoned action (TRA), which implies that intentions are proximal cognitive antecedents of actions or behavior. TAM determines that attitudes toward the usefulness and ease of use of an innovative technology are factors in its adoption and use [21]. In TPB, intentions index the motivation to perform a specific action and are determined by three constructs: attitudes (ATT), subjective norm (SN), and perceived behavioral control (PBC). The PBC construct extends TPB from TRA to account for requisite resources necessary for performing a behavior [7]. The SN construct represents an individual's beliefs as to whether a specific behavior is accepted and encouraged by people who are important to her or him [7]. In general, ATT represents an individual's overall evaluation of a specific behavior. Within the context of this research study, ATT constitutes an individual's beliefs that taking security measures is a desirable behavior that helps to enhance the protection of smartphones. Given that TAM is tailored for modeling user acceptance of IS objects, we

adapted both attitudinal TAM constructs, perceived usefulness (PU) and perceived ease of use (PEOU), to explain the attitude's impact on behavioral intention. More specifically, in our case, PU determines the degree to which a smartphone user believes that using specific security measures will enhance the protection level of his or her smartphone. The second attitudinal TAM construct, PEOU, denotes the degree to which a smartphone user believes that using security measures for smartphones will be effortless. If a smartphone user perceives the result of a certain behavior as being positive, he or she will form positive attitudes towards the adoption or use of this specific security measure. In comparison to PBC, PEOU represents the individual beliefs about the degree of effort applied, while PBC can be seen as a control belief and situational perception. A smartphone user might perceive that a specific security measure is easy to use, but could feel that she or he does not have control over the adoption or use. As mentioned above, smartphones have different types of security measures in place. Therefore, we decided to determine these behavioral constructs by regarding multiple security measure rather than a single one. Because there is little research in this field yet, we believe that a more global focus on security measures is beneficial for practitioners and researchers alike.

3. Research Model and Hypotheses

Personality research shows that personality traits vary in their respective relevance, but are resistant to transformation [22]. Prior meta-analytic evidence has demonstrated that specific FFM traits are more relevant in explaining different factors of behavior than others [19]. Therefore, specific personality traits are hypothesized to be related to some, but not each and every one of the cognitive constructs. A hypothesized relationship is relevant when it is appropriate, grounded in, and supported by theoretical and empirical research studies.

The aim of this study is to provide a general link between personality traits, cognitive factors, and the respective behavior. Therefore, behavioral intentions are the dependent variable in our integrated model (**Figure 1**).

Assessing intentions rather than actual behavior is theoretically and technically justified. Despite criticism that most critical limitation of TAM or TPB studies is the use of self-reported data (e.g. [23]), several authors have shown a strong and consistent relationship between behavioral intention and actual behavior (e.g. [24]). In our case, the technical measurement of the actual usage of security measures is argued to be difficult due to the sensitive context of information security (e.g. [25] and the large and diverse sample sizes [26]. Despite theoretical agreement that PU, PEOU, SN and PBC predicts behav-

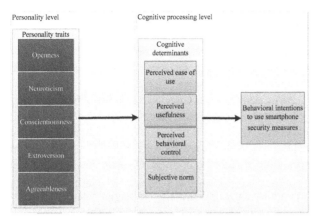

Figure 1. Integrated Research Model.

ioral intentions, prior research has shown a strong and consistent empirical relationship between these constructs (e.g. [4,8]).

Hypothesis (H) 1a-1d: PEOU (H1a), PU (H1b), SN (H1c) and PBC (H1d) are positively associated with the behavioral intention toward the use of security measures

Individuals with an open personality are characterized as being adventurous, creative, intelligent, imaginative, unconventional, and receptive to new and innovative ideas [17]. Associated with various cognitive skills and abilities in individuals, openness is characterized as the motivational tendency to critically examine information, reflection on ideas, and the cognitively differentiated interpretation of information in multiple scenarios [27]. A high degree of openness, with its facets of a deeper scope of awareness and less conscious in tradition [22], promotes that smartphone users deal with potential security risks that might affect their smartphones. This is expected to result in a positive judgment about the utility of security measures in general. These facets and cognitive processes are hypothesized to lead to positive attitudes and values towards the perceived ease of use and usefulness of security measures. Those individuals who are high in openness are less concerned with the change implicit in adopting a new technology [8]. In their meta-analytic review, Judge *et al.* [20] demonstrated that openness is positively related to self-efficacy and the motivation toward the accomplishment of self-set targets. In addition, Barrick *et al.* [19] emphasized that openness is positively related in learning experiences and proficiency. Therefore, more open smartphone users will find it easy to use a security measure and will form positive attitudes towards their own learning experience and capacity to perform.

H2a-c: Openness is positively associated with attitudes towards the perceived ease of use (H2a), perceived usefulness (H2b), and perceived behavioral control of security measures (H2c)

Neuroticism is characterized by anxiety, pessimism,

hostility, and personal insecurity [17]. Individuals who score high in neuroticism tend to avoid situations of taking control and show low motivation toward goal-setting [20]. In addition, prior research demonstrated that one of the facets of neuroticism, anxiety, is negatively related to computer self-efficacy [28]. As a result, neurotic smartphone users tend to feel insecure or nervous that they do not have control over using a security measure. Further, Devaraj *et al.* [8] have shown that emotionally stable individuals, the counterpart of neurotic individuals, are likely to view innovative technical advances as being helpful and important. Due to a lack of confidence and optimism, we expect that if a highly neurotic smartphone user views the use of security measures with skepticism, he or she will form negative attitudes, because it is believed that a potential action cannot make a significant difference in protecting their smartphone.

H3a, b: Neuroticism is negatively associated with the attitude towards perceived usefulness (H3a) and perceived behavioral control of security measures (H3b).

Conscientiousness, a personality trait that is associated with intrinsic motivation to achieve, competence, persistence, and being careful, is one of the most important traits within the research of information security behavior [1,29]. Prior research emphasized a positive relationship between conscientiousness and mindfulness in IT innovations [27], and a positive relation to security concerns [30]. Conscientious smartphone users tend towards purposeful and careful reactions before prematurely employing inefficient security measures. In particular, conscientious smartphone users are more likely to be intrinsically motivated to use security measures to protect their smartphones. This cognitive processing is expected to result in a positive attitude toward the usefulness of the security measure. In addition, individuals with high levels of conscientiousness are more likely to take responsebility [17]. Together with the facet of self-control and due to the tendency of intrinsic motivation to perform, we posit that conscientiousness will interact with PBC in determining behavioral intentions. If a smartphone user forms positive beliefs in his or her capacity to use security measures, conscientiousness will increase those beliefs and result in positive behavioral intentions to use these security measures.

H4a: Conscientiousness is positively associated with the attitude towards the perceived usefulness of security measures.

H4b: Conscientiousness moderates the relationship between the attitude perceived behavioral control and behavioral intentions to use security measures.

Individuals who score high in extraversion are characterized as being cheerful, energetic, gregarious, ambitious and optimistic [19]. In addition, they seek out new excitements and opportunities [31] and value interpersonal relationships [19]. For example, in training situations, research results indicate that extraverted individuals are more likely to be active and involved in opportunities to provide and obtain information in specific situations [19]. Extraverted individuals tend to perform a specific behavior that is viewed as being desirable by significant others. In this regard, we expect that extraverted smartphone users will form positive intentions to use security measures as long as significant others think that this is acceptable.

*H*5: Extraversion moderates the relationship between subjective norm and behavioral intention to use security measures.

Agreeableness is the trait that implies cooperating, nurturing other individuals, and being helpful and considerate [17]. Prior meta-analytic evidence has demonstrated that agreeableness, like extraversion, is particularly relevant when performance involves interaction with other people [19]. Korukonda [32] demonstrated that agreeableness is negatively related to computer anxiety. Individuals high in agreeableness are sensitive towards other's thoughts and opinions. Therefore, it is hypothesized that agreeable smartphone users will reveal themselves to use security measures when significant others think the same as they do. This leads to the assumption that agreeableness acts as a moderator of the relationship between subjective norm and intention towards the use of security measures.

*H*6: Agreeableness moderates the relationship between subjective norm and behavioral intentions to use security measures.

4. Research Methodology

4.1. Explorative Data Collection Procedure

Kotulic and Clark [33] emphasized that collecting acceptable empirical organizational data in this sensitive context of information security is quite challenging. To gain an acceptable number of observations, we decided to use a student sample. The rationale for using a student sample was to gather acceptable explorative data, given our unique focus on personality traits and behavioral cognition models. The objective of this study is to shed light in the explanation of cognitive processes of smartphone users that lead to specific behavior towards security measures. Personality traits are shown to be relatively stable across situations in an individual's lifespan, especially beyond adulthood [17]. Therefore, a student sample is adaptable into an organizational context. Another reason is that younger individuals, mostly represented through students, have been shown to use mobile devices most frequently [22,34] and are more open to all kinds of innovations and are often the first to adopt them [35]. Although we acknowledge the criticism of the use

of student samples due to their limited representativeness or external validity, the appropriateness and usefulness of student samples in the specific context of personality traits and information security has been demonstrated in different research studies (e.g. [22]).

Participants were contacted via university social networks, email, and closed groups in social networks (e.g. Facebook, Xing). Participation was voluntary and no course credits or incentives were given. But participation was motivated by a promise to share the results. The survey was hosted using a secure university-based tool; anonymity and confidentiality were guaranteed. All questionnaires were completed with a web-based survey. A total of 526 undergraduate and graduate business students from a large university participated. Gender was nearly equally balanced with 40% male and 60% female. The largest percentage (65%) of respondents was in the age group of 21 - 29. About 86% of the sample indicated that they use apps, messaging, e-mails, and make calls multiple times a day, indicating that these individuals are experienced smartphone users. In order to ensure a high level of validity, only those questionnaires that were entirely complete were used in the study. The final sample frame contained 435 responses that can be considered sufficient. **Table 1** provides an overview of the demographic statistics.

Table 1. Demographic statistics.

Criteria	Frequency	Percentage
Gender		
Male	174	40
Female	261	60
Range of age		
<21	84	19.3
21 to 29	284	65.3
30 to 39	33	7.6
40 to 49	18	4.1
50 to 59	9	2.1
>59	7	1.6
Level of education		
Student	23	5.3
Secondary modern school	5	1.1
High school diploma	48	11
Higher education entrance qualification	199	45.7
University degree	159	36.6
Not stated	1	0.2

To test for non-response bias, we compared those who responded within a few days with late respondents using t-test comparison of means for measurement items. No significant differences between the early and late respondents could be identified, so non-response bias was not an issue in this study.

4.2. Operationalization of Measurement Items and Instrumentation

The items for constructs were adapted with the help of validated items from literature whenever possible. Personality was measured using the validated 44-item BFI inventory developed by John et al. [10]. In contrast to the 240 item NEO-PI-R or the 60-item NEO-FFI [17], the BFI is advantageous due to its short and succinct phrasing, which is less time consuming for respondents. The behavioral constructs for mobile security were multi-item scales (see Appendix **Table 2**). All items were measured using a five-point Likert scale. In concordance with prior literature, subjective norm was regarded as a formative construct because it is comprised of causal items [36]. The items occur independently of the others within this construct [37]. All other items in the study were modeled as reflective. To increase content validity, measurement items for both formative and reflective constructs were based on validated prior literature. In addition, the complete questionnaire was pre-tested with nine faculty members and PhD students who were skilled in quantitative research methods.

4.3. Data Analysis and Results

Empirical data were analyzed using the component-based structural equation modeling approach of partial least squares (PLS) [38]. PLS is the preferred option in explorative studies of complex research relationships [38] and for studies during the early stages of theory building [3]. In addition, we chose PLS to handle the presence of a large number of measures and the combination of latent reflective and formative variables [39]. Model testing and measurement validation were conducted using SmartPLS (Version 2.0 M3).

Following the validation guidelines from Chin [38] and Straub et al. [40] for reflective measurement models, we made use of convergent validity, discriminant validity, and reliability. With regard to individual item reliability, the factor loadings of each item were assessed on its respective construct. Recommendations for threshold levels of item reliability range from a minimum loading of 0.4 [40] to ideally 0.707 as proposed by Chin [38]. The item reliability analysis of personality traits showed that some items had low factor loadings. This phenomenon is known in personality research [41]. Since we focus on the global dimensions rather than the single facets, re-

moving items is appropriate. After purification, the lowest item loading on its respective underlying construct was 0.62 (agreeableness) so that every item was near the recommended ideal threshold of 0.707. To confirm internal consistency, composite reliability (CR) was measured. All constructs met the minimum threshold of 0.70 (lowest CR is PU with a CR of 0.79), which is considered to be sufficient [42]. To ensure convergent validity of constructs, average variance extracted (AVE) for each construct was above the minimum threshold of 0.50 (lowest AVE is extraversion with an AVE of 0.59). For adequate discriminant validity, the square root of the AVE for each construct exceeded the correlation values in the correlation matrix [42].

Regarding the formative measure, we first ensured the content validity by using validated past empirical studies. To ensure that multicollinearity was not present in this study, we used variance inflation factor (VIF) statistic. A VIF of ten or below is required [38]. Since the VIF value was 1.01, no multicollinearity could be observed. In addition, all weights of formative indicators were significant at p < 0.01 (lowest t-value 2.98).

5. Discussion

The aim of this study was to examine how personality traits influence the cognitive determinants of users' intention with respect to smartphone security measures. It was shown that personality traits are influential in determining core constructs of TPB and TAM. **Figure 2** provides the estimates of the path coefficients and a summary of the results of hypotheses. As predicted by TPB, TAM, and in consistence with our expectations and the results of prior studies in information security research (e.g. [4,8]), a smartphone user's intention is strongly influenced by the core constructs PU ($\beta = 0.329$; p < 0.001), SN ($\beta = 0.281$; p < 0.001), and PBC ($\beta = 0.395$; p < 0.001). In more detail, smartphone users' intentions to use security measures are mainly motivated by their beliefs about the usefulness and whether the use is under their control. The results also imply that social influence

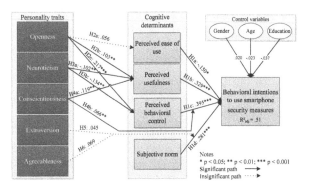

Figure 2. Results of PLS structural equation model analysis.

determines the intentions to use security measures. A smartphone user is likely to use security measures if she or he perceives that significant others are using the same security measure. Contrary to TAM, H1a is not supported. A negative significant influence of PEOU to INT is identified. Upon reflection, this result can be the phenomenon of other external variables, influencing the relationship between PEOU and INT. For example, Venkatesh and Bala [43] highlighted the sensitivity of potential moderators that influence the relationship between PEOU and INT. The authors found that experience moderated the effect of PEOU and INT such that the effect becomes weaker with an increase in user experience levels [43]. It is possible that the relationship between PEOU and INT might be more complex than a linear relationship. Overall the cognitive determinants accounted for a significant proportion of the variance in INT (R^2_{adj} = 0.51).

Further, the results of our study indicate that the cognitive determinants of security measures vary depending on different personality traits. More specifically, out of the nine hypothesized relationships between personality traits and cognitive determinants and behavioral intentions, six significant relationships were identified. Openness was hypothesized to have a positive relationship to PEOU, PU, and PBC. Due to the facets of, for example, a higher scope of awareness, open smartphone users are found to form positive beliefs about the usefulness of potential security measures. In addition, facets such as being intelligent and willingness to learn [19] make smartphone users believe in their own ability to use different security measures. A significant relationship between openness and PEOU could not be identified. As mentioned above, other external variables such as experience might influence the relationship between openness and PEOU. Devaraj et al. [8] pointed out that the relationship between openness and attitudinal constructs might be more complex than a simple linear relationship. The authors justified their argumentation by demonstrating that openness and attitudinal constructs were not significant, while a direct positive relationship to behavioral intention exists. Turning to neuroticism, the results indicate that neuroticism has a negative impact on PU and PBC. Prior research stated that neurotic individuals tend to avoid taking control of a situation; this research study confirms this relationship. Additionally, neurotic smartphone users are more skeptical and form negative beliefs towards the usefulness of a security measure and their own ability to take control of using a security measure. Turning to conscientiousness, both hypotheses are supported. These results are not surprising, since conscientiousness has been shown to be an important personality trait in information security research [1].

Agreeable and extraverted smartphone users are hypothesized to influence the relationship between SN and INT. In prior research, it was pointed out that in a situation that requires interpersonal interaction, both traits appear to show a high predictive validity [19]. However, prior research has shown that self-efficacy, or in the case of this study, PBC, eliminates the effect of extraversion on behavioral intention [31]. Therefore, a reason for H6 not being supported can be the strong impact of PBC on INT. Another reason can be the peculiarity of extravertsion with the desire to gain social status. Within the context of smartphone security measures, social pressure does not affect the social cues within this personality trait. On the other hand, agreeableness shows its facets in interpersonal interactions, especially in situations that involve helping and cooperating with others [19]. Social pressure to use security measures refers to the extent to which the use of a security measure is perceived as enhancing a smartphone user's image or status in a social system. Agreeableness may show its facets more in helping and supporting others. Agreeable smartphone users are more willing to help others, but may not necessarily feel compelled to use security measures because of social pressure.

6. Implications and Recommendations

This study makes theoretical and practical contributions to the emerging knowledge of behavioral issues in regard to the use of mobile security measures. Literature in information security investigated both personality and cognitive factors to explain different behaviors in each human being. With the exception of Devaraj et al. [8] and Nov and Ye [9], who based their work on TAM, research has not focused on understanding the main personal determinants of cognitive key factors that influence intended behavior. Further, to the best of our knowledge, this is the first study that combines personality traits and mediated cognitive factors to intended behavioral outcome in a mobile security context. Knowing that personality traits are stable over time, results indicate that cognitive factors about the overall acceptance of smartphone security measures are influenced by personality traits in different ways. Therefore, the current research demonstrates a more complete, integrated, and coherent view of the acceptance of security measures. These results can spur other researchers to examine personality traits together with other established behavioral models, such as general deterrence theory or protection motivation theory, in information security research.

On the more practical side, this study sheds light on different kinds of smartphone users and their cognitive processes that result in intended behavior. The applied cognitive factors are associated with intentions to use a security measure, and to actual use behavior. In the current debate of consumerization (e.g. [44]), organizations can benefit from our findings that different kinds of individuals are likely to form positive attitudes and intentions towards security measures by developing preventative strategies. While personality traits are stable over time, cognitive factors such as beliefs about the perceived usefulness or perceived behavioral control can be directly enhanced. Practitioners should attempt to adapt these findings and design specified user training.

7. Limitations and Future Research

The study is subject to following limitations: First, as this study is based on a student sample of smartphone users, the results cannot be generalized to the entire smartphone user's population. The rationale for using student samples is explained in section 3.1 and has been evaluated to be appropriate for the purpose of this study. We encourage validation of our findings with other population segments. Further, despite the use of actual behavior, this study is based on self-reported information that measures behavioral intentions. Due to the sensitive context of security measures and the investigated object of smartphones, which can be seen as an object of privacy, it is difficult to obtain data about actual behavior. To focus more on the gap between behavioral intention and actual behavior, and to link that with the FFM, one option to alleviate this limitation is to use scenario techniques [26]. Providing broader information about hypothetical information security situations and indirectly asking about attitudes towards security measures might allow researchers to get a better impression of a smartphone user's true behavior. Further, respondents are from a German university. In regard to cross-national differences in personality, it is likely that smartphone users from other countries have different attitudes about or reactions to the protection of their smartphones. Future studies could integrate cultural differences by expanding into a more international context.

8. Conclusion

This paper presents a first attempt at investigating how personality traits of smartphone users affect cognitive determinants for the use of security measures. Recent studies have acknowledged the influence of personality traits on IS success outcome factors; however, incorporating personality traits from smartphone users' perspective into determinants of behavioral intention to use security measures have largely been ignored. Personality is measured by the FFM; the determinants of behavioral intention are adapted from TPB and TAM, the latter is represented by PEOU and PU. Results indicate that personality traits influence smartphone security measures' usage. For example, openness, neuroticism, and conscientiousness are found to have a significant influence on smartphone users' beliefs towards the usefulness of a security measure. In addition, the core cognitive determinants of behavioral intentions are all found to significantly influence the intention to use security measures.

REFERENCES

[1] J. Shropshire, M. Warkentin, A. C. Johnston and M. B. Schmidt, "Personality and IT security: An Application of the Five-Factor Model," *Proceedings of the 12th Americas Conference on Information Systems, Acapulco (Mexico)*, Acapulco, 4-6 August 2006, pp. 3443-3449.

[2] W. Wang, "How Personality Factors Affects Continuance Intention: An Empirical Investigation of Instant Messaging," *Proceedings of the 14th Pacific Asia Conference on Information Systems*, Taipei, 9-12 July 2010, p. 113.

[3] H. H. Teo, K. K. Wei and I. Benbasat, "Predicting Intention to Adopt Interorganizational Linkages: An Institutional Perspective," *MIS Quarterly*, Vol. 27, No. 1, 2003, pp. 19-49.

[4] C. L. Anderson and R. Agarwal, "Practicing Safe Computing: A Multimethod Empirical Examination of Home Computer User Behavioral Intention," *MIS Quarterly*, Vol. 34, No. 4, 2010, pp. 613-643.

[5] B. Lebek, J. Uffen, M. Neumann, B. Hohler and M. H. Breitner, "Employees' Information Security Awareness and Behavior: A Literature Review," *Proceedings of the 45th Hawaii International Conference on System Science, Maui (USA)*, Wailea, 7-10 January 2013, pp. 2978-2987.

[6] M. Fishbein and I. Ajzen, "Belief, Attitude, Intention and Behavior," John Wiley, New York, 1975.

[7] I. Ajzen, "Theory of Planned Behavior," *Organizational Behavior and Human Decision Processes*, Vol. 50, No. 2, 1991, pp. 179-211.

[8] S. Devaraj, R. F. Easley and J. M. Crant, "How Does Personalty Matter? Relating Five-Factor Model to Technology Acceptance and Use," *Information Systems Research*, Vol. 19, No. 1, 2008, pp. 93-115.

[9] O. Nov and C. Ye, "Personality and Technology Acceptance: Personal Innovativeness in IT, Openness and Resistance to Change," *Proceedings of the 41st Hawaii International Conference on System Science, Big Island (USA)*, Waikoloa, 7-10 January 2008, p. 448.

[10] O. P. John, E. M. Donahue and R. L. Kentle, "The Big Five Inventory—Version 4a und 54," Institute of Personality and Social Research, University of California, Berkeley, 1991.

[11] R. A. Botha, S. M. Furnell and N. L. Clarke, "From Desktop to Mobile: Examining the Security Experience," *Computer and Security*, Vol. 28, No. 3-4, 2009, pp. 130-137.

[12] Z. Tu and Y. Yuan, "Understanding User's Behaviours in Coping with Security Threat of Mobile Devices Loss and Theft," *Proceedings of the 45th Hawaii International Conference on System Science*, Maui, 4-7 January 2012, pp. 1393-1402.

[13] R. W. Smith and A. Pridgen, "STAAF: Scaling Android Application Analysis with a Modular Framework," *Proceedings of the 45th Hawaii International Conference on System Sciences*, Maui, 4-7 January 2012, pp. 5432-5440.

[14] J. D'Arcy, A. Hovav and D. Galletta, "User Awareness of Security Countermeasures and Its Impact on Information Systems Misuse," *Information Systems Research*, Vol. 20, No. 1, 2009, pp. 79-98.

[15] N. L. Clarke andS. M. Furnell, "Authentication of Users on Mobile Telephones—A Survey of Attitudes and Practices," *Computer & Security*, Vol. 24, No. 7, 2005, pp. 519-527.

[16] N. Ben-Asher, N. Kirschnick, H. Sieger, J. Meyer and S. Möller, "On the Need for Different Security Methods on Mobile Phones," *Proceedings of the 13th International Conference on Human Computer Interaction with Mobile Devices and Services*, Stockholm, 30 August-2 September 2011, pp. 465-473.

[17] P. Costa, R. McCrae and D. Dye, "Facet Scales for Agreeableness and Conscientiousness: A Revision of the NEO Personality Inventory," *Personality Individual Differences*, Vol. 9, No. 12, 1991, pp. 887-898.

[18] G. W. Allport, "Pattern and Growth in Personality," Holt, Rinehart & Winston, New York, 1961.

[19] M. R. Barrick, M. K. Mount and T. A. Judge, "Personality and Performance at the Beginning of the New Millennium: What Do We Know and Where Do We Go Next?" *International Journal of Selection & Assessment*, Vol. 9, No. 1-2, 2001, pp. 9-29.

[20] T. A. Judge, J. E. Bono, R. Ilies and M. W. Gerhardt, "Personality and Leadership: A Qualitative and Quantitative Review," *Journal of Applied Psychology*, Vol. 87, No. 4, 2002, pp. 765-780.

[21] F. D. Davis, "Perceived Usefulness, Perceived Ease of Use, and User Acceptance of Information Technology," *MIS Quarterly*, Vol. 13, No. 3, 1989, pp. 319-339.

[22] I. Junglas, N. Johnson and C. Spitzmüller, "Personality Traits and Concern of Privacy: An empirical Study in the Context of Location-Based Services," *European Journal of Information Systems*, Vol. 17, No. 4, 2008, pp. 387-402.

[23] Y. Lee, K. A. Kozar and K. R. T. Larsen, "The Technology Acceptance Model: Past, Present, and Future," *Communications of the AIS*, Vol. 12, 2003, pp. 752-780.

[24] V. Venkatesh, M. G. Morris, G. B. Davis and F. D. Davis, "User Acceptance of Information Technology: Toward a Unified View," *MIS Quarterly*, Vol. 27, 3, 2003, pp. 425-478.

[25] R. Sharma and P. Yetton, "The Contingent Effects of Management Support and Task Interdependence on Successful IS Implementation," *MIS Quarterly*, Vol. 27, No. 4, 2003, pp. 533-556.

[26] B. Bulgurcu, H. Cavusoglu and I. Benbasat, "Information Security Policy Compliance: An Empirical Study of Rationality-Based Beliefs and Information Security Awareness," *MIS Quarterly*, Vol. 34, No. 3, 2010, pp. 523-548.

[27] S. Goswami, H. H. Teo and H. C. Chan, "Decision-Maker Mindfulness in IT Adoption: The Role of Informed Culture and Individual Personality," *Proceedings of the 30th International Conference on Information Systems*, Phoenix, 15-18 December 2009, p. 203.

[28] D. R. Compeau and C. A. Higgins, "Computer Self-Efficacy: Development of a Measure and Initial Test," *MIS Quarterly*, Vol. 19, No. 2, 1995, pp. 189-211.

[29] Q. Hu, T. Dinev, P. Hart and D. Cooke, "Top Management Championship and Individual Behavior towards Information Security: An Integrative Model," *Proceedings of the 16th European Conference on Information Systems*, Galway, 9-11 June 2008, pp. 1310-1321.

[30] G. Bansal, "Security Concerns in the Nomological Network of Trust and Big5: First Order vs. Second Order," *Proceedings of the 32nd International Conference on Information Systems*, Shanghai, 7 December 2011, Paper 9.

[31] J. C. McElroy, A. R. Hendrickson, A. M. Townsend and S. M. DeMarie, "Dispositional Factors in Internet Use: Personality versus Cognitive Styles," *MIS Quarterly*, Vol. 31, No. 4, 2007, pp. 809-820.

[32] A. R. Korukonda, "Differences that do Matter: A Dialectic Analysis of Individual Characteristics and Personality Dimensions Contributing to Computer Anxiety," *Computers in Human Behavior*, Vol. 23, No. 4, 2007, pp. 1921-1942.

[33] A. G. Kotulic and J. G. Clark, "Why There Aren't More Information Security Research Studies," *Information & Management*, Vol. 41, No. 5, 2004, pp. 597-607.

[34] S. Okazaki, "What Do We Know About Mobile Internet Adopters? A Cluster Analysis," *Information and Management*, Vol. 43, No. 2, 2006, pp. 127-141.

[35] H. Dai, A. F. Salam and R. King, "Service Convenience and Relational Exchange in Electronic Mediated Environment: An Empirical Investigation," *Proceedings of the 29th International Conference on Information Systems*, Paris, 14-17 December 2008, pp. 1-20.

[36] A. C. Johnston and M. Warkentin, "Fear Appeals and Information Security Behaviours: An Empirical Study," *MIS Quarterly*, Vol. 34, No. 3, 2010, pp. 549-566.

[37] C. B. Jarvis, S. B. MacKenzie and P. M. Podsakoff, "A Critical Review of Construct Indicators and Measurement Model Misspecification in Marketing and Consumer Research," *Journal of Consumer Research*, Vol. 30, No. 2, 2003, pp. 199-218.

[38] W. W. Chin, "Issues and Opinion on Structural Equation Modeling," *MIS Quarterly*, Vol. 29, No. 3, 1998, pp. 7-16.

[39] S. Petter, D. Straub and A. Rai, "Specifying Formative Constructs in Information Systems Research," *MIS Quarterly*, Vol. 31, No. 4, 2007, pp. 623-656.

[40] W. Straub, M. C. Boudreau and D. Gefen, "Validation

Guidelines for IS Positivist Research," *Communications of the AIS*, Vol. 13, No. 24, 2004, pp. 380-427.

[41] W. Renner, "A Psychometric Analysis of the NEO Five-Factor Inventory in an Austrian Sample," *Review of Psychology*, Vol. 9, No. 1, 2002, pp. 25-31.

[42] D. Gefen, D. W. Straub and M. C. Boudreau, "Structural Equation Modeling and Regression: Guidelines for Research Practice," *Communications of the AIS*, Vol. 4, No. 7, 2000, pp. 1-80.

[43] V. Venkatesh and H. Bala, "Technology Acceptance Model 3 and a Research Agenda on Interventions," *Decision Sciences*, Vol. 39, No. 2, 2008, pp. 273-315.

[44] F. Weiß and J. M. Leimeister, "Consumerization-IT Innovations from the Consumer Market as a Challenge for Corporate IT," *Business and Information Systems Engineering*, Vol. 4, No. 6, 2012, pp. 363-366.

Appendix

Table 2. Questionnaire items.

Item	Measure (translated from German)
Behavioral intention (e.g. Venkatesh *et al.*, 2003; Davis, 1989; Ajzen, 1991; Anderson and Agarwal, 2010)	
INT1	I intend to continuously engage in security measures for my smartphone
INT2	I will execute data-backups on my smartphone in intervals of less than 3 months
INT3	I plan to change my smartphone PIN-authentication in regular intervals
INT4	I intend to execute updates for firmware and apps in regular intervals
INT5	I intend to receive information about new security measures for my smartphone in the near future
Perceived ease of use (e.g. Venkatesh, 2000; Venkatesh and Davis, 2000)	
PEOU1	I think the enabling of security measures like PINs is easy for most people
PEOU2	I think most people execute regular updates of apps and firmware
PEOU3	I think with modern smartphones, most people can easily execute backups
PEOU4	A lot of expertise is needed to implement security measures on a smartphone
Perceived usefulness (e.g. Venkatesh, 2000; Venkatesh and Davis, 2000)	
PU1	I think PIN-authentication for my smartphone is fundamental
PU2	I would only use a lot of functions on my smartphone if I perceived my data to be safe
PU3	I consider data backups to be very important to effectively avoid data loss
Subjective norm (e.g. Ajzen, 1991; Johnston and Warkentin, 2010; Venkatesh, 2003)	
SN1	People in my closer environment think I should protect the data on my smartphone, for example via regularly backups
SN2	I know a lot of people who use PIN-authentication or similar security measures on their smartphone
SN3	People who influence my behavior use different security measures to protect their smartphones
Perceived behavioral control (e.g. Compeau and Higgins, 1995)	
PBC1	It is easy for me to enable PIN-authentication on my smarthphone
PBC2	I always need someone to assist when I want to change security settings on my smartphone
PBC3	Constant updates for apps and firmware are easy for me
PBC4	Executing data backups is entirely under my control

11

A Formal Model of Conformity and Security Testing of Inheritance for Object Oriented Constraint Programming

Khalid Benlhachmi, Mohammed Benattou

Laboratory of Research in Computer Science and Telecommunications,
Faculty of Science, Ibn Tofail University, Kenitra, Morocco

ABSTRACT

This paper presents an approach for extending the constraint model defined for conformity testing of a given method of class to its overriding method in subclass using inheritance principle. The first objective of the proposed work is to find the relationship between the test model of an overriding method and its overridden method using the constraint propagation. In this context the approach shows that the test cases developed for testing an original method can be used for testing its overriding method in a subclass and then the number of test cases can be reduced considerably. The second objective is the use of invalid data which do not satisfy the precondition constraint and induce valid output values for introducing a new concept of test called secure testing. The implementation of this approach is based on a random generation of test data and analysis by formal proof.

Keywords: Conformity Test; Security Test; Constraints Resolution; Formal Specification; Inheritance

1. Introduction

The principle of testing is to apply input events to the Implementation under Test (IUT) and to compare the observed output events to the expected results. A set of input events and its corresponding results is generally called test case and can be generated from the IUT specification. The purpose of testing methods is to find the failures that are not detected during system normal operation and to define the relationship between the specifications and implementations of entities under test. Indeed, in object oriented modeling, a formal specification defines operations by collections of equivalence relations and is often used to constrain class and type, to define the constraints on the system states, to describe the pre- and post-conditions on operations and methods, and to give constraints of navigation in a class diagram. The object oriented constraints (OOC) are specified by formal languages as OCL [1] and JML [2], and are used for generating test data from formal specifications [3]. The proposed test oracles in the industry are satisfied with the conformity test methods, and are carried out by generating test data that conform to the pre-condition constraint. However, a false pre-condition may induce both valid post-condition and invariant at the same time. A correctly implemented testing method should eliminate cases of invalid data which lead to valid results.

In this context, this paper introduces in the first instance an optimizing approach to minimize the test sequences used for testing the conformity of an overriding method in object oriented models. The main idea of this work is the use of a technique that generates test data by exploiting the existing test sequences. Indeed, it is important to reuse the test result of overridden methods for testing the conformity of the overriding methods during inheritance operation. That is why our approach specifies all cases of conformity of an overriding method by using data extracted from conformity testing of the original methods. The second contribution of our approach is the definition of a security testing based on the generation of invalid input data which induce valid output values. Indeed, in this paper we show how we can use the valid data extracted from the pre-condition constraint to test the conformity of an overriding method, and how the data which does not satisfy the precondition can be used to test the security of similar methods. Our test oracle enables to detect anomalies in invalid inputs that imply valid results.

The work presented in this paper allows to extend the

constraint model defined in [4] for modeling the specification of an overriding method in subclass using inheritance principle. This work is based on our model of similarity concept [5,6] for testing the conformity and the security of overriding methods from test results of the original methods. The main objective is to reduce the number of test cases by using the test result developed in parent classes, and to integrate the invalid data in test process. We present firstly, the relationship between the test model of overridden and overriding methods, and we show how to use the constraint model for extracting the possible cases of test values. Secondly, we show how it is possible to exploit the invalid data that do not satisfy the precondition constraint and induce valid post-conditions.

This paper is organized as follows: in Section 2 we present related works and similar approaches for generating test data from a formal specification, in Section 3 we describe theoretical aspects of our test process, and we define our test formal model of constraints, in Section 4 we present how the testing formal model can be used to generate data for testing the conformity of overriding methods during inheritance operation, in Section 5 we present our approach of security testing that strengthens the conformity testing, and we show how the security testing of an overriding method can be deduced from its overridden method in parent class. Finally, in Section 6 we describe our approach with an example of conformity and security testing for an object oriented model.

2. Related Works

Most works have studied the problem of relating types and subtypes with behavioral specification in an object oriented paradigm. These proposed works show how the contracts are inherited during method overriding and how the testing process can use the formal specification. In [4], we have presented the definition of a formal model of constraint, illustrating the relationship between pre-conditions, post-conditions and invariants of methods, and we have formalized a generic constraint of a given individual method of class that contains all constraints into a single logical predicate. The given model translates algebraically the contract between the user and the called method.

In [5], we have developed a basic model for the concept of methods similarity, the test is based only on a random generation of input data. In [6], we have generalized the basic model of similarity using analysis of partition and formal proof. In [7], the authors propose a randomly generation of test data from a JML specification of class objects. They classify the methods and constructors according to their signature (basic, extended constructors, mutator, and observer) and for each type of

individual method of class, a generation of test data is proposed. In [8], the paper describes specially the features for specifying methods, related to inheritance specification; it shows how the specification of inheritance in JML forces behavioral sub-typing.

The work presented in [9] shows how to enforce contracts if components are manufactured from class and interface hierarchies in the context of Java. It also overcomes the problems related to adding behavioral contracts to Object Oriented Languages, in particular, the contracts on overriding methods that are improperly synthesized from the original contracts of programmer in all of the existing contract monitoring systems. The work is based on the notion of behavioral sub-typing; it demonstrates how to integrate contracts properly, according to the notion of behavioral sub-typing into a contract monitoring tool for java. In [10], the authors treat the problem of types and subtypes with behavioral specifications in object oriented world. They present a way of specification types that makes it convenient to define the subtype relation. They also define a new notion of the subtype relation based on the semantic properties of the subtype and super-type. In [11], they examine various notions of behavioral sub-typing proposed in the literature for objects in component-based systems, where reasoning about the events that a component can raise is important.

All the proposed works concerning the generation of test data from formal specification or to test the conformity of a given method implementation, use only the constraint propagation from super to subclass related to subtype principle and do not exploit the test results of the original method. As an example, several test oracles used in industry as JML compiler can generate the conformity test of an overriding method even if its original method in the parent class does not conform to its specification. Our approach shows that this type of test is unnecessary and can be removed, and presents how we can reduce the test cases by using the test values developed for testing the original methods in a parent class. The main difference between our work and other related works is the definition of the security testing. Indeed, the test methods have focused only on valid inputs satisfying the precondition, and do not integrate the invalid data in test process. Our approach shows how we can use the valid and invalid data extracting from the pre-condition to test the conformity and the security of overridden and overriding methods.

3. Formal Model of Constraint

This section presents a formal model of the generalized constraint defined in [4] which provides a way for modeling the specification of an overriding method by inheritance from a super-class. Indeed, we establish a series of theoretical concepts in order to create a solid basis for testing the conformity of overriding methods in subclasses using the test result of the original methods.

3.1. Constraint Propagation in Inheritance

In [4] we have presented the definition of a formal model of constraint, illustrating the relationship between the pre-condition P, the post-condition Q of a method m and the invariant Inv of the class C: this constraint H is a logical property of the pair (x,o) (x is the vector of parameters $\left(x=(x_1,x_2,\cdots,x_n)\right)$ and o is the receiver object) such that:

$$H(x,o): P(x,o) \Rightarrow \left[Q(x,o) \wedge Inv(o)\right], (x,o) \in E \times I_c$$

where I_c is the set of instances of the class C and E the set of input vectors of m.

Indeed, the invocation of a method m is generally done by reference to an object o and consequently, m is identified by the couple (x,o). The logical implication in the proposed formula means that: each call of method with (x,o) satisfying the precondition P and the invariant before the call, (x,o) must necessarily satisfy the post-condition Q and the invariant Inv after the call. In the context of this work, we assume that the object which invokes the method under test is valid (satisfying the invariant of its class), thus, the objects used at the input of the method under test are generated from a valid constructor. This justifies the absence of predicate Inv of the object o before the call to m in the formula H (**Figure 1**).

The purpose of this paragraph is to establish a series of theoretical rules in order to evolve the constraint H of a method m of a super-class during the operation of inheritance. We consider a method m of a class C_2 which inherits from the class C_1 such that m overrides a method of C_1. The original method and its overriding method in the subclass C_2 will be denoted respectively by $m^{(1)}$, $m^{(2)}$. $(P^{(1)},Q^{(1)})$ denote respectively the pre-condition, the post-condition of the method $m^{(1)}$, and $Inv^{(1)}$ the invariant of C_1; and (P'_2,Q'_2) denote respectively the specific pre-condition, post-condition of the overriding method $m^{(2)}$, and Inv'_2 the specific invariant of the class C_2. $(P^{(2)},Q^{(2)})$ denote respectively the pre-condition, the post-condition of the method $m^{(2)}$, and $Inv^{(2)}$ the invariant of C_2 (**Figure 2**).

The results of this paragraph are based on the works of Liskov, Wing [12] and Meyer [13] who have studied the problem relating to types and subtypes with behavioral

specification in an object oriented (OO) paradigm. Indeed, a derived class obeys the Liskov Substitution Principle (LSP) if for each overriding method $m^{(2)}$, the pre-condition $P^{(2)}$ is weaker than the pre-condition $P^{(1)}$ of the overridden method $\left(P^{(1)} \Rightarrow P^{(2)}\right)$, the post-condition $Q^{(2)}$ is stronger than the post-condition $Q^{(1)}$ of the overridden method $\left(Q^{(2)} \Rightarrow Q^{(1)}\right)$, and the class invariant $Inv^{(2)}$ of the subclass C_2 must be equal to or stronger than the class invariant $Inv^{(1)}$ of the C_1 $\left(Inv^{(2)} \Rightarrow Inv^{(1)}\right)$.

As a result of LSP:

The pre-condition $P^{(2)}$ of $m^{(2)}$ is the disjunction of $P^{(1)}$ and the specific pre-condition P'_2 of $m^{(2)}$ (**Figure 2**):

$$P^{(2)} \Leftrightarrow \left(P^{(1)} \vee P'_2\right) \tag{1}$$

The post-condition $Q^{(2)}$ of $m^{(2)}$ is the conjunction of the post-condition $Q^{(1)}$ of $m^{(1)}$ and the specific post-condition Q'_2 of $m^{(2)}$ (**Figure 2**):

$$Q^{(2)} \Leftrightarrow \left(Q^{(1)} \wedge Q'_2\right) \tag{2}$$

The invariant $Inv^{(2)}$ of the class C_2 is the conjunction of the invariant $Inv^{(1)}$ of C_1 and the specific invariant Inv'_2 of C_2 (**Figure 2**):

$$Inv^{(2)} \Leftrightarrow \left(Inv^{(1)} \wedge Inv'_2\right) \tag{3}$$

Based on the definition of the generalized constraint, we have:

The constraint of $m^{(1)}$:

$$H^{(1)}(x,o): P^{(1)}(x,o) \Rightarrow \left[Q^{(1)}(x,o) \wedge Inv^{(1)}(o)\right],$$
$$(x,o) \in E \times I_{c_1}$$

The constraint of $m^{(2)}$:

$$H^{(2)}(x,o): P^{(2)}(x,o) \Rightarrow \left[Q^{(2)}(x,o) \wedge Inv^{(2)}(o)\right],$$
$$(x,o) \in E \times I_{c_2}$$

Using (1), (2), (3) the constraint of $m^{(2)}$ will have the following form:

$$H^{(2)}: \left[P^{(1)} \vee P'_2\right] \Rightarrow \left[Q^{(1)} \wedge Inv^{(1)} \wedge Q'_2 \wedge Inv'_2\right]$$

In our approach, the specification $\left(P^{(2)},Q^{(2)},Inv^{(2)}\right)$ of $m^{(2)}$ is constituted by:

Two inputs: the Basic Input $\left(BI = P^{(1)}\right)$ and the Specific Input $\left(SI = P'_2\right)$ of $m^{(2)}$.

Two outputs: Basic Output $\left(BO = \left(Q^{(1)},Inv^{(1)}\right)\right)$ and the Specific Output $\left(SO = (Q'_2,Inv'_2)\right)$ of $m^{(2)}$.

This induces 4 possible combinations of I-O: (BI,BO), (BI,SO), (SI,BO), (SI,SO).

3.2. Constraint Model of Overriding Methods

The aim of this paragraph is to construct a formal model of an overriding method by generalizing the constraint

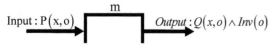

Input : $P(x,o)$ — m — Output : $Q(x,o) \wedge Inv(o)$

Figure 1. Specification of a method m.

Class C_1

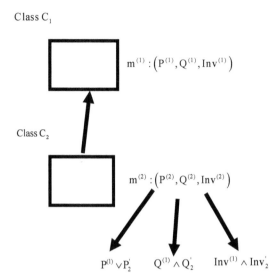

$$m^{(1)} : \left(P^{(1)}, Q^{(1)}, Inv^{(1)}\right)$$

Class C_2

$$m^{(2)} : \left(P^{(2)}, Q^{(2)}, Inv^{(2)}\right)$$

$$P^{(1)} \vee P_2' \qquad Q^{(1)} \wedge Q_2' \qquad Inv^{(1)} \wedge Inv_2'$$

Figure 2. Constraints of $m^{(1)}$ and $m^{(2)}$.

model of the original methods. In achieving this goal, we should define a specific constraint of inheritance and also study the compatibility between the overriding methods and original methods in the parent class.

In this sense, we had proposed in [5,6] the definition of similarity concept for assuring if the overriding method $m^{(2)}$ has the same behavior as its original version $m^{(1)}$ in the super-class relatively to their common specification $\left(P^{(1)}, Q^{(1)}, Inv^{(1)}\right)$. Indeed, the implementation in the subclass must override the implementation in the super class by providing a method $m^{(2)}$ that is similar to $m^{(1)}$. We propose firstly the definition of a constraint $H_{(SI,SO)}$ allowing a partial view of the overriding method $m^{(2)}$ in the class C_2. Secondly, we determine the relationship between the constraints $H^{(2)}$, $H^{(1)}$ and $H_{(SI,SO)}$.

The constraint $H_{(SI,SO)}$ specifies the logical relationship between the input specific predicate P_2' of $m^{(2)}$ and the output predicates $\left(Q_2', Inv_2'\right)$ specific to $m^{(2)}$:

Definition 1: (*Constraint $H_{(SI,SO)}$*)

We define the constraint $H_{(SI,SO)}$ of an overriding method $m^{(2)}$ of a sub-class C_2 as a logical property of the pair $(x,o) \in E \times I_{C_2}$ such that:

$$H_{(SI,SO)}(x,o) : P_2'(x,o) \Rightarrow \left[Q_2'(x,o) \wedge Inv_2'(o)\right]$$

where I_{C_2} is the set of instances of C_2, and E is the set of parameters vector of $m^{(2)}$.

The logical implication in the proposed formula means that: each call of method with (x,o) satisfying the specific precondition P_2 before the call, (x,o) must necessarily satisfy the specific post-condition Q_2' and the specific invariant Inv_2' after the call.

In the same way, we put:

$$H_{(BI,SO)}(x,o) : P^{(1)}(x,o) \Rightarrow \left[Q_2'(x,o) \wedge Inv_2'(o)\right]$$

And

$$H_{(SI,BO)}(x,o) : P_2'(x,o) \Rightarrow \left[Q^{(1)}(x,o) \wedge Inv^{(1)}(o)\right]$$

The relationship between $H^{(1)}$ and $H^{(2)}$ for the two similar methods $m^{(1)}$ and $m^{(2)}$ in classes C_1 and C_2 is shown in the following theorem:

Theorem 1:

$$\left[H^{(2)} \Leftrightarrow \left(H^{(1)} \wedge H_{(SI,SO)}\right)\right] \quad (R)$$

Proof: Using the following result:

$$\left[(a \vee b) \Rightarrow (c \wedge d)\right]$$
$$\Leftrightarrow \left[(a \Rightarrow c) \wedge (a \Rightarrow d) \wedge (b \Rightarrow c) \wedge (b \Rightarrow d)\right]$$

We have:

$$\left[\left(P^{(1)} \vee P_2'\right) \Rightarrow \left(\left(Q^{(1)} \wedge Inv^{(1)}\right) \wedge \left(Q_2' \wedge Inv_2'\right)\right)\right]$$
$$\Leftrightarrow \left[\left(P^{(1)} \Rightarrow \left(Q^{(1)} \wedge Inv^{(1)}\right)\right) \wedge \left(P^{(1)} \Rightarrow \left(Q_2' \wedge Inv_2'\right)\right)\right.$$
$$\left. \wedge \left(P_2' \Rightarrow \left(Q^{(1)} \wedge Inv^{(1)}\right)\right) \wedge \left(P_2' \Rightarrow \left(Q_2' \wedge Inv_2'\right)\right)\right]$$

Therefore, we have the following result:

$$\left[H^{(2)} \Leftrightarrow \left(H^{(1)} \wedge H_{(BI,SO)} \wedge H_{(SI,BO)} \wedge H_{(SI,SO)}\right)\right]$$

In principle, the method $m^{(2)}$ is not intended to provide the services (SI,BO) and (BI,SO) however $m^{(2)}$ must guarantee the services (BI,BO) (**Figure 3**) and (SI,SO) (**Figure 4**). Consequently, we put: $H_{(BI,SO)} = 1$ and $H_{(SI,BO)} = 1$.

Finally, (R) is equivalent to

$$\left[H^{(2)} \Leftrightarrow \left(H^{(1)} \wedge H_{(SI,SO)}\right)\right].$$

The constraints $H^{(1)}$, $H_{(SI,SO)}$, and the relation (R) form the theoretical basis that will be used to test the conformity of overriding methods in subclasses from the test result of their original methods in the parent classes.

4. Conformity Testing

The formal model of test proposed in [4] defines the no-

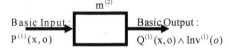

Figure 3. Constraint *BI-BO* of an overriding method.

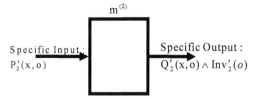

Figure 4. Constraint *SI-SO* of an overriding method.

tion of method validity in a basic class and constitutes a way to generate test data for conformity. In a conformity test, the input data must satisfy the precondition of the method under test. In this context, we are particularly interested in valid input values (*i.e.* the pairs (x,o) that satisfy the precondition P). The conformity test for a method means that if a pre-condition is satisfied at the input, the post-condition and the invariant must be satisfied at the output. The purpose of this section is to generalize the model of [4-6] in order to test the conformity of an overriding method $m^{(2)}$ in a derived class by using the elements of conformity test of its original method $m^{(1)}$ in the super-class.

In [4], we have tested the conformity of methods in a basic class without taking into account the inheritance relationship: the model of test generates random data at the input of a method using elements of the valid domain which satisfy the precondition of the method under test. This test stops when the constraint H becomes False $(H(x,o)=0)$ or when the maximum threshold of the test is reached with H satisfied.

Definition 2: (*Valid method*)

A method m of class C is valid or conforms to its specification if for each $(x,o) \in E \times I_c$, the constraint H is satisfied: $\forall (x,o) \in E \times I_c : H(x,o)=1$

In other words, for a valid method: $\forall (x,o) \in E \times I_c :$ If (x,o) satisfies the precondition P then this (x,o) must satisfy the post-condition Q and the invariant Inv.

The conformity test of $m^{(2)}$ requires the following steps:

- *Step* 1: a conformity test of a basic constructor of class C_2. This step is necessary for using valid objects at the input of the method under test.
- *Step* 2: a similarity test of $m^{(1)}$ and $m^{(2)}$ relatively to $\left(P^{(1)},Q^{(1)},Inv^{(1)}\right)$.

We assume that the test of step 2 showed that $m^{(1)}$ and $m^{(2)}$ are similar.

The conformity test process of the overriding method $m^{(2)}$ relatively to $H^{(2)}$ is based on the test result of $m^{(1)}$ relatively to $H^{(1)}$ and the test result of $m^{(2)}$ relatively to $H_{(SI,SO)}$ (*Theorem* 1).

The conformity test of $m^{(1)}$ induces two cases: $m^{(1)}$ conforms to its specification or $m^{(1)}$ is not in conformity with its specification:

- *Case* 1: The method $m^{(1)}$ *is not in conformity with its specification*
  We have the following result:
  Theorem 2:
  If the overridden method $m^{(1)}$ in parent class C_1 is not in conformity with its specification $\left(P^{(1)},Q^{(1)},Inv^{(1)}\right)$ then any similar method $m^{(2)}$ in a subclass is not in conformity with its specification $\left(P^{(2)},Q^{(2)},Inv^{(2)}\right)$.
  Proof:
  We assume that the method $m^{(1)}$ is not in conformity

with its specification. This means (*Def.* 2) that:

$$\exists (x_0,o_0) \in E \times I_c : H^{(1)}(x_0,o_0)=0$$

The object o_0 is an instance of the class C_1. We consider an object o_0' of the subclass C_2 that has the same values as the object o_0 for attributes of C_1 And therefore, the object o_0' has the same behavior as o_0 in a context of C_1 and consequently:

$$\exists (x_0,o_0') \in E \times I_{C_2} : H^{(1)}(x_0,o_0')=0$$

We apply the relationship (R) (*Theorem* 1) on the pair (x_0,o_0') of the domain $E \times I_{C_2}$:

$$(R) \Leftrightarrow \left[H^{(2)}(x_0,o_0') \Leftrightarrow \left(0 \wedge H_{(SI,SO)}(x_0,o_0')\right) \right]$$
$$\Leftrightarrow \left[H^{(2)}(x_0,o_0') \Leftrightarrow 0 \right]$$

This means: $\exists (x_0,o_0') \in E \times I_{c_2} : H^{(2)}(x_0,o_0')=0$

This shows (*Def.* 2) that the method $m^{(2)}$ is not in conformity with its specification.

- *Case* 2: The method $m^{(1)}$ conforms to its specification
  In this case, we have (*Def.* 2):

$$\forall (x,o) \in E \times I_{c_1} : H^{(1)}(x,o)=1$$

Using $\left(E \times I_{c_2} \subset E \times I_{c_1}\right)$, we have:

$$\forall (x,o) \in E \times I_{c_2} : H^{(1)}(x,o)=1$$

The relationships (R) in theorem 1 implies:

$$\left[H^{(2)}(x,o) \Leftrightarrow \left(1 \wedge H_{(SI,SO)}(x,o)\right) \right] \Leftrightarrow \left[H_{(SI,SO)}(x,o) \right]$$

Therefore, we must to test $m^{(2)}$ relatively to $H_{(SI,SO)}$:

- $m^{(2)}$ *is not in conformity with* $H_{(SI,SO)}$
  We have in this case, the following result:
  Theorem 3:
  If the overriding method $m^{(2)}$ of the subclass C_2 is not in conformity relatively to its specific constraints $\left(P_2',Q_2',Inv_2'\right)$, then the method $m^{(2)}$ is not in conformity with its global specification $\left(P^{(2)},Q^{(2)},Inv^{(2)}\right)$.
  Proof:
  We assume that the method $m^{(2)}$ does not satisfy its specific constraint $H_{(SI,SO)}$:

$$\exists (x_0,o_0) \in E \times I_{c_2} : H_{(SI,SO)}(x_0,o_0)=0$$

Applying the relationship (R):

$$\left[H^{(2)}(x_0,o_0) \Leftrightarrow \left(H^{(1)}(x_0,o_0) \wedge 0\right) \right]$$
$$\Leftrightarrow \left[H^{(2)}(x_0,o_0) \Leftrightarrow 0 \right]$$

and consequently: $\exists (x_0,o_0) \in E \times I_{c_2} : H^{(2)}(x_0,o_0)=0$

This induces that $m^{(2)}$ is not in conformity with its global specification (*Def.* 2).

- $m^{(2)}$ *conforms to its specific constraint* $H_{(SI,SO)}$
  We have in this case, the following result:

Theorem 4:

If the overridden method $m^{(1)}$ of the class C_1 conforms to its specification, and its similar method $m^{(2)}$ in the subclass C_2 conforms to the specific constraint $H_{(SI,SO)}$, we deduce that the overriding method $m^{(2)}$ conforms to its global specification.

Proof:

In this case, we have:

$$\forall (x,o) \in E \times I_{c_2} : H^{(1)}(x,o) = 1 \quad \text{and} \quad H_{(SI,SO)}(x,o) = 1$$

The relationships (R) implies: $\left[H^{(2)}(x,o) \Leftrightarrow (1 \wedge 1) \right]$

This means: $\forall (x,o) \in E \times I_{c_2} : H^{(2)}(x,o) = 1$

We deduce that the overriding method $m^{(2)}$ conforms to its global specification (*Def.* 2).

5. Security Testing

5.1. Formal Model of Security Testing

The realized tests for conformity consider that the input data satisfy the precondition. However, a false pre-condition may induce both a post-condition and an invariant which are valid. A correctly testing of implementation of a method should reject cases of invalid data which provide valid results. Most of test oracles do not integrate the invalid data in test process. This section presents a complementary test aimed to study the invalid inputs of a method that conforms to its specification. Indeed, an anomaly difficult to be detected arises when a couple (x,o) does not satisfy the pre-condition P is accepted and induces both a post-condition Q and invariant Inv that are valid at the output. Our approach allows resolving these anomalies by the introduction of a complementary test for each method m that conforms to its specification. On the theoretical level, we are looking for strengthening the current constraint H in order to integrate this type of test.

Consider a method m of class C such that: o the receiver object and x the vector of parameters.

Definition 3: (*Secure method*)

The method m is secure relatively to its specification if it satisfies the following conditions:

- It conforms to its specification.
- For each invalid couple (x,o) of input (does not satisfy the pre-condition: $P(x,o) = 0$), the post-condition Q and the invariant Inv should not be both valid in output: $(Q(x,o) \wedge Inv(o) = 0)$.

As is shown in **Table 1**, the constraint H defined above for conformity test takes in the security test the following form:

$$\forall (x,o) \in E \times I_c : P(x,o) \Leftrightarrow \left[Q(x,o) \wedge Inv(o) \right]$$

We note:

$$H_{security}(x,o) : P(x,o) \Leftrightarrow \left[Q(x,o) \wedge Inv(o) \right]$$

Table 1. Truth cases of H and $H_{security}$.

P	Q	Inv	$H : P \Rightarrow (Q \wedge Inv)$	$H_{security} : P \Leftrightarrow (Q \wedge Inv)$
1	1	1	1	1
1	1	0	0	0
1	0	1	0	0
1	0	0	0	0
0	0	0	1	1
0	0	1	1	1
0	1	0	1	1
0	1	1	1	0

In this test, we assume that with an invalid input, we can expect only an invalid result: any valid result coming from an invalid input indicates the presence of a security problem into the method implementation.

Theorem 5: The method m is secure relatively to its specification, if: $\forall (x,o) \in E \times I_c : H_{security}(x,o) = 1$.

5.2. Algorithm of Security Testing

The main aim of security testing algorithm is the use of the proposed security testing model for checking if the method under test is secure relatively to its specification. We assume that the method under test is conforming to its specification. The test data generation requires that the input values generated must not satisfy the pre-condition $(P = 0)$. The execution of each security test algorithm stops when the constraint $H_{security}$ becomes false $(H_{security}(x,o) = 0)$ or when we reach the threshold of test with $H_{security} = 1$. In the **Figure 5**, the constant N is an input value and $(A_{21}, A_{22}, A_{23}, A_{24})$ is the partition of the invalid input domain of the method m:

$$A_{21} = \left\{ (x,o) \in E \times I_c \,/\, \left(P(x,o), Q(x,o), Inv(o) \right) = (0,0,0) \right\}$$

$$A_{22} = \left\{ (x,o) \in E \times I_c \,/\, \left(P(x,o), Q(x,o), Inv(o) \right) = (0,0,1) \right\}$$

$$A_{23} = \left\{ (x,o) \in E \times I_c \,/\, \left(P(x,o), Q(x,o), Inv(o) \right) = (0,1,0) \right\}$$

$$A_{24} = \left\{ (x,o) \in E \times I_c \,/\, \left(P(x,o), Q(x,o), Inv(o) \right) = (0,1,1) \right\}$$

5.3. Security Testing in Inheritance

The purpose of this paragraph is to test the security of an overriding method $m^{(2)}$ relatively to its global specification $\left(P^{(2)}, Q^{(2)}, Inv^{(2)} \right)$ in a derived class C_2 using the

```
do{
    do{
    for ( xᵢ in set of parameters of m)
    {xᵢ=generate(Eᵢ);}
    x= (x₁,x₂,…,xₙ);o = generate_object();
        }while(P(x,o));
    invoke"o.m(x)"
    if( !Q(x,o)&& !Inv(o))
    A₂₁.add(x,o);
    elseif( !Q(x,o)&&Inv(o))
    A₂₂.add(x,o);
    elseif( Q(x,o)&& !Inv(o))
    A₂₃.add(x,o);
    else A₂₄.add(x,o)
    }while(A₂₁.size()<N  &&  A₂₂.size()<N  &&  A₂₃.size()<N
    &&  A₂₄.isEmpty());
```

Figure 5. Security test algorithm of the method m.

elements of security test of its original method $m^{(1)}$ in the super-class C_1.

Definition 4: (*Security of $m^{(2)}$ relatively to* $\left(P^{(1)}, Q^{(1)}, Inv^{(1)}\right)$

An overriding method $m^{(2)}$ is secure relatively to its inherited specification $\left(P^{(1)}, Q^{(1)}, Inv^{(1)}\right)$ if:

- $m^{(2)}$ conforms to its inherited specification $\left(P^{(1)}, Q^{(1)}, Inv^{(1)}\right)$.
- For each couple (x,o) in the invalid input domain of $m^{(2)}$ $\left((P^{(1)} \vee P'_2)(x,o)=0\right)$, the post-condition $Q^{(1)}$ and the invariant $Inv^{(1)}$ should not be both valid in output of $m^{(2)}$ $\left(Q^{(1)}(x,o) \wedge Inv^{(1)}(o)=0\right)$.

Definition 5: (*Security of an overriding method $m^{(2)}$ relatively to* $\left(P'_2, Q'_2, Inv'_2\right)$).

An overriding method $m^{(2)}$ is secure relatively to its own specification $\left(P'_2, Q'_2, Inv'_2\right)$ if:

- $m^{(2)}$ conforms to its own specification $\left(P'_2, Q'_2, Inv'_2\right)$.
- For each couple (x,o) in the invalid input domain of $m^{(2)}$ $\left(\left(P^{(1)} \vee P'_2\right)(x,o)=0\right)$, the post-condition Q'_2 and the invariant Inv'_2 should not be both valid in output of $m^{(2)}$ $\left(\left(Q'_2(x,o) \wedge Inv'_2\right)(o)=0\right)$.

Definition 6: (*Security of an overriding method $m^{(2)}$ relatively to its global specification* $\left(P^{(2)}, Q^{(2)}, Inv^{(2)}\right)$)

An overriding method $m^{(2)}$ is secure relatively to its global specification $\left(P^{(2)}, Q^{(2)}, Inv^{(2)}\right)$ if and only if:

- $m^{(2)}$ is secure relatively to its inherited specification $\left(P^{(1)}, Q^{(1)}, Inv^{(1)}\right)$.
- $m^{(2)}$ is secure relatively to its own specification $\left(P'_2, Q'_2, Inv'_2\right)$.

Theorem 6:

An overriding method $m^{(2)}$ is secure relatively to its global specification $\left(P^{(2)}, Q^{(2)}, Inv^{(2)}\right)$ if:

- $m^{(2)}$ conforms relatively to its global specification $\left(P^{(2)}, Q^{(2)}, Inv^{(2)}\right)$.
- For each invalid couple (x,o) of input (does not satisfy the pre-condition $\left(P^{(2)}(x,o)=0\right)$, the post-condition $Q^{(2)}$ and the invariant $Inv^{(2)}$ should not be both valid in

output of $m^{(2)}$ $\left(Q^{(2)}(x,o) \wedge Inv^{(2)}(o)=0\right)$.

Theorem 7:

An overriding method $m^{(2)}$ (that conforms to its global specification) is not secure relatively to this specification if

$$\exists(x,o) \in E \times I_{C_2} : \left[\left(P^{(1)} \vee P'_2\right)(x,o)=0\right]$$

in input of $m^{(2)}$ and

$$\left[\left(\left(Q^{(1)} \wedge Inv^{(1)}\right)(x,o)=1\right) \vee \left(\left(Q'_2 \wedge Inv'_2\right)(x,o)=1\right)\right]$$

in output of $m^{(2)}$.

The security test of $m^{(2)}$ relatively to its global specification $\left(P^{(2)}, Q^{(2)}, Inv^{(2)}\right)$ is performed only if the conformity test of $m^{(2)}$ relatively to $\left(P^{(2)}, Q^{(2)}, Inv^{(2)}\right)$ is validated. We consider that $m^{(1)}$ and $m^{(2)}$ are in conformity with their specifications, and we assume that the security test of $m^{(2)}$ starts when the security testing of $m^{(1)}$ is completed. Indeed, the security test of $m^{(1)}$ induces two cases: $m^{(1)}$ is secure relatively to its specification or $m^{(1)}$ is not secure relatively to its specification:

- *Case 1:* $m^{(1)}$ is not secure relatively to its specification.

We assume that the method $m^{(1)}$ is not secure relatively to its specification. This means (*Def. 3 and Th. 5*) that:

$$\left(\exists(x_0,o_0) \in E \times I_{C_1} : H^{(1)}_{security}(x_0,o_0)=0\right)$$

The object o_0 is an instance of the class C_1. We consider an object o'_0 of the subclass C_2 that has the same values as the object o_0 for attributes of C_1 and therefore, the object o'_0 has the same behavior as o_0 in a context of C_1 and consequently:

$$\left(\exists(x_0,o'_0) \in E \times I_{C_2} : H^{(1)}_{security}(x_0,o'_0)=0\right)$$

i.e.

$$\left[\left[P^{(1)}(x_0,o'_0)=0 \text{ in input of } m^{(1)}\right] \text{ and}\right.$$
$$\left.\left[\left(Q^{(1)} \wedge Inv^{(1)}\right)(x_0,o'_0)=1 \text{ in output of } m^{(1)}\right]\right]$$

$m^{(1)}$ and $m^{(2)}$ are similar, then we have:

$$\left[\left[P^{(1)}(x_0,o'_0)=0 \text{ in input of } m^{(2)}\right] \text{ and}\right.$$
$$\left.\left[\left(Q^{(1)} \wedge Inv^{(1)}\right)(x_0,o'_0)=1 \text{ in output of } m^{(2)}\right]\right]$$

We have two cases: $P'_2(x_0,o'_0)=0$ or $P'_2(x_0,o'_0)=1$

- $P'_2(x_0,o'_0)=0$.

In this case, we have:

$$\left[\left[\left(P^{(1)} \vee P'_2\right)(x_0,o'_0)=0 \text{ in input of } m^{(2)}\right] \text{ and}\right.$$
$$\left.\left[\left(Q^{(1)} \wedge Inv^{(1)}\right)(x_0,o'_0)=1 \text{ in output of } m^{(2)}\right]\right]$$

Consequently the method $m^{(2)}$ is not secure relatively

to $\left(P^{(1)}, Q^{(1)}, Inv^{(1)}\right)$ (*Def.* 4).

Finally, this shows (*Th.* 7) that the method $m^{(2)}$ is not secure relatively to its global specification $\left(P^{(2)}, Q^{(2)}, Inv^{(2)}\right)$.

• $P_2'\left(x_0, o_0'\right) = 1$

In this case, we have: $\left(\left(P^{(1)} \vee P_2'\right)\left(x_0, o_0'\right) = 1\right)$

Consequently the couple $\left(x_0, o_0'\right)$ is in the valid input domain: the security of $m^{(2)}$ cannot be deduced from the security test of $m^{(1)}$ (**Figure 6**).

• *Case* 2: $m^{(1)}$ is secure relatively to its specification.

In this case, we must test the method $m^{(2)}$ relatively to its own specification $\left(P_2', Q_2', Inv_2'\right)$ (**Figure 6**).

6. Evaluation

We evaluate the correctness of our approach by implementing the algorithm of conformity and security testing for inheritance. We consider for example of conformity and security testing the methods $withdraw^{(1)}$ and $withdraw^{(2)}$ of the class *Account*1 and *Account*2 (**Figure 7**).

The constraints $H^{(1)}$ and $H^{(2)}$ of $withdraw^{(1)}$ and $withdraw^{(2)}$ in an algebraic specification are shown in the **Figure 8** ($x = x_1$, $o_{(a)}$ and $o_{(b)}$ are respectively the object o after and before the call of the method):

• Conformity testing for $withdraw^{(2)}$ and $withdraw^{(1)}$

We test firstly the similarity of $withdraw^{(2)}$ and $withdraw^{(1)}$ on the common valid domain CVD
$\left(CVD = \left\{(x, o) \in E \times I_{C_2} / P^{(1)}(x, o) = 1\right\}\right)$: for each (x, o) that satisfy the common precondition of $withdraw^{(1)}$ and $withdraw^{(2)}$ $\left(P^{(1)}(x, o) = 1\right)$, the condition of the block if {…} (method $withdraw^{(2)}$ in **Figure 7**) is not satisfied, and thus the block if {…} is not executed, this means that the method $withdraw^{(2)}$ does exactly the same thing as

```
If (m⁽¹⁾ is secure relatively to (P⁽¹⁾,Q⁽¹⁾,Inv⁽¹⁾))
   If (m⁽²⁾ is secure relatively to(P₂',Q₂',Inv₂'))
      -m⁽²⁾ is secure relatively to (P⁽²⁾,Q⁽²⁾,Inv⁽²⁾)
   Else
      -m⁽²⁾ is not secure relatively to (P⁽²⁾,Q⁽²⁾,Inv⁽²⁾)
   EndIf
Else
   -Generate (x₀,o₀)∈E×I_C1 / H_security⁽¹⁾(x₀, o₀)=0
   -Generate (x₀,o₀')∈E×I_C2 / o₀' has the same attributes
    values as o₀
   If (P₂'(x₀,o₀')=0)
      - m⁽²⁾ is not secure relatively to (P⁽²⁾,Q⁽²⁾,Inv⁽²⁾)
   Else
      -Indeterminate Form
   EndIf
EndIf
```

Figure 6. Security test cases for an overriding method.

```
class Account1
{      protected double bal;
       /* bal is the account balance */
       public Account1(double x1)
       {this.bal=x1;}
       public void withdraw (int x1)
       {this.bal=this.bal - x1;}
}
class Account2 extends Account1
{      private double InterestRate;
       public Account2(double x1, double x2)
       {super(x1); this.InterestRate=x2;}
       public void withdraw (int x1)
       {super.withdraw(x1);
           if ((x1>bal) && (x1<(bal/InterestRate)))
           this.bal=this.bal-(this.InterestRate)*x1;
           InterestRate = InterestRate/2;}
}
```

Figure 7. *Account*1 and *Account*2 classes.

the method $withdraw^{(1)}$ (**Figure 7**). As a result thereof, $withdraw^{(2)}$ and $withdraw^{(1)}$ are similar on the valid domain CVD.

The second test concerns the conformity testing of $withdraw^{(2)}$ that is based on the conformity testing of $withdraw^{(1)}$:

• Conformity Testing for $withdraw^{(1)}$

In order to test the conformity of $withdraw^{(1)}$ in class *Account*1, we generate randomly x_1 and the balance values in the interval $(-200,200)$ with $N = 100$ (**Table 2**):

The test result shows that for 100 iterations the constraint $H^{(1)}$ is always true $\left(H^{(1)} = 1\right)$, we can deduce that the $withdraw^{(1)}$ method is valid (**Table 2**). In this case it is necessary to test the method $withdraw^{(2)}$ relatively to its own constraint $H_{(SI,SO)}$:

• Conformity testing for $withdraw^{(2)}$ relatively to $H_{(SI,SO)}$

In order to test the method $withdraw^{(2)}$ relatively to the constraint $H_{(SI,SO)}$, we use an analysis with proof. The testing by proof of the method $withdraw^{(2)}$ relatively to the constraint $H_{(SI,SO)}$ is used to strengthen the randomly testing .Indeed, we must have for satisfying the specific output (SO) :

◦ The specific post-condition Q_2' must be satisfied.

◦ The specific invariant Inv_2' must be satisfied.

The constraint Q_2' is always satisfied (**Figures 7** and **8**), however we must proof that Inv_2' is satisfied.

For each created object o_0, we have : ($0 \leq$ InterestRate$_0$ ≤ 0.3) where InterestRate$_0$ is the initial value assigned to InterestRate when creating the object o_0, and InterestRate$_{(n)}$ is the value of InterestRate after n operations of type $withdraw^{(2)}$ in an execution sequence.

We have:

$$\left[\text{InterestRate}_{(n)} = \frac{\text{InterestRate}_{(n-1)}}{2}\right], n \geq 1$$

Table 2. Result of a conformity test of *withdraw*$^{(1)}$

Iteration number:	x	o	P$^{(1)}$(x,o)	H$^{(1)}$(x,o)
1	29	*Account*1(70)	1	1
2	42	*Account*1(93)	1	1
3	79	*Account*1(187)	1	1
...	...	...	...	...
....	....	....	....	....
.....	.....	.....	.....	.....
98	31	*Account*1(104)	1	1
99	18	*Account*1(86)	1	1
100	68	*Account*1(151)	1	1

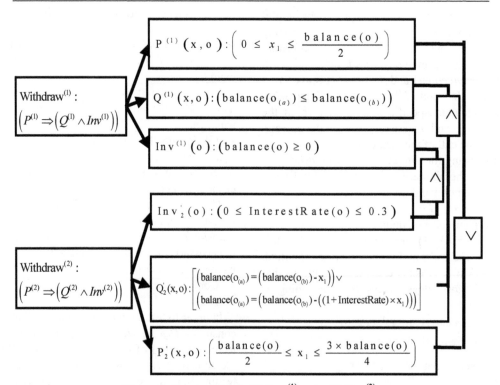

Figure 8. Constraints of *withdraw*$^{(1)}$ **and** *withdraw*$^{(2)}$**.**

where *n* is number of withdrawals (**Figure 7**).

The geometric series proposed is written in the general case as follows:

$$\left[\text{InterestRate}_{(n)} = \frac{\text{InterestRate}_{(0)}}{2^n} \right],$$

with $n \geq 0$ and $(0 \leq \text{InterestRate}_0 \geq 0.3)$

We deduce that:

$$\left[\forall n : \left(0 \leq \text{InterestRate}_{(n)} \leq 0.3 \right) \right]$$

And consequently, the specific invariant is always satisfied (**Figure 8**). This leads to the conclusion that the

method *withdraw*$^{(2)}$ is in conformity to $H_{(SI,SO)}$, and we can deduce that *withdraw*$^{(2)}$ is in conformity with its global specification.

- Security testing for *withdraw*$^{(2)}$ and *withdraw*$^{(1)}$

For security testing, we test firstly the similarity of withdraw methods on the common invalid domain *CID*

$$\left(CID = \left\{ (x,o) \in E \times I_{C_2} \, / \, \left(P^{(1)} \vee P_2' \right)(x,o) = 0 \right\} \right)$$

For this we generate randomly x_1 and the balance values in the interval (–200,200) with the threshold limit *N* =100 (**Table 3**).

The test result shows that for 100 iterations the size of the similarity set *Sim* is exactly the threshold limit of the test. We can conclude that the methods $withdraw^{(2)}$ and $withdraw^{(1)}$ are similar on the domain CID relatively to $\left(P^{(1)}, Q^{(1)}, Inv^{(1)}\right)$ (**Table 3**).

In the last paragraph, we have showed that $withdraw^{(2)}$ and $withdraw^{(1)}$ are in conformity with their specifications and are similar on the common invalid domain. For testing the security of the overriding method $withdraw^{(2)}$, we must testing the security of the overridden method $withdraw^{(1)}$ (**Figure 6**):

- Security Testing for $withdraw^{(1)}$ relatively to $\left(P^{(1)}, Q^{(1)}, Inv^{(1)}\right)$

We generate in the **Table 4** the security test cases for the overridden method $withdraw^{(1)}$ relatively to $\left(P^{(1)}, Q^{(1)}, Inv^{(1)}\right)$:

For the first four iterations, we have:

$$x_1 > \text{balance}(o) > \frac{\text{balance}(o)}{2},$$

i.e. $P^{(1)}(x,o) = 0$ and it induces to a false invariant $\left(\text{balance}(o) < 0\right)$ at the output, i.e. $H_{securty}^{(1)}(x,o) = 1$. In the iteration 5, we have for

$$(x,o) = \left(137, Account1(180)\right):$$

$$\frac{\text{balance}(o)}{2} < x_1 < \text{balance}(o),$$

Table 3. Similarity test of the *withdraw* methods on *CID*.

Itration number	x	o	$\left(P^{(1)} \vee P_2'\right)(x,o)$	$(x,o) \in$
1	117	$Account2(96,0.24)$	0	Sim
2	94	$Account2(83,0.18)$	0	Sim
3	173	$Account2(147,0.01)$	0	Sim
...	...	...	...	...
....	....	....	...	....
.....	......	...	...	.....
98	102	$Account2(120,0.17)$	0	Sim
99	88	$Account2(72,0.1)$	0	Sim
100	131	$Account2(159,0.22)$	0	Sim

Table 4. Security test of $withdraw^{(1)}/(P^{(1)}, Q^{(1)}, Inv^{(1)})$.

Iteration number	x_1	O	$P^{(1)}(x,o)$	$H_{securty}^{(1)}(x,o)$
1	113	$Account1(87)$	0	1
2	176	$Account1(138)$	0	1
3	91	$Account1(42)$	0	1
4	101	$Account1(73)$	0	1
5	137	$Account1(180)$	0	0

i.e. $P^{(1)}(x,o) = 0$, and this induces $Q^{(1)}(x,o) = 1$ and $Inv^{(1)}(x,o) = 1$, i.e. $H_{securty}^{(1)}(x,o) = 0$. Indeed, our implementation cannot reject this situation and conesquently the overridden method $withdraw^{(1)}$ under test which is conforming to its specification, is considered not secure relatively to the same specification.

- Security Testing for $withdraw^{(2)}$ relatively to $\left(P^{(2)}, Q^{(2)}, Inv^{(2)}\right)$

According to the **Figure 6**, we have for $(x,o) = \left(137, Account1(180)\right)$ the method $withdraw^{(1)}$ is not secure, we consider for example the object o' of the class $Account2$ that has the same balance value $\left(o' = Account2(180,0.19)\right)$ and we must determinate the truth value of $P_2'(x,o)$ (**Figure 6**).

We have:

$$\left[\left(\frac{1}{2}\right) \times 180 \leq 137 \leq \left(\frac{3}{4}\right) \times 180 \text{ is false}\right]$$

i.e. $P_2'(x,o) = 0$ (**Figure 8**).

Finally, we can deduce that $withdraw^{(2)}$ is not secure relatively to $\left(P^{(2)}, Q^{(2)}, Inv^{(2)}\right)$ (**Figure 6**).

7. Conclusions

This paper introduces an approach to reduce the test sequences used for testing the conformity of an overriding method during inheritance operation in object oriented models. The key idea of this work is the use of a technique that generates test data by exploiting the existing test sequences. Indeed, for the sub-classes methods that have the same behavior as their corresponding methods in a parent class, it is possible to reuse the data extracted from the conformity testing of an overridden method for testing the conformity of its overriding method.

The main contribution of our approach is the definition of a security testing that generates invalid input values not satisfying the precondition constraint. Indeed, the test methods have focused only on valid inputs satisfying the pre-condition, and do not integrate the invalid data in test process. We think that a correctly implemented testing method should eliminate cases of invalid data which lead to valid results. Our approach shows how we can use the valid and invalid data extracted from the pre-condition to test the conformity and security of overridden and overriding methods.

We present firstly the relationship between the test model of overridden methods and overriding methods, and we show how the use of existing test sequences can make the generation of the test data during inheritance less expensive. Secondly, we present our approach of security testing based on data not satisfying the precondition constraint.

REFERENCES

[1] B. K. Aichernig and P. A. P. Salas, "Test Case Generation by OCL Mutation and Constraint Solving," *Proceedings of the International Conference on Quality Software*, Melbourne, September 19-20, 2005, 2005, pp. 64-71.

[2] F. Bouquet, F. Dadeau, B. Legeard and M. Utting, "Symbolic Animation of JML Specifications," *International Conference on Formal Methods*, Vol. 3582, Springer-Verlag, 2005, pp. 75-90.

[3] M. Benattou, J.-M. Bruel and N. Hameurlain, "Generating Test Data from OCL Specification," *Proceedings of the ECOOP'2002 Work-Shop on Integration and Transformation of UML Models (WITUML'2002)*, 2002.

[4] K. Benlhachmi, M. Benattou and J.-L. Lanet, "Génération de Données de Test Sécurisé à Partir d'une Spécification Formelle par Analyse des Partitions et Classification," *Proceedings of the International Conference on Network Architectures and Information Systems Security (SAR-SSI 2011)*, La Rochelle, 18-21 May 2011, pp. 143-150.

[5] K. Benlhachmi and M. Benattou, "A Formal Model of Similarity Testing for Inheritance in Object Oriented Software," *Proceedings of the IEEE International Conference (CIST'2012)*, Fez, 24-26 October 2012, pp. 38-42.

[6] K. Benlhachmi and M. Benattou, "Similarity Testing by Proof and Analysis of Partition for Object Oriented Specifications," *Journal of Theoretical and Applied Information Technology*, Vol. 46, No. 11, 2012, pp. 461-470.

[7] Y. Cheon and C. E. Rubio-Medrano, "Random Test Data Generation for Java Classes Annotated with JML Specifications," *Proceedings of the 2007 International Conference on Software Engineering Research and Practice*, Volume II, 25-28 June 2007, Las Vegas, pp. 385-392.

[8] G. T. Leavens, "JML's Rich, Inherited Specification for Behavioral Subtypes," Iowa State University, Ames, 2006.

[9] R. B. Findler, M. Latendresse and M. Felleisen, "Behavioral Contracts and Behavioral Subtyping," Foundations of Software Engineering, Rice University, Houston, 2001.

[10] B. H. Liskov and J. M. Wing, "A Behavioral Notion of Subtyping," *MIT Laboratory for Computer Science, Carnegie Mellon University, ACM Transactions on Programming Languages and Systems*, Vol. 16, No. 6, 1994, pp. 1811-1841.

[11] G. T. Leavens and K. K. Dhara, "Concepts of Behavioral Subtyping and a Sketch of their Extension to Component-Based Systems," In: G. T. Leavens and M. Sitaraman, Eds., *Foundations of Component-Based Systems*, 2000, pp. 113-135.

[12] B. H. Liskov and J. Wing, "Behavioral Subtyping Using Invariants and Constraints," Technical Report CMU CS-99-156, School of Computer Science, Carnegie Mellon University, Pittsburgh, 1999.

[13] B. Meyer, "Object Oriented Software Construction," Prentice Hall, Upper Saddle River, 1988.

12

Technology of Secure File Archiving in the Uniformly Random Distributed Archive Scheme

Ahmed Tallat, Hiroshi Yasuda, Kilho Shin
Applied Information Engineering, Tokyo Denki University, Tokyo, Japan

ABSTRACT

This paper investigates the security features of the distributed archive scheme named Uniformly Random Distributed Archive (URDA). It is a simple, fast and practically secure algorithm that meets the needs of confidentiality and availability requirements of data. URDA cuts a file archived into fragments, and distributes each fragment into randomly selected $n - k + 1$ storages out of n storages. As the result, users only need to access at least k storages to recover original file, whereas stolen data from $k - 1$ storages cannot cover original file. Thus, archived files are nothing but sequences of a large number of fixed length fragments. URDA is proved of disappearing both characters and biased bits of original data in archived files, indicating the probabilities of both a fragment and a bit appearing at particular position are uniformly constant respectively. Yet, through running experiments, we found out the risk of likelihood that URDA might be vulnerable to bit pattern attack due to the different ratios of characters appearing in real world files. However, we solved the problem by modifying URDA with variable fragment lengths, which results in that all the bits in revealed sequences are distributed uniformly and independently at random.

Keywords: Cloud Computing; Archive; Secret Sharing; Character Set

1. Introduction

Cloud computing is attracting attentions of people of a wide variety of fields including users, service providers and facility manufacturers. From the users' point of view, the most attractive advantages of cloud computing must be the ubiquity and affordability of services that cloud computing can realize. Since cloud computing is constructed on top of the Internet, users can take advantage of services anytime and anywhere. The recent rapid spread of mobile computing certainly enhances the demands for the ubiquity of service provision. On the other hand, the affordability of cloud computing is based on exploitation of public infrastructures. The Internet itself is apparently public good, and cloud computing is enlargeing its scope to computational powers and storages that are available in the Internet. For example, the data backup services provided by data center companies are very expensive, and small and middle-sized enterprises cannot afford them. In contrast, the same services are now being provided at significantly lower prices based on cloud computing.

Thus, the advantages of cloud computing are due to the fundamental idea of exploiting the Internet and public goods existing in the Internet. This, however, can produce disadvantages as well. In particular, in terms of se-

curity, the Internet has serious problems. ISO 17799 [1] determines that confidentiality, integrity and availability (CIA) are the three important factors in considering security issues, and the Internet has vulnerability in all of them: Communication over the Internet is in principle subject to eavesdropping and tampering; Nobody controls the overall the services of the Internet, and cutoff and delay of communication can happen anytime. Furthermore, we cannot deny the possibility that the providers of services are malicious. Although cryptographic technology will provide us with strong countermeasures with respect to confidentiality and integrity, we need different technologies to solve the issue of availability.

Let's consider a data backup service based on cloud computing. A user uploads his or her data to the Internet for the backup purpose, and the data are distributed across many inexpensive storages unknown to the user. Different storage providers operate different storages under different policies. Even their connectivity may vary. Thus, the user can have a problem when he or she needs to restore the data. In the worst case scenario, it is still possible that some of storage providers have ceased their services without notification, and therefore, a part of the backup data has been lost forever.

To solve this problem of availability, storing data with redundancy is probably the only solution, and we have already had technologies to realize availability by redundant storing.

RAID [2] (Redundant Array of Inexpensive Disks) is daily use technology, and combines more than one physical hard disks into a single logical unit by distributing the whole data mostly with redundancy across multiple disks, which is necessary in case of data lost; A failed disk is replaced by a new one, and the lost data will be built from the remaining data and the redundancy such as parity data. This technology enables computer users to achieve high level storage reliability from PC-class components.

Although RAID is appropriate to apply to "home" servers, it has evidently issues in its scalability. In particular, RAID can accept failures of only one (RAID 3 and 5) or two disks, and will not be able to apply to the Internet, where users may lose access to more than two storages.

The technology known as "secret sharing" also provide a method to distribute secret information with redundancy: For $n > k > 0$, n members have their shares derived from a secret, and the secret will be completely reconstructed when k members exhibit their own shares; By contrast, collusion of $(k - 1)$ members will reveal none or only a few bits of the secret. This property of secret sharing is referred to as k-out-of-n threshold secrecy. The initial (k, n) threshold secret sharing scheme (SSS) known in the literature were independently invented by Adi Shamir [3] and George Blackley [4] in 1979, and since then the scheme has been widely studied and applied on a variety of fields. (for example, Rabin [5], Bai [6,7], Blundo [8], He [9], Wang [10]).

Although these schemes support the severe requirement of k-out-of-n threshold secrecy, their computational complexity is extremely high, and it cannot show practical performance when applied to archive of bulky data: data should be fragmented into a number of fragments so that they are short enough to be dealt with by the secret sharing algorithms, and the algorithms need heavy computation such as modular exponentiation and matrix manipulation in calculating shares from each fragment.

The recent technology of P2P also provides the function of storing data with redundancy. P2P aims at sharing decentralized resources (CPU, storage, bandwidth and contents) of each participant, while eliminating conventional centralized unit to provide browsing and downloading, and thus the participants are both consumer and provider of the resources in distributed networks. The principle is simply uploading and downloading simultaneously and continuously, and the acceleration of data transferring can be improved significantly by downloading desired pieces simultaneously with random order from multiple providers that treat distributed contents as

sequence of pieces through fragmenting them into sequences. We already have several P2P based global storage products (for example, OceanStore [11] and PAST [12]).

The most important problem of the P2P technology when applying to our purpose should be its extremely low efficiency in storage spaces and bandwidth. The initial aim of P2P is to realize sharing data among an unspecified number of people, and hence, data are exchanged and stored with very high redundancy exceeding the necessity for the backup purpose.

In our previous work [13], we investigated a simple scheme, called the uniformly random distributed archive scheme (URDA). The algorithm of URDA is extremely simple and easy: The original data is fragmented into a number of tiny fragments (several bits long), and each fragment is distributed across $n - k + 1$ storages out of n storages: The most important feature of URDA consists in that the selection of the $n - k + 1$ storages is dominated by a completely random process: Storages are selected uniformly and independently at random per fragment. By this, URDA meets the condition of k-out-of-n threshold robustness: that is, even if the owner of the data loses access to $k - 1$ storages of the entire n storages, the user can restore the original data from the data fragments retrieved from the remaining k storages.

In terms of confidentiality, it has been revealed in previous work that URDA has a couple of remarkable properties.

1) Except for bits existing in the very narrow neighborhood of the start and the end of the original file, the probability that a guess on the position where a particular fragment of the original file appears in a distributed backup file is very small, and almost constant.

2) When assuming that the original data consists of ASCII characters selected at random from the entire possible values, the probability that a particular bit pattern appears at a particular position in a distri- buted backup file is independent of the position. To be precise, we can theoretically derive the following formula.

$$\Pr\left[b_t = \cdots = b_{t-l} = 0\right] \approx \frac{1}{8}\left(\frac{l+1}{2^l} + \frac{7-l}{2^{l+1}}\right) = \frac{l+9}{2^{l+4}} \qquad (1)$$

The symbol b_t represents the t-th bit from the head of the backup data, and the formula holds unless the bit falls into narrow neighborhoods of the head and the tail of the distributed backup file.

The first property implies that, if attackers do not take advantage of biases of bit patterns in the original data, they cannot guess the contents of the original data from the distributed backup data. On the other hand, in the second property, we take ASCII data as an instance, and show that the evident bias of bit patterns, that is, 0 appears every eight bits, disappears in distributed backup files. Thus, these properties indicate the possibility that URDA can provide confidentiality of a certain degree, without relying on cryptographic techniques. This would be an important advantage of URDA in terms of time-efficiency of the scheme.

In this paper, we further investigate the second property. In the real world, any text files have particular biases in the distributions of bit patterns, and the theoretical conclusion of URDA might not hold true for data in the real world. We struggle with this problem through experiments.

In the experiments, we downloaded 200 ASCII files from the Internet, applied URDA to these files to generate 1000 backup files, and looked into the statistical features of the backup files. First, we found that the Equation (1) still holds true for the backup files we investigated in our experiments. This was verified by performing the one-sample t-test: It has turned out that the "null" hypothesis that the Equation (1) does hold cannot be rejected even with a large significance level. Secondly, we synthetically generated 200 random ASCII files and 1000 backup files in the same way as for the downloaded ASCII files. Then, we compared between the synthetic and the real backup files in terms of the variance of the distributions of the particular bit pattern. The result this time showed that the null hypothesis can be rejected with the significance level 0.05 by the F-test. This means that the distributions of bit patterns between the real and synthetic backup files are different, and therefore, we cannot deny the possibility that a clever attacker can invent an effective pattern analysis to guess the original contents from the contents of the backup files.

Based on the result of this experiment, we modified the algorithm of URDA so that the length of fragments are to be determined at random per fragment, and performed the same experiment using this modified URDA. The result was surprising. The two groups of distributions, one for the real backup files generated by the modified URDA and the other for the synthetic backup files, are concluded to be the same. To be precise, even with a large significance level, we could not reject the null hypotheses that claim that the distributions are the same as Gaussian distributions. This consequence is significant: The backup files of real ASCII files generated by the modified URDA are indistinguishable from the synthetic backup files. By definition, the synthetic backup files show the uniform randomness in terms of bit pattern distributions, and hence, we can conclude backup files generated by the modified URDA are secure against bit pattern analysis.

Following Section 2 describes some related studies followed by URDA scheme proposed in previous paper for the consistency of the paper, and it also includes analyses of security feature of URDA. Section 3 clarifies problem that the paper is tackling, and provides solution by running experiments and applying statistical methods. We conclude the paper with future work in section 4.

2. Distributed Archive Schemes

In this section, we provide a brief review over the data storage techniques of redundancy known in the literature, and then describe URDA proposed in our previous work.

2.1. Distributed Schemes in Storage Pools

Digital high density recording technologies have made a variety of data recorded in storage medium. As a result, the form of utilizing storage devices has been greatly changed, and a variety of home appliances, computers/ servers, and even micro device in mobiles have become to have their own storages and to utilize them at a higher level.

However, with the advent of the Internet the need of sharing information made rapid increase of data in terms of variability and amount, which in turn led to creation of high technical processing power of computers and also posed strong demand to the scale of flexibility of storages for these ever-increasing data. Since there are limits of computational power and capacity within conventional devices having attached to individual storages inside, they are no longer able to meet the need the way of data being accessed, stored and shared. Furthermore, tracking and backing up files distributed into a variety of storages constitute significant hardship. Some storage techniques [14] try to address these problems by allowing all the files to be stored in a single, secure storage that can be accessed by other clients and servers regardless of the operating systems from anywhere within the same domain.

However, independency of storages and servers is costly in terms of updating, managing and running. Thus, the conception of "storage pool" [15] aims at providing the scale of flexibility to solve the problems by allowing servers to utilize storage capacity from the pool so that virtual hard disk drives can be dedicated to servers based on their needs without buying extra storage to each of them individually. The storage pool is also known as a dedicated storage network, because it is separated and independent from servers, allowing several servers to connect one drive and vise verse. Same as the independent storage, drive enclosure in the storage pool can hold any number of drives with a variety of types and expand on demand. Mostly the variety of drives has a central control unit to manage all the Input/output and they are equipped with some technical schemes for providing security and recoverability in case of disaster or system failure.

However, to guarantee the availability, integrity and confidentiality of the data stored in storage medium is not easy task. Because every system is vulnerable to certain damages caused by natural, physical and technical attacks, and thus these data can be lost, delayed or even stolen. Redundancy probably is the only feasible solution to address the issues. The fastest method to realize redundancy is replication [16], which distributes redundantly copied fragments of data across infrastructure, but it is space inefficient, and p2p is a typical example of the replication-based systems. Another resilient method is erasure coding that splits data into n fragments, which are then further redundantly encoded into k additional fragments using parity, matrix, polynomial etc. Thus, k specifies the level of resiliency or Maximum Distance Separable (MDS), where $k = $ MDS.

Despite their values, widespread utilities, and reliabilities due to the capabilities of meeting the various needs for disaster recoveries, they all have drawbacks in terms of heavy cost and complex computational procedures. Because they use matrices, cryptography and heavy mathematical calculation etc. for producing redundancy, and applying them to large amount of data is very expensive, due to extremely time-consuming computational requirements, and even they are relatively inflexible, due to the complexity and difficulty of meeting various levels of desired security requirements as needed. What is more, dealing with cloud computing environment, for example for the purpose of backup of datacenter, is not easy with these schemes, due to lack of utilization of cost-effect readiness to use available storages provided. Thus, the currently heavy set-up cost and computational complexity cause significant hardship to utilize currently available storage services in order to realize secure backup services.

2.2. URDA-Uniformly Random Distributed Archive Scheme

In order to address aforementioned issues of current techniques when applying them to cloud computing in the context of robustness and security, and to provide affordable backup techniques, we have introduced URDA in our previous work.

The outline of the algorithm of URDA is as follows: URDA first fragment the source file to archive into multiple tiny fragments, and then distributes each fragment to $n - k + 1$ destination storages selected out of the entire n storages. The $n - k + 1$ storages are selected uniformly and independently at random per fragment. Thus, the source file is distributed across n storages, and each fragment is archived at exactly $n - k + 1$ different storages. The simple image of URDA is shown in **Figure 1**.

To be specific, URDA consists of a smartcard and a host (e.g. client/server software), and they communicate with each other through a standardized interface like IC card interface [17], Near Field Communication [18] and Infrared Link Access Protocol [19]. The role of the smartcard is to generate random distribution keys taking advantage of the key generator RNG_K receiving seeds from the seed generator RNG_S, both RNG_K and RNG_S are installed inside the smartcard, whereas the host fragments the source file, duplicates the fragments, and distributing the copies generated across multiple storages, following the indication by the random distribution keys. In the following, we give a brief description of the archival and retrieval phases of URDA. The flow chart of the algorithm is shown in **Figure 2**.

(1) *Archival phase*: The role of the smart card in the archival phase is to generate a series of distribution keys and to transmit them to the host. The algorithm of the smart card in the archival phase is as follows;

1) Receive the START_ARCHIVAL signal accompanying the identifier of the source file through the card-host interface. The identifier is denoted by crr_fid.

2) Generate a random seed taking advantage of RNG_S. The seed is denoted by crr_seed.

3) Store the pair of crr_fid and crr_seed in the internal

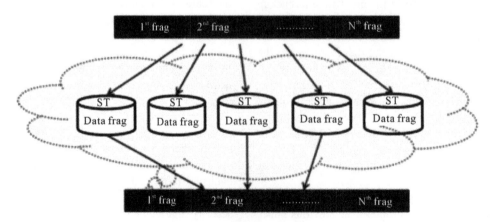

Figure 1. The simple image of URDA ($n = 5$, $k = 3$).

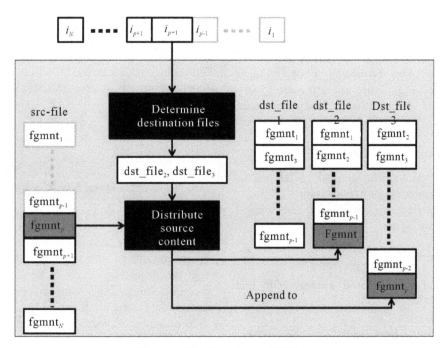

Figure 2. The flow chart of URDA.

database. The pair will be used in the retrieval phase.

4) Input crr_seed into RNG_K.

5) Let RNG_K generate a random number, which is an index to determine the $(n; k)$-distribution key to be used by the host. The smart card outputs the random number to the host program.

6) Repeat Step 5 until it receives the END_OF_FILE signal from the host program.

On the other hand, the role of the host program in the archival phase is to distribute the contents of the source file over n destination files.

1) Fragment the source file into the b-bit long fragments of $fgmnt_1, \cdots, fgmnt_{last}$, and create a pointer p to indicate the current fragment $fgmnt_p$. The initial value of p is 1.

2) Send the START_ARCHIVAL signal to the smart card.

3) Receive an index i_p from the smart card.

4) Identify the distribution with index i_p. The distribution key determines the set of $n - k + 1$ destination files to which the current fragment $fgmnt_p$ is to be appended.

5) Take away the current fragment $fgmnt_p$ from the source file, and increment the pointer p by 1.

6) Append the fragment $fgmnt_p$ to the destination files determined in Step 4.

7) Repeat the steps from 3 to 6 until all the fragments are taken away from the source file.

8) Send the END_OF_File signal to the smart card.

9) The host program sends the resultant n destination files to n storages via networks.

(2) *Retrieval phase*: The algorithm of the smartcard in the retrieval phase is as follows:

1) Receive the START_RETRIEVAL signal accompanying the identifier crr_fid of the target file from the host program.

2) Look up crr_fid in the internal database, and retrieve the seed crr_seed paired with crr_fid.

3) Input crr seed into RNGK.

4) Output the random numbers i_p that RNGK generates to the host program.

5) Repeat Step 4 until the END_OF_FILE signal is received.

On the other hand, algorithm of the host is described as follows.

1) Fragment the destination files into b-bit length fragments, create a pointer for each destination file. Initially, each pointer is set so that it indicates the first fragment.

2) Send the START_RETRIEVAL signal to the smart card.

3) Receive an index i_p from the smart card. The initial value of p shall be 1.

4) Determine the set of $n - k + 1$ destination files in which the current fragment $fgmnt_p$ are included.

5) For each of the destination files determined in Step 4, take away the fragment indicated by the pointer associated with the destination file, and change the pointer so that it points the next fragment.

6) Append $fgmnt_p$ to the source file, and increment p by 1.

7) Repeat the steps of 3 to 6 until all of the destination files are empty.

The size of the resultant destination files is exactly $(n - k + 1)$ times as great as the original size of the source file and the expected size of each destination file is $(n-k+1)/n$ times smaller than the size of the source file, and thus it supports (k,n) robustness and (k,n) security, which means that downloading from k storages is enough to recover original file and that even $(k-1)$ storages are attacked, the stolen data cannot cover total amount of the file.

2.3. Security Features of URDA

In this clause, we summarize the security features of URDA that are presented in our previous work.

The probability that a specific fragment is not included in any of specific r storages is

$$\frac{n-k+1}{n} * \frac{n-k}{n-1} * \cdots * \frac{n-k-r}{n-r-1}$$

Thus, if r storages are compromised, the probability that all of the fragments are revealed is

$$\left(1-\prod_{i=1}^{r}\frac{n-k-i}{n-i-1}\right)^{N} \qquad (2)$$

N is the total number of the fragments. When $r \ge k$, the Equation (2) is 1, whereas, when $r < k$, it approaches 0, as N increases. This implies the k-out-of-n threshold secrecy: Even if $k - 1$ storages are compromised, the entire original contents will not be revealed.

Definition 1. Let N and m denote the number of fragments in a source file and a revealed sequence, and a and j denote the positions of a fragment in both the source file and the revealed sequence $(N \ge a \ge 1, m \ge j \ge 1)$ respectively. Then we define that $\mathbf{Match}(a, j; N, m)$ denotes the probability that a fragment at the position of a in the source file appears at the position of j in the revealed sequence.

When a is fixed and j moves, following holds for the maximum value of $\mathbf{Match}(a, j; N, m)$.

$$\underset{j \in \{1, \cdots, m\}}{\mathbf{argmax}\,\mathbf{Match}}(a, j; N, m) = \left\{\left\lceil \frac{am}{N+1} \right\rceil, \left\lfloor \frac{am}{N+1} \right\rfloor + 1\right\}$$

Thus, the maximum of $\mathbf{Match}(a, j; N, m)$ when a is fixed and j moves, is given by the following formula.

$$\mathbf{Match}\left(a, \frac{am}{N+1}; N, m\right) \approx \frac{m}{N\sqrt{\pi}} \cdot \left(\frac{N-1}{(a-1)(N-a)}\right)^{1/4} \qquad (3)$$

The minimum value of the equation can be reached at $a = \frac{N-1}{2}$, and **Figure 3** is its simulation result for the value of $N = 10^3, 10^4, 10^5, 10^6$ and $\frac{m}{N} = \frac{3}{4}$.

Thus, we can conclude that the security against identifying the position of a fragment is uniformly small except the fragments located in heads and tails. Furthermore, obtaining further safety can be possible by adding dummy data at the heads and tails.

Next, we run a thought experiment. In the experiment, we see that the certain significant pattern of the bit distribution of ASCII text files disappears in archived backup files. For the ASCII text files to use in the experiment, we assume that ASCII characters in the files are selected uniformly and independently at random per character from the entire possible values. Therefore, the bit distribution of the files is as follows: The most significant bit (MSB) of every byte is always 0, whereas the remaining bits are distributed uniformly and independently at random. Then, we define

$$\bar{q}(j, \rho) = \sum_{a \bmod 8 = \rho} \mathbf{Match}(a, j; N, m)$$

to represent the probability that $a \bmod 8 = \rho$ holds when fgmnt_j is a copy of fgmnt_a. Then, the probability that the ρ-th bit $(\rho = 1, \cdots, 7)$ of fgmnt_j is 0 turns out to be

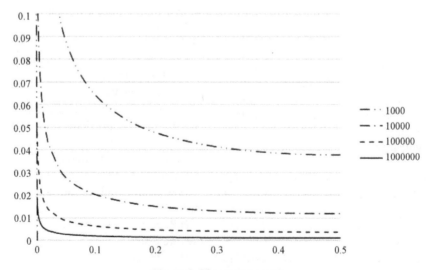

Figure 3. Simulation result

$$\Pr\left[b_{7j+\rho}=0\right]=\overline{q}(j,\rho)+\left(1-\overline{q}(j,\rho)\right)\cdot\frac{1}{2} \quad (4)$$

A remarkable fact is that $\overline{q}(j,\rho)\approx\frac{1}{8}$ holds except for narrow neighborhoods of $j=1$ and $j=m$. Hence, when t is not close to 1 or m, we have the following approximation.

$$P\left[b_t=\cdots=b_{t-l}=0\right]\approx\frac{1}{8}\left(\frac{l+1}{2^l}+\frac{7-l}{2^{l+1}}\right)=\frac{l+9}{2^{l+4}}$$

Through the same computation as above, we have the following.

Corollary 1. When t is not close to 1 or m, $\Pr\left[b_t=\beta_t,\cdots,b_{t+l}=\beta_{t+l}\right]$ is approximately constant.

Corollary 2. When t is not close to 1 or m, $\Pr\left[b_t=\beta_t,\cdots,b_{t+l}=\beta_{t+l}\right]$ is approximately constant.

Corollary 1 and 2 imply that most of the bits in the revealed contents look almost the same in the attacker's eye.

3. Problem and Solution

In following sections, through identifying the problem, we provide particular solutions to address it. To proceed, we investigate experimentally on ASCII characters to see if bit patterns of source files can be disappeared in archived files, and further demonstrate that practical security of plain text archiving can be obtain by varying fragment length in bit distribution.

3.1. Identified Problems

Our previous work, assuming that source files include only ASCII characters selected uniformly and independently at random, we mathematically proved that an archived file consisting of seven-bit-long fragments shows uniformly constant distributions with respect to the probabilities that particular bit patterns appear in it. To be precise, we let $C_1\cdots C_L$ be the byte contents of a file, where c_i is an ASCII character selected uniformly at random from the entire space of ASCII characters. Then, we apply URDA to this file by setting the fragment length to be seven bits, and hence, the file content is fragmented into seven-bit-long fragments. The resulting archived files are collections of these fragments. Focusing on one of the archived files, we proved that the probability $\Pr\left[b_{t-\ell}=\beta_{-l},b_{t-\ell+1}=\beta_{-l+1},\cdots,b_t=\beta_0\right]$ is approximately constant regardless of the choice of t, unless t is too small or too large. b_t denotes the bit at the position t in the archived file, and $\beta_{-\ell}\beta_{-\ell+1},\cdots,\beta_0$ is an arbitrary bit pattern with $\beta_{-i}\in\{0,1\}$. This means that we can view the archived file as secure against bit pattern analysis, since the source file does not include any bit pattern except that the bit 0 appears every 8 bits, and this

pattern proves to disappear in the archived file.

On the other hand, text files found in the real world, even when they consist of ASCII characters, cannot help including biases in the distribution of characters. Thus, the hypothesis of the aforementioned investigation does not necessarily hold, and hence, it is not certain that the conclusion of the investigation holds true for the real files.

The problem that we solve in this paper is first to investigate whether the property that we proved in our previous work also holds true for real files that include biases in the distributions of characters. Then, we will answer the question whether URDA is secure against bit pattern analysis when applied to real files.

3.2. How to Solve the Problem

To solve this problem, we run experiments with a large number of files that we obtain from the internet.

To be specific, we download ASCII files from diverse sites to apply URDA to these files, and then investigate the distributions of bit patterns that appear in the resulting archived files. We first examine whether the mean of the probabilities that particular bit patterns (in the experiments, we focus on four bit patterns that are sequences of 0) is identical to what was theoretically derived in Equation (1).

When we naturally assume that the probabilities observed follow Gaussian distributions, it is not sufficient to investigate only the means. We have to investigate the variances as well. For this purpose, in addition to the files obtained from the Internet, we generate synthetic ASCII files based on the uniformly random process: For each position in a file, an ASCII character is selected uniformly and independently at random. Then we compare the distributions of the probabilities of the same bit patterns between the archived files generated from the downloaded files and those derived from the synthetic files. The comparison will be made in terms of the means and the variances, since we assume that the distributions follow Gaussian distribution. Since the synthetic files are generated based on the same probabilistic model as what Equation (1) was based on, and since we concluded that such files are secure against bit pattern analysis, this comparison shows an answer to the question whether the same conclusion with respect to confidentiality holds true for real ASCII files.

3.3. URDA with the Setting of the Fragment Length = 7 bits

The procedures to run the experiment are given as follows.

1) Find 200 ASCII files in the Internet, and download them.

2) Apply URDA to the downloaded files with $n = 5$ and $k = 3$, and hence, obtain 1000 archived files, each of which is at least 100 KB length. Here, we set the fragment length to be seven bits as specified in Section 2.2.

3) For $t = 1$ to 400,000, count the number n_t of occurrence of $b_t = \cdots = b_{t-\ell} = 0$ for $\ell = 0,1,2,3$ over the 1,000 archived files, and calculate $\Pr[b_t = \cdots = b_{t-\ell} = 0]$ by $\dfrac{n_t}{1000}$. Thus, we have 400,000 scores of $\Pr[b_t = \cdots = b_{t-\ell} = 0]$ for each $\ell = 0,1,2,3$ respectively.

We plot these scores in the graphs of **Figure 4**.

Yet we are still unable to estimate whether the mathematical formula can also apply to the real world biased ASCII files with fixed fragment length, without evaluating dispersion of the scores from means.

3.4. Statistical Tests

According to the mathematical evaluation given in URDA in previous work, the scores vary drastically when t is small (the position is close to the head of the files), but they quickly converge to Equation (1).

In fact, when looking at **Figure 4**, the scores observed in this experiment seem to follow this rule: The values of $\dfrac{l+9}{2^{l+4}}$ are 0.5625, 0.3125, 0.1719 and 0.0938 respectively for $l = 0,1,2,3$. In the following, we will investigate this, that is, whether the scores observed in fact follow the statistically calculated mathematical formula proved in previous work.

3.4.1. Examining the Means
By the one-sample t-test, we investigate whether the

population means underlying the observed scores are identical to the test means calculated by Equation (1).

The null hypothesis here is of course that the population means are identical to the test means. **Table 1** shows the results of one-sample t-test.

The t statistics are calculated from the equation $t = \dfrac{\overline{x} - \mu}{\dfrac{s}{\sqrt{n}}}$, where $\overline{x}, \mu, n$ and s stand for the sample mean, test mean, sample size and standard deviation of the sample respectively. From **Table 1**, we see that we cannot reject the null hypothesis even with very large significance level, say 0.2: Typically, we use the significance level 0.05 or 0.01. Hence, we can reasonably guess that the null hypothesis is right, that is, the population means are identical to the theoretical value calculated by Equation (1).

3.4.2. Examining the Variances
In the previous clause, we see that the population means are identical to the theoretical means calculated from Equation (1). This result alone, however, is insufficient, since this result tells nothing about how the scores vary around the means. Thus, we have to investigate whether the population variances are sufficiently small. The problem here is that, unlike the calculation of means, we do not have a formula to give the theoretical expectation for the variances. As an alternative method, we generate synthetic files that are generated based on the same probability model as the mathematical model that underlies Equation (1), and compare the scores obtained from the experiment and the scores derived from these synthetic files.

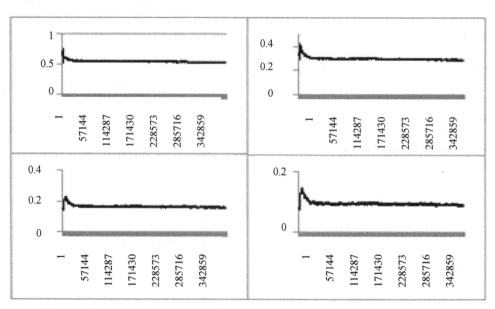

Figure 4. Fixed-fragment-length $\Pr[b_t = \cdots = b_{t-l} = 0]$ ($l = 0,1,2,3, t = 1, \cdots, 400,000$).

Table 1. Comparing of observed scores and test means.

	$\Pr[b_t = 0]$	$\Pr[b_t, b_{t+1} = 0]$	$\Pr[b_t, \cdots, b_{t+2} = 0]$	$\Pr[b_t, \cdots, b_{t+3} = 0]$
Sample Mean	$\bar{x}_f = 0.5707$	$\bar{x}_f = 0.3082$	$\bar{x}_f = 0.1718$	$\bar{x}_f = 0.0948$
Test Mean	$\bar{x}_f = 0.5625$	$\bar{x}_f = 0.3125$	$\bar{x}_f = 0.1719$	$\bar{x}_f = 0.0938$
T-Statistics	$T_f = -0.706$	$T_f = 0.4928$	$T_f = 0.0107$	$T_f = -0.167$
TINV	$T = 1.66$	$T = 1.66$	$T = 1.66$	$T = 1.66$
P-Value	$T_{tail} = 0.482$	$T_{tail} = 0.623$	$T_{tail} = 0.992$	$T_{tail} = 0.868$

To be specific, we generate 200 files that include only ASCII characters selected uniformly and independently at random regardless of the position of the characters. Then, we apply Step 2 and 3 of Section 3.3 to obtain 400,000 scores for each of $\ell = 0, 1, 2, 3$. We call these scores test scores to distinguish them from the sample scores generated in Section 3.3.

To verify this statistically, we apply two-sample F-test to the sample scores and the test scores. Consequently, the null hypothesis to use should be that the population variances underlying the sample scores are identical to those underlying the test scores.

Table 2 shows the result of the test, where σ_f^2 and $\sigma_t^2, \bar{x}_f$ and $\bar{x}_t$ are the variances and the means of the sample scores and the test scores, respectively. According to **Table 2**, we see that the variance σ_f^2 is greater than σ_t^2, while the means x_f and x_t are very close to each other. When investigating the P-values presented in the table with the significance level 0.05, we see that the null hypothesis should be rejected for all cases of $\ell = 0, 1, 2, 3$. Thus, when we apply URDA to ASCII files downloaded from the Internet with the fixed fragment length seven bits, the resulting archived files will not be explained by the mathematical model that is a basis of Equation (1). In other words, we cannot prove that the archived files generated by URDA with the aforementioned setting are secure against the bit pattern analysis, and we cannot recommend use of URDA with this setting.

3.5. URDA with the Setting of the Fragment Length = Variable

As seen in the above, using URDA with the fixed fragment length cannot be recommended from the security point of view. In this clause, we investigate the security of URDA with a different setting, that is, we assume that the fragment length is variable, and is selected at random per fragment in the range of 1 to 32 bits.

For the experiment, we use the same ASCII files stated in Section 3.3. The difference consists in Step 2, and we run URDA with the setting of the fragment length =

variable.

In the same way as Section 3.3, we obtain 400,000 sample scores for each of $\ell = 0, 1, 2, 3$, and plot them in **Figure 5**.

At a glance, the means of the sample scores are identical to their theoretically expected values of

$\Pr[b_t = \cdots = b_{t-\ell} = 0] = \dfrac{l+9}{2^{l+4}}$, and the variances have be-

come smaller compared with the case of the fixed fragment length. In the following, we verify these observations by means of statistics.

3.5.1. Examining the Means

In the same way as the previous subsection, we apply the one-sample t-test to verify that the population means of the sample scores are identical to the theoretical expectation.

Table 3 shows that the P-values obtained are large (the minimum is 0.188), and we cannot reject the null hypotheses with a small significance level, for example, 0.05. Hence the population means of the target probabili-

ties are identical to the values given by $\dfrac{l+9}{2^{l+4}}$ for

$\ell = 0, 1, 2, 3$.

3.5.2. Examining the Variances

As shown in **Table 4**, the variances of the sample scores are close to those of the test scores, which are the scores generated in Section 3.3 using the synthetic ASCII files. If this is true, this will be a clear contrast with the former case where we ran URDA with the fixed fragment length. In the following, we verify that the population variances of the sample scores and the test scores are identical to each other by means of the two-sample F-test.

Table 4 shows that the P-values obtained are large (the smallest is 0.1704), and we cannot reject the null hypotheses with a small significance level, for example, 0.05.

As a consequence, we can conclude that the population variances that underlie the sample scores and the test scores are identical to each other.

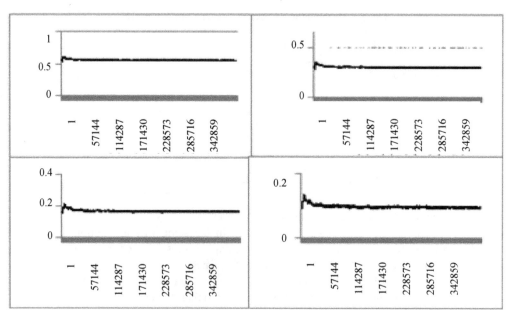

Figure 5. Variable-fragment-length $\Pr[b_t = \cdots = b_{t-l} = 0]$ (l = 0,1,2,3, t = 1, $\cdots$, 400,000).

Table 2. Comparing of fixed variances and test variances.

	$\Pr[b_t = 0]$	$\Pr[b_t, b_{t+1} = 0]$	$\Pr[b_t, \cdots, b_{t+2} = 0]$	$\Pr[b_t, \cdots, b_{t+3} = 0]$
Sample Variance	$\sigma_f^2 = 0.0135$	$\sigma_f^2 = 0.0078$	$\sigma_f^2 = 0.0078$	$\sigma_f^2 = 0.0036$
Test Variance	$\sigma_f^2 = 0.0036$	$\sigma_t^2 = 0.0045$	$\sigma_t^2 = 0.0019$	$\sigma_t^2 = 0.0014$
Sample Mean	$\bar{x}_f = 0.5707$	$\bar{x}_f = 0.3082$	$\bar{x}_f = 0.1718$	$\bar{x}_f = 0.0948$
Test Mean	$\bar{x}_t = 0.5617$	$\bar{x}_t = 0.3103$	$\bar{x}_t = 0.1721$	$\bar{x}_t = 0.0923$
F-Value	1.53	1.72	2.64	2.61
Critical Value	$O_{tail} = 1.39$	$O_{tail} = 1.39$	$O_{tail} = 1.39$	$O_{tail} = 1.39$
	$T_{tail} = 1.49$	$T_{tail} = 1.49$	$T_{tail} = 1.49$	$T_{tail} = 1.49$
P-Value	$T_{tail} = 0.036$	$T_{tail} = 0.007$	$T_{tail} = 0.000002$	$T_{tail} = 0.000004$

Table 3. Comparing of variable means and test means.

	$\Pr[b_t = 0]$	$\Pr[b_t, b_{t+1} = 0]$	$\Pr[b_t, \cdots, b_{t+2} = 0]$	$\Pr[b_t, \cdots, b_{t+3} = 0]$
Test Mean	$\bar{x}_t = 0.5625$	$\bar{x}_t = 0.3125$	$\bar{x}_t = 0.1719$	$\bar{x}_t = 0.0938$
Sample Mean	$\bar{x}_r = 0.5511$	$\bar{x}_r = 0.3031$	$\bar{x}_r = 0.1712$	$\bar{x}_r = 0.0938$
TINV	$T = 1.66$	$T = 1.66$	$T = 1.66$	$T = 1.66$
T-Statistics	$T_r = 1.067$	$T_r = 1.3261$	$T_r = 0.1437$	$T_r = -0.021$
P-Value	$T_{tail} = 0.288$	$T_{tail} = 0.188$	$T_{tail} = 0.886$	$T_{tail} = 0.983$

Table 4. Comparing of variable variances and test variances.

	$\Pr[b_t = 0]$	$\Pr[b_t, b_{t+1} = 0]$	$\Pr[b_t, \cdots, b_{t+2} = 0]$	$\Pr[b_t, \cdots, b_{t+3} = 0]$
Sample Variances	$\sigma_r^2 = 0.0115$	$\sigma_r^2 = 0.0051$	$\sigma_r^2 = 0.0025$	$\sigma_r^2 = 0.0015$
Test Variances	$\sigma_t^2 = 0.0088$	$\sigma_t^2 = 0.0045$	$\sigma_t^2 = 0.0019$	$\sigma_t^2 = 0.0014$
Sample Mean	$\bar{x}_r = 0.5511$	$\bar{x}_r = 0.3031$	$\bar{x}_r = 0.1712$	$\bar{x}_r = 0.0938$
Test Mean	$\bar{x}_p = 0.5617$	$\bar{x}_p = 0.3103$	$\bar{x}_p = 0.1721$	$\bar{x}_p = 0.0923$
F-Value	0.7694	0.89	0.7583	0.9458
Critical Value	$O_{\text{tail}} = 1.39$	$O_{\text{tail}} = 1.39$	$O_{\text{tail}} = 1.39$	$O_{\text{tail}} = 1.39$
	$T_{\text{tail}} = 1.49$	$T_{\text{tail}} = 1.49$	$T_{\text{tail}} = 1.49$	$T_{\text{tail}} = 1.49$
P-Value	$T_{\text{tail}} = 0.194$	$T_{\text{tail}} = 0.549$	$T_{\text{tail}} = 0.1704$	$T_{\text{tail}} = 0.7823$

3.6. Summary of This Experiments

In our previous work, assuming that source files include ASCII characters selected uniformly and independently at random per character, we have mathematically proved that an archived file consisting of seven-bit-long fragments shows uniformly constant distributions with respect to the probabilities that particular bit patterns appear. In other words, we can view the archived file as secure against the bit pattern analysis. On the other hand, the distributions of characters that appear in files of the real world are certainly biased, and hence, it was not certain that the same conclusion holds true when applying URDA to files of the real world with the same setting. To investigate this problem, we first compared the following two scenarios in terms of the means and variances of the probability distribution of some particular bit patterns.

- Apply URDA to files taken from the Internet with the setting of seven-bit-long fragments.
- Apply URDA to synthetic files generated so that every ASCII character appears with the same probability regardless of the position in the files.

As we expected, the means of the probability are identical to their theoretical expectation of $\dfrac{l+9}{2^{l+4}}$ for $\ell = 0, 1, 2, 3$, but the variances for the first scenario are significantly larger than those for the second scenario. Therefore, we cannot deny the possibility that there exist some clever attacks that take advantage of this difference in the variance.

Hence, we ran the same experiments after modifying the first scenario. In the new scenario, the length of each fragment is not fixed, but is determined at random between 1 bit to 32 bits per fragment. The results of the comparison is surprising, we cannot detect statistically significant differences in either the means or the vari-ances between the scores for the downloaded and randomly fragmented ASCII files and those for the synthetic ASCII files. In other words, we cannot statistically distinguish between the archived files generated from the downloaded files and the synthetic files.

Thus, we cannot conclude that use of URDA with the fixed fragment length is secure, while use of URDA with the randomly variable fragment length is secure against bit pattern analysis.

4. Conclusion and Future Work

We investigated whether the formula

$$P[b_t = \cdots = b_{t-l} = 0] \approx \frac{l+9}{2^{l+4}}$$

applies to real ASCII text files that include biases in the distributions of characters. Applying URDA to downloaded text files by fragmenting the files into seven bit long, we found that the resulting archived files might be vulnerable to bit pattern analysis attacks. Thus, in the same way as the previous experiment, we ran another experiment by modifying URDA in the way how to select fragment lengths, that is, the length of each fragment is determined at random per fragment between 1 bit to 32 bits, and showed this modified URDA with the randomly variable fragment length is secure against the bit pattern analysis.

As the next step, we will investigate the security of URDA when applied to text files that include a variety of character sets and their corresponding code units. We will specify the significance of biased bits in these code units, which includes their actual representation in storages and how it affects security issues in plain text archiving. Consequently we need to testify, by stochastically determining the size b per fragment, whether we can obtain similar conclusion for various kinds of source files with various bit distributions. In addition, we also investigate some sorts of file existed in the real world that are said close to random files like video, image and compressed files etc.

REFERENCES

[1] http://www.iso.org/iso/iso_catalogue/catalogue_tc/catalog ue_detail.htm?csnumber=39612

[2] P. M. Chen, E. K. Lee, G. A. Gibson, R. H. Katz and D. A. Patterson, "Aid: High-performance, Reliable Secondary Storage," *ACM Computing Surveys*, Vol. 26, No. 2, 1994, pp. 145-185.

[3] A. Shamir, "How to Share a Secret," *Communication of ACM*, Vol. 22, No. 11, 1979, pp. 612-613.

[4] G. Blakley, "Safeguarding Cryptographic Keys," 1979 *Proceedings of the National Computer Conference*, New York, 4-7 July 1979, p. 313.

[5] M. O. Rabin, "Efficient Dispersal of Information for Security, Load Balancing, and Fault Tolerance," *Journal of the ACM*, Vol. 36, No. 2, 1989, pp. 335-348.

[6] L. Bai, "A Strong Ramp Secret Sharing Scheme Using Matrix Projection," *Proceedings of the 2006 International Symposium on a World of Wireless, Mobile and Multimedia Networks*, New York, 26-29 July 2006, pp. 652-656.

[7] L. Bai and X. K. Zou, "A Proactive Secret Sharing Scheme in Matrix Projection Method," *International Journal of Security and Networks*, Vol. 4, No. 4, 2009, pp. 201-209.

[8] C. Blundo, "Alfredo de Santis and Ugo Vaccaro, Efficient Sharing of Many Secrets," Springer Verlag, Berlin, 1993.

[9] J. M. He and E. Dawson, "Multistage Secret Sharing Based on One-Way Function," *Electronic Letters*, Vol. 30, No. 19, 1994, pp. 1591-1592.

[10] K. Wang, X. K. Zou and Y. Sui, "A Multiple Secret Sharing Scheme Based on Matrix Projection," *Proceedings of the 33rd Annual IEEE International Computer Software and Applications Conference*, Seattle, 20-24 July 2009, pp. 400-405.

[11] S. Rhea, C. Wells, P. Eaton, D. Geels, B. Zhao, H. Weatherspoon and J. Kubiatowicz, "Maintenance-Free Global Data Storage," *IEEE Internet Computing*, Vol. 5, No. 5, 2001, pp. 40-49.

[12] A. Rowstron and P. Druschel, "Storage Management and Caching in PAST, a Large-Scale, Persistent Peer-to-Peer Storage Utility," *Proceeding SOSP*'01 *Proceedings of the Eighteenth ACM Symposium on Operating Systems Principles*, Banff, 21-24 October 2001, pp. 188-201.

[13] A. Tallat, K. Shin, H. Lee and H. Yasuda, "Some Remarkable Property of the Uniformly Random Distributed Archive Scheme," *Advances in Information Sciences and Service Sciences*, Vol. 4, No. 11, 2012, pp. 114-124.

[14] Cisco System, "Storage Networking 101," Cisco System, San Jose, 2001.

[15] International Business Machines Corporation, "Introduction to Storage Area Networks," 2012. http://www.redbooks.ibm.com/

[16] S. Ratnasamy, P. Francis, M. Handley, R. Karp and S. Shenker, "A scalable Content-Addressable Network", *SIGCOMM* '01 *Proceedings of the* 2001 *Conference on Applications, Technologies, Architectures, and Protocols for Computer Communications*, 2001, pp. 161-172.

[17] International Organization for Standardization, "ISO/IEC 7816 Series: Identification Cards-Integrated Circuits(s) Cards with Contacts," International Organization for Standardization, Geneva, 1999.

[18] International Organization for Standardization, "ISO/IEC 18092-3: Information Technology-Telecomunications and Information Exchange between Systems-Near Field Communication-Interface and Protocol (NFCIP-1)," International Organization for Standardization, Geneva, 2004.

[19] IBM Corporation, "Infrared Data Association: Serial infrared Link Access Protocol (IrLAP) Version.1.1," IBM Corporation, New York, 1996.

13

Attacks on Anonymization-Based Privacy-Preserving: A Survey for Data Mining and Data Publishing

Abou-el-ela Abdou Hussien[1], Nermin Hamza[2], Hesham A. Hefny[2]
[1]Department of Computer Science, Faculty of Science and Humanities, Shaqra University, Shaqra, KSA
[2]Department of Computer and Information Sciences, Institute of Statistical Studies and Research, Cairo University, Giza, Egypt

ABSTRACT

Data mining is the extraction of vast interesting patterns or knowledge from huge amount of data. The initial idea of privacy-preserving data mining PPDM was to extend traditional data mining techniques to work with the data modified to mask sensitive information. The key issues were how to modify the data and how to recover the data mining result from the modified data. Privacy-preserving data mining considers the problem of running data mining algorithms on confidential data that is not supposed to be revealed even to the party running the algorithm. In contrast, privacy-preserving data publishing (PPDP) may not necessarily be tied to a specific data mining task, and the data mining task may be unknown at the time of data publishing. PPDP studies how to transform raw data into a version that is immunized against privacy attacks but that still supports effective data mining tasks. Privacy-preserving for both data mining (PPDM) and data publishing (PPDP) has become increasingly popular because it allows sharing of privacy sensitive data for analysis purposes. One well studied approach is the k-anonymity model [1] which in turn led to other models such as confidence bounding, l-diversity, t-closeness, (α,k)-anonymity, etc. In particular, all known mechanisms try to minimize information loss and such an attempt provides a loophole for attacks. The aim of this paper is to present a survey for most of the common attacks techniques for anonymization-based PPDM & PPDP and explain their effects on Data Privacy.

Keywords: Privacy; k-Anonymity; Data Mining; Privacy-Preserving Data Publishing; Privacy-Preserving Data Mining

1. Introduction

Although data mining is potentially useful, many data holders are reluctant to provide their data for data mining for the fear of violating individual privacy. In recent years, study has been made to ensure that the sensitive information of individuals cannot be identified easily. One well studied approach is the k-anonymity model [1] which in turn led to other models such as confidence bounding, l-diversity [2], (α,k)-anonymity [3], t-closeness [4]. These models assume that the data or table T contains: (1) a quasi-identifier (QID), which is a set of attributes (e.g., a QID may be {Date of birth, Zipcode, Sex}) in T which can be used to identify an individual, and (2) sensitive attributes, attributes in T which may contain some sensitive values (e.g., HIV of attribute Disease) of individuals. Often, it is also assumed that each tuple in T corresponds to an individual and no two tuples refer to the same individual. All tuples with the same QID value form an equivalence class, which we call QID-EC. The table T is said to satisfy k-anonymity if the size of every equivalence class is greater than or equal to k. The intuition of k-anonymity is to make sure that each individual is indistinguishable from other k − 1 individuals. In this paper, we present some attacks for anonymization-based PPDM & PPDP and explain their effects. The paper is organized as follows: Section 2 explains anonymity models, Section 3 presents related research directions, Section 4 discusses anonymization-based attacks, and Section 4 concludes the paper and presents future works.

2. Anonymity Models

k-anonymization techniques have been the focus of intense research in the last few years. In order to ensure anonymization of data while at the same time minimizing the information loss resulting from data modifications, several extending models are proposed, which are discussed as follows.

2.1. k-Anonymity

k-anonymity [1] is one of the most classic models, which technique that prevents joining attacks by generalizing and/or suppressing portions of the released microdata so that no individual can be uniquely distinguished from a group of size k. In the k-anonymous tables, a data set is k-anonymous ($k \geq 1$) if each record in the data set is indistinguishable from at least ($k - 1$) other records within the same data set. The larger the value of k, the better the privacy is protected. k-anonymity can ensure that individuals cannot be uniquely identified by linking attacks. Let T (*i.e.* TABLE) is a relation storing private information about a set of individuals. The attributes in T are classified in four categories: an identifier (AI), a sensitive attribute (SA), quasi-identifier attributes (QI) and other unimportant attributes. For example, we have a raw medical data set as in **Table 1**. Attributes sex, age and postcode form the quasi-identifier. Two unique patient records 1 and 2 may be re-identified easily since their combinations of sex, age and postcode are unique. The table is generalized as a 2-anonymous table as in **Table 2**. This table makes the two patients less likely to be re-identified.

However, while k-anonymity protects against identity disclosure, it does not provide sufficient protection against attribute disclosure by the homogeneous attack and the background knowledge attack.

2.2. Extending Models

Since k-anonymity does not provide sufficient protection

Table 1. Raw medical data set.

AI		QI		SA
Name	Sex	Age	Postcode	Illness
Bill	M	20	13000	Flu
Ken	M	24	13500	HIV
Linda	F	26	16500	Fever
Mary	F	28	16400	HIV

Table 2. A 2-anonymos data set of Table 1.

AI		QI		SA
Name	Sex	Age	Name	Sex
Bill	M	[20,24]	13*00	Flu
Ken	M	[20,24]	13*00	HIV
Linda	F	[26,28]	16*00	Fever
Mary	F	[26,28]	16*00	HIV

against attribute disclosure. The paper in [2] proposes the model of l-diversity. The notion of l-diversity attempts to solve this problem by requiring that each equivalence class has at least l well-represented value for each sensitive attribute. The technology of l-diversity has some advantages than k-anonymity. Because k-anonymity dataset permits strong attacks due to lack of diversity in the sensitive attributes. In this model, an equivalence class is said to have l-diversity if there are at least l well-represented value for the sensitive attribute. Because there are semantic relationships among the attribute values, and different values have very different levels of sensitivity. An extending model called t-closeness is proposed in [3], which requires that the distribution of a sensitive attribute in any equivalence class is close to the distribution of the attribute in the overall table. That is, a table is said to have t-closeness if all equivalence classes have t-closeness. The paper in [4] extends the k-anonymity model to the (α,k)-anonymity model to limit the confidence of the implications from the quasi-identifier to a sensitive value (attribute) to within a in order to protect the sensitive information from being inferred by strong implications. After anonymization, in any equivalence class, the frequency (in fraction) of a sensitive value is no more than α. The paper in [5] proposes such a k-anonymization model for transactional databases. Assuming that the maximum knowledge of an adversary is at most m items in a specific transaction, it wants to prevent him from distinguishing the transaction from a set of k published transactions in the database. LeFevre *et al.* in [6] propose the notion of multidimensional k-anonymity [7] where data generalization is over multi-dimension at a time, and [8] extend multidimensional generalization to anonymize data for a specific task such as classification. Recently, m-invariance is introduced by Xiaokui Xiao and Yufei Tao in [9] in order to effectively limit the risk of privacy disclosure in re-publication. The paper in [10] proposes a generalization technique called HD-composition to offer protection on serial publishing with permanent sensitive values. It involves two major roles, holder and decoy. Decoys are responsible for protecting permanent sensitive value holder which is a dynamic setting. According k-anonymity does not take into account personal anonymity requirements, personalized anonymity model is also introduced in [11]. The core of the model is the concept of personalized anonymity, *i.e.*, a person can specify the degree of privacy protection for her/his sensitive values.

3. Related Research Areas

Several polls [12,13] show that the public has an increased sense of privacy loss. Since data mining is often a key component of information systems, homeland security systems [14], and monitoring and surveillance systems [15], it gives a wrong impression that data mining is a technique for privacy intrusion. This lack of trust has become an obstacle to the benefit of the technology. For example, the potentially beneficial data mining research project, Terrorism Information Awareness (TIA), was terminated by the US Congress due to its controversial procedures of collecting, sharing, and analyzing the trails left by individuals [14].

Motivated by the privacy concerns on data mining tools, a research area called privacy-reserving data mining (PPDM) emerged in 2000 [16,17]. The initial idea of PPDM was to extend traditional data mining techniques to work with the data modified to mask sensitive information. The key issues were how to modify the data and how to recover the data mining result from the modified data. The solutions were often tightly coupled with the data mining algorithms under consideration. In contrast, privacy-preserving data publishing (PPDP) may not necessarily tie to a specific data mining task, and the data mining task is sometimes unknown at the time of data publishing. Furthermore, some PPDP solutions emphasize preserving the data truthfulness at the record level, but PPDM solutions often do not preserve such property.

PPDP Differs from PPDM in Several Major Ways as Follows

1) PPDP focuses on techniques for publishing data, not techniques for data mining. In fact, it is expected that standard data mining techniques are applied on the published data. In contrast, the data holder in PPDM needs to randomize the data in such a way that data mining results can be recovered from the randomized data. To do so, the data holder must understand the data mining tasks and algorithms involved. This level of involvement is not expected of the data holder in PPDP who usually is not an expert in data mining.

2) Both randomization and encryption do not preserve the truthfulness of values at the record level; therefore, the released data are basically meaningless to the recipients. In such a case, the data holder in PPDM may consider releasing the data mining results rather than the scrambled data.

3) PPDP primarily "anonymizes" the data by hiding the identity of record owners, whereas PPDM seeks to directly hide the sensitive data. Excellent surveys and books in randomization [16,18-23] and cryptographic techniques [17,24,25] for PPDM can be found in the existing literature.

A family of research work [26-33] called privacy-preserving distributed data mining (PPDDM) [17] aims at performing some data mining task on a set of private databases owned by different parties. It follows the principle of Secure Multiparty Computation (SMC) [34,35], and prohibits any data sharing other than the final data mining result. Clifton et al. [17] present a suite of SMC operations, like secure sum, secure set union, secure size of set intersection, and scalar product, that are useful for many data mining tasks. In contrast, PPDP does not perform the actual data mining task, but concerns with how to publish the data so that the anonymous data are useful for data mining. We can say that PPDP protects privacy at the data level while PPDDM protects privacy at the process level. They address different privacy models and data mining scenarios.

In the field of statistical disclosure control (SDC) [18, 36], the research works focus on privacy-preserving publishing methods for statistical tables. SDC focuses on three types of disclosures, namely identity disclosure, attribute disclosure, and inferential disclosure [37]. Identity disclosure occurs if an adversary can identify a respondent from the published data. Revealing that an individual is a respondent of a data collection may or may not violate confidentiality requirements. Attribute disclosure occurs when confidential information about a respondent is revealed and can be attributed to the respondent. Attribute disclosure is the primary concern of most statistical agencies in deciding whether to publish tabular data [37]. Inferential disclosure occurs when individual information can be inferred with high confidence from statistical information of the published data. Some other works of SDC focus on the study of the non-interactive query model, in which the data recipients can submit one query to the system. This type of non-interactive query model may not fully address the information needs of data recipients because, in some cases, it is very difficult for a data recipient to accurately construct a query for a data mining task in one shot. Consequently, there are a series of studies on the interactive query model [38-40], in which the data recipients, including adversaries, can submit a sequence of queries based on previously received query results. The database server is responsible to keep track of all queries of each user and determine whether or not the currently received query has violated the privacy requirement with respect to all previous queries. One limitation of any interactive privacy-preserving query system is that it can only answer a sublinear number of queries in total; otherwise, an adversary (or a group of corrupted data recipients) will be able to reconstruct all but $1 - o(1)$ fraction of the original data [41], which is a very strong violation of privacy. When the maximum number of queries is reached, the query service must be closed to avoid privacy leak. In the case of the non-interactive query model, the adversary can issue only one query and, therefore, the non-interactive query model cannot achieve the same degree of privacy defined by Introduction the interactive model. One may consider that privacy-reserving data publishing is a special case of the non-interactive query model.

4. Anonimization-Based Attacks

In this paper, we study the case where the adversary has some additional knowledge about the mechanism involved in the anonymization and launches an attack based on this knowledge. We distinguish heir between both PPDM and PPDP attacks.

4.1. Privacy-Preserving Data Publishing PPDP Attacks

In this section we present Attacks for anonimization-based attacks in privacy-preserving data publishing and we study mainly minimality attack.

Minimality Attack
In **Table 3(a)**, assume that the QID values of q1 and q2 can be generalized to Q and assume only one sensitive attribute "disease", in which HIV is a sensitive value. For example, q1 may be {Nov 1930, Z3972, M}, q2 may be {Dec 1930, Z3972, M} and Q is {Nov/Dec 1930, Z3972, M}. (Note that q1 and q2 may also be generalized values). A tuple associated with HIV is said to be a sensitive tuple. For each equivalence class, at most half of the tuples are sensitive. Hence, the table satisfies 2-diversity. As observed in LeFevre et al. [2005], existing approaches of anonymization for data publishing have an implicit principle: "For any anonymization mechanism, it is desirable to define some notion of minimality". Intuitively, a k-anonymization should not generalize, suppress, or dis- tort the data more than it is necessary to achieve k-ano- nymity". Based on this minimality principle, **Table 3(a)** will not be generalized. In fact the aforesaid notion of minimality is too strong since almost all known anonymization problems for data publishing are NP-hard, many existing algorithms are heuristical and only attain

local minima. We shall later give a more relaxed notion of the minimality principle in order to cover both the optimal as well as the heuristical algorithms. For now, we assume that mimimality principle means that a QID-EC will not be generalized unnecessarily. Next, consider a slightly different table, **Table 3(b)**. Here, the set of tuples for q1 violates 2-diversity because the proportion of the sensitive tuples is greater than 1/2. Thus, this table will be anonymized to a generalized table by generalizing the QID values as shown in **Table 3(c)** by global recoding [11]. In global recoding, all occurrences of an attribute value are recoded to the same value. If local recoding [Sweeney, 2002a; Aggarwal et al., 2005a, 2005b] is adopted, occurrences of the same value of an attribute may be recoded to different values. Such an anonymization is shown in **Table 3(d)**. These anonymized tables satisfy 2-diversity. The question we are interested in is whether these tables really protect individual privacy. In most previous works [Sweeney, 2002b; LeFevre et al., 2006, 2005; Xiao and Tao, 2006b], the knowledge of the adversary involves an external table T^e. such as a voter registration list that maps QIDs to individuals. As in many previous works, we assume that each tuple in T^e maps to one individual and no two tuples map to the same individual. The same is also assumed in the table T to be published. Let us first consider the case when T and T^e are mapped to the same set of individuals. **Table 4(a)** is an example of T^e. Assume further that the adversary knows the goal of 2-diversity, s/he also knows whether it is a global or local recoding, and **Table 4(a)** is available as the external table T^e. With the notion of minimality in anonymization, the adversary reasons as follows: From the published **Table 3(c)**, there are 2 sensitive tuples in total. From T^e, there are 2 tuples with QID = q1 and 5 tuples with QID = q2. Hence, the equivalence class for q2 in the original table must already satisfy 2-diversity, because even if both sensitive tuples have QID = q2, the proportion of sensitive values in the class for q2 is only 2/5.

Table 3. 2-diversity: Global and local recoding.

QID	Disease	QID	Disease	QID	Disease	QID	Disease
q1	HIV	q1	HIV	Q	HIV	Q	HIV
q1	non-sensitive	q1	HIV	Q	HIV	Q	HIV
q2	HIV	q2	non-sensitive	Q	non-sensitive	Q	non-sensitive
q2	non-sensitive	q2	non-sensitive	Q	non-sensitive	Q	non-sensitive
q2	non-sensitive	q2	non-sensitive	Q	non-sensitive	q2	non-sensitive
q2	non-sensitive	q2	non-sensitive	Q	non-sensitive	q2	non-sensitive
q2	non-sensitive	q2	non-sensitive	Q	non-sensitive	q2	non-sensitive
(a)	Good table	(b)	Bad table	(c)	Global	(d)	Local

Table 4. T^e: External table available to the adversary.

QID	QID	Name	QID	QID	Name
q1	q1	Andre	q1	q1	Andre
q1	q1	Kim	q1	q1	Kim
q2	q2	Jeremy	q2	q2	Jeremy
q2	q2	Victoria	q2	q2	Victoria
q2	q2	Ellen	q2	q2	Ellen
q2	q2	Sally	q2	q2	Sally
q2	q2	Ben	q2	q2	Ben
q4	q4	Tim			
q4	q4	Joseph			
(a) Individual QID	(b)	multiset	**(c) Individual QID**	(d)	multiset

Since generalization has taken place, at least one equivalence class in the original table T must have violated 2-diversity, because otherwise no generalization will take place according to minimality. The adversary concludes that q1 has violated 2-diversity, and that is possible only if both tuples with QID = q1 have a disease value of "HIV". The adversary therefore discovers that Andre and Kim are linked to "HIV". In some previous works, it is assumed that the set of individuals in the external table T^e can be a superset of that for the published table. **Table 4(c)** shows such a case, where there is no tuple for Tim and Joseph in **Table 3(a)** and **Table 3(b)**. If it is known that q4 cannot be generalized to Q (e.g., q4 = {Nov 1930, Z3972, F} and Q = {Jan/Feb 1990, Z3972, M}), then the adversary can be certain that the tuples with QID = q4 are not in the original table. Thus, the tuples with QID = q4 in Te do not have any effect on the previous reasoning of the adversary and, therefore, the same conclusion can be drawn. We call such an attack based on the minimality principle a minimality attack.

***Observation* 1.** If a table T is anonymized to T^* which satisfies l-diversity, it can suffer from a minimality attack. This is true for both global and local recoding and for the cases when the set of individuals related to T^e is a superset of that related to T. In the preceding example, some values in the sensitive attribute Disease are not sensitive. Would it help if all values in the sensitive attributes are sensitive? In the tables in **Table 5**, we assume that all values for Disease are sensitive. **Table 5(a)** satisfies 2-diversity but **Table 5(b)** does not. Suppose anonymization of **Table 5(b)** results in **Table 5(c)** by global recoding and **Table 5(d)** by local recoding.

The adversary is armed with the external table **Table 4(c)** and the knowledge of the goal of 2-diversity, s/he can launch an attack by reasoning as follows: With 5 tuples for QID = q2 and each sensitive value appearing at most twice, there cannot be any violation of 2-diversity for the tuples with QID = q2. There must have been a violation for QID = q1. For a violation to take place, both tuples with QID = q1 must be linked to the same disease. Since HIV is the only disease that appears twice, Andre and Kim must have contracted HIV.

***Observation* 2.** Minimality attack is possible whether the sensitive attribute contains non-sensitive values or not. Recall that the intended objective of 2-diversity is to make sure that an adversary cannot deduce with a probability above 1/2 that an individual is linked to any sensitive value. Thus, the published tables violate this objective. The previous attacks to Andre would also be successful if the knowledge of the external table **Table 4(a)** is replaced by that of a multiset of the QID values as shown in **Table 4(b)** plus the QID value of Andre; or if **Table 4(c)** is replaced by the multiset in **Table 4(d)** plus the QID value of Andre. Note that the multisets in **Tables 4(b)** and **(d)** are inherently available in the published data if the bucketization technique as in Xiao and Tao [2006a], Zhang *et al.* [2007], or Martin *et al.* [2007] is used.

***Observation* 3.** The minimality attacks to an individual t would also be successful if the knowledge of the external table T^e (which is either a superset of individuals of the published table or not) is replaced by that of a multiset of the QID values of the external table T^e plus the QID value of t. A strong requirement of 3-diversity is used to achieve the original intended requirement of 2-diversity.

It is natural to ask whether there is a privacy breach if the data publisher generalizes the table a little more than minimal. In this case, we say that the anonymization algorithm follows a near to minimality principle. Suppose the intended objective is to generate a table which satisfies a privacy requirement of 2-diversity. Under the near

Table 5. 2-diversity (where all values in Disease are sensitive): Global and local recoding.

Disease	QID	Disease	QID	Disease	QID	Disease	QID
HIV	Q	**HIV**	**Q**	HIV	q1	**HIV**	**q1**
HIV	Q	**HIV**	**Q**	HIV	q1	**Lung Cancer**	**q1**
Gallstones	Q	**Gallstones**	**Q**	Gallstones	q2	**Gallstones**	**q2**
Lung Cancer	Q	**Lung Cancer**	**Q**	Lung Cancer	q2	**HIV**	**q2**
Ulcer	q2	**Ulcer**	**Q**	Ulcer	q2	**Ulcer**	**q2**
Alzheimer	q2	**Alzheimer**	**Q**	Alzheimer	q2	**Alzheimer**	**q2**
Diabetes	q2	**Diabetes**	**Q**	Diabetes	q2	**Diabetes**	**q2**
Ulcer	q4	**Ulcer**	**q4**	Ulcer	q4	**Ulcer**	**q4**
Alzheimer	q4	**Alzheimer**	**q4**	Alzheimer	q4	**Alzheimer**	**q4**
(a)	**Good table**	(b)	Bad table	**(c)**	**Global**	(d)	Local

to minimality principle, the publisher generates a table which satisfies a stronger privacy requirement of 3-diversity. Again we assume that the adversary knows that the algorithm adopted guarantees 3-diversity while minimizing the information loss. Does a published table which satisfies 3-diversity guarantee that the probability that an individual is linked to a sensitive value is at most 1/2? The answer is interestingly no. Consider **Table 6**. Suppose our original intended privacy requirement is 2-diversity because we want to guarantee that the probability that an individual is linked to a sensitive value is at most 1/2. Based on the near to minimality principle, a stronger 3-diversity is attained instead. **Table 6(a)** satisfies 3-diversity but **Table 6(b)** does not. Thus, **Tables 6(c)** and **6(d)** are generated by global recoding and local recoding, respectively. By similar arguments, with the knowledge of a strong requirement 3-diversity and **Table 6(c)**, the adversary can also deduce that the probability that an individual with QID value = q1 is equal to 2/3 which is greater than the intended maximum disclosure probability of 1/2. This is because the two HIV values must be linked to the tuples with QID = q1. Otherwise, there will be no violation of 3-diversity and there is no need for generalization. Similar arguments can be made to **Table 6(d)**. We call this kind of attack the near-to-minimality attack.

Observation **4.** Near-to-minimality attack is possible when the anonymization algorithm follows the near to minimality principle. From the preceding discussion, we described the attack by minimality and the attack by near-to-minimality are successful under the principles of minimality principle and near-to-minimality principles used in the anonymization algorithm. Both are based on some knowledge about the algorithm, let us call an attack based on such knowledge an attack by mechanism. Hence minimality or near-minimality attack are under

this bigger class of attack.

4.2. Privacy-Preserving Data Mining (PPDM) Attacks

Various attacks are addressed from a privacy-preserving perspective. In the following subsections the most common attacks are discussed.

4.2.1. Background Knowledge Attack
Recently, Xiao and Tao [42] introduced Anatomy as an alternative anonymization technique to generalization. Anatomy releases all the quasi-identifier and sensitive data directly into two separate tables. For example, the original table shown in **Table 7** is decomposed into two tables, the quasi-identifier table (QIT) in **Table 8(a)** and the sensitive table (ST) in **Table 8(b)**. The QIT table and the ST table are then released. The authors also proposed an anatomizing algorithm to compute the anatomized tables. The algorithm first hashes the records into buckets based on the sensitive attribute, *i.e.*, records with the same sensitive values are in the same bucket. Then the algorithm iteratively obtains the ! buckets that currently have the largest number of records and selects one record from each of the ! buckets to form a group. Each remaining record is then assigned to an existing group.

We show background knowledge attack on the anatomized tables. Suppose Alice knows that Bob's record belongs to the first group in **Table 8(b)** where the two sensitive values are "prostate cancer" and "ovary cancer", then Alice immediately knows that Bob has "prostate cancer". The apparent diversity does not help provide any privacy, because certain values can be easily eliminated. This problem is particularly acute in the Anatomy approach. The anatomizing algorithm randomly picks records and groups them together (rather than grouping

Table 6. Illustration of near to minimality principle.

Disease	QID	Disease	QID	Disease	QID	Disease	QID
HIV	Q	**HIV**	**Q**	HIV	q1	**HIV**	**q1**
HIV	Q	**HIV**	**Q**	HIV	q1	**non-sensitive**	**q1**
non-sensitive	Q	**non-sensitive**	**Q**	non-sensitive	q1	**non-sensitive**	**q1**
non-sensitive	Q	**non-sensitive**	**Q**	non-sensitive	q2	**HIV**	**q2**
non-sensitive	Q	**non-sensitive**	**Q**	non-sensitive	q2	**non-sensitive**	**q2**
non-sensitive	Q	**non-sensitive**	**Q**	non-sensitive	q2	**non-sensitive**	**q2**
non-sensitive	q2	**non-sensitive**	**Q**	non-sensitive	q2	**non-sensitive**	**q2**
non-sensitive	q2	**non-sensitive**	**Q**	non-sensitive	q2	**non-sensitive**	**q2**
non-sensitive	q2	**non-sensitive**	**Q**	non-sensitive	q2	**non-sensitive**	**q2**
(a)	**Good table**	(b)	Bad table	(c)	**Global**	(d)	Local

Table 7. Original patients table.

Disease	Sex	Age	ZIP Code	
Ovarian Cancer	F	29	47677	1
Ovarian Cancer	F	22	47602	2
Prostate Cancer	M	27	47678	3
Flu	M	43	47905	4
Heart Disease	F	52	47909	5
Heart Disease	M	47	47906	6
Heart Disease	M	30	47605	7
Flu	M	36	47673	8
Flu	M	32	47607	9

Table 8. (a) The quasi-identifier table (QIT); (b) The sensitive table (ST).

(a)

Disease	Sex	Age	ZIP Code	
1	F	29	47677	1
1	F	22	47602	2
1	M	27	47678	3
2	M	43	47905	4
2	F	52	47909	5
2	M	47	47906	6
3	M	30	47605	7
3	M	36	47673	8
3	M	32	47607	9

(b)

Group-ID	Disease	Count
1	Ovarian Cancer	2
1	Prostate Cancer	1
2	Flu	1
2	Heart Disease	2
3	Heart Disease	1
3	Flu	2

records with similar quasi-id values together). Therefore, it is likely that one may be grouping records with incompatible sensitive attribute values together.

4.2.2. Unsorted Matching Attack

This attack is based on the order in which tuples appear in the released table. While we have maintained the use of a relational model, and so the order of tuples cannot be assumed, in real-world use this is often a problem. It can be corrected of course, by randomly sorting the tuples of the solution. Otherwise, the release of a related table can leak sensitive information.

From **Figure 1** we can see that this attack is based on the order in which tuples appear in the released table.

Solution: Random shuffling of rows.

4.2.3. Complementary Release Attack

It is more common that the attributes that constitute the quasi-identifier are themselves a subset of the attributes released. As a result, when a k-minimal solution, which we will call table T is released, it should be considered as joining other external information. Therefore, subsequent releases of generalizations of the same privately held information must consider all of the released attributes of T a quasi-identifier to prohibit linking on T, unless of course, subsequent releases are themselves generalizations of T.

From **Figure 2** we find that Different releases can be linked together to compromise k-anonymity.

Solution:

1) Consider all of the released tables before release the new one, and try to avoid linking.

2) Other data holders may release some data that can be used in this kind of attack. Generally, this kind of attack is hard to be prohibited completely.

Race	Zip	Race	Zip	Race	Zip
Asian	02138	Person	02138	Asian	02130
Asian	02139	Person	02139	Asian	02130
Asian	02141	Person	02141	Asian	02140
Asian	02142	Person	02142	Asian	02140
Black	02138	Person	02138	Black	02130
Black	02139	Person	02139	Black	02130
Black	02141	Person	02141	Black	02140
Black	02142	Person	02142	Black	02140
White	02138	Person	02138	White	02130
White	02139	Person	02139	White	02130
White	02141	Person	02141	White	02140
White	02142	Person	02142	White	02140
PT		**GT1**		**GT2**	

Figure 1. Demonstrate unsorted matching attack.

4.2.4. Temporal Attack

Data collections are dynamic. Tuples are added, changed, and removed constantly. As a result, releases of generalized data over time can be subject to a temporal inference attack.

From **Figures 3(a)**, **(b)** and **(c)**, we see that adding or removing tuples may compromise k-anonymity protection.

Solution: Subsequent releases must use the already released table.

4.2.5. Homogeneity Attack and Background Knowledge Attack

In this subsection we present two major attacks, the homogeneity attack and background knowledge attack [43], along with unsorted matching attack, complementary release attack and temporal attack, and we show that how they can be used to compromise a k-anonymous dataset.

Problem	ZIP	Gender	Birth Date	Race	Problem	ZIP	Gender	Birth Date	Race
Short of breath	02141	male	1965	black	Short of breath	02141	male	1965	black
Chest pain	02141	male	1965	black	Chest pain	02141	male	1965	black
Painful eye	02138	female	1965	black	Painful eye	0213*	female	1965	Person
wheezing	02138	female	1965	black	wheezing	0213*	female	1965	person
obesity	02138	female	1964	black	obesity	02138	female	1964	black
Chest pain	02138	female	1964	black	Chest pain	02138	female	1964	black
Short of breath	02138	male	1960-69	white	Short of breath	0213*	male	1964	White
hypertension	02139	human	1960-69	white	hypertension	0213*	female	1965	person
obesity	02139	human	1960-69	white	obesity	0213*	male	1964	white
fever	02139	human	1960-69	white	fever	0213*	male	1964	white
vomiting	02138	male	1960-69	white	vomiting	02138	male	1967	white
backpain	02138	male	1960-69	white	backpain	02138	male	1967	white
		GT1					GT3		

Problem	ZIP	Gender	Birth Date	Race	Problem	ZIP	Gender	Birth Date	Race
Short of breath	02141	male	9/20/1965	black	Short of breath	02141	male	1965	black
Chest pain	02141	male	2/14/1965	black	Chest pain	02141	male	1965	black
Painful eye	01238	female	10/23/1965	black	Painful eye	02138	female	1965	black
wheezing	01238	female	8/24/1965	black	wheezing	02138	female	1965	black
obesity	02138	female	11/7/1964	black	obesity	02138	female	1964	black
Chest pain	02138	female	12/1/1964	black	Chest pain	02138	female	1964	black
Short of breath	02139	male	10/23/1964	White	Short of breath	02138	male	1964	white
hypertension	02139	female	3/15/1965	White	hypertension	02139	female	1965	white
obesity	02139	male	8/13/1964	white	obesity	02139	male	1964	white
fever	02139	male	5/5/1964	white	fever	02139	male	1964	white
vomiting	02138	male	2/13/1967	white	vomiting	02138	male	1967	white
backpain	02138	male	3/21/1967	white	backpain	02138	male	1967	white
		PT					LT		

Figure 2. Different releases for Micro-Data.

(a)

Problem	ZIP	Gender	Birth Date	Race
Short of breath	02141	male	9/20/1965	black
Chest pain	02141	male	2/14/1965	black
Painful eye	01238	female	10/23/1965	black
wheezing	01238	female	8/24/1965	black
obesity	02138	female	11/7/1964	black
Chest pain	02138	female	12/1/1964	black
Short of breath	02139	male	10/23/1964	White
hypertension	02139	female	3/15/1965	White
obesity	02139	male	8/13/1964	white
fever	02139	male	5/5/1964	white
vomiting	02138	male	2/13/1967	white
back pain	02138	male	3/21/1967	white

PT

(b)

Problem	ZIP	Gender	Birth Date	Race
Short of breath	02141	male	1965	black
Chest pain	02141	male	1965	black
Painful eye	0213*	female	1965	Person
Wheezing	0213*	female	1965	person
Obesity	02138	female	1964	black
Chest pain	02138	female	1964	black
Short of breath	0213*	male	1964	White
Hypertension	0213*	female	1965	person
Obesity	0213*	male	1964	white
Fever	0213*	male	1964	white
Vomiting	02138	male	1967	white
back pain	02138	male	1967	white

GT1

(c)

Problem	ZIP	Gender	Birth Date	Race
Short of breath	02141	male	1965	black
Chest pain	02141	male	1965	black
Painful eye	02138	female	1965	black
wheezing	02138	female	1965	black
obesity	02138	female	1964	black
Chest pain	02138	female	1964	black
Short of breath	02138	male	1960-69	white
hypertension	02139	human	1960-69	white
obesity	02139	human	1960-69	white
fever	02139	human	1960-69	white
vomiting	02138	male	1960-69	white
back pain	02138	male	1960-69	white

Figure 3. Adding or removing tuples; (a) black 9/7/65 male 02139 headache, black 11/4/65 male 02139 rash; (c) black 1965 male 02139 rash; black 1965 male 02139 headache.

So here new definition arise l-diversity. l-diversity provides privacy even when the data publisher does not know what kind of knowledge is possessed by the adversary. The main idea behind l-diversity is the requirement that the values of the sensitive attributes are well-represented in each group.

Even when sufficient care is taken to identify the QI, the k-anonymity is still vulnerable to attacks. The common attacks are unsorted matching attacks, complementary release attacks and temporal attacks. Fortunately, these attacks can be prevented by some best practices. But the two major attacks, Homogeneity and Background attacks disclose the individuals' sensitive information. K-anonymity does not protect against attacks based on background knowledge because k-anonymity can create groups that leak information.

Observation: k-anonymity does not provide privacy in case of Homogeneity and Background attacks.

Homogeneity Attack: Suppose A and B are enemies and A wants to infer B's medical status which is present in **Table 9**. A knows B's ZIP Code is 13053 and his age is 35. So using this knowledge A knows that B's records belong from record no. 9,10,11,12 have Cancer. So A concludes that B has Cancer. This situation or attack is implies that k-anonymity can create groups which are responsible for leakage of information. This happens due to the lack of diversity in the sensitive attribute. This problem suggests that in addition to k-anonymity, the disinfected table should also ensure "diversity" all tuples that share the same values of their quasi-identifiers should have diverse values for their sensitive attributes.

Background Knowledge Attack: Suppose C and D are two aggressive neighbors and C wants to infer D's private data, let the medical status, from the private table PT. **Table 9** shows a 4-anonymous private table with patient micro data which satisfies k-anonymity. So for a single value, C finds 3 more values. So if he wants to infer D's medical status, he has four options for disease. This is k-anonymity principle. But C knows some general details about D as his ZIP Code is 14853 and age above 50. So using these values as quasi-identifiers, C concludes that D's record is present in records 5,6,7,8. But here C has three options of disease, Cancer, Heart Disease and Viral infection. Here C uses his background knowledge and concludes that D has Heart Disease because D has low blood pressure and he avoids fatty meals.

So, we can say that k-anonymity does not protect against attacks based on background knowledge. We have demonstrated (using the homogeneity and background knowledge attacks) that a k-anonymous table may disclose sensitive information. Since both of these attacks are plausible in real life, we need a stronger definition of privacy that takes into account diversity and background knowledge. The k-anonymity may suffer

Table 9. 4-anonymous inpatient microdata.

SENSITIVE	NONSENSITIVE			S. NO
Medical Status	Nationality	Age	Zip Code	
Heart Disease	*	<30	130**	1
Heart Disease	*	<30	130**	2
Viral Infection	*	<30	130**	3
Viral Infection	*	<30	130**	4
Cancer	*	≥40	1485*	5
Heart Disease	*	≥40	1485*	6
Viral Infection	*	≥40	1485*	7
Viral Infection	*	≥40	1485*	8
Cancer	*	3*	130**	9
Cancer	*	3*	130**	10
Cancer	*	3*	130**	11
Cancer	*	3*	130**	12

with this aspect also.

5. Conclusion

This paper presents a survey for most of the common attacks techniques for anonymization-based PPDM & PPDP and explains their effects on Data Privacy. k-anonymity is used for security of respondents identity and decreases linking attack in the case of homogeneity attack a simple k-anonymity model fails and we need a concept which prevent from this attack solution is l-diversity. All tuples are arranged in well represented form and adversary will divert to l places or on l sensitive attributes. l-diversity limits in case of background knowledge attack because no one predicts knowledge level of an adversary. It is observe that using generalization and suppression we also apply these techniques on those attributes which doesn't need this extent of privacy and this leads to reduce the precision of publishing table. e-NSTAM (extended Sensitive Tuples Anonymity Method) [44] is applied on sensitive tuples only and reduces information loss, this method also fails in the case of multiple sensitive tuples. Generalization with suppression is also the causes of data lose because suppression emphasize on not releasing values which are not suited for k factor. Future works in this front can include defining a new privacy measure along with l-divesity for multiple sensitive attribute and we will focus to generalize attributes without suppression using other techniques which are used to achieve k-anonymity because suppression leads to reduce the precision of publishing table.

REFERENCES

[1] P. Samarati and L. Sweeney, "Protecting Privacy When Disclosing Information: k-Anonymity and Its Enforcement through Generalization and Suppression," Technical Report SRI-CSL-98-04, 1998.

[2] A. Machanavajjhala, J. Gehrke, *et al.*, "1 -Diversity: Privacy beyond k-Anonymity," *Proceeding of ICDE*, April 2006.

[3] N. Li, T. Li and S. Venkatasubramanian, "t-Closeness: Privacy Beyond k-Anonymity and l-Diversity," *Proceedings of ICDE*, 2007, pp. 106-115.

[4] R. C. Wong, J. Li, A. W. Fu, *et al.*, "(α,k)-Anonymity: An Enhaned k-Anonymity Model for Privacy-Preserving Data Publishing," In: *Proceedings of the 12th ACM SIGKDD*, ACM Press, New York, 2006, pp. 754-759.

[5] M. Terrovitis, N. Mamoulis and Kalnis, "Privacy Preserving Anonymization of Set-Valued Data," *VLDB*, Auckland, 2008, pp. 115-125.

[6] K. LeFevre, D. J. DeWitt and R. Ramakrishnan, "Incognito: Efficient Full-Domain k-Anonymity," In: *Proceedings of the ACM SIGMOD International Conference on Management of Data*, Baltimore, June 2005, pp. 49-60.

[7] X. Ye, L. Jin and B. Li, "A Multi-Dimensional K-Anonymity Model for Hierarchical Data, Electronic Commerce and Security," 2008 *International Symposium*, Beijing, August 2008, pp. 327-332.

[8] K. LeFevre, D. J. DeWitt and R. Ramakrishnan, "Workload-Aware Anonymization," *Proceedings of the 12th ACM SIGKDD International Conference on Knowledge Discovery and Data Mining*, Philadelphia, August 2006, pp. 277-286.

[9] X. Xiao and Y. Tao, "M-Invariance: Towards Privacy-Preserving Re-Publication of Dynamic Datasets," In: *Proceedings of SIGMOD*, ACM Press, New York, 2007, pp. 689-700.

[10] Y. Bu, A. Wai-Chee Fu, *et al.*, "Privacy-Preserving Serial Data Publishing By Role Composition," *VLDB*, Auckland, 2008, pp. 845-856.

[11] X. Xiao and Y. Tao, "Personalized Privacy Preservation, Proceedings of ACM Conference on Management of Data (SIGMOD)," ACM Press, New York, 2006, pp. 785-790.

[12] "Business for Social Responsibility," BSR Report on Privacy, 1999. http://www.bsr.org/

[13] B. Krishnamurthy, "Privacy vs. Security in the Aftermath of the September 11 Terrorist Attacks," November 2001. http://www.scu.edu/ethics/publications/briefings/privacy.html

[14] J. W. Seifert, "Data Mining and Homeland Security: An Overview," CRS Report for Congress, (RL31798), January 2006. http://www.fas.org/sgp/crs/intel/RL31798.pdf

[15] T. Fawcett and F. Provost, "Activity Monitoring: Noticing Interesting Changes in Behavior," *Proceedings of the 5th ACM International Conference on Knowledge Discovery and Data Mining (SIGKDD)*, San Diego, 1999, pp. 53-62.

[16] R. Agrawal and R. Srikant, "Privacy-Preserving Data Mining," *Proceedings of ACM International Conference on Management of Data (SIGMOD)*, Dallas, 2000, pp. 439-450.

[17] C. Clifton, M. Kantarcioglu, J. Vaidya, X. Lin and M. Y. Zhu, "Tools for Privacy-Preserving Distributed Data Mining," *ACM SIGKDD Explorations Newsletter*, Vol. 4, No. 2, 2002, pp. 28-34.

[18] N. R. Adam and J. C. Wortman, "Security Control Methods for Statistical Databases," *ACM Computer Surveys*, Vol. 21, No. 4, 1989, pp. 515-556.

[19] S. Agrawal and J. R. Haritsa, "A Framework for High-Accuracy Privacy-Preserving Mining," *Proceedings of the 21st IEEE International Conference on Data Engineering (ICDE)*, Tokyo, April 2005, pp. 193-204.

[20] A. Evfimievski, "Randomization in Privacy-Preserving Data Mining," *ACM SIGKDD Explorations Newsletter*, Vol. 4, No. 2, 2002, pp. 43-48.

[21] K. Liu, H. Kargupta and J. Ryan, "Random Projection-Based Multiplicative Perturbation for Privacy-Preserving Distributed Data Mining," *IEEE Transactions on Knowledge and Data Engineering (TKDE)*, Vol. 18, No. 1, 2006, pp. 92-106.

[22] A. Shoshani, "Statistical Databases: Characteristics, Problems and Some Solutions," *Proceedings of the 8th Very Large Data Bases (VLDB)*, Mexico City, September 1982, pp. 208-213.

[23] V. S. Verykios, E. Bertino, I. N. Fovino, L. P. Provenza, Y. Saygin and Y. Theodoridis, "State-of-the-Art in Privacy Preserving Data Mining," *ACM SIGMOD Record*, Vol. 3, No. 1, 2004, pp. 50-57.

[24] B. Pinkas, "Cryptographic Techniques for Privacy-Preserving Data Mining," *ACM SIGKDD Explorations Newsletter*, Vol. 4, No. 2, 2002, pp. 12-19.

[25] J. Vaidya, C. W. Clifton and M. Zhu, "Privacy-Preserving Data Mining," 2006.

[26] W. Du, Y. S. Han and S. Chen, "Privacy-Preserving Multivariate Statistical Analysis: Linear Regression and Classification," *Proceedings of the SIAM International Conference on Data Mining (SDM)*, Florida, 2004.

[27] W. Du and Z. Zhan, "Building Decision Tree Classifier on Private Data," *Workshop on Privacy, Security, and Data Mining at the 2002 IEEE International Conference on Data Mining*, Maebashi City, December 2002.

[28] A. W. C. Fu, R. C. W. Wong and K. Wang, "Privacy-Preserving Frequent Pattern Mining across Private Databases," *Proceedings of the 5th IEEE International Conference on Data Mining (ICDM)*, Houston, November 2005, pp. 613-616.

[29] M. Kantarcioglu and C. Clifton, "Privacy-Preserving Data Mining of Association Rules on Horizontally Partitioned Data," *IEEE Transactions on Knowledge and Data Engineering (TKDE)*, Vol. 16, No. 9, 2004, pp. 1026-1037.

[30] M. Kantarcioglu and C. Clifton, "Privately Computing a

Distributed K-Nn Classifier," *Proceedings of the 8th European Conference on Principles and Practice of Knowledge Discovery in Databases* (*PKDD*), Pisa, September 2004, pp. 279-290.

[31] J. Vaidya and C. Clifton, "Privacy-Preserving Association Rule Mining in Vertically Partitioned Data," *Proceedings of the 8th ACM International Conference on Knowledge Discovery and Data Mining* (*SIGKDD*), Edmonton, 2002. pp. 639-644.

[32] J. Vaidya and C. Clifton, "Privacy-Preserving k-Means Clustering over Vertically Partitioned Data," *Proceedings of the 9th ACM International Conference on Knowledge Discovery and Data Mining* (*SIGKDD*), Washington, 2003, pp. 206-215.

[33] Z. Yang, S. Zhong and R. N. Wright, "Privacy-Preserving Classification of Customer Data without Loss of Accuracy," *Proceedings of the 5th SIAM International Conference on Data Mining* (*SDM*), Newport Beach, 2005, pp. 92-102.

[34] A. C. Yao, "Protocols for Secure Computations," *Proceedings of the 23rd IEEE Symposium on Foundations of Computer Science*, Washington DC, 1982, pp. 160-164.

[35] A. C. Yao, "How to Generate and Exchange Secrets," Proceedings of the 27*th Annual IEEE Symposium on Foundations of Computer Science*, 1986, pp. 162-167.

[36] R. Brand, "Microdata Protection through Noise Addition," *Inference Control in Statistical Databases, From Theory to Practice*, London, 2002, pp. 97-116.

[37] Confidentiality and Data Access Committee, "Report on Statistical Disclosure Limitation Methodology," Technical Report 22, Office of Management and Budget, December 2005.

[38] A. Blum, C. Dwork, F. McSherry and K. Nissim, "Practical Privacy: The Sulq Framework," *Proceedings of the 24th ACM Symposium on Principles of Database Systems* (*PODS*), Baltimore, June 2005, pp. 128-138.

[39] I. Dinur and K. Nissim, "Revealing Information While Preserving Privacy," *Proceedings of the 22nd ACM Symposium on Principles of Database Systems* (*PODS*), San Diego, June 2003, pp. 202-210.

[40] C. Dwork, "Differential Privacy: A Survey of Results," *Proceedings of the 5th International Conference on Theory and Applications of Models of Computation* (*TAMC*), Xi'an, April 2008, pp. 1-19.

[41] A. Blum, K. Ligett and A. Roth, "A Learning Theory Approach to Non-Interactive Database Privacy," *Proceedings of the 40th annual ACM Symposium on Theory of Computing* (*STOC*), Victoria, 2008, pp. 609-618.

[42] X. Xiao and Y. Tao, "Anatomy: Simple and Effective Privacy-Preservation," *Proceedings of the International Conference on Very Large Data Bases* (*VLDB*), Seoul, 2006, pp. 139-150.

[43] N. Maheshwarkar, K. Pathak and V. Chourey, "Privacy Issues for k-Anonymity Model," *International Journal of Engineering Research*, Vol. 1, No. 4, 2011, pp. 1857-1861.

[44] X. Hu, Z. Sun, Y. Wu, W. Hu and J. Dong, "k-Anonymity Based on Sensitive Tuples," *First International Workshop on Database Technology and Applications*, Wuhan, 25-26 April 2009, pp. 91-94.

14

A Forensic Traceability Index in Digital Forensic Investigation

Siti Rahayu Selamat*, **Shahrin Sahib, Nor Hafeizah, Robiah Yusof, Mohd Faizal Abdollah**
Faculty of Information and Communication Technology, Universiti Teknikal Malaysia Melaka, Melaka City, Malaysia

ABSTRACT

Digital crime inflicts immense damage to users and systems and now it has reached a level of sophistication that makes it difficult to track its sources or origins especially with the advancements in modern computers, networks and the availability of diverse digital devices. Forensic has an important role to facilitate investigations of illegal activities and inappropriate behaviors using scientific methodologies, techniques and investigation frameworks. Digital forensic is developed to investigate any digital devices in the detection of crime. This paper emphasized on the research of traceability aspects in digital forensic investigation process. This includes discovering of complex and huge volume of evidence and connecting meaningful relationships between them. The aim of this paper is to derive a traceability index as a useful indicator in measuring the accuracy and completeness of discovering the evidence. This index is demonstrated through a model (*TraceMap*) to facilitate the investigator in tracing and mapping the evidence in order to identify the origin of the crime or incident. In this paper, tracing rate, mapping rate and offender identification rate are used to present the level of tracing ability, mapping ability and identifying the offender ability respectively. This research has a high potential of being expanded into other research areas such as in digital evidence presentation.

Keywords: Digital Forensic Investigation; Traceability; Tracing Rate; Mapping Rate; Offender Identification Rate; Forensic Traceability Index; Trace Pattern

1. Introduction

Forensic or forensic science is the term given to an investigation of a crime using scientific means or used to describe crime detection in general. It is the application of a broad spectrum of sciences to answer questions of interest to a legal system. The emergence of forensic comes from the incidence of criminal, illegal and inappropriate behaviors.

The field of forensic science is vast. The majority of the public are probably exposed to only a few different types of forensic. A sub-discipline of forensic known as digital forensic is developed to investigate any digital devices in the detection of crime. With the development of modern computers, network and the internet, computer-related crimes have become a threat to society because of the immense damage it can inflict while at the same time it has reached a level of sophistication. This sophistication makes tracking the sources difficult.

This paper highlights the tracking issues or also known as traceability aspects due to the complexity of the crime in digital forensic investigation process. The current tra-

ceability of cybercrimes basically allows two consequences. First is to identify the scope of an attack instead of the actual attacker and second is to assess the liability of an organization [1]. However, according to [1-3], there was a critical need to deal with issue of origin identification and cross referencing in investigation process. Hence, traceability is not only important to avoid misleading in decision making but also to ensure the valuable information collected is complete and accurate. A methodology to overcome the traceability issue in digital forensic investigation process is developed by introducing the evidence tracing and mapping procedures. These procedures were later used to formulate the traceability index. The ability to trace and map the evidence complete and accurately could assist in practitioner decision making.

2. Related Work

2.1. Digital Forensic Investigation Framework

A common definition of digital forensic is the use of scientifically derived and proven methods toward the process of preservation, collection, validation, identification,

*Corresponding author.

analysis, interpretation, documentation, and presentation of digital evidence which is derived from the digital sources [4]. The purpose of these processes is to facilitate the reconstruction of events or to help anticipate illegal actions. [5] had simplified the definition as the process of preservation, identification, extraction, documentation and interpretation of computer media for evidentiary and (or) root cause analysis.

Though to some researchers the digital forensic is inclusive of computer forensic, network forensic, software forensic and information forensic, but it is largely used interchangeably with computer forensic [3]. Computer forensic implies a connection between computers, the scientific method, and crime detection. It includes devices other than general-purpose computer systems such as network devices, cell phones, and other devices with embedded systems. There are over hundreds of digital forensic investigation procedures developed in digital forensic investigation practices. An organization tends to develop its own procedures and some focused on the technology aspects such as data acquisition or data analysis [6]. Most of these procedures were developed in tackling different technology used in the inspected device. As a result, when underlying technology of the target device changes, new procedures have to be developed. However, [7,8] stated that the process of the investigation should be incorporated with the basic procedures in forensic investigation which are preparation, investigation and presentation. A categorization of investigation process was done in [9] to group and merge the similar activities or processes in five phases that provide the same output. The phases are: Phase 1 (Preparation), Phase 2 (Collection and Preservation), Phase 3 (Examination and Analysis), Phase 4 (Presentation and Reporting), and Phase 5 (Disseminating the case). The researcher also proposed a mapping process of digital forensic investigation process model to eliminate the redundancy of the process involved in the model and standardize the terms used in achieving the investigation goal.

The analysis emphasized that most of the frameworks consist of Phase 2 (Collection and Preservation), Phase 3 (Examination and Analysis), and Phase 4 (Presentation and Reporting) except Phase 1 and Phase 5. The analysis also propose that even though, Phase 1 and Phase 5 are not included in some of the framework, the study of [7,10-17] indicate the needs of both phases to confirm the completeness of the investigation. The purpose of Phase 1 comes in two objectives: 1) to approve that an investigation process can start and run in a proper procedure, and 2) to protect the chain of the evidence. The purpose of Phase 5 is to avoid the possibility of the incomplete investigation and lack of improvement in investigation procedures. From the analysis, it shows that an appropriate digital forensic investigation framework should at least consist of: Preparation Phase, Collection and Preservation Phase, Examination and Analysis Phase, Presentation and Reporting, and Disseminating the case. From the work done in [9], this paper focused on the Collection and Preservation Phase which has been identified as one of the critical phases of the digital forensic investigation process model. The Collection and Preservation Phase is where the digital evidence is identified, collected and preserved which then is analyzed and extracted to be presented in a court of law. However, to make it acceptable in court, there are two issues to be considered: the digital evidence itself and the collection process.

2.2. Characteristic Issues of Digital Evidence

[18] addressed four issues of digital evidence itself. First, the digital evidence is in a disorganized form and as such it can be very difficult to handle and not all of them is obviously readable by human. For example, a hard drive platter contains messy pieces of information mixed together and layered on top of each other over time. Because of that, only a small portion of the information is relevant to the case which makes it necessary to extract useful pieces, fit them together and translate them into a form that can be interpreted. Second, digital evidence generally is an abstraction of some event or digital object and can be seen as residual data that give a partial view of what occurred in the incident being investigated. Third, digital evidence can be maliciously altered or changed during collection without leaving any obvious trace indicating that alteration has taken place. This is due to the fact that computer data can be easily manipulated. Lastly, traditional evidences are created and retrieved as a single record but in a great majority of modern cases, it involves computerized system where evidence is created or retrieved from different records and sources.

2.3. Managing Issues in the Collection Process of Digital Evidence

In the collection process, the issues are the approach on collecting, analyzing and presenting the evidence. During collection process, the evidence is related to the aspect on how the evidence is searched, collected, analyzed, presented and documented without tampering the evidence and preserving the chain of evidence. In analyzing the evidence, the issue is about the aspect on the process of analysis. These cover all aspects such as the tools that are used for the analysis, the person responsible for the analysis and the integrity of the evidence. During the analysis process, the analysis tools used must be legally accepted, performed by experts or qualified person, and the evidence is not tampered. The issue on presenting the evidence is concerned with the approach of presenting and documenting the evidence in an understandable manner to non-technical person such as jury and judge.

Another problem during the collection process is the diversity of devices. In network, these devices generate a huge volume of evidence [19-21]. This situation leads to difficulty in identifying sources of the potential evidence or in tracing the evidence as stated in [22]. As it is important to obtain acceptable evidence in the court of law, the investigation must be successfully performed without tampering the evidence and also able to prove the evidence is legitimate. To solve the problem mentioned above, the ability to track, link and preserve the chain of evidence in huge volume of evidence is crucial. Hence, the traceability is one of the important elements during the digital forensic investigation process in identifying the origin and become the first challenge in the investigation as mentioned in [1-3].

2.4. The Tracing and Mapping in Digital Forensic Traceability

Traceability gives meaningful information through the study of the related links. The collected digital evidence must give appropriate information or meanings to the collector. The information cannot be attained via single digital evidence as it is meaningless [23-26]. Therefore, to avoid meaningless information, the link between the collected digital evidence must be identified. The objective of traceability is to identify and track real or imaginary objects through a process chain [28]. Given the origin of an object, traceability provides the opportunity to track a chain of events, or to predict process outcomes. The definition of traceability can be broad due to the complexity of it processes and the way it implemented [29,30]. For example, in networks, traceability refers to how difficult it is to establish the source and destination of communications on computers and communication networks.

In this paper, traceability is defined as the ability to trace and map the events of an incident from different sources in order to obtain useful evidence and well managed. In order to have the evidence well managed, the works of [31-33] suggested that traceability can be established from the source evidence to its lower level evidence and from the lower level evidence back to their sources. This situation brings the concept of forward and backward traceability or called as bidirectional traceability approach as discussed by [33,34]. The concept was used and further extend as an enhanced traceability model discussed in [35]. The discussed traceability model consists of definition, production and extraction. This model established the concepts of trace and map within the traceability: The process of establishing the structures is referred as tracing the digital evidence, whereas the

process of putting the structure according to the hypothesis/scenario is referred as mapping the digital evidence. Next, the construction of tracing and mapping procedures from the model are explained.

3. Method

In this section, the experimental design to establish the trace and map concepts in traceability from the perspective of digital forensic investigation is presented. It is note that while the traceability model is adapted from other domain, the model structure is able to be implemented in digital forensic investigation due to its compatibility and capability. We present the data collection and data analysis through a controlled experiment for data scenario using malware intrusion. The findings from the analysis will be used as the primary guideline to establish the generic incident trace pattern. The components of the trace pattern are used to formulate the traceability index for digital forensic investigation process.

3.1. Inquisition of Incident Scenario

In this research, a controlled experiment is designed to run the worm intrusion, to collect logs from each of the devices involved and to design the intrusion scenario. The design is motivated by [36]. In Rahmani et al. research, the experiment is focusing on DDoS attack that involves few processes which are declare attack setup, run selected attack, collect logged MIB variables and analyze result. It consists of four processes: Network Environment Setup, Attack Activation, Incident Log Collection and Incident Log Analysis as described in [37, 38].

In this experiment, the worm intrusion is launched and the intrusion activities are captured in the selected logs which are personal firewall log, security log, system log, application log, IDS log, tcpdump and Wireshark log. The researchers have collected all logs generated during the experiment and nine intrusion scenarios are derived based on the log analysis are identified. For the purpose of this paper, Scenario A as depicted in **Figure 1** is selected as the example. **Figure 1** illustrates the incident scenarios of Blaster A (Scenario A). In this incident scenario, the attack is activated in host *Mohd* and this host is successfully exploited all hosts except for hosts *Ramly*, *Abdollah*, *Roslan* and *Sahib*. Subsequently, one of the infected hosts, *Selamat* has organized an attack on host *Ramly*. In this incident scenario, the hosts that are marked with 1,354,444 and 69 are indicated as have been successfully being exploited by the attacker and have been infected. The hosts that are marked with 135 and 4444 demonstrated the attacker has already opened the backdoor but has not successfully transferred the exploit codes through *port* 69.

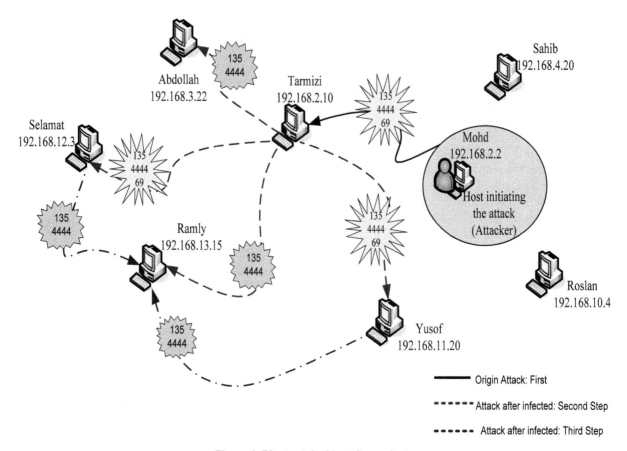

Figure 1. Blaster A incident-Scenario A.

3.2. Identification of Incident Trace Pattern

An attack pattern is defined as a mechanism to capture and communicate at the attacker perspective that shows the common methods for exploiting software, system or network [39-41]. It describes how an attack is performed, how the security pattern is enumerates to defeat the attack, and how to trace an attack once it has occurred [42,43]. It provides a systematic description of the attack goals and attack strategies to defend and trace the attack. Attack patterns can guide forensic investigators in searching the evidence. This also helps them at the data collection phase to determine and identify all the components to be collected, decide the priority of the data, find the location of the components and collect data from each of the component during the investigation process [43]. In general, attack pattern is very important in providing a way to protect the system from any potential attack. The existing researches done by [39-43] reveal an attack pattern is a type of pattern that focuses on the attacker perspective while victim perspective is omitted. In forensic view, both perspectives are important. A victim or attacker can be identified based on the traces data found in the attack pattern analysis. In forensic, these traces data are represent in the form of trace pattern to determine how a crime is being committed.

Trace pattern is defined as a regular way of process discovering the origin or starting point of a scenario that has happened. It is an essential element in helping investigator in finding evidence of crime or incident. For example, in a digital crime the evidence can be found in any digital devices. The objective of these patterns is to provide clear view on how an attack is performed and its impact.

Based on the previous work done in [37,38,44,45], three generic malware incident trace pattern for victim perspective, attacker perspective and multistep attacker perspective are established by observing the traces leave on the selected logs. For example, the generic malware incident trace pattern for victim perspective is depicted in **Figure 2**.

Figure 2 depicts the *generic malware incident trace pattern* for victim perspective consists of the incident traces (evidence) from host level and network level. In host level, three main events of the incident occur. The events are *scan event*, *exploit event* and *impact/effect event*. In this level, the *scan event* and *exploit event* occur in the *personal firewall log*. Whereas the incident traces of the *impact/effect event* are found in the *system log*, *application log* and *security log*.

In this research, the *personal firewall log* is identified

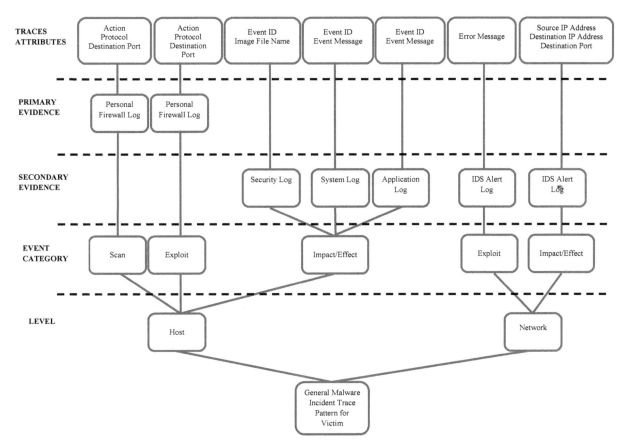

Figure 2. Generic malware incident trace pattern-victim perspective.

as the *primary evidence* and the generic attributes of this log are *action*, *protocol* and *destination port*. The *security log*, *application log* and *system log* are considered as the *secondary evidence* and the generic attributes of these logs are *event id*, *image filename* and *event message*.

In network level, only two main events occurred namely *exploit event* and *impact/effect event*. In this level, the *exploit event* and *impact/effect event* exist in the IDS *alert log*. This IDS *alert log* is considered as *secondary evidence* and the generic attributes of this log are *error message*, s*ource IP address*, *destination IP address* and *destination port*. The attribute of *error message* indicates the exploiting activities and the attributes of s*ource IP address*, *destination IP address* and *destination port* indicate the impact of the attack that shows the offender of the incident (*victim*, *attacker* or *multi-step attacker*).

In contrast, the *generic malware incident trace pattern* for attacker perspective consists of incident traces from host level and network level. In these levels, three events (*scan*, *exploit* and *impact/effect*) of the incidents occur at the host level and two events (*scan* and *impact/effect*) occur at the network level. The events at the network level show the difference between the *generic malware incident trace pattern* for victim perspective and *generic malware incident trace pattern* for attacker perspective.

In victim perspective, it consists of *exploit event* and *impact/effect event* as highlighted in **Figure 2** with the traces attributes are *source IP address*, *destination IP address*, *destination port* and *error message* compared to attacker perspective trace pattern, it consists of *scan event* and *impact/effect event* with the traces attributes are *error message* and *source IP address*. The *generic malware incident trace pattern* for multistep attacker perspective is similar to the *generic malware incident trace pattern* for victim perspective except for *impact/effect* in network log. The considered traces attributes are only *destination IP address* and *destination port* for victim; and *error message* and *source IP address* for multistep attacker incident trace pattern.

3.3. Constructing Tracing and Mapping Procedures

The generic malware *victim*, *attacker* and *multi-step attacker incident trace pattern* then are used in formulating the tracing and mapping evidence procedures to demonstrate the ability of trace and map evidence (traceability) in digital forensic investigation process. Tracing evidence procedures are necessary in order to extract the incident traces from the logs [46]. However, the extracted traces are meaningless without knowing the relation between those traces; hence identifying the relationships are important. These relationships can be identified by mapping or linking process [47].

In this research, mapping the evidence is connecting or linking all traces discovered from the tracing activities by correlating the traces with the origin of the traces. The purpose of this mapping is to provide evidence that can answer the questions about the incident occurred. The mapping also is an aid to diagnostic the decision regarding to the incident. Due to the important of tracing and mapping evidence in digital forensic investigation process, the tracing and mapping procedures are formulated based on the proposed generic malware incident trace pattern as shown in **Figures 3** and **4** respectively.

As shown in **Figure 3**, the tracing processes are initially started at the *personal firewall log* followed by *security log*, *system log*, *application log* and IDS *alert log*. The aim of these tracing processes is to examine the traces left in the logs by focusing the traces of three main events of an incident which are *scan, exploit and impact/effect*. *Scan* events can only be found in *personal firewall log*, while *exploit* events can be found in both *personal firewall log* and IDS *alert log*. The *impact/effect* events can be found in *system, security* and *application logs*.

For example, the tracing procedure for tracing the incident traces from the *personal firewall log* starts with tracing the traces attributes identified in the proposed generic incident trace pattern. The traces attributes are perspective *IP address, action, protocol* and *destination*

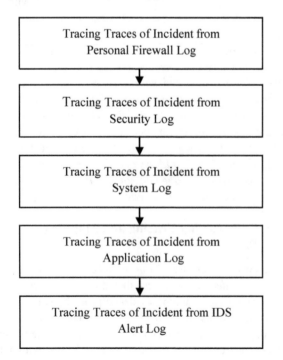

Figure 3. Tracing procedures for tracing evidence of malware incident.

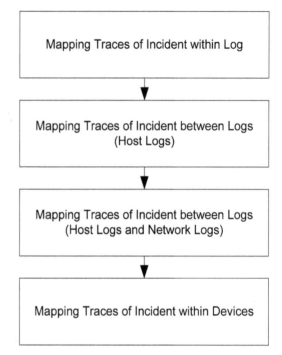

Figure 4. Mapping procedures of incident traces.

port. The perspective *IP address* refers to the *destination IP address* or the *source IP address* of the perspective. *Action* indicates the perspective is trying to open the connection. *Protocol* and *destination port* show an attack is attempted to establish the communication. In this tracing process, any relevant set of traces that consist of *destination port* (x), *action* (y) and *protocol* (z) that are found in the *personal firewall log* is assigned as trace P.

The tracing begin with some assumptions:

Let $Dp(x)$ = the set of all vulnerable destination ports that is used by malware in the incident

Let $Act(y)$ = the set of all actions that is used by malware in the incident

Let $Pr(z)$ = the set of all protocols that is used by malware in the incident

Let $P_n(x,y,z)$ = set of traces in personal firewall log

A predicate is established that defines the traces as below:

$$\forall x \forall y \forall z \big((Dp(x) \wedge Act(y) \wedge Pr(z)) \rightarrow \exists P_n(x,y,z) \big) \ (1)$$

which can defines that for all vulnerable destination port x, action y and protocol z, there exists trace of an incident from personal firewall log, such that $P_n(x,y,z)$.

The incident traces found from the tracing procedures are then mapped to show the relationship of the evidence of the incident discovered during the investigation process. The mapping procedures are depicted in **Figure 4**.

Figure 4 illustrates the mapping procedures of the incident traces discovered from the tracing process. Firstly, the traces that are discovered from the tracing process are mapped within logs. For example, the traces discovered in *personal firewall log* are mapped with the traces discovered in the same log.

Secondly, the traces that are mapped from the first mapping process are further mapped between logs. For example, the traces discovered in *personal firewall log* are mapped to the traces discovered in *security log*.

Thirdly, the traces that are mapped from the second mapping process are further mapped to the logs that are in different level of communication layer. For example, the traces mapped from the host logs (*personal firewall log, security log, system log and application log*) are further mapped to network log (IDS *alert log*).

Finally, the traces that are mapped from the third mapping process are further mapped within devices. For example, the mapped traces that belong to the same devices will be mapped and merged to the same devices. In this research, the traces will be tagged for each new mapped trace. The objective of this tagging is to show the traces are already mapped between one trace to another trace either belongs to same log (within log), different logs (between logs), same level (host logs), different level (host and network logs) or same devices (within devices).

For example, in the mapping procedures for mapping traces of incident between logs (host log), the identified incident traces from specified host log are mapped within the same host. This mapping is required to identify the

relationship of the relevant incident traces at host level. In this process, the traces of incident in *security log* SE_m are firstly mapped to the incident traces in *system log* SY_m. The traces that are mapped are assigned to a new mapped trace $TM(SE_m, SY_m)$. These traces, $TM(SE_m, SY_m)$ are further mapped with the incident traces in *personal firewall log* P_m to produce a new mapped trace and assigned the trace as $TM(SE_m, SY_m, P_m)$. Finally, the mapped traces $TM(SE_m, SY_m, P_m)$ are further mapped with *application log* AP_m to produce the complete mapped traces from host log and assigned as $TM(SE_m, SY_m, P_m, AP_m)$.

In this research, the *security log* is identified as one of the important logs for malware incident; therefore the unmapped traces of incident in *security log* also are mapped with the traces of incident in *personal firewall log*. This mapping process produces a new mapped traces and assigned as $TM(SE_n, P_m, AP_m)$. Hence, these mapping procedures can produce three types of mapped traces that consist of traces of incident from logs selected in this research: $TM(SE_m, SY_m, P_m, AP_m), TM(SE_n, P_m, AP_m)$ and $TM(SE_m, SY_m, P_m, AP_m)$. These mapping procedures are summarized as illustrated in **Figure 5**.

These tracing and mapping procedures have been implemented on the proposed model in the previous work

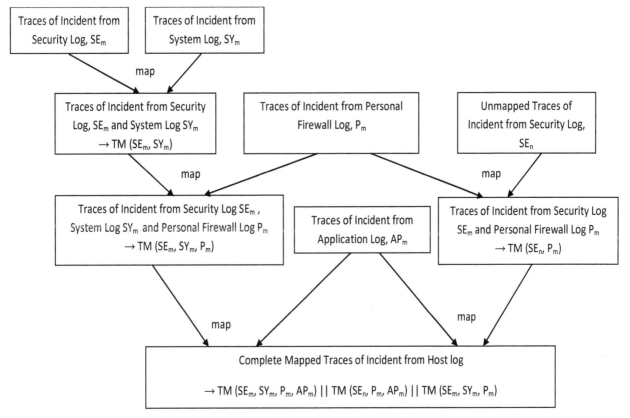

Figure 5. Mapping procedures for host incident traces.

done and discussed in [35,48]. A prototype version is developed in order to demonstrate the proposed model that called as *TraceMap* and can benefit the digital forensic investigation research and community. The *TraceMap* consist of generic trace pattern structure, tracing and mapping procedure, and offender identification procedure. Twelve datasets are seed into the *TraceMap* implementation and the result is generated as an incident report.

4. Results

The objective of this section is to identify the ability of the tracing and mapping procedures in the *TraceMap* implementation to discover the incident traces. This could facilitate the investigator in identifying the origin of the incident. In this research, three main capabilities need to be measured to identify the effectiveness of the *TraceMap*. The capabilities are tracing capability, mapping capability and offender identification capability. Thus, the metrics for evaluation are formulated and further discussed in next subsection paper.

4.1. Forensic Traceability Measurement

According to [49], there is a need for security metrics in digital forensic that: 1) meet legal requirements for measureable reliability, authenticity, accuracy and precision, 2) based on a sound scientific methodology properly applied, and 3) have a basis provided for independent testing. Unfortunately, the digital forensic metric is not yet formulated and there is no industry consensus that a judge and jury can rely upon as adequate to support a claim and meet legal requirements for measurable reliability, authenticity, accuracy, and precision. These are currently elusive and must be constructed on a case-by-case basis. Due to this reason, it is possible to transfer concepts from another research area to build a metric to be used in the current research as described in [50]. Therefore, this research is proposed to transfer concepts from another research area to build a metric to measure the effectiveness of the tracing evidence (incident traces), mapping evidence (incident traces), and identifying the origin of the incident.

Two metrics from other research domain, namely information retrieval and IDS information theory is explained to be used to build a metric for digital forensic. The aim is to measure the capability of tracing the incident traces and to measure the capability of mapping the incident traces in the *TraceMap* respectively.

In the concept of information retrieval, two metrics are used to measure the information retrieval; recall and precision. In the field of information retrieval, precision is the fraction of retrieved documents that are relevant to the search whereas recall is the fraction of the documents

that are relevant to the query that are successfully retrieved [51]. This concept has been used in measuring the performance of the digital forensic investigation tools such as FTK^{TM} and Encase^{TM} by measuring the query precision and query recall [52]. However, the classic precision-recall trade-off dilemma is that as recall increases, the query precision decreases. While digital forensic seeks recall rates at or near 100%, query precision is usually low [53]. Thus, based on the aim of transferring the concept of information retrieval mentioned previously, the recall metric is adapted due to the aim of the tracing evidence (incident traces) in this research is to retrieve all relevant incident traces to the hypothesis (query). This metric is used to measure the capability of tracing evidence (incident traces) and later known as *Tracing Rate* (TC_R).

Tracing Rate (TC_R) is the ratio of relevant traces discovered (output), $N_{relevant\_traces}$ and the total traces (input), N_{total_traces}. This metric is represented as in Equation (2):

$$TC_R = \frac{N_{relevant\_traces}}{N_{total\_traces}} \qquad (2)$$

where:

$N_{relevant\_traces}$ is the number of relevant traces discovered (output) from all potential sources of evidence.

N_{total_traces} is the number of the traces (input) from all potential sources of evidence.

Equation (2) is used to evaluate the effectiveness of the tracing process of the *TraceMap*. The result from this evaluation is used to demonstrate the capability of tracing evidence (incident traces) for digital forensic investigation process.

[54] uses the concepts of information theory to motivate an information theoretic metric for IDS. This metric is used to measure the capability of detecting the intrusion which is known as Intrusion Detection Capability (C_{ID}). C_{ID} is the ratio of mutual information between IDS input and output $I(X,Y)$ and the entropy $H(X)$ of the input that can be expressed as $C_{ID} = I(X,Y)/H(X)$. The mutual information $I(X;Y)$ corresponds to the intersection of the information in X with the information in Y. The entropy $H(X)$ is the sum of the mutual information of X and Y. Thus, based on the aim of transferring the concept of information theory used for IDS mentioned previously, this metric is adapted in this research, in which the mutual information $I(X;Y)$ is referred to the relevant incident traces that are mapped or connected. As a result, this metric is used to measure the capability of mapping the incident traces and is later known as *Mapping Rate* (MP_R).

Mapping Rate (MP_R) is the ratio of the output traces that are relevant and mapped, $N_{relevant\_map\_traces}$ and the input traces that are relevant, $N_{relevant\_traces}$. This metric is represented as in Equation (3):

$$MP_R = \frac{N_{relevant\_map\_traces}}{N_{relevant\_traces}} \qquad (3)$$

where:

$N_{relevant\_map\_traces}$ is the number of traces that is part of incident is relevant and mapped

$N_{relevant\_traces}$ is the number of the traces relevant traces

Equation 3 is used to evaluate the effectiveness of the mapping procedures of the *TraceMap* on mapping the relevant traces of the incident within and between *sources of evidence*. The result from the evaluation is used to demonstrate the capability of mapping the incident traces for digital forensic investigation process.

In order to identify the evidence origin, there is a need to determine the rate of successfully origin found from the mapped traces. To achieve this, another metric is proposed named as *Offender Identification Rate (OI_R)*. This metric is significant in identifying the offenders (perspectives) of the incident. The *Offender Identification Rate (OI_R)* is the ratio of mapped incident traces that are matched with the incident trace pattern, $N_{tracepattern\_traces}$ and the number of traces that are relevant and mapped, $N_{relevant\_map\_traces}$. This metric is represented as in Equation (4):

$$OI_R = \frac{N_{tracepattern\_traces}}{N_{relevant\_map\_traces}} \qquad (4)$$

where:

$N_{tracepattern\_traces}$ is the number of mapped traces that can match with the perspective incident trace pattern.

$N_{relevant\_map\_traces}$ is the number of the traces that is relevant and mapped.

Equation (4) is used to evaluate the effectiveness of the *TraceMap* and the result from the evaluation is used to demonstrate the capability of identifying the offender or the origin of the incident.

4.2. The Significant Findings of Tracing Process

According to [52,53], the percentage of tracing rate and mapping rate imply the effectiveness level of the *TraceMap*. To be specific, in order to indicate it effectiveness, the range of the rate percentage of TC_R should be at or near 100% [52]. However, to the best of our knowledge, the range of rate percentage of MP_R has not been mentioned specifically in any research. Thus, in this paper, to show the accuracy of the incident traces, the level of MP_R rate should be close to TC_R rate.

The effectiveness of the tracing process, mapping process and offender identification process is measured using the metrics proposed in this research. The metrics

are *Tracing Rate (TC_R)*, *Mapping Rate (MP_R)* and *Offender Identification Rate (OI_R)*. The objective of tracing is to discover the relevant incident traces of the incident. By using the proposed TC_R metric, the results show the *TraceMap* is able to discover the relevant incident traces and could answer the incident from the range of 82.60% to 99.17%. The relevant traces discovered to the irrelevant traces discovered are compared as depicted in **Figure 6**.

The graph in **Figure 6** shows that there is significant result in relevant incident traces especially in DS7, DS8 and DS9. Overall, using the *TraceMap*, the relevant traces are 82.60% to 99.17% while irrelevant traces are 0.83% to 17.40%. It means that out of 100 reported potential evidence for Incident A, the probability of successfully evidence traced as relevant to that particular incident is as maximum as 99%.

4.3. The Comprehensiveness of Mapping Process

In this research, the process of mapping is divided into four stages. The stages are mapping the incident traces within log, mapping the incident traces between logs (host logs), mapping the incident traces between logs (network logs) and mapping the incident traces within devices (hosts). In this process, the result from each stage becomes the input to the next stage. For example, the result obtained from the first stage (mapping incident traces within log) will be used as the input to the second stage (mapping incident traces between logs). For each stage, the mapping rates are measured using the mapping metric as in Equation (4). The summary of the result generated is depicted in **Table 1**.

In **Table 1**, the second column (Stage 1) demonstrates the process of mapping the incident traces within host logs or sensor logs in which the percentage of the mapping rates are in the range of 82.60% to 99.96%. These rates show most of the relevant incident traces discovered has been mapped. It shows the number of traces that are relevant and mapped is consistent to the number of relevant traces discovered. These results indicate the effectiveness of the mapping process for mapping the incident traces within logs in which the most significant result shown in DS4, DS5 and DS6 with the percentage of mapping rates are 99.90%, 99.95% and 99.96% respectively.

The third column (Stage II) demonstrates the mapping process of the incident traces between logs. The result in this column implies that the incident traces from the mapping incident traces within log is the most relevant traces to be mapped. It shows that all relevant traces discovered from different *sources of evidence* are the most relevant traces that can be mapped between the logs belong to the same devices or hosts with the percentage of

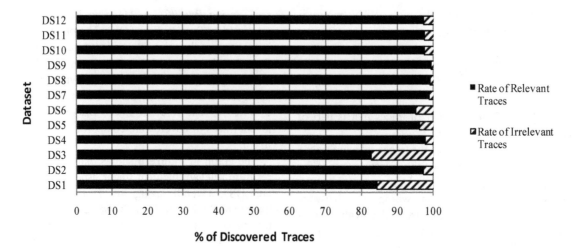

Figure 6. Rates of Relevant and Irrelevant Traces of Incident.

Table 1. Summary of mapping rate (MP_R).

Dataset	Stage 1	Stage II	Stage III	Stage IV
	% of Mapping Rate MP_R	% of Mapping Rate MP_R	% of Mapping Rate, MP_R	% of Mapping Rate, MP_R
DS1	97.61	100.00	69.57	100.00
DS2	97.08	100.00	82.86	100.00
DS3	82.60	100.00	66.67	100.00
DS4	99.90	100.00	81.48	100.00
DS5	99.95	100.00	87.80	100.00
DS6	99.96	100.00	63.89	100.00
DS7	99.31	100.00	77.27	100.00
DS8	99.21	100.00	78.38	100.00
DS9	98.92	100.00	74.29	100.00
DS10	99.29	100.00	93.62	100.00
DS11	99.10	100.00	78.57	100.00
DS12	99.14	100.00	85.71	100.00

the mapping rates are at 100%. These results indicate the process of mapping the incident traces between logs for host logs are effective and capable to map all relevant traces successfully.

The fourth column (Stage III) depicts the percentage of the *Mapping Rate* (MP_R) achieved in this process is in the range of 66.67% to 93.62% with the highest rate is obtained from Dataset 10 (DS10) and the lowest rate is obtained from Dataset 3 (DS3). These rates show the incident traces from network log is not probable to be mapped with the incident traces from host. These also reveal that it is difficult to prove the incident has happened based on the evidence provided from network and this cause the origin identification of the incident become

difficult. These findings show that some of the traces from the network log are considered as false alarm which is unrelated with the traces discovered in the host log. Even though the percentage of the mapping rate in this stage indicates a low rate because only one dataset has achieved the high percentage which is 93.62% compared to other dataset (66.67% to 87.80%). But, this mapping process is still effective since the mapping procedure in this stage is able to determine the relationship between traces from host log and traces from network log.

Finally, the last column (Stage IV) shows the percentage of the MP_R is 100% for all dataset evaluated. These rates demonstrate the results from the third mapping process are the most relevant traces of the incident. The rates also show the mapping process is completed in which all relevant incident traces are mapped.

4.4. The Use of Trace Pattern for Successfulness Offender Identification

The purpose of metric used in this process is to measure the effectiveness of *TraceMap* to assist the investigator in identifying all potential offenders involved in incident. In this research, the offender is named as perspective; *victim*, *attacker* and *multi-step attacker* (*victim/attacker*). The *Offender identification Rate* (OI_R) is calculated using Equation 3 and the result generated is shows in **Table 2**.

As shown in **Table 2**, the percentage rate for offender identification calculated from DS1 is 100% which indicates the offender has been successfully identified from all relevant incident traces mapped and matched with the hypothesis formulated at the beginning of the investigation process.

In the case of DS1, seven offenders (perspectives) are identified with four of them are victims, one attacker and two are multi-step attacker (victim/attacker). Although the percentage of the OI_R is 100% for all datasets as depicted in **Table 2**, three (DS2, DS3 and DS12) out of twelve dataset are unsuccessful in identifying the true attacker. These results are gained due to the traces identified are not documented in any logs selected in this research. However, in such cases, the attacker can still be identified by analyzing the multi-step attacker (victim/attacker) traces.

5. Derivation of Traceability Metric in Digital Forensic Investigation Process

As shown in Section IV, the traceability metric in this research, consists of *Tracing Rate* (*TC_R*), *Mapping Rate* (*MP_R*) and *Offender Identification Rate* (*OI_R*).
where:

n as the maximum number of stage and i as the current stage

$N_{relevant\_traces}$ is the number of relevant traces discovered (output) from all potential sources of evidence

N_{total_traces} is the number of the traces (input) from all potential sources of evidence

$N_{relevant\_map\_traces}$ is the number of traces that is part of incident that is relevant and mapped

$N_{relevant\_traces\_TC}$ is the number of the traces relevant traces discovered (output) given by TC

$N_{relevant\_map\_traces\_MP\_stage\_of\_n}$ is the number of traces that is part of incident is relevant and mapped given by MP at the stage n

$N_{relevant\_traces\_MP}$ is the number of the traces relevant traces discovered (output) given by MP

$N_{tracepattern\_traces}$ is the number of mapped traces that can match with the perspective incident trace pattern,

given by $N_{relevant\_map\_traces\_MP\_stage\_of\_n}$

Hence, the whole metric for traceability in digital forensic investigation process is derived as follow:

Tracing process equation:

$$TC = \frac{N_{relevant\_traces}}{N_{total\_traces}} \qquad (5)$$

TC is used as N relevant traces in $MP_{stage\_of\_i}$ for mapping process.

Mapping process Equation for stage $1 \cdots n$:

$$MP_{stage\_of\_i} = \frac{N_{relevant\_map\_traces}}{N_{relevant\_traces\_TC}} \qquad (6)$$

$$MP_{stage\_of\_i+1}$$

$$= \frac{N_{relevant\_map\_trace\_MP\_stage\_of\_i+1}}{N_{relevant\_traces\_TC} - N_{relevant\_map\_trace\_MP\_stage\_of\_i}} \qquad (7)$$

Therefore, the generic mapping process equation:

$$MP = \frac{N_{relevant\_map\_traces}}{N_{relevant\_traces}} \qquad (8)$$

In order to complete the traceability of forensic, the identification of the origin is determined by the offender identification equation:

$$OI = \frac{N_{relevant\_map\_traces\_MP\_stage\_of\_n}}{N_{relevant\_map\_traces\_MP} - N_{relevant\_map\_trace\_MP\_Stage\_of\_n}} \qquad (9)$$

$$\infty = \frac{N_{tracepattern\_traces}}{N_{relevant\_map\_traces}} \qquad (10)$$

Thus, a traceability index for digital forensic investigation process named as *Forensic Traceability Index* is defined as:

$$TraceIndex_{forensic} = \left(TC, \sum_{i=1}^{n} MP, OI \right) \qquad (11)$$

where the output of TC is used as the input of MP and the result of MP is used to identify the *OI*.

This $TraceIndex_{forensic}$ is a useful indicator in measuring the accuracy and the completeness of evidence. The results obtained prove that the *TraceMap* is an effective model that supports the tracing and mapping evidence to overcome the traceability problem in digital forensic investigation process.

6. Conclusions

This paper introduces an approach to overcome traceability issues in digital forensic investigation process. The approach which consists of generic trace pattern, and tracing and mapping procedure was embedded in a model named as *TraceMap*. This *TraceMap* is used to provide an effective way to trace and map digital evi-

Table 2. Summary of offender identification rate (OI_R).

Dataset	Total Relevant and Mapped Traces $N_{relevant\_map\_traces}$	Total Trace Pattern Traces $N_{tracepattern\_traces}$	% of Offender Identification OI_R	Offender Identified		
				Victim	Attacker	Multi-step Attacker
DS1	7	7	100.00	4	1	2
DS2	7	7	100.00	3	0	4
DS3	8	8	100.00	5	0	3
DS4	4	4	100.00	2	1	1
DS5	4	4	100.00	1	1	2
DS6	4	4	100.00	2	1	1
DS7	4	4	100.00	1	1	2
DS8	8	8	100.00	2	1	5
DS9	7	7	100.00	2	1	4
DS10	8	8	100.00	4	1	3
DS11	8	8	100.00	5	1	2
DS12	8	8	100.00	5	0	3

dence in digital forensic investigation process specifically in collection and preservation phase. Thus, it facilitates the investigator in formulating the hypothesis, identifying, tracing, mapping and presenting the digital evidence.

In this *TraceMap*, the identification of offender is based on three primary events of incident which are *scan*, *exploit* and *impact/effect*. It could help the investigator in providing complete and accurate digital evidence to identify the origin of the incident.

The results obtained in the experiment demonstrates the *TraceMap* is able to discover the evidence, able to connect or map the evidence and able to identify the origin of the incident. These abilities are demonstrated through the result obtained using three metrics: *Tracing Rate* (TC_R) *Mapping Rate* (MP_R) and *Offender Identification Rate* (OI_R).

The *Tracing Rate* (TC_R) are used to demonstrate the ability of discovering the evidence, *Mapping Rate* (MP_R) is used to demonstrate the ability of mapping the evidence and *Offender Identification Rate* (OI_R) is used to demonstrate the ability of identifying the origin of the incident.

Based on these metrics, traceability index ($TraceIndex_{forensic}$) is derived that can be used in digital forensic investigation process to help the practitioner in measuring the accuracy and completeness of the evidence discovery. This research has a high potential of being expanded into other research areas such as in digital evidence presentation.

7. Acknowledgements

This research was kindly supported by Universiti Teknikal Malaysia Melaka and Ministry of Higher Education Malaysia.

REFERENCES

[1]   E. Casey and G. L. Palmer, "Digital Evidence and Computer Crime," 2nd Edition, Elsevier Academic Press, Cambridge, 2004.

[2]   D. Birk and C. Wegener, "Technical Issues of Forensic Investigations in Cloud Computing Environments," *Proceedings of the 6th International Workshop on Systematic Approaches to Digital Forensic Engineering*, 26-26 May 2011, Oakland, pp. 1-10.

[3]   P. Stephenson, "A Comprehensive Approach to Digital Incident Investigation," *Information Security Technical Report*, Vol. 8, No. 2, 2003, pp. 42-54.

[4]   G. Palmer, "A Road Map for Digital Forensic Research," Technical Report (DTR-T001-01) for Digital Forensic Research Workshop (DFRWS), New York, 2001.

[5]   W. Kruse and J. Heiser, "Computer Forensics: Incident Response Essentials," Addison Wesley, Indianapolis, 2002.

[6]   A. Brill and M. Pollitt, "The Evolution of Computer Forensic Best Practices: An Update on Programs and Publications," *Journal of Digital Forensic Practice*, Vol. 1, No. 1, 2006, pp. 3-11.

[7]   M. Kohn, J. Eloff and M. Olivier, "Framework for a Digital Forenisc Investigation," *Proceedings of the Information Security South Africa (ISSA) 2006 from Insight to Foresight Conference*, Sandton, 5-7 July 2006, pp. 1-7.

[8]   S. Satpathy, S. K. Pradhan and B. B. Ray, "A Digital

Investigation Tool based on Data Fusion in Management of Cyber Security Systems," *International Journal of Information Technology and Knowledge Management*, Vol. 2, No. 2, 2010, pp. 561-565.

[9]   S. S. Rahayu, Y. Robiah and S. Shahrin, "Mapping Process of Digital Forensic Investigation Framework," *International Journal of Computer Science and Network Security*, Vol. 8, No. 10, 2008, pp. 163-169.

[10] V. Baryamureeba and F. Tushabe, "The Enhanced Digital Investigation Process Model," *Proceedings of the Digital Forensic Research Workshop (DFRWS)*, 11-13 August 2004, Baltimore, pp. 1-9.

[11] B. Carrier and E. Spafford, "Getting Physical with the Digital Investigation Process," *International Journal of Digital Evidence*, Vol. 2, No. 2, 2003, pp. 1-21.

[12] S. Ó. Ciardhuáin, "An Extended Model of Cybercrime Investigations," *International Journal of Digital Evidence*, Vol. 3, No. 1, 2004, pp. 1-22.

[13] M. Roger, "DCSA: Applied Digital Crime Scene Analysis," Handbook of Information Security, New York, 2006.

[14] M. Reith, C. Carr and G. Gunsch, "An Examination of Digital Forensic Models," *International Journal of Digital Evidence*, Vol. 1, No. 3, 2002, pp. 1-12.

[15] N. L. Beebe and J. G. Clark, "A Hierarchical, Objectives-Based Framework for the Digital Investigations Process," *Proceedings of the Digital Forensic Research Workshop (DFRWS)*, Baltimore, 11-13 August 2004, pp. 146-166.

[16] F. C. Freiling and B. Schwittay, "A Common Process Model for Incident Response and Computer Forensics," *Proceedings of the Conference on IT Incident Management and IT Forensics*, Stuttgart, 11-13 September 2007, pp. 1-21.

[17] S. Perumal, "Digital Forensic Model Based on Malaysian Investigation Process," *International Journal of Computer Science and Network Security*, Vol. 9, No. 8, 2009, pp. 38-44.

[18] S. Rekhis, J. Krichene and N. Boudriga, "Cognitive-Maps Based Investigation of Digital Security Incident," *Proceedings of the Third International Workshop on Systematic Approaches to Digital Forensic Engineering*, Oakland, 22 May 2008, pp. 25-40.

[19] S. L. Garfinkel, "Digital Forensics Research: The next 10 Years," *Journal of Digital Investigation*, Vol. 7, 2010, pp. S64-S73.

[20] T. Lindsey, "Challenges in Digital Forensics," The Digital Forensic Research Workshop (DFRWS), New York, 2006.

[21] K. Nance, B. Hay and M. Bishop, "Digital Forensics: Defining a Research Agenda," *Proceedings of the 42nd Hawaii International Conference on System Sciences*, Big Island, 5-8 January 2009, pp. 1-6.

[22] C. Shields, O. Frieder and M. Maloof, "A System for the Proactive, Continuous and Efficient Collection of Digital Forensic Evidence," *Journal of Digital Investigation*, Vol. 8, 2011, pp. S3-S13.

[23] A. Ahmad, "The Forensic Chain-of-Evidence Model: Improving the Process of Evidence Collection in Incident Handling Procedures," *Proceedings of the 6th Asia Conference on Information Systems (PACIS 2002)*, 2-4 September 2002, Tokyo pp. 1-5.

[24] V. H. Bhat, P. G. Rao, R. V. Abhilash, P. D. Shenoy, K. R. Venugopal and L. M. Patnaik, "A Data Mining Approach for Data Generation and Analysis for Digital Forensic Application," *IACSIT International Journal of Engineering and Technology*, Vol. 2, No. 3, 2010, pp. 314-319.

[25] G. Giova, "Improving Chain of Custody in Forensic Investigation of Electronic Digital Systems," *International Journal of Computer Science and Network Security*, Vol. 11, No. 1, 2011, pp. 1-9.

[26] J. Herrerias and R. Gomez, "A Log Correlation Model to Support the Evidence Search Process in a Forensic Investigation," *Proceedings of the 2nd International Workshop on Systematic Approaches to Digital Forensic Engineering (SADFE'07)*, Bell Harbor, 10-12 April 2007, pp. 31-42.

[27] P. Sommer, "Intrusion Detection Systems as Evidence," *Computer Networks*, Vol. 31, No. 23, 1999, pp. 2477-2487.

[28] P. Oghazi, B. Palsson and K. Tano, "An Attempt to Apply Traceability to Grinding Circuits," *Proceedings of the Conference in Mineral Processing*, Lulea, 6-7 February 2007, pp. 169-183.

[29] R. Clayton, "Anonymity and Traceability in Cyberspace," Ph.D. Thesis, University of Cambridge, Cambridge, 2005.

[30] E. Golan, B. Krissoff, F. Kuchler, L. Calvin, K. Nelson and G. Price, "Traceability in the U.S. Food Supply: Economic Theory and Industry Studies," Department of Agriculture, Washington DC, 2004.

[31] G. Zemont, "Towards Value-Based Requirements Traceability," Master Thesis, DePaul University, Chicago, 2005.

[32] M. Narmanli, "A Business Rule Approach to Requirements Traceability," Master Thesis, Middle East Technical University, Ankara, 2010.

[33] Morckos, M. "Requirements Traceability," Report for School of Computer Science, University of Waterloo, Waterloo, 2011.

[34] L. Westfall, "Bidirectional Requirements Traceability," White Paper, The Westfall Team, Dallas, 2006.

[35] S. R. Selamat, R. Yusof, S. Sahib, M. F. Abdollah, M. Z. Mas'ud and I. Roslan, "Adapting Traceability in Digital Forensic Investigation Process," *Proceedings of the Malaysian Technical Universities International Conference on Engineering and Technology (MUiCET 2011)*, Johor, 13-15 November 2011, pp. 1-8.

[36] C. Rahmani, M. Sharifi and T. Tafazzoli, "An Exprimental Analysis of Proactive Detection of Distributed Denial of Service Attacks," *Proceedings of the IIT Kanpur Hacker's Workshop (IITKHACK04)*, Kanpur, 23-24 February 2004, pp. 37-44.

[37] S. R. Selamat, R. Yusof, S. Sahib, M. F. Abdollah, M. Z. Masud and I. Roslan, "Tracing Technique for Blaster Attack," *International Journal of Computer Science and Information Security*, Vol. 4, No. 1, 2009, pp. 1-8.

[38] S. R. Selamat, R. Yusof, S. Sahib, M. Z. Masud, I. Roslan and M. F. Abdollah, "Scenario Based Worm Trace Pattern Identification Technique," *International Journal of Computer Science and Information Security*, Vol. 7, No. 1, 2010, pp. 1-9.

[39] S. R. Selamat, R. Yusof, S. Sahib, M. Z. Masud, M. F. Abdollah and Z. Z. Abidin, "Advanced Trace Pattern for Computer Intrusion Discovery," *Journal of Computing*, Vol. 2, No. 6, 2010, pp. 200-207.

[40] G. Hoglund and G. McGraw, "Exploiting Software: How to Break Code," Addison-Wesley/Pearson, Indianapolis, 2004.

[41] A. Moore, R. Ellison and R. Linger, "Attack Modeling for Information Security and Survability. Technical Note (CMU/SEI-2001-TN-001) for Software," Carnegie Mellon University, Pittsburgh, 2001.

[42] B. Sean and S. Amit, "Introduction to Attack Patterns," 2006. https://buildsecurityin.us-cert.gov/

[43] Fernandez, E., Pelaez, J. and M. Larrondo-Petrie, "Attack Patterns: A New Forensic and Design Tool," *Advances in Digital Forensics III, Proceeding of Third Annual IFIP WG 11.9 International Conference of Digital Forensics*, 28-31 January 2007, Cozumel, pp. 345-357.

[44] K. Kent, S. Chevalier, T. Grance and H. Dang, "Guide to Integrating Forensic Techniques into Incident Response," National Institute of Standards and Technology (NIST), Gaithersburg, 2006,

[45] R. Yusof, S. R. Selamat, S. Sahib, M. F. Abdollah, M. Z. Masud and M. Ramly, "An Improved Traditional Worm Attack Pattern," *Proceedings of the 4th International Symposium on Information Technology* 2010 (*ITSIM* 2010), Kuala Lumpur, 17 June 2010, pp. 1067-1072.

[46] R. Yusof, S. R. Selamat, S. Sahib, M. F. Abdollah, M. Z. Mas'ud and M. Ramly, "A New Malware Attack Pattern Generalization," *Proceedings of the Malaysian Technical Universities International Conference on Engineering and Technology* (*MUiCET* 2011), Johor, 13-15 November 2011, pp. 20-29.

[47] J. Velasco, "A Guide to Electronic Evidence Collection Methodologies," White Paper, RenewData Corporation, Austin, 2007.

[48] A. Hassanzadeh and B. Sadeghiyan, "A Data Correlation Method for Anomaly Detection Systems using Regression Relations," *Proceedings of the* 1*st International Conference on Future Information Networks*, Beijing, 14-17 October 2009, pp. 242-248.

[49] S. R. Selamat, R. Yusof, S. Sahib, N. H. Hassan, M. Z. Mas'ud, and Z. Z. Abidin, "Traceability in Digital Forensic Investigation Process," *Proceedings of the IEEE Conference on Open Systems*, Langkawi, 25-28 September 2011, pp. 101-106.

[50] F. Cohen, "Metrics for Digital Forensics," *Proceedings of the MiniMetriCon Conference*, 14 February 2011, San Francisco, pp. 1-22.

[51] T. Holz, "Security Measurements and Metrics for Networks," *Dependability Metrics*: *Advanced Lectures Notes in Computer Science* (*LNCS*), Vol. 4909, 2008, pp. 157-165.

[52] A. Al-Dallal and R. S. Abdulwahab, "Achieving High Recall and Precision with HTLM Documents: An Innovation Approach in Information Retrieval," *Proceedings of the World Congress on Engineering* (*WCE* 2011), London, 6-8 July 2011, pp. 1-6.

[53] N. L. Beebe and J. G. Clark, "Digital Forensic Text String Searching: Improving Information Retrieval Effectiveness by Thematically Clustering Search Results," *Journal of Digital Investigation*, Vol. 4, 2007, pp. S49-S54.

[54] G. Peterson, S. Shenoi and N. Beebe, "Digital Forensic Research: The Good, the Bad and the Unaddressed," *Advances in Digital Forensics V*, Vol. 306, 2009, pp. 17-36.

[55] G. Gu, P. Fogla, D. Dagon, W. Lee and B. Skoric, "Towards an Information-theoretic Framework for Analyzing Intrusion Detection Systems," *Proceedings of the* 11*st European Symposium on Research in Computer Security* (*ESORICS*'06), Hamburg, 18-20 September 2006, pp. 1-20.

15

A Novel Solution to Handle DDOS Attack in MANET

Meghna Chhabra[1], **Brij Gupta**[1*], **Ammar Almomani**[2]

[1]School of Computing Science & Engineering, Galgotias Universiy, Greater Noida, India
[2]Faculty of Computing and Information Technology, North Jeddah Branch, King Abdulaziz University, Jeddah, Saudi Arabia

ABSTRACT

Distributed Denial of Service (DDoS) attacks in the networks needs to be prevented or handled if it occurs, as early as possible and before reaching the victim. Dealing with DDoS attacks is difficult due to their properties such as dynamic attack rates, various kinds of targets, big scale of botnet, etc. Distributed Denial of Service (DDoS) attack is hard to deal with because it is difficult to distinguish legitimate traffic from malicious traffic, especially when the traffic is coming at a different rate from distributed sources. DDoS attack becomes more difficult to handle if it occurs in wireless network because of the properties of ad hoc network such as dynamic topologies, low battery life, multicast routing, frequency of updates or network overhead, scalability, mobile agent based routing, and power aware routing, etc. Therefore, it is better to prevent the distributed denial of service attack rather than allowing it to occur and then taking the necessary steps to handle it. This paper discusses various the attack mechanisms and problems due to DDoS attack, also how MANET can be affected by these attacks. In addition to this, a novel solution is proposed to handle DDoS attacks in mobile ad hoc networks (MANETs).

Keywords: DDoS Attack; MANET; AODV; DSR; Flooding Attack; Botnet

1. Introduction

In view of the increasing demand for wireless information and data services, providing faster and reliable mobile access is becoming an important concern. Nowadays, not only mobile phones, but also laptops and PDAs are used by people in their professional and private lives. These devices are used separately for the most part that is their applications do not interact. Sometimes, however, a group of mobile devices form a spontaneous, temporary network as they move closer. This allows us to share information in the form of documents, presentations even when we are on the move or in a meeting [1]. This kind of spontaneous, temporary network referred to as mobile ad hoc networks (MANETs) sometimes just called ad hoc networks or multi-hop wireless networks, play an important role in our present life and will continue to help us in near future.

A mobile ad hoc network (MANET) is a spontaneous network that can be established without any fixed infrastructure or a topology. This means that all its nodes behave as routers and take part in its discovery and maintenance of routes *i.e.* nodes within each other's radio range communicate directly via wireless links, while those that are not in each other's radio range use other nodes as relays. Its routing protocol has to be able to manage with the new difficulties that an ad hoc network creates such as nodes mobility, limited power supply, quality of service, bandwidth issues, changing topology and security issues. These challenges set new requirements on MANET routing protocols and make them more vulnerable to attacks [2].

Ad hoc networks have a wide array of military and commercial applications. They are ideal in situations where installing an infrastructure network is not possible or when the purpose of the network is too transient or even for the reason that the previous infrastructure network was destroyed. Because of its ad hoc infrastructure, decentralized and dynamic topology, loopholes such as limited bandwidth, limited memory and limited battery power, it is very hard to achieve security. There are many solutions exist which cope up against loopholes and provide security up to a certain level in wired network but these solutions are not always suitable for wireless environment. Therefore ad-hoc network has its own issues and challenge over security, which cannot be tackled by the available wired security mechanism.

---

*Corresponding author.

In MANETs, all the participating nodes are involved in the routing process. Since conventional routing protocols are designed for predefined infrastructure networks, which cannot be used in mobile ad hoc networks, so the new classes of routing protocols, *i.e.* ad hoc routing protocols were designed to accomplish the requirement of less infrastructure ad hoc network. In comparison to guided and unguided media, most of the traditional applications do not provide user level security schemes based on the fact that physical network wiring provides some level of security. The routing protocol sets the upper limit to security in any packet network. If routing is misdirected, the entire network will be paralyzed. This problem makes ad hoc networks more complex as the routing usually needs to trust on the trustworthiness of all nodes that are participating in the routing process [3].

One of the recent and biggest cyber attacks has been reported on Netflix, this is because broadband router has been subverted and "Digital N-bombs" slows the Internet worldwide. The attackers were throwing so much of the digital traffic that popular site like Netflix have reportedly disrupted access. Mathew Prince, chief executive of CloudFlare, one of firms dealing with "nuclear bombs" said it's easy to cause so much damage. Spamhaus, an anti-spam organization, was hit by a wave of digital traffic that knocked its website offline.

Spamhaus's work is believed to have launched the massive DDoS, attack to bring down to bring down the anti-spam group. The attackers sent a series of data requests to DNS severs, which help to direct web traffic around the world. After receiving legitimate requests (as these servers are accessed by authorized users), the servers responded by sending the required data to Spamhaus, which could not deal with the information that suddenly arrived. The attack was so large that it began clogging up the DNS servers, which in turn slowed down the Internet worldwide. The congestion was so heavy that it overwhelmed the DNS routers [4]. A flood of request to view a site at the same time will exceed its capacity-stopping it from loading. Spamhaus greater capacity turning to CloudFlare, spread traffic over larger bandwidth. However the attackers began targeting their attacks so they would be concentrated. Hence, the connection slowed down.

Recent wireless research indicates that the wireless MANET presents a larger security problem than conventional wired and wireless networks. Distributed Denial of Service (DDoS) attacks has also become a problem for users of computer systems connected to the Internet. A DDoS attack is a distributed, large-scale attempt by malicious users to flood the victim network with an enormous number of packets. This exhausts the victim network of resources such as bandwidth, computing power, etc. The victim is unable to provide services to its legiti-

mate clients and network performance is greatly deteriorated [5].

Rest of the paper is organized as follows: Section 2 describes related work, Section 3 presents over of DDoS attacks, Section 4 describes MANET overview, Section 5 describes proposed prevention scheme, and finally, Section 6 concludes the paper and discusses some future work.

2. Related Work

In paper [6], Lu Han describes that the wireless ad hoc networks were first unfolded in 1990's. Mobile ad hoc networks have been widely researched for many years. Mobile ad hoc networks are collection of two or more devices equipped with wireless communications and networking capability The Wireless ad hoc Networks do not have gateway rather every node can act as the gateway. Although, lots of research is done in this field, but the question is often raised, whether the architecture of mobile ad hoc networks is a fundamental flawed architecture.

Kamanshis Biswas in [7] mentioned that Mobile Ad Hoc Network (MANET) is a collection of communicating devices or nodes that wish to communicate without any fixed infrastructure. The nodes in MANET themselves are responsible for dynamically finding out other nodes in the network to communicate. Although ad hoc network is used for commercial uses due to their certain unique characteristics, but the main challenge is the vulnerability to security attacks. A number of challenges like dynamic network topology, stringent resource constraints, shared wireless medium, open peer-to-peer network architecture etc., are posed in MANET. As MANET is widely spread for the property of its capability in forming temporary network without any fixed infrastructure or centralized topology, security challenges has become a main concern to provide secure communication.

Andrim Piskozub in [8] gives main types of DoS attacks which flood victim's communication channel bandwidth, is carried out their analysis and are offered methods of protection from these attacks. The DDoS attacks are considerably more effective than their DoS-counterparts because they allow performing such attacks simultaneously from several sites, that makes this attack more efficient and complicates searches of attacker. Attacker uses the client program, which, in turn, interacts with the handler program. The handler sends commands to the agents, which perform actual DoS attacks against indicated system-victim. This paper also describes various countermeasures that should be taken to prevent the network from DDoS attack.

Xianjun Geng in [9] describe that the notorious, crippling attack on e-commerce's top companies in February 2000 and the recurring evidence of active network scanning, a sign of attackers looking for network weaknesses all over the Internet, are harbingers of future Distributed Denial of Service (DDoS) attacks. They signify the continued dissemination of the evil daemon programs that are likely to lead to repeated DDoS attacks in the foreseeable future. This paper gives information about the weaknesses in the network that DDoS attacks exploit the technological futility of addressing the problem solely at the local level.

In [10], Vicky Laurens *et al.* describe that due to financial losses caused by Distributed Denial of Service (DDoS) attacks; most defense mechanisms have been deployed at the network where the target server is located. This paper believes that this paradigm should change in order to tackle the DDoS threat in its basis: thwart agent machines participation in DDoS attacks. Paper consists of developing an agent to monitor the packet traffic rate (outgoing packets/incoming packets).The deployment is based upon characterizing TCP connections; normal TCP connections can be characterized by the ratio of the sent packets to the received packets from a given destination. The result shows that the traffic ratio values usually give larger values at the beginning of the run when there are not enough packets to make a decision that whether or not the traffic is legitimate. A low value for threshold allows for faster detection of attack, but also increases the false-positives.

In [11] Stephen M. Specht describe that Distributed Denial of Service (DDoS) attacks have become a large problem for the systems connected to the Internet. DDoS attackers take control over secondary victim systems and use them to launch a coordinated large-scale attack against primary victim systems. As a result of new countermeasures that are developed to prevent or mitigate DDoS attacks, attackers are constantly developing new methods to cheat on these new countermeasures.

This paper gives us information about DDoS attack models and proposed taxonomies to characterize the DDoS attacks, the software attacking tools used, and the possible countermeasures those are available. The taxonomy shows the similarities and patterns in different DDoS attacks, including new derivative attacks. It is essential, that as the Internet and Internet usage expand, more comprehensive solutions and countermeasures to DDoS attacks be developed, verified, and implemented more effectively and precisely. Thus, this paper describes that DDoS attacks make a networked system or service unavailable to legitimate users. These attacks are an annoyance at a minimum, or can be seriously damaging if a critical system is the primary victim. Loss of network resources causes economic loss, work delays, and loss of communication between network users. Solutions must be developed to prevent these DDoS attacks.

Qiming Li in his paper [12], mention that Distributed Denial of Service (DDoS) attacks pose a serious threat to service availability of the victim network by severely degrading its performance. There has been significant interest in the use of statistical-based filtering to defend against and mitigate the effect of DDoS attacks. Under this approach, packet census is monitored to classify normal and abnormal behavior. Under attack, packets that are classified as abnormal are dropped by the filter that guards the victim network. This paper gives the effectiveness of DDoS attacks on such statistical-based filtering in a general context where the attackers are smart. They first give an optimal policy for the filter when the statistical behaviors of both the attackers and the filter are static. Next, this paper considers cases where both the attacker and the filter can dynamically change their behavior, possibly depending on the perceived behavior of the other party.

In [13], the authors introduced a dynamic DoS attack, the one which can be characterized by exploiting the node mobility, dynamic power control, and compromised nodes to launch new DoS attacks dynamically. The authors have discussed static and dynamic DoS attacks. The DoS attacks launched on data link layer and on the layer above it, *i.e.* network layer is called as static DoS attack. Malicious nodes may be able to move around the entire network, to adjust transmission power dynamically, or even launch DoS attacks by compromising their cooperative neighbors.

In [14], the authors proposed a model to characterize the DDoS flooding attack and its traffic statistics. Also, they proposed an analytical model for looking for specific patterns of the attack traffic, aiming to check if there is an anomaly in the traffic and whether the attack is the DDoS attack and to find out the time when the attack is launched. The main aim of flooding attack is to paralyze the entire network by inserting overwhelming attack traffic (e.g. RREQ broadcasting) into the MANET. The advantage of this method is to detect DDoS attacks more effectively by traffic pattern identification proposed in their work.

In [15], the authors proposed a system which consists of a client detector and a server detector for producing warning of a DDoS attack. The client detector uses a Bloom filter-based detection scheme to generate accurate detection results and it consumes minimal storage and computational resources. Its main task is to monitor the TCP control packets entering and leaving a network. The detection scheme is developed from a modified hash table. The server detector, in an active state, assists the warning by sending requests to legitimate hosts. With the help of client detectors, a server detector can detect an upcoming DDoS attack at an early stage.

Antonio Challita in [16] describe different types of DDoS attacks, present recent DDoS defense methods and propose a unique approach to handle DDoS attack. Based on common defense principles and taking into account a number of DDoS attacks, the author find out several defense methods and categorize them according to several criteria. This paper proposes a simple-to integrate DDoS victim based defense method, Packet Funneling, whose main aim is to mitigate the effect of attack on the victim. In this approach, heavy traffic is checked before being passed to its destination node, thus preventing congestion in the network. This method is simple to integrate, requires no association between nodes, causes no overhead, and adds delays only in case of heavy network loads. The proposed packet funneling approach promises to be a suitable means of coping with DDoS traffic, with easy integration at lesser cost.

Mobile ad hoc networks are expected to be widely used in the near future. However, they are vulnerable to various security issues because of their dynamic characteristics. Malicious flooding attacks are the lethal attacks on mobile ad hoc networks. These attacks can severely occlude an entire network. To defend against these attacks, the authors propose a novel defence mechanism in mobile ad hoc networks. The proposed scheme increases the number of legitimate packet processing at each node and thus improves the end-to-end packet delivery ratio.

From the above literature survey, it is being concluded that the security attacks in MANETs can be categorized as active attacks and passive attacks.

- Active Attack is an attack when attacker node has to bear some energy costs in order to perform the threat. Nodes that perform active attacks with the aim of causing harm to other nodes by causing network outage are considered as malicious.
- Passive Attacks are mainly with the purpose of saving energy selfishly. Nodes that cause passive attacks with the aim of saving battery life for their own communications are considered to be selfish.

Various types of attacks in MANETs are: Modification, Impersonation, Fabrication, Eavesdropping, Replay, Denial of Service, Malicious Software, Lack of Cooperation, Denial of Service attack, and distributed denial of service attack. A number of proposals have been given

by different researchers to handle these attacks but none crossed the benchmark because of dynamic characteristics of the MANET. A perfect solution needs to be proposed to handle the attacks and prevent the sensitive data of the user from mishandling.

Most ad hoc routing protocols are vulnerable to two categories, called external attacks and internal attacks. Internal attacks are initiated and executed by authorized node in the network, where as external attacks are performed by the node that they are not authorized to participate in the network. Another classification of attacks is related to protocol stacks, for instance, network layer attacks and some network layer attacks [17] are listed below in **Table 1** [18].

3. DDoS Attack Overview

3.1. DDoS Attack Components

A DDoS (Distributed Denial-of-Service) attack is a distributed, large-scale attempt by malicious users to flood the victim network with an enormous number of packets. This kills the victim network of resources such as bandwidth, computing power, etc. The victim becomes unable to provide services to its legitimate clients and network performance is greatly affected. In brief, as the name suggests, the service to a legitimate user is being denied of the service by a malicious users by sending a large number of unwanted packets on a network or a single computer. The distributed format adds the "many to one" dimension that makes these attacks more difficult to prevent. A distributed denial of service attack is composed of four elements. First, it involves a victim, *i.e.*, the target host that has been chosen to receive the brunt of the attack. Second, it involves the presence of the attack daemon agents. These are agent programs that actually conduct the attack on the target victim. Attack agents are usually installed on host computers. These attacker agents or the secondary victims affect both the target and the host computers [19-22].

The task of deploying these attack daemons requires the attacker to gain access and infiltrate the host computers. The third component of a distributed denial of

Table 1. Various network layer attack.

Type of Attack	Description
Wormhole	Tunneling the packets using private high speed network.
Byzantine	Selectively drop packets by making routing loops, forwarding packets through non-optimal paths with compromised nodes.
Rushing	Quickly forwards the control messages to gain access to the network.
Resource consumption	It injects the packets to get more network resource.
Location disclosure	Attacker discloses the privacy of a network by knowing the location of a node.
Blackhole	Drops the packets by sending false route reply messages to the route request.

service attack is the control master program. Its task is to coordinate the attack. Finally, there is the real attacker, the mastermind behind the attack. By using a control master program, the real attacker can stay behind the scenes of the attack. The DDoS attack components and procedure is shown in **Figure 1**. The following steps take place during a distributed attack [2,19]:

- The real attacker sends an "execute" message to the control master program.
- The control master program receives the "execute" message and propagates the command to the attack daemons under its control.
- Upon receiving the attack command, the agent machines begin the attack on the victim.

3.2. Distributed Cooperative Architecture of DDoS Attacks

Before real attack traffic reaches the victim, the attacker must communicate with all its DDoS agents. Therefore, there must be control channels present in between the agent machines and the attacker machine. This cooperation between the two requires all agents to send traffic based on the commands received from the attacker. The attack network consists of the three components: attacker, agents, and control channels. In attack networks are divided into three types: the agent-handle model, the Internet Relay Chat (IRC)-based model and the reflector model [20,23].

The agent-handler model consists of three components: attacker, handlers, and agents. **Figure 2** illustrates the typical architecture of the agent handler model. The main attacker sends control messages to the previously compromised agents through a number of handlers, guiding

them to produce unwanted traffic to send it to the victim [2].

The only difference between the architecture of IRC-based model and the agent-handler model is in the former case, an IRC communication channel is used to connect the main attacker to agent machines [24], which is shown in **Figure 3**.

In the attack network architecture of the reflector model, the reflector layer creates a major difference from the basic DDoS attack architecture. In the request messages, the agents changes the source address field in the IP header to the victim's address and thus replace the real agents' addresses. Then, the reflectors will in turn generate response messages to the victim. As a result, the flooding traffic that finally reaches the victim computer or the victim network is not from a few hundred agents, but from a million reflectors. An exceedingly diffused reflector-based DDoS attack raises the bar for tracing out the real attacker by hiding the attacker behind a large number of reflectors [24].

3.3. DDoS Attack Taxonomy

There are a wide variety of DDoS attacks [22]. Two types of DDoS attacks are: Active and passive attack. Packet dropping is a type of passive attack in which node drops some or all of data packets sent to it for further forwarding even when no congestion occurs. There are two main classes of DDoS attacks: bandwidth depletion and resource depletion attacks. The classification of various DDoS attacks is shown in the **Figure 4**.

3.3.1. Bandwidth Depletion Attacks
A Bandwidth Depletion Attack is designed to flood the

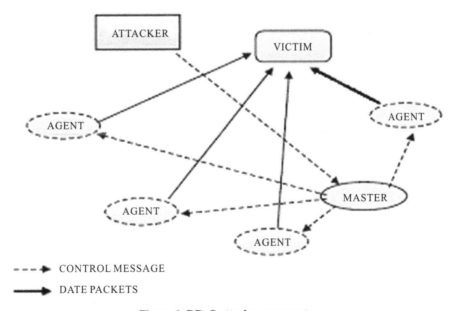

Figure 1. DDoS attack components.

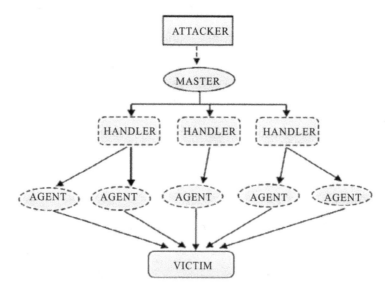

Figure 2. Typical DDoS architecture (the agent handler model).

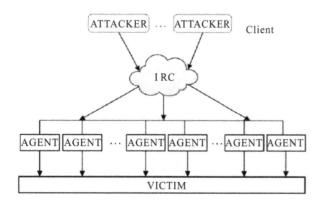

Figure 3. Architecture of IRC based DDoS attack.

victim network with unwanted traffic that prevents legitimate traffic from reaching the primary victim. Bandwidth depletion attacks can be characterized as flood attacks and amplification attacks [25,26].

1) Flood Attacks

In a *flood attack*, zombies send a large volume of traffic to a victim system, so as to congest the victim system's network bandwidth with IP traffic. The victim system slows down, crashes, or suffers from saturated network bandwidth, thereby preventing access by an authorized user. Flood attacks can be launched using both UDP (User Datagram Protocol) and ICMP (Internet Control Message Protocol) packets [27].

In a *UDP Flood attack*, a large number of UDP packets are sent to either random or specified ports on the victim system. The victim system tries to process the incoming data to determine which applications have requested data. If the victim system is not having any applications on the targeted port, it will send an ICMP packet to the sending system indicating a "destination

port unreachable" message [28].

Often, the attacking DDoS tool will also spoof the source IP address of the attacking packets. This helps the secondary victims in hiding their identity since return packets from the victim system are not sent back to the zombies, but are sent back to the spoofed addresses. UDP flood attacks may also fill the bandwidth of connections located around the victim system.

An *ICMP flood attack* is initiated when the zombies send a huge number of ICMP_ECHO_REPLY packets ("ping") to the victim system. These packets flag the victim system to reply to this message and the combination of traffic saturates the bandwidth of the victim's network connection. During this attack, the source IP address of the ICMP packet may also be spoofed [29,30].

2) Amplification Attacks

In amplification attack the attacker or the zombies send messages to a broadcast IP address, using this to cause all systems in the subnet reached by the broadcast address to send a reply to the victim system. The broadcast IP address feature is found on most routers; when a sending system specifies a broadcast IP address as the destination address, the routers replicate send the broadcast message directly, or use the agents to send the broadcast message to increase the volume of attacking traffic. If the attacker decides to send the broadcasting message directly, this attack helps the attacker with the ability to use the systems within the broadcast network as zombies without any need to install any agent software [2].

A DDoS *Smurf attack* is a type of an amplification attack where the attacker sends packets to a network amplifier, with the return address changed to the victim's IP address. The attacking packets are typically ICMP ECHO REQUESTs, which are packets (similar to a

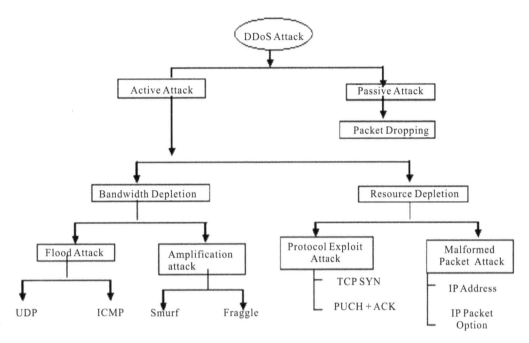

Figure 4. DDoS attack taxonomy.

"ping") that request the receiver to generate an ICMP ECHO REPLY packet [31]. The amplifier sends the ICMP ECHO REQUEST packets to all of the systems within the broadcast address range, and each of these systems will return an ICMP ECHO REPLY to the target victim's IP address. This type of attack amplifies the original packet tens or hundreds of times [32].

Another example is the DDoS *Fraggle attack*, where the attacker sends packets to a network amplifier, using UDP ECHO packets [33]. There is a variation of the Fraggle attack where the UDP ECHO packets are sent to the port that supports character generation, with the return address spoofed to the victim's echo service creating an infinite loop [34]. The UDP Fraggle packet will target the character generator in the systems reached by the broadcast address. These systems generate a character to send to the echo service in the victim system, which will send an echo packet back to the character generator, and the process repeats. This attack can generate more bad traffic and cause more damage than a Smurf attack.

3.3.2. Resource Depletion Attacks

A Resource Depletion Attack is an attack that is designed to tie up the resources of a victim system making the victim unable to process legitimate requests for service. DDoS resource depletion attacks involve the attacker sending packets that misuse network protocol communications or are malformed. Network resources are tied up so that none are left for legitimate users [35].

1) Protocol Exploit Attacks

We give two examples, one misusing the TCP SYN

(Transfer Control Protocol Synchronize) protocol, and the other misusing the PUSH + ACK protocol.

In a DDoS *TCP SYN attack*, the attacker gives instructions the zombies to send tons of TCP SYN requests to a victim server so as to tie up the server's processor resources, and hence prevent the server from responding to the requests from legitimate user. The TCP SYN attack exploits the three-way handshake between the sending machine and the receiving machine by sending a huge number of TCP SYN packets to the victim system with changed source IP addresses, so the victim system responds to a non requesting system with the ACK + SYN. When a large volume of SYN requests are being processed by a server and none of the ACK + SYN responses are returned, the server eventually runs out of the computing resources such as the processor and memory resources, and is unable to respond to legitimate users [35].

In a *PUSH + ACK attack*, the attacking agents send TCP packets with the PUSH and ACK bits set to one. These triggers in the TCP packet header instruct the victim system to unload all data in the TCP buffer and send an acknowledgement message when complete. If this process is repeated with a number of agent machines, the receiving system cannot process the large volume of incoming packets and the victim system will eventually crash.

2) Malformed Packet Attacks

A *malformed packet attack* is an attack where the attacker instructs the zombies to send incorrectly formed IP packets to the victim system in order to crash it. There are at least two types of malformed packet attacks [2,35].

In an *IP address attack*, the packet contains the same source and destination IP addresses. This can confuse the victim system and can cause it to crash. In an *IP packet options* attack, a malformed packet may randomize the optional fields within an IP packet and set all quality of service bits to one so that the victim system must use additional processing time to analyze the traffic. If this attack is multiplied, it can exhaust the processing ability of the victim system [2].

3.4. DDoS Attack Mechanism

As one of the major security problems in the current Internet, a denial-of-service (DoS) attack always attempts to prevent the victim from serving legitimate users. A distributed denial-of-service (DDoS) attack is a DoS attack which relies on multiple compromised hosts in the network to attack the victim. There are two types of DDoS attacks. The First type of DDoS attack aims at attacking the victim node so as to drop some or all of the data packets for further forwarding even when there is no congestion in the network, is known as Malicious Packet Dropping-based DDoS attack [36]. The second type of DDoS attack is based on a huge volume of attack traffic, which is known as a Flooding-based DDoS attack [36]. A flooding-based DDoS attack tries to clog the victim's network bandwidth and other resources with real-looking but unwanted IP data. As a result of which, the legitimate IP packets cannot reach their destination node.

To amplify the effects and hide real attackers, DDoS attacks can be run in two different distributed and parallel ways. In the first one, the attacker compromises a number of agents and manipulates the agents to send attack traffic to the victim node. The second method makes it even more difficult to determine the attack sources because it uses reflectors. For example, a Web server can be reflector because it will return a HTTP response packet after receiving a HTTP request packet. The attacker sends request packets to servers and fakes victim's address as the source address. Therefore, the servers will send back the response packets to the real victim. If the number of reflectors is large enough, the victim network will suffer exceptional traffic congestion [37].

Problems Due to DDoS Attacks:

- DDoS attack is an attempt to make a computer resource inaccessible to its legitimate users.
- The bandwidth of the Internet and a LAN may be consumed unwontedly by DDoS, by which not only the intended computer, but also the entire network suffers.
- Slow network performance (opening files or accessing web sites) due to DDoS attacks.
- Unavailability and inability to access a particular web site due to DDoS attacks.

- Gradual increase in the number of fake emails received due to DDoS attacks.

4. Mobile Ad Hoc Network (MANET) Overview

4.1. MANET Overview

A mobile ad hoc network (MANET) consists of a number of mobile hosts to carry out its basic functions like packet forwarding, routing, and service discovery without the help of an established infrastructure. Each node of an ad hoc network depends on another node in forwarding a packet to its destination, because of the limited range of each mobile host's wireless transmissions. An ad hoc network uses no centralized administration. This ensures that the network will not stop its functioning just because one of the mobile nodes moves out of the range of the others. Because of the limited transmitter range of the nodes, multiple hops need to cooperate to reach other nodes. Every node in an ad hoc network must be willing to forward packets to other nodes. Thus, every node acts both as a host and as a router. The topology of ad hoc networks varies with time as nodes move in and out of the network. This topological instability requires a routing protocol to run on each node to create and maintain routes among the nodes [38].

Mobile Ad hoc Networks' Usages: Wireless ad-hoc networks are mainly used in areas where a wired network infrastructure cannot fit in due to reasons such as cost or convenience. It can be very quickly deployed to support emergency requirements, connectivity on the go, short-term needs, and coverage in undeveloped areas. Any day-to-day application such as electronic email and file transfer can be considered to be easily deployable within an ad hoc network environment.

In addition to this, there is no need to focus on the wide range of military applications possible with ad hoc networks. Even the technology was initially developed for the military applications. In such situations, the ad hoc networks having self-organizing capability can be effectively used where other technologies either fail or cannot be deployed effectively. Some well-known ad hoc network applications are:

Collaborative Work: For some business environments, the need for collaborative computing is sometimes more important outside office environments than inside. Moreover, it is often the case where people really need to have meetings to cooperate and exchange information on a project.

- *Crisis-Management Applications*: These arise as a result of natural disasters where the entire communications infrastructure is disordered and restoring communications quickly is essential. By using ad hoc networks, it becomes easy and quick to establish a communication channel than required for wired communications.

- *Personal Area Networking and Bluetooth*: A personal area network (PAN) is a short-range, localized network where nodes are usually associated with someone. These nodes could be attached to a pulse watch, belt, and so on. In such scenarios, mobility is only a major consideration when interaction among several PANs is the main issue.

Mobile Adhoc Network Usage and Characteristics: MANETs have a number of characteristics and challenges which are as follows [39]:

- *Dynamic topologies*: Nodes are free to move anywhere in the network. Thus, the network topology changes randomly and rapidly at unpredictable times, which is the main characteristic of a MANET.
- *Bandwidth-constrained, variable capacity links*: Wireless links will continue to have considerably lower capacity than their hardwired counterparts. Also, the actual throughput of wireless communications, after calculating for the effects of multiple accesses, multipath routing, noise, and interference conditions, is lesser than a radio's maximum transmission rate.
- *Energy-constrained operation*: The nodes in a MANET may depend on batteries or other exhaustible means for their energy. For these nodes, an important optimization criteria system design may be energy saving.
- *Security*: Mobile wireless networks are highly prone to physical security threats because of its hop by hop routing, multipath routing and dynamically changing topology. Therefore, an increase in possibility of different attacks should be carefully considered.

Security goals for MANET: Security is an important issue for ad hoc networks especially for the more security-sensitive applications used in military and critical networks. An ad hoc network can be considered secure if it holds the following attributes:

- *Availability*: Ensures that the network manages to provide all services despite denial of service attacks. A denial of service attack can be launched at any layer of an ad hoc network. On the physical and media access control layer a malicious user can employ jamming in order to interfere with signals in the physical layer. On the network layer, a malicious user can disrupt the normal operation of the routing table in various ways that are presented in a following section. Lastly, on the higher layer, a malicious user can bring down high-level services such as the key management service.
- *Confidentiality*: Ensures that certain information is never disclosed to unauthorized users. This attribute is mostly desired when transmitting sensitive infor-

mation such as military and tactical data. Routing information must also be confidential in some cases when the user's location must be kept secret.

- *Integrity*: Guarantees that the message that is transmitted reaches its destination without being changed or corrupted in any way. Message corruption can be caused by either a malicious attack on the network or because of radio propagation failure.
- *Authentication*: Enables a node to be sure of the identity of the peer with which it communicates. When there is no authentication scheme a node can masquerade as some other node and gain unauthorized access to resources or sensitive information.
- *Non-repudiation*: Ensures that the originator of a message cannot refuse sending this message. This attribute is useful when trying to detect isolated compromised nodes.

4.2. Manet Routing Protocols

The routing protocols in ad hoc networks may be categorized as proactive routing protocols, reactive routing protocols, and hybrid routing protocols [40].

- Proactive Routing Protocols are those protocols, in which the routes are maintained to all the nodes, including those nodes to which packets are not sent. An example of proactive routing protocols in ad hoc networks is Optimized Link State Routing Protocol (OLSR).
- Reactive Routing Protocols are those protocols in which the route between the two nodes is constructed only when the communication occurs between the two nodes. Such type of routing protocols is ad hoc On Demand Distance Vector Routing Protocol (AODV) and Dynamic Source Routing Protocol (DSR) [41].
- Hybrid Routing Protocols are those protocols in which the combined approach of proactive routing and reactive routing are used for the route generation between the nodes. The Zone Routing Protocol (ZRP) is such a hybrid reactive/proactive routing protocols.

Figure 5 shows the categorization of various mobile ad hoc network routing protocols and their subtypes [42].

4.3. Overview of AODV Routing Protocol

The Ad Hoc On-Demand Distance Vector (AODV) routing protocol [43,44] is built on the Dynamic Destination Sequenced Distance-Vector (DSDV) algorithm. AODV is a betterment of DSDV because it typically minimizes the number of required broadcasts by creating routes on a demand basis, and does not maintain a complete list of routes as in the DSDV algorithm [43]. AODV is classified as a pure on-demand route finding system, since nodes that are not on a selected path do not maintain routing information nor do they participate in the routing

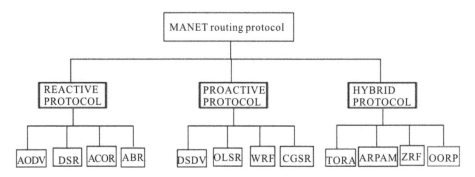

Figure 5. MANET routing protocols.

table maintenance. In general, the operations in AODV can be classified into two phases: the route construction phase and the route maintenance phase. The main work in route construction phase is to create a route from source node to destination node while in route maintenance phase, the main work is to rebuild a route between source and destination nodes since the previous found route may be broken due to the nodes movement.

In the route construction phase, when a source node wants to send packets to a destination node and there is no valid route between the source node and the destination node, the source node commences a path discovery process to locate the destination node. The source node will broadcast a route request (RREQ) packet to explore a route to the destination. AODV uses the destination sequence number to ensure that all routes are loop-free and contain the most recent route information [43].

During the route discovery process, each intermediate node that gets the RREQ packet will again broadcast this packet to its neighbors. The duplicate copies of the same RREQ message that is received by an intermediate node will be discarded. Once the RREQ reaches the destination or an intermediate node with a fresh route to the destination is located, the destination or the intermediate node will send a route reply (RREP) packet back to the source along the reverse routing path [42].

Figure 6 shows the process of route discovery in AODV. In **Figure 6(a)**, the source node broadcast RREQ packet to its neighbor, and so on, while in **Figure 6(b)**, the destination node send the RREP packet back to the source node.

Advantages:
- The main advantage of this protocol is that routes are established on demand or as when needed and destination sequence numbers are used to check the freshness of the route in the network.
- The connection setup delay is less. Another advantage of AODV is that it creates no extra traffic for communication along existing links.
- Thirdly, distance vector routing is simple, and doesn't require much memory or calculation.

Disadvantages:

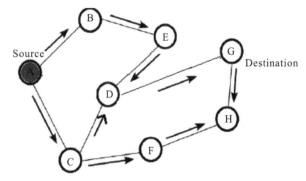

(a) RREQ Broadcast

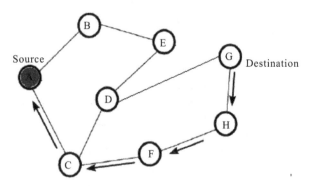

(b) RREP Forwarded Path

Figure 6. AODV route discovery.

- AODV requires more time to establish a connection as before sending data packets, route to the destination is searched and the initial communication to establish a route is heavy.
- Other disadvantages of this protocol is that intermediate nodes can lead to inconsistent routes if the source sequence number is very old and the intermediate nodes have a higher but not the latest destination sequence number, thereby having stale entries.
- Thirdly, multiple RREP packets in response to a single RREQ packet can lead to heavy control overhead.

4.4. Flooding Attacks in MANET

The Flooding attack procedure was proposed in [45].

Flood attacks occur when a network or service becomes incapable of providing service to its clients, thereby causing incomplete connection requests. By flooding a server or host with connections that cannot be completed, the flood attack eventually tries to fill the host's memory buffer thereby not accepting further connections, which causes a Denial of Service attack. To reduce congestion, the protocol has already adopted some methods which are briefly described as follows.

1) Firstly, the number of RREQ that a node can originate per second is limited. Secondly, after broadcasting a RREQ packet, the initiator node will wait for a ROUTE REPLY. If a route is not received within round-trip milliseconds, the node may try again to discover a route by broadcasting another RREQ; until it reaches a maximum of retry times at the maximum TTL value. Time intervals between repeated attempts by a source node at route discovery for a single destination must satisfy a binary exponential back off. The first time a source node broadcasts a RREQ, it waits until the round-trip time for the receiving the ROUTE REPLY (RRPEP) packet [45-48].

2) But for the second RREQ, the time to wait for the ROUTE REPLY should be calculated according to a binary exponential backoff, by which the waiting time now becomes twice of round trip time.

3) Thirdly, The RREQ packets are broadcasted in an incremental ring to reduce the overhead caused by flooding the whole network. At first, the packets are flooded in a small area confined by a small starting time-to-live (TTL) in the IP headers. After RING TRA-VERSAL TIME, if no ROUTE REPLY is received, the forwarding area is enlarged by increasing the TTL by a fixed value.

The procedure is repeated until a ROUTE REPLY is received which means that a route has been found. In the flooding attack, the attack node violates the above rules to exhaust the network resources. Firstly, the attacker will produce many IP addresses which do not exist in the networks if he knows the scope of the IP addresses in the networks. As no node can return ROUTE REPLY packets for these ROUTE REQUESTs, the reverse route in the nodes' route table will be conserved longer than normal. If the attacker cannot get the scope of IP addresses in the network, he can just choose random IP addresses. Secondly, the attacker successively originates mass RREQ messages with these void IP addresses as destination and tries to send excessive RREQ without considering the RREQ RATELIMIT, that is, without waiting for the ROUTE REPLY or waiting a round-trip time. Besides, the TTL of RREQ is set up to a maximum at the beginning without using an expanding ring search method. Under such attack, the whole network will be full of RREQ packets from the attacker. The communication bandwidth and other node resources will be ex-

hausted by the flooded RREQ packets. For example, the storage of route table is limited. If the large amounts of RREQ packets are arriving in a very short time, the storage of the route table in the node will be used up soon so that the node cannot receive new RREQ packets any more [45-47]. **Figure 7** shows the flooding attack mechanism in MANET.

4.5. Effect of Flooding Attacks

Flooding Attack can seriously degrade the performance of reactive routing protocols and affect a node in the following ways. This was proposed in [48].

4.5.1. Degrade the Performance in Buffer

The buffer used by the routing protocol may exceed the limit since a reactive protocol needs to buffer data packets when the RREQ packets are being sent by the source node. Also, if a large number of data packets originating from the application layer are actually unreachable, genuine data packets in the buffer may be replaced by these unreachable data packets, based on the buffer management scheme used.

4.5.2. Degrade the Performance in Wireless Interface

Depending on the design of the interface of wireless network, the buffer used by the wireless network interface may overflow due to the large number of RREQs sent in the route discovery process. Similarly, genuine data packets may be dropped if routing packets have higher priority over data packets.

4.5.3. Degrade the Performance in RREQ Packets

Since RREQ packets are broadcasted into the entire network, the increased number of RREQ packets in the network leads to more collision in MAC layer and thereby congestion in the network and delays for the data

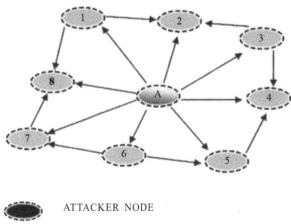

ATTACKER NODE

RREQ FLOODING PATH

Figure 7. The RREQ flooding attack.

packets. Protocols like TCP that is sensitive to round trip times and congestion in the network gets affected.

4.5.4. Degrade the Performance in Lifetime of MANET

Since MANET nodes are likely to be power and bandwidth constrained, useless RREQ packets transmission can reduce the lifetime of the network also incurring additional overheads of authenticating a large number of RREQs. The following metrics can be used to evaluate the performance of flooding attack.

- Packet loss rate: The ratio of the number of packets dropped by the nodes divided by the number of packets originated by the application layer continuous bit rate (CBR) sources. The packet loss ratio is important as it describes the loss rate that can be seen by the transport protocols, which in turn affects the maximum throughput that the network can support. The metric characterizes both the completeness and correctness of the routing protocol.
- Average delay: Average of delay incurred by all the packets which are successfully transmitted.
- Throughput: Average number of packets per second X packet size.
- Average number of hops: Total length of all routes divided by the total number of routes.

5. Proposed Prevention Technique

A broadcast is a data packet that is to be delivered to multiple hosts. Broadcasts can be done at the data link layer and the network layer. Packets that are broadcasted at data-link layer are sent to all hosts attached to a particular physical network whereas the packets that are broadcasted to network layer are sent to all hosts attached to a particular logical network.

Since, broadcast packets are destined to all hosts; the goal of the router is to control unnecessary proliferation of broadcast packets. Cisco routers support two kinds of broadcasting, the directed broadcast and the flooded one. In a directed broadcast, a packet is sent to a specific network or series of networks, whereas a flooded broadcast is a packet meant for every network or for every node in the network [36].

Taking the example of flooding broadcast which cause DDoS attack. A nasty type of DDoS attack is the Smurf attack, which is made possible mainly because of the network devices that respond to ICMP echoes sent to broadcast addresses. The attacker node sends a large amount of ICMP traffic to a broadcast address and uses a victim's IP address as the source IP so the replies from all the devices that respond to the broadcast address will flood the victim. The surprising part of this attack is that the attacker uses a low-bandwidth connection to kill a high-bandwidth connection. The amount of traffic sent by the attacker is multiplied by a numeric value equal to the number of hosts behind the router that reply to the ICMP echo packets.

The attacker sends a number of ICMP echo packets to the router at 128 Kbps. The attacker, before sending them, modifies the packets by changing the source IP to the IP address of the victim's computer so replies to the echo packets will be sent to that address [36]. The destination address of the packets is a broadcast address of the so-called bounce site. If the router is (mis-) configured to forward these broadcasts to hosts on the other side of the router all this host will reply. That would mean N × 128 Kbps of ICMP replies will revert back to the victim's system, which would effectively disable its 512 Kbps connection. Besides the target system, the *intermediate* router is also a victim, and thus also the hosts in the bounce site. A similar attack that uses UDP echo packets instead of ICMP echo packets is called a Fraggle attack [36].

IP Broadcast is used in AODV routing Protocols to broadcast RREQ packets on all the nodes in the network. Flood attack occurs because of initiating lots of RREQ packets in the network so that network becomes congested and no bandwidth is available to send packets. Hence, we need to keep a check on the number of the RREQs which are broadcast to all nodes.

We put a threshold value on the number of packets, which can be sent by a node and if a node exceeds the threshold value then it will be considered as an attacker node.

In the detection technique, each node comes into processing. For each attack, the node that runs the corresponding detection rule is the "monitoring" node, and the node whose behavior is being analyzed (*i.e.*, the possible attacking or misbehaving node) the "monitored" node. The monitoring node is a 1-hop neighborhood of the "monitored" node. For Flooding, only the attack type, but not the attacker, can be identified by a monitoring node.

The monitoring node will send a "Hello" packet to its next neighborhood node, *i.e.* the monitored node and will wait for its reply. If it does not get reply within the set interval then the node being monitored is flooded node that is the victim node. Later, the id of this node will be disabled and the entry of victim node will be deleted from the routing tables of all nodes. After finding the nodes, we handle it by finding the path in which attack is being executed and sum up the broadcast ids whose effect will be nullified. Code for the technique will be implemented in neighbor management function, Get Broadcast ID function and finalize function of aodv.pc file. **Figure 8** describes the procedure of the proposed model in the form of a flow chart.

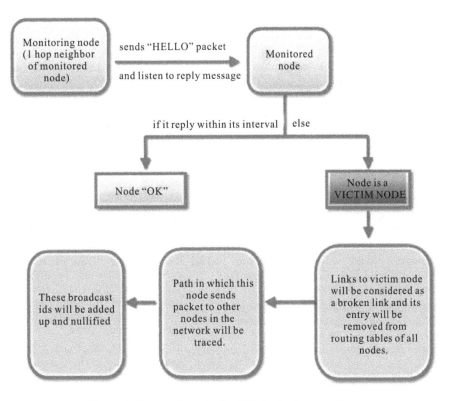

Figure 8. Proposed model for DDoS attack prevention.

6. Conclusion

Mobile ad hoc network is an infrastructure less network due to its capability of operating without the support of any fixed infrastructure. Security plays a vital role in MANET due to its applications like battlefield or disaster-recovery networks. MANETs are more vulnerable compared to wired networks due the lack of a trusted centralized authority and limited resources. There is an urgent need to develop a scheme to handle DDoS attack in mobile ad hoc network. We have discussed the various the attack mechanisms and problems due to DDoS attack, also how MANET can be affected by these attacks, in this paper. In addition to this, a novel solution is proposed to handle DDoS attacks in mobile ad hoc networks (MANETs).

REFERENCES

[1] C. S. R. Murthy and B. S. Manoj, "Ad-Hoc Wireless Networks Architectures and Protocols," Prentice Hall Communications Engineering and Emerging Technologies Series, Pearson Education, Upper Saddle River, 2004.

[2] S. K. Sarkar, T. G. Basavaraju and C. Puttamadappa, "Ad-Hoc Mobile Wireless Networks: Principles, Protocols, and Applications," Auerbach Publications, Boca Raton, 2008.

[3] S. Taneja and A. Kush, "A Survey of Routing Protocols in Mobile Ad Hoc Networks," *International Journal of Innovation, Management and Technology*, Vol. 1, No. 3, 2010, ISSN: 2010-0248.

[4] D. Lee, "Global Internet Slows after Biggest Attack in History," 2013.
http://www.bbc.co.uk/news/technology-21954636

[5] B. B. Gupta, R. C. Joshi and M. Misra, "Defending against Distributed Denial of Service Attacks: Issues and Challenges," *Information Security Journal: A Global Perspective*, Vol. 18, No. 5, 2009, pp. 224-247.

[6] B. Han, H. H. Fu, L. Lin and W. Jia, "Efficient Construction of Connected Dominating Set in Wireless Ad Hoc Networks," *IEEE International Conference on Mobile Ad-Hoc and Sensor Systems*, Fort Lauderdale, 25-27 October 2004, pp. 570-572,

[7] K. Biswas and Md. Liaqat Ali, "Security Threats in Mobile Ad-Hoc Network," Master Thesis, Blekinge Institute of Technology, Blekinge, 2007.

[8] A. Piskozub, "Denial of Service and Distributed Denial of Service Attacks," *Proceedings of the International Conference on Modern Problems of Radio Engineering, Telecommunications and Computer Science*, Lviv-Slavsko, 18-23 February 2002, pp. 303-304.

[9] X. J. Geng and A. B. Whinston, "Defeating Distributed Denial of Service Attacks," *IT Professional*, Vol. 2, No. 4, 2000, pp. 36-41.

[10] V. Laurens, "Detecting DDoS attack traffic at the Agent Machines," *Canadian Conference on Electrical and Computer Engineering*, CCECE'06, Ottawa, 7-10 May 2006, pp. 2369-2372.

[11] S. M. Specht, "Distributed Denial of Service: Taxonomies of Attacks, Tools and Countermeasures," *ISCA 17th*

International Conference on Parallel and Distributed Computing Systems, San Francisco, 15-17 September 2004, pp. 543-550.

[12] Q. M. Li, "On the Effectiveness of DDoS Attacks on Statistical Filtering," INFOCOM 2005, 24th Annual Joint Conference of the IEEE Computer and Communications Societies, Miami, 13-17 March 2005, pp. 1373-1383.

[13] F. Xing and W. Y. Wang, "Understanding Dynamic Denial of Service Attacks in Mobile Ad Hoc Networks," Military Communications Conference, MILCOM 2006, Washington DC, 23-25 October 2006, pp. 1-7.

[14] Y. H. Guo and M. Simon, "Network Forensics in MANET: Traffic Analysis of Source Spoofed DoS Attacks," Fourth International Conference on Network and System Security, Melbourne, 1-3 September 2010, pp. 128-135.

[15] B. Xiao, W. Chen and Y. Xian, "A Novel Approach to Detecting DDoS Attacks at an Early Stage," The Journal of Supercomputing, Vol. 36, No. 3, 2006, pp. 235-248.

[16] A. Challita, M. El Hassan, S. Maalouf and A. Zouheiry, "A Survey of DDoS Defense Mechanisms," FEA Student Conference, 2004.
http://webfea-lb.fea.aub.edu.lb/proceedings/2004/SRC-ECE-39.pdf

[17] P. Joshi, "Security Issues in Routing Protocols in Manets at Network Layer," Procedia Computer Science, Vol. 3 2011, pp. 954-960.

[18] K. S. Madhusudhananaga Kumar and G. Aghila, "A Survey on Black Hole Attacks on AODV Protocol in MANET," International Journal of Computer Applications, Vol. 34, No. 5, 2011, pp. 23-30.

[19] E. Alomari, S. Manickam, B. B. Gupta, S. Karuppayah and R. Alfaris, "Botnet-based Distributed Denial of Service (DDoS) Attacks on Web Servers: Classification and Art," International Journal of Computer Applications, Vol. 49, No. 7, 2012, pp. 24-32.

[20] B. B. Gupta, M. Misra and R. C. Joshi, "FVBA: A Combined Statistical Approach for Low Rate Degrading and High Bandwidth Disruptive DDoS Attacks Detection in ISP Domain," Proceedings of 16th IEEE International Conference on Networks (ICON-2008), New Delhi, 12-14 December 2008, pp. 1-4.

[21] A. Srivastava, B. B. Gupta, A. Tyagi, A. Sharma and A. Mishra, "A Recent Survey on DDoS Attacks and Defense Mechanisms," Proceedings of the First International Conference on Parallel, Distributed Computing Technologies and Applications (PDCTA-2011), Tirunelveli, 23-25 September 2011, pp. 570-580.

[22] B. B. Gupta, R. C. Joshi and M. Misra, "ANN Based Scheme to Predict Number of Zombies Involved in a DDoS Attack," International Journal of Network Security (IJNS), Vol. 14, No. 1, 2012, pp. 36-45.

[23] J. Lo, et al., "An IRC Tutorial," 1997.
http://www.irchelp.org/irchelp/irctutorial.html#part1

[24] V. Paxson, "An Analysis of Using Reflectors for Distributed Denial-of-Service Attacks," ACM SIGCOMM Computer Communication Review, Vol. 31, No. 3, 2001, pp.

38-47.

[25] R. Guo, G. R. Chang, R. D. Hou, Y. H. Qin, B. J. Sun, A. Liu, Y. Jia and D. Peng, "Research on Counter Bandwidth Depletion DDoS Attacks Based on Genetic Algorithm," Third International Conference on Natural Computation, ICNC 2007, Haikou, 24-27 August 2007, pp. 155-159,.

[26] H.-J. Kim, R. B. Chitti and J. S. Song, "Handling Malicious Flooding Attacks through Enhancement of Packet Processing Technique in Mobile Ad Hoc Networks," Journal of Information Processing Systems, Vol. 7, No. 1, 2011, pp. 137-150.

[27] U. D. Khartad and R. K. Krishna, "Route Request Flooding Attack Using Trust Based Security Scheme in Manet," International Journal of Smart Sensors and Ad Hoc Networks (IJSSAN), Vol. 1, No. 4, 2012, p. 27.

[28] P. J. Criscuolo, "Distributed Denial of Service Trinoo, Tribe Flood Network, Tribe Flood Network 2000, and Stacheldraht, CIAC-2319," Department of Energy Computer Incident Advisory Capability (CIAC), UCRL-ID-136939, Rev.1, Lawrence Livermore National Laboratory, Livermore, 2000.

[29] S. Bellovin, M. Leech and T. Taylor, "ICMP trace back messages," Internet Draft: draft-ietf-itrace-01.txt, Work in Progress, 2001.

[30] H. X. Tan, "Framework for Statistical Filtering against DDoS Attacks in MANETs," Second International Conference on Embedded Software and Systems, Xi'an, 16-18 December 2005, 8 pp.

[31] TFreak, 2003.
www.phreak.org/archives/exploits/denial/smurf.c

[32] Fed CIRC, "Defense Tactics for Distributed Denial of Service Attacks," Federal Computer Incident Response Center, Washington DC, 2000.

[33] TFreak, "fraggle.c," 2003.
www.phreak.org/archives/exploits/denial/fraggle.c

[34] M. J. Martin, "Router Expert: Smurf/Fraggle Attack Defense Using SACLS," Networking Tips and Newsletters, 2002.

[35] A. Mishra, B. B. Gupta and R. C. Joshi, "A Comparative Study of Distributed Denial of Service Attacks, Intrusion Tolerance and Mitigation Techniques," European Intelligence and Security Informatics Conference, EISIC 2011, 12-14 September 2011, pp. 286, 289.

[36] Y. Chaba, Y. Singh and P. Aneja, "Performance Analysis of Disable IP Broadcast Technique for Prevention of Flooding-Based DDoS Attack in MANET," Journal of Networks, Vol. 4, No. 3, 2009, pp. 178-183.

[37] S. A. Arunmozhi and Y. Venkataramani, "DDoS Attack and Defense Scheme in Wireless Ad Hoc Networks," International Journal of Network Security & Its Applications, Vol. 3, No. 3, 2011, 6 pp.

[38] A. Sun, "The Design and Implementation of Fisheye Routing Protocol for Mobile Ad Hoc Networks," Master Thesis, Massachusetts Institute of Technology, Cambridge, 2002.

[39] A. Nayyar "Enhanced Anomaly Detection IDS-Based Scheme for Dynamic MANET On-Demand (DYMO)

Routing Protocol for MANETS," *International Journal of Computer Science and Mobile Computing*, Vol. 2, No. 4, 2013, pp. 384-390.

[40] P. Misra, "Routing Protocols for Ad Hoc Mobile Wireless Networks," 2006. http://www.cse.wustl.edu/~jain/cis788-99/adhoc_routing/

[41] D. Johnson, D. Maltz and J. Broch, "DSR the Dynamic Source Routing Protocol for Multihop Wireless Ad Hoc Networks," In: C. E. Perkins, Ed., *Ad Hoc Networking*, Addison-Wesley Longman Publishing Co., Inc., Boston, 2001, pp. 139-172.

[42] C. E. Perkins, E. M. Belding-Royer and S. R. Das, "Ad Hoc On-Demand Distance Vector (AODV) Routing," *2nd IEEE Workshop on Workshop Mobile Computing Systems and Applications*, New Orleans, 25-26 February 1999, pp. 90-100.

[43] S. Saraeian, F. Adibniya, M. G. Zadeh and S. A. Abtahi, "Performance Evaluation of AODV Protocol under DDoS Attacks in MANET," *World Academy of Science, Engineering and Technology*, Vol. 45, 2008, p. 501.

[44] G. S. Tomar, T. Sharma, D. Bhattacharyya and T.-H. Kim,

"Performance Comparision of AODV, DSR and DSDV under Various Network Conditions: A Survey," 2011 *International Conference on Ubiquitous Computing and Multimedia Applications*, Daejeon, 13-15 April 2011, pp. 3-7.

[45] C. CenGen, "Allocations for Mobile Ad Hoc Network (MANET) Protocols," IANA, Marina del Rey, 2009.

[46] P. Ning and K. Sun, "How to Misuse AODV: A Case Study of Inside Attacks against Mobile Ad-Hoc Routing Protocols," *Proceedings of the 2003 IEEE Workshop on Information Assurance United States Military Academy*, West Point, New York, 18-20 June 2003, pp. 60-67.

[47] M. Y. Dangore and S. S. Sambare, "A Survey on Detection of Blackhole Attack Using AODV Protocol in MANET," *International Journal on Recent and Innovation Trends in Computing and Communication*, Vol. 1, No. 1, 2013, pp. 55-61.

[48] M. B. Guddhe and M. U. Kharat, "Core Assisted Defense against Flooding Attacks in MANET," 2009. http://www.nsnam.org

16

A Multi-Leveled Approach to Intrusion Detection and the Insider Threat

Rita M. Barrios

Computer Information Systems, Cyber Security, University of Detroit Mercy Detroit, Detroit, USA

ABSTRACT

When considering Intrusion Detection and the Insider Threat, most researchers tend to focus on the network architecture rather than the database which is the primary target of data theft. It is understood that the network level is adequate for many intrusions where entry into the system is being sought however it is grossly inadequate when considering the database and the authorized insider. Recent writings suggest that there have been many attempts to address the insider threat phenomena in regards to database technologies by the utilization of detection methodologies, policy management systems and behavior analysis methods however, there appears to be a lacking in the development of adequate solutions that will achieve the level of detection that is required. While it is true that Authorization is the cornerstone to the security of the database implementation, authorization alone is not enough to prevent the authorized entity from initiating malicious activities in regards to the data stored within the database. Behavior of the authorized entity must also be considered along with current data access control policies. Each of the previously mentioned approaches to intrusion detection at the database level has been considered individually, however, there has been limited research in producing a multileveled approach to achieve a robust solution. The research presented outlines the development of a detection framework by introducing a process that is to be implemented in conjunction with information requests. By utilizing this approach, an effective and robust methodology has been achieved that can be used to determine the probability of an intrusion by the authorized entity, which ultimately address the insider threat phenomena at its most basic level.

Keywords: Bayesian Belief Network; Database; Insider Threat; Intrusion Detection

1. Introduction

As far back as the 1970's, detection of a data breach at the database level by an authorized insider (also known as the insider threat), has been an issue that has plagued the information technology community. The research put forth addresses the insider threat issue by presenting a multileveled approach to Database Intrusion Detection.

1.1. The Insider Threat

The theft and exposure of the critical data components that resides in a relational database by the authorized insider is on the rise [1].

An authorized insider can be defined as an individual who has been granted privileges to utilize or modify the critical data components. This entity can be characterized as an entity that chooses to abuse their role to perform malicious activities. It is because of this type of threat that has given visibility to the need for an automated solution that enables detection of this type of breach [10,20]. While the insider threat presents a trust issue that cannot be solved with this research, the framework as

presented did, however, aid in the reduction of exposure when the motivations and subsequent actions of the trusted user can no longer be relied upon.

Finding those trusted entities that are capturing the confidential data components is a task that is difficult at best [1,2]. Identification can encompass a complex decision making process on several levels of abstraction which includes having an understanding of the daily non-threatening, functional actions of the users as identified in the usage logs as well as the measuring those actions against the defined access control policies associated with the related user classification [3]. The challenge within this scope becomes how identification can be successfully accomplished to distinguish between the dynamic and valid usages of the data components vs. the abuse situation. With the introduction of an automated and robust extension to the current research in database Intrusion Detection Systems (IDS), it is possible to overcome this challenge.

With this challenge in mind, the research presented focused on a novel combination of established methodologies in data mining, policy identification and abuse identification in an attempt identify inappropriate behavior as demonstrated by the authorized users of a relational database. Additionally, there are two secondary objectives presented in this research. The first being the creation of a supervised learning component of the presented Database Intrusion Detection Systems (dIDS) to determine the validity of the "normal" behavior and the latter is to develop the definition of the behaviors that were needed to identify, classify and respond to the introduction of new transactions. These objectives are realized by the pairing of the defined access control and security policies with the usage behaviors as found in the database logs.

1.2. Relevance

When the theft of critical data components is successfully executed by the authorized insider, corporate trust begins to deteriorate among its consumer base as well as exposes the organization to various legal issues due to the violation of local, state and/or federal laws and regulations.

This phenomena occurred recently when [4] reports that the data breach of 2008 at T. J. Maxx is expected to realize costs of more than 10 times the original estimate to a record $4.5 billion. This is about $100 per consumer record for each of the 45 million credit card account numbers stolen over an 18-month period [4]. It is expected that the cost associated with the breach to lower profits by $118 million in the first quarter of FY 08 [4].

The insider threat is considered significant, since there have been many cases presented in the literature where a security breach had been successfully accomplished by the actions of an internal user when there has been an advanced level of authorization granted. Statistics as presented in a study by [1], which had been conducted by the FBI in 2006 identified approximately 52% of the respondents had reported unauthorized use of information resources by internal users along with 10% of the respondents unsure if they had been exposed. Further, judicial proceedings as presented by [5] as well as is documented in industry publications as presented by [4] suggests that there is a significant degree of loss to those victim organizations where there has been an exposure of data as a result of inside. Reference [5] also presents a case where a senior database administrator (DBA) had pled guilty to stealing 8.5 million consumer information records over a five-year period, which subsequently had been sold for approximately $580 k. Reference [5] further exposes the problem of the insider threat by presenting a case where the directors of admissions and computer center operations at a Manhattan college were indicted on charges of fraud after setting up an operation where people who had never attended the college paid

between $3 k and $25 k to obtain forged academic transcripts. As can been seen, the anomaly of the insider threat is consider a cross-cutting concern as it is not restricted to a single industry but can encompass all types information systems.

Many researchers tend to focus on a single aspect of the overall solution to database intrusion detection. It is not clear as to why the merging of the two critical components of transaction validation and abusive activity validation has not been attempted to create a well-rounded and complete solution even though many researchers do recognize the need for both components [2,3,6-8]. With this obvious omission, it appears as if this type of multileveled solution may in and of itself, pose a task that is too difficult to accomplish.

1.3. Guide to the Paper

The research presented takes on the following progression. Section 2 presents a brief but through review of the literature associated with research on database intrusion detection, digital rights management and data mining for behavior patterns. Section 3 presents a brief account of the methodologies that were employed to successfully implement the framework while Section 4 presents the post implementation findings. Section 5 concludes this work with a summary of research presented along with an examination of future works to be achieved.

2. Prior Research

2.1. Access Controls

Although advancement in database access controls has made significant progress towards securing data that resides within the database, there are still limitations of how much can be prevented when considering the insider threat phenomena. This becomes apparent given that the majority of the strides made thus far are focused on addressing the functions of proper authorizations. Since the insider is already authorized these methods will not prevent the theft and/or exposure of the data components [9].

2.2. Intrusion Detection Methodologies

Intrusion Detection Systems (IDS) have been a focused research subject for decades with significant attention given at the start of the 21st century. It was at this time that [10,11] as well as others began to present the foundational concepts in formalized research and publications. Because of the clarity presented in the [11] research, the discussions presented in the following paragraph are centralized around this work however; the seminal works are identified as well as the basis for [11] study. It should be noted that the research presented in the [10] study follows the same presentation as [11] whereby the seminal works form the foundational concepts.

IDS can be defined as a system with a goal to defend a system by raising an alarm when the protocol detects that there has been a security violation [11,12]. With this in mind, [10,11] as well as the seminal works in intrusion detection, identify two primary principles in the IDS model, anomaly detection and signature detection [12,13]. Anomaly detection is defined as flagging all abnormal behavior as an intrusion [10,12-14]. While Signature detection is defined as flagging behavior that is relatively, close in comparison of some defined, known pattern of an intrusion that has been previously defined to the IDS [10-13].

2.3. IDS Implementation

When implementing IDS the focus must be on the three primary components: the audit data, detector model and output that will be used in the follow-up process. The detector model and its underlying principles is the primary component of the system [10-19]. Additionally, IDS protocol is further categorized base on the type of intrusion recognized by the system. These categorizations are defined as follows: The Well-Known intrusion that identifies a static well-defined pattern discernible with the intrusion being executed in a predictable fashion. The Generalized intrusion is similar to the Well-Known category but is variable by nature. Lastly, the Unknown intrusion is identified by a weak coupling between the intrusion and a system flaw. This intrusion category is the most difficult to understand [5]. It is this category, the Unknown Intrusion that is the focal point of the presented research when coupled with the insider threat phenomena.

2.4. Database Intrusion Detection Systems

Historic as well as current research in the area of IDS and access control methodologies does not support the identification of intrusions at the database level [3,6,7,16]. As can been seen, most notably in a study presented by [11] on threat monitoring, there are three classes of database users: 1) The masquerader who has gained access to the system by impersonating an authorized user; 2) The legitimate user who misuses his/her authority; 3)The clandestine user who is operating in stealth mode and nearly undetectable. As [11] notes, the legitimate user can be most difficult to detect using standard audit trail data, as abnormal behavior is difficult to detect when the occurrence is minimal or when the standard rules of operation are often subject to exceptions and modifications. If the access control methods are the focal point, a misconception that simply having the right levels of access control applied to the data components as defined by [16] is suf-

ficient to protect the data or that these methods will function as a deterrent to abusive access behavior. However, given statistics as noted previously on data breaches involving the legitimate user, it is understood in the industry that standard IDS with standard access control is not enough to prevent the insider threat risk. When taken in context with a legitimate user, these forms of detection and access control often fall short in detecting the abusive behavior [3,6,7,16].

Often, the developers of the common IDS make a false assumption that an entity accessing critical data is authenticated and authorized via external supporting automated security measures. These external authentication/ authorization methods reside primarily at the networking and/or operating system level. Another assumption is that authorization and authentication is a failsafe and always successfully identifies the entity as behaving in a trustworthy manner based on the high user database level access [6,7].

To aid in the closure of the gap between access rights, information protection and levels of responsibility, research in the area of the authorized insider threat risk as it relates to the capture of the critical data components has started to take shape. As seen in the [1] study an attempt is made to identify the person making a request for information via usage of the DBMS audit logs to determine whether the requestor is functioning within the boundaries of their security capacity. Again, as presented by [8] an attempt is made at identifying suspect actions via the usage of a quantitative measurement of transaction violations as had been mapped from the Database Management System (DBMS) audit logs. This measurement determines whether the requestor is making a "legal" request [8]. However, both of these studies fall just short of the proactive, dynamic and automatic identification of an abusive use of the data components by the authorized insider.

As previously noted, [20] attempts to identify the unauthorized insider by constructing a Networked Bayesian Network (NBN). This was done in an attempt to project the probability of an intrusion when critical data components are linked within a transaction. The deficient factors identified in this study are the authors' base assumption that 50% of all insiders are attempting to breach the system, leading the reader to conclude that the assumption is an unrealistic expectation given that there are no documented references in the study that lends itself to this percentage. In addition, the authors [4] realize that their proposed method is ineffective when applied to the authorized insider threat risk. However, if applied properly and with additional controls such as the use of the corporate access controls and security policies, this deficiency may be resolved. In addition to the inability of being able to identify an intrusion when executed by the authorized insider, the current research as demonstrated above produces a mutually exclusive view on abuse identification of the authorized user and the identification of a potentially harmful transaction when in actuality the two components should be working to compliment one another's strengths [1,6,7,8,20]. Therefore, the research put forth begins to fill the gap that exists between the concepts of malicious transaction and abusive action identification by expanding these concepts to incorporate the defined access control, security policies as well as the behavior of the authorized user to identify a viable, proactive solution that is both dynamic and automated.

3. Methodology

The foundations of this study were focused on three primary facets. The first was the research proposed by [21] with their methodologies of mining association rules within a large set of data using the Apriori Hybrid Algorithm. The methodologies put forth by [14] in the area of utilizing the Stochastic Gradient Boosting and the Bayesian Belief Network algorithms to determine probabilities was the second pillar for this study. Thirdly, current methodologies utilized in the dynamic maintenance area of security policy, known as Digital Rights Management (DRM) served as the final pillar to secure the foundation of this research. Along with the novel approach to database intrusion detection that guided the presented research, a series of modified Intrusion Detection System heuristics has been presented to provide a solid foundation for the acceptance of the results of the approach. The following paragraphs outline how these objectives were achieved.

3.1. Development Approach

The process began with the Trusted User initiating a transaction. Within the context of this study, whether the transaction is initiated via internal or external means has not been addressed but is considered in future work. Once the transaction has entered the presented dIDS system, several processes were initiated to determine the probability of an intrusion. The results from the probability assessment were stored in the dIDS repository for future reference by the dIDS. At this time, the transaction continued on to its completion since this study was focused on intrusion detection and not intrusion prevention. Future work focuses on extending the work presented into the intrusion prevention research area within the context of the database environment.

3.2. Association Rules

Following the building of the data repository that housed the various dIDS signatures, generation of the dIDS

training data dependencies signatures was the next logical step. As in most organizations, certain data components are dependent upon other data components. Often usage outside of the normal transactional scope is an anomaly in and of itself. For instance, the retrieval of only a consumer name data component really does not garner one much information however if that same consumer name component is used in tandem with the corresponding consumer address component, one can make inferences about the data that was retrieved. It then makes sense if the selection of certain data components is without their complimentary counterpart, one can reasonably conclude that an intrusion may be occurring. However, obtaining the data dependencies can be a daunting task given that there may be thousands of various data component combinations open to selection. As [22] have reasoned, often times, in intrusion detection, the training data is developed utilizing a significant amount of expert information about the system and often times this domain knowledge is difficult to obtain. Continuing with the implementation of the [21] Apriori Hybrid Algorithm to mine the association rules, the difficulty of the domain expertise is greatly reduced. Following the acquisition of the training data, it is then subsequently used to identify known intrusions. As [5] point out there is a direct relationship between the quality of the intrusion detection model and the quality of the training data obtained thru various data mining techniques. With this quality concern in mind, the study presented in this research utilized an Apriori Hybrid Algorithm in order to determine the most appropriate data dependency signatures (or rule associations) since there can be a high correlation between the combinations of the data components. Utilization of this type of algorithm is common during a data mining operations when obtaining a selection of relevant facts (data components) where the members have a high degree of correlation [21]. Application of the algorithm in this regard helped to limit the creation of data component combinations to only those where the historical pattern has been consistently demonstrated throughout the data. Once developed, the application of the algorithm to the TPC-C data occurs in order to determine which data components appear to be of significance for the processing environment of the prototype dIDS. Since the creation of the training data is a generic process, utilization of the algorithm to process the historical data in order to determine the data component significance is appropriate. As such, it is also appropriate to apply the training algorithm to a variety of input data following the definition of the components within the pool of information to develop newly identified association rules.

To begin this novel approach to database intrusion detection, an unsupervised learning process was initially employed in a data-mining environment to establish the baseline rules, which developed the data association rules that established the behavior correlations. Rule associations algorithms are well researched as noted above. These methods are considered the standard in data mining when trying to establish data correlations. The Apriori Algorithm as implemented by [23] is said to be the most popular of these types of mining operations [24]. However, an extension to this algorithm as developed by [23], called the Apriori Hybrid was utilized in the development of the initial data signatures because of its wide acceptance within the data mining community. This is due in part to the algorithm's quality levels when mining user behavior, patterns of access and the assigned classifications from historical data [24]. To implement the Association Rule algorithm, two steps are taken into account to satisfy the user-specified minimum support and the user-specified minimum confidence in parallel [23]. These two steps are as follows:

- Apply the minimum support to find all frequent item sets in the database
- Form the rules using the frequent item sets as defined in the first step and minimum confidence constraint.

Typically, the first step is more challenging since it involves searching all item combinations. Given the growth rate of the item set can be expressed as a potential for exponential growth depending on the number of items in the item set, a method of deterring this growth can be found with the implementation of the downward-closure property of the support constraint [23,24]. This property guarantees that for a frequent item set, all of its subsets are frequent and therefore for an infrequent item set, all of its supersets must be infrequent.

Since the Apriori Hybrid Algorithm exploits the best features of both the Apriori and the Apriori TID in addition to being one of the most popular of the Association Rules algorithms as noted by [24], its foundational properties have been employed in the presented research.

3.3. Probability of Intrusion

As evidenced in historical and current research, fuzzy logic and/or neural networks have been successfully used to determine whether an intrusion has been encountered [3]. Since "normal" behaviors are often known within the data processing environments and patterns of behavior can be established from the historical information, the utilization of a similar approach to the neural network IDS solution can be implemented utilizing the more defined decision tree methodology to determine the probability of an intrusion.

The data gathered during the data mining process as outlined above was then utilized to refine the prototype system by utilizing the supervised Stochastic Gradient

Boosting decision tree process to establish the probability of whether a given signature as created by the Apriori Hybrid Algorithm is considered an intrusion [14,25].

It should be noted that the recommend practice as suggested by [25], is to perform both the Stochastic Gradient Boosting tree creation as well as a single tree. This is because the Stochastic Gradient Boosting method is more like a "black box" methodology that is highly accurate however; it is difficult to visualize the relationships established during the process [25]. This recommendation of running both methods has been followed in the presented research to ensure the most complete information can be realized in building the model's accuracy as well as being able to fully understand the relationships.

Once the prototype had been successfully built with the association rules based on the Apriori Hybrid Algorithm as well as the detection signatures as identified in the Stochastic Gradient Boosting methodology, this same learning process was employed to account for new entities making requests for information. Upon the discovery of a new entity, the behavior signature repository was updated accordingly with relevant data.

3.4. Current Security Policies

In most organizations, the ability to dynamically create and maintain acceptable use policies tends to be an extensive and resource intensive process. For most, the development life cycle goes thru an iteration of steps ultimately ending up at the point where the policy must be published [12]. Today, most organizations' view on publishing the policy's modifications requires the updating of web pages, hard copy documents as well as applying any needed updates to the information systems via physical code modifications. Since a process so resource intensive can take weeks or even months to realize, often times, it is near impossible to determine if a violation of policy has occurred until sometime later. In recent times, the application of digital rights management systems (DRM) to allow for policy development and distribution is taking shape [26]. A DRM system is a system that allows for the management of the actions and entity can perform on a digital resource (the data) as well as controlling the usages of the resource within the information system. As [26] notes the ability to specify and manage the rights of an entity is one of the most important features of the DRM. Unlike standard authorization mechanisms, the DRM is meant to give specific rights to specific entities for a specific amount of time [26]. Bringing this notion of the DRM into the context of this research by building a DRM-like repository allowed for dynamic, real-time policy development that can be accessed at will by the presented intrusion detection system.

3.5. Detection of Abusive Activities with the Bayesian Approach

Since the Bayesian Belief Network (BBN) methodology employs a reasoning mechanism that the enables the determination of the probability of an event occurring when various factors are present, usage of the BBN is the most effective method of detection for this study.

The usage of BBN has been supported in recent literature as a viable method of intrusion detection. In [27] study, the Bayesian approach combined with a visualization component is defined to create an interactive intrusion detection system in an attempt to reduce the number of false positives presented in current intrusion detection systems. Again, in the [28] study, the Bayesian approach is applied to improve the effectiveness of the detection mechanism in the presented intrusion detection system for a mobile ad hoc network. Reference [20] used the Bayesian approach to expand the independent environment variables often present in intrusion detection to propose a networked Bayesian Network to understand the correlation between these environmental variables which may be used to identify an intrusion within a relational database. Therefore, with the objectives of this research endeavor in mind and in keeping with current research, the probabilistic approach of utilizing the BBN where the conditional probability and the causality relationships between the variables as defined have been applied to the presented intrusion detection system. Since the dIDS does have knowledge of the acceptable behaveiors, relevant security polices as well as the data dependencies, the BBN can make a reasonable assumption of the probability that an intrusion has occurred even when presented with new information.

Implementation of the BBN took the following path in the research presented. Initially, the data mined as described in the preceding paragraphs was used to identify the variables (nodes) of concern for the detection model as well as their association rules. With this information, the Directed Acyclic Graphs (DAG) was developed to visualize the conditional properties of the relationships presented. Following the creation of the DAGs the probabilities for each node was developed.

3.6. Information Flow Overview

The flow of information within the presented research and identified in **Figure 1** is as follows which is similar

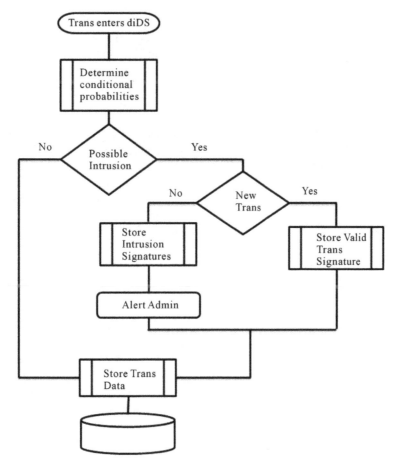

Figure 1. Information flow diagram.

to the [20] study. Each of the contributing factors, which include environment, policy as well as data component combinations were given a conditional probability. If the computed probability of the information request, (given the identified variables), fell within an acceptable range, the transaction was identified as not being an intrusion. However, if the probability fell outside of the acceptable range, the transaction was defined, as a potential intrusion where by further steps were completed in an attempt to make a determination as to whether or not the "true" intrusion flag is accurate. These further steps include looking into the system to determine if there are any new applications as well as users accessing the system. Should this situation present itself where the dIDS encounters a "new" entity, the signatures of the entity were stored for utilization in future detection processes. Should the system identify an actual intrusion, in addition to storing the intrusion signatures, the transaction was flagged as an intrusion that should be further examined.

It should be noted that in order to determine the most optimal thresholds, various probability thresholds were utilized. This aided in the determination of the level that the presented research is most effective with the goal being that the model should employ the most restrictive threshold possible while maintaining an acceptable level of detection.

3.7. Management of New Information

The research as is presented does not suggest that the flagged transactions should be prevented from completing its processing cycle. This decision should be left the system administrators given the business model in which the database operates. Future work focuses on extending this research into an intrusion prevention model to facilitate the prevention of potentially harmful transactions from reaching the database.

Continuing on to the acceptance of the new information within the dIDS, "new" data was collected via the development of a simulated payment processing application, where the necessary data components were established and persisted in a relational database. In addition, this subset of "new" data was utilized to develop the intelligent features needed to enable the system to automatically identify the new entity and "learn" from that new relationship for future reference.

To begin, a SQL Server 2008 Enterprise Edition database was created modeling the TPC-97 data structures. Give that one of the objectives of this research was to implement the Database Intrusion Detection System (dIDS) in an environment that supports the very large database (VLDB) concepts, the TPC-97 was selected as the data model of choice given its ability to support large amounts of data and transactions.

In order to generate a significant amount of data for the TPC-97 model, a data-generator software product was purchased under a research license via Red Gate Software, Ltd., a private limited company located in the UK. This software, called Data Generator, was specifically developed for the SQL Server environment to generate meaningful test data. To support this functionality, the generation of 1 million customer accounts as well as supporting order entry information, which included the customer order history using the primary keys of the schema's table object occurred. Following the build of the baseline TPC-97 objects, the specific tables for the intrusion detection system were generated along with the incoming transactions. The policy and entity information was manually entered using standard INSERT statements of the SQL query language given that the data was not complex in nature. To support incoming transactions to the TPC-97 database, 925 random transactions were generated based on the policies of the database. Following the requirements definition of the experiment the Apriori Hybrid algorithm was implemented in the Java programming language and applied against the TPC-97 database to determine the most common patterns of data contained within the data. These patterns served as the baseline patterns used in the dIDS.

To begin the process, the generated transactions were sequentially read into the dIDS where an attempt was made to seek out any existing patterns previously identified as well as any policies that may be set in place to govern the transaction processing. If the policy and pattern were found within the signature repository, the transaction was identified as being proper. However, if only a portion or no information was gathered about the transaction, it was subjected to further scrutiny by first going thru the Stochastic Gradient Boosting algorithm to understand the probability of an intrusion based on the transactional statically defined components such as the data relationships and defined policies. If the transaction continued to be identified as an intrusion by exceeding the pre-defined threshold, the transaction was then subjected to the Bayesian Belief Net algorithm to determine the probability that an intrusion was occurring based on the uncertainty of the environment and the prior behavior of the requestor. It should be understood that the requestor could be either a human or an electronic source. Should the transaction continue to be identified as an intrusion, it was flagged as an intrusion then logged as such in the signature table to be used in the analysis of future transactions. Manual verification and validation was then applied to determine whether the transaction was a true intrusion or classified as a false positive.

To support the learning component, if the transaction was not classified as an intrusion, it was also logged in the signature table along with the information to identify the transaction as a potential new signature. Like the intrusions that were identified during the probability of intrusion calculations, a manual verification and validation process was applied to determine the validity of the new log entry.

Since the availability of a standardized set of metrics used to measure intrusion detection at the level of the database are not readily available, the NIST algorithms that are used to measure network intrusion detection systems were modified to consider the database environment.

Instead of using the network packet as the focus of the measurements as is done in network intrusion detection systems, this research focused the attention on the incoming transaction that are requesting database services. This insider entity was defined to take on the role of an authorized application user, a Database Administrator or an automated program that requests database resources. These roles were defined in the additional database objects that were built to support the intrusion detection system. No programmatic distinction was made during the development of the functional dIDS as to which entity was requesting the information meaning that the policy definitions were the driving force in the identification of the requesting entity.

4. Findings

Intrusion detection at the database level remains a new concept within industry and research. Attempting to find a relevant study to measure the presented research against was difficult. That said, the [5] study was selected as a measurement due to similarities in methodology. In the [5] study, the authors built user profiles of normal behavior as a baseline to detect anomalies. In addition, included in the [5] study was the deployment of the Bayesian approach to estimate probabilities to strengthen their intrusion detection process. Given these commonalities, the information presented in this study served to create the goal measurements for the presented work. Other studies on database intrusion detection identified in this research had a significant enough difference in approach and methodology that they could not be used to create a reasonable and like objective value.

The metrics identified in [7] are presented at a degree of abstraction higher than what was useful for this study. Therefore, the data identified in [7] was expanded and mined in an effort to make visible enough natural detail to provide a reasonable comparison to the presented work. Given that in [7] the successful detection rate was identified at 38.38%, it also served as the baseline for successful detection in this study. The presented study achieved similar results that fell within the range of

<61.62% for false responses and ≥38.38% positive responses.

Additionally and where applicable, specific baseline measurement values identified in [7] were adopted and included in accordance with the Information Assurance Directorate (IAD)-US Government Protection Profile for Intrusion Detection Systems as described in [7,28,29,31]. Specifically, these measurements inclusive as quailtative measurements that relate directly to the accuracy of the detection model as defined in the following.

4.1. Coverage

Coverage (c) is determined by the rate which IDS can successfully identify an attack under ideal conditions. The original measurement as identified by [29] is concerned with detecting and measuring the number of unique attacks. This measurement, in a signature-based system, is achieved by verifying the number of valid signatures (s) and mapping them to a standard naming schema. The entering transaction (t) is then measured against the known signatures to determine if the transacttion exists within the signature baseline. If the transaction does exist, it is then considered a valid request for information since it meets the criteria of an authorized entity. If the signature does not exist, it is considered a successful recognition of an anomaly and counted in the measurement as noted in Equation (1). To support database intrusion detection in regards to the authorized insider, the measurement presented was adapted to focus attention on the rate by which IDS can identify an anomaly that has been initiated by authorized insiders at various levels of authorization. Therefore, only transactions that are initiated by a trusted user are considered in the measurement. This measurement achieved a rate of ≥38.38% as is indicated using the data presented in [7].

$$c = \sum (t \notin s)/s \qquad (1)$$

4.2. Probability of Detection

This measurement determines the detection rate (d) of attacks correctly detected (b) by an IDS in a given environment during a particular period (T) in minutes [29]. As with the Coverage measurement, probability of detection assumes that various types of attacks were measured. Given that this study is focused on one type of attack, the measurement was adjusted to focus on the various levels of authorization of the information requestor as opposed to the various types of attacks. Given that the false positive rate is directly related to the detection rate, care must be given to ensure that the scenarios are exact and consistent when used in both measurements. This measurement, in accordance with the baseline data set as presented in [7] achieved a rate of measurement of ≥38.38%

of correctly identified attacks.

$$d = \left(\frac{b}{t}\right) * T \qquad (2)$$

4.3. Volume of Data

This measurement determines the difference in the volume of data (v) the dIDS can manage when presented with a large mass of transactions as compared with the pre IDS implementation. While data as presented in the NIST IR-7007 identifies the number packet/second for the network IDS, when put into the context of this study, the transaction will be the unit of measure. Additionally, this measurement will identify the change of data volume pre and post dIDS implementation in order to identify any latency issues that may be present.

Given that this measurement is very subjective to the system environment, the initial transaction sets were processed without the implementation of the dIDS to capture the rate of processing using the maximum (m) volume of data. This measurement was considered the baseline processing rate. Following the establishment of the baseline measurement, the same transaction set was processed through the implementation of the dIDS (i) to determine the change in processed transactions through the dIDS implementation. The pre and post IDS expressions used to calculate this measurement, m and i can be defined as follows:

- m = Tpre/s where Tpre is the number of pre-IDS transactions and s is the elapsed processing time (in seconds) for the transaction set
- i = Tpost/s where Tpost is the number of post-IDS transactions and s is the elapsed processing time (in seconds) for the transaction set

Pre-IDS results show 408.38 as the volume of data transactions per second. Overall the system performed as expected with the greatest latency observed at iteration 4 with 309.67 as the volume of data transactions per second or a delta of 98.71 transactions.

$$v = m - i \qquad (3)$$

4.4. Adaptability Rate

The Adaptability (a) Rate measurement determines the rate by which the presented dIDS was able to identify new, valid (v) transactions and new, authorized users (u). It is presented, as an aggregate and identified as total new (n) transactions. Note that new information always carries a higher rate of false positives when introduced to the dIDS and this will be reflected in the development of this measurement. The anticipated adaptability rate was achieved at ≥25% of new transactions identified.

The threshold values for the Adaptability Rate were manually modified in the code as the iterations progressed through the testing phase. The policy tables were also modified manually to test the response of the dIDS and its ability to recognize changes and permissions.

Transaction volume was not considered in the intrusion probability calculation in an effort to keep the intrusion process independent from the input. This allowed the system to recognize a normalized range of probabilities regardless of transaction volume during the intrusion detection process. As the metrics contained within this research demonstrate, the probability range remained stable and consistent throughout the testing phase.

Using the generated data, the Apriori Hybrid data mining Algorithm was deployed using the SPMF software created by [30]. The resulted in an in the generation of 13,199 patterns of data. Examination of these patterns reflect a support of <0.8 and creating less meaningful information. Often patterns were generated that had no value in the intrusion detection process. To avoid this, the threshold of pattern utilization was set at ≥0.8. The results were 14 common behavior patterns and 95 data patterns. Within the data patterns 14 common fields were identified. These results were then utilized as the baseline signature of the dIDS system.

To support the incoming transaction set, 925 incoming transactions were generated using the Data Generator software. However, the study only used 115% or 12.5% of the amount of input that [7] used, the sample reduction did not affect the testing since the study is focused on the percentage of transactions identified as an intrusion and not the volume. Additionally, the following results can further be inferred to account for the larger dataset.

The data was generated based on the behaviors identified in the Apriori Hybrid data mining process. The patterns mined were determined to be the valid signatures while the remaining. Using the valid signatures patterns as the catalyst, both valid and invalid transactions were generated.

Monitoring and subsequent analysis of incoming transactions will determine probability of intrusion by identifying the tokens in a transaction. Tokens are included the action SELECT, INSERT, UPDATE, DELETE as well as the individual columns, with the identity of the requesting entity and WHERE and SET clauses, (when present). Once identified, these tokens were then compared to policy tables to determine if they were contained in an existing policy. If the transaction is validated based on the information in the policy tables, the transaction was considered a non-intrusion. If not validated, the intrusion process will be triggered.

Once triggered, the intrusion process will compare the incoming transaction to the database transaction logs in an attempt to identify a new, valid signature. The method of identifying the information contained within the logs was implemented by way of a dynamically generated

SELECT statement where a probability was computed based on how many of the tokens were found on a single log entry when taking into account the environmental factors (as previously noted). Next a probability was generated using the Stochastic Gradient Boosting algorithm. If the result was greater than 0.75, the transaction was marked as a new signature; otherwise it was subjected to further scrutiny. The 0.75 probability threshold used to identify a new signature was established at a high value since a transaction that is not yet considered valid can hold a higher degree of risk.

If the transaction was not validated in the new signature identification process, the transaction was subjected to the intrusion detection process. Unlike the new signature identification process, logs do not support the intrusion transaction. To refine the intrusion probability the transaction's probability of intrusion was computed by the Stochastic Gradient Boosting algorithm. This allowed control over the refinement of the threshold level. Then the transaction was subjected to further refinement using the Bayesian Belief Net algorithm. If the probability of this primary review was below the threshold, it was deemed as a non-intrusion event and added to the signature table as a validated signature. Should the incoming transaction require further analysis the same principle as identified for the stochastic Gradient Boosting Algorithm was applied to the application of the Bayesian Belief Net algorithm. If this probability computation resulted in a value that was above the control threshold, the transaction was deemed an intrusion and logged to the intrusion table to be used in the on-going signature identification process. There were six (6) iterations of the transaction cycle performed during the testing phase using the various threshold values.

$$a = (u + v)/n \qquad (4)$$

5. Conclusions and Future Work

5.1. Conclusions

Based on the information provided to the dIDS model, the following conclusions have been drawn. Identification of "good" vs. "malicious" transactions is greatly dependent upon the information contained within the transaction itself, the log information, the number of rows being impacted by the database request and the policies pertaining to the entity making the request and the behavior of the requesting entity. Without consideration of each of these components within the context of each other, it cannot be accurately determined if the authorized insider is behaving as expected.

When using the Stochastic Gradient Boosting algorithm alone, when compared to using both algorithms to reach a finer degree of analysis, is less effective than use both algorithms together in a single process when attempting to identify an intrusive transaction. By using both algorithms within the same intrusion process, the number of false-positives was markedly reduced.

Several types of transactions were introduced to indicate a new entity; the system was able to identify the new entity as the testing iterations progressed regardless of what the threshold rate was set at. When policy changes were introduced, the system correctly identified the intrusion and non-intrusion state.

Overall, the system presented proved very successful. Each goal with the exception of the maintaining the latency factor at a steady rate was met. Further research in the area of maintaining or reducing the latency of a Database intrusion detection system is warranted.

As has been observed, to use one methodology in an attempt to identify the insider threat phenomena in the context of the database environment, that supports a reasonable probability measurement, cannot be considered a complete solution. The uncertainty of the requestor's prior behavior must take into consideration along with the complete set of data and environmental factors in order to reach the conclusion that the insider is behaving beyond the boundaries as stated within defined security policies.

This research also observed that it is possible to leave the system in unattended learning environment in order to determine the probability of intrusion when the system is presented with new information as long as the other factors as noted are considered.

5.2. Future Works

The success of this research was based upon the research of many other researchers in not only intrusion detection but in the database technologies as well.

This research simply laid the foundations for future work to be investigated with respect to Database intrusion detection systems. To further the positive results presented, it can be expected that research in the following areas will build upon what has been presented in the preceding sections.

The presented research was based upon current research in intrusion detection models. Some of these models are utilized at the network level while others are at the database level. While intrusion detection does aid in the discovery of potential intrusions, it still requires a manual decision to be made by an intrusion administrator as to whether the incoming database request can be definitively considered a non-intrusion event. This is most often accomplished by some form of human intervention. Expansion of this study to move from an intrusion detection model to an intrusion prevention model allows for an expansion in the research area which enables the next generation of database security to be realized.

Latency continues to be a concern whenever one considers the implementation of a component that forces extra work on the database. This is unavoidable as every layer of security requires some degree of computing power. At the database level of the technology stack, this latency is most often evident in the response times associated with the database request given that the system is asking the database for more information in an attempt to make a sustainable decision as to the state of the intrusion event.

In addition, since this study assumed that the database environment must be a complete system, more information on history, behavior and policy will need to be maintained in order to have a robust database intrusion model. By the nature of more data, latency will continue to grow, as more resources in terms of data and input/output processes will be utilized during the detection process. By moving the intrusion model to the database engine level, the system will be inherently faster since there will be less of the technology stack to traverse which ultimately reduces the latency time.

6. Acknowledgements

The author would like to thank Dr. Cannady for his guidance in the development of this research and Anthony Beshouri for his keen eye for refinement.

REFERENCES

[1]   J. Fonseca, M. Vieira and H. Madeira, "Online Detection of Malicious Data Access Using DBMS Auditing," Association for Computing Machinery, New York, 2008.

[2]   A. Kamra, E. Bertino and G. Lebanon, "Mechanisms for Database Intrusion Detection and Response," Association for Computing Machinery, New York, 2008.

[3]   S. Castano, M. Fugini, G. Martella and P. Samarati, "Database Security", Association for Computing Machinery, New York, 1994.

[4]   S. Gaudin, "Computer Crimes Charged in College Cash-for-Grades Scheme, 2007.
http://www.informationweek.com/story/showArticle.jhtml?a

[5]   J. Vijayan, "DBA Admits to Theft of 8.5m Records," 2007.
http://www.computerworld.com/action/article.do?command=viewArticleBasic&articleId=308611&source=rss_topic82

[6]   Y. Hu and B. Panda, "A Data Mining Approach for Database Intrusion Detection," Association for Computing Machinery, New York, 2004.

[7]   K. Ilgun, A. Kamra, E. Tertzi and E. Bertino, "Detecting Anomalous Access Patterns in Relational Databases," *The VLDB Journal*, Vol. 17 No. 5, 2007, pp. 1603-1077.

[8]   G. Lu, J. Yi and K. Lü, "A Dubiety-Determining Based

[9]   E. Shmueli, R. Vaisenberg, Y. Elovici and C. Glezer, "Database Encryption: An Overview of Contemporary Challenges and Design Considerations", *ACM SIGMOD Record*, Vol. 38 No. 3, 2009, pp. 29-34.

[10] J. Allen, A. Christie, W. Fithen, J. McHugh, J. Pickel and E. Stoner, "State of Practice of Intrusion Detection Technologies," Carnegie Mellon University, Pittsburgh, 2000.

[11] S. Axelsson, "Intrusion Detection Systems: A Survey and Taxonomy," Chalmers University of Technology, Goteborg, 2000.

[12] S. Kumar and E. H. Spafford, "An Application of Pattern Matching in Intrusion Detection," Purdue University, Lafayette, 1994.

[13] S. E. Smaha, "Tools for Misuse Detection," Information Systems Security Association, Portland, 1993.

[14] G. E. Leipins and H. S. Vaccaro, "Anomaly Detection: Purpose and Framework," *Proceedings of 12th National Computer Security Conference*, 1989, pp. 495-504.

[15] H. Debar, M. Becke and D. Siboni, "A Neural Network Component for an Intrusion Detection System," *Proceedings of IEEE Computer Society Symposium on Security and Privacy*, Oakland, 4-6 May 1992, pp. 240-250.

[16] D. E. Denning, "An Intrusion Detection Model", *IEEE Transactions on Software Engineering*, Vol. 13 No. 2, 1993, pp. 222-232.

[17] T. F. Lunt, A. Tamru, F. Gilham, R. Jagannathan, C. Jalai, P. G. Newman, H. S. Javitz, A. Valdes and T. D. Garvey, "A Real-time Intrusion Detection Expert System (IDES)", Final Technical Report for SRI Project 6784, 1992.

[18] R. A. Kemmerer and P. A. Porras, "State Transition Analysis: A Rule-based Intrusion Detection Approach," *IEEE Transactions on Software Engineering*, Vol. 21 No. 3, 1995, pp. 181-199.

[19] H. S. Venter, M. S. Oliver and J. H. P. Eloff, "PIDS: A Privacy Intrusion Detection System" *Internet Research*, Vol. 14 No. 5, 2004, pp. 360-365.

[20] X. An, D. Jutla and N. Cercone, "A Bayesian Network Approach to Detecting Privacy Intrusion," *Proceedings of 2006 International Conferences on Web Intelligence and Intellgent Agent Technology Workshop*, Hongkong, 18-22 December 2006, pp. 73-76.

[21] R. Agrawal and P. Srikant, "Fast Algorithms for Mining Association Rules in Large Databases," Morgan Kaufmann Publishers, San Francisco, 1994.

[22] Z. Yu, J. J. Tsai and T. Weigert, "An Adaptive Automatically Tuning Intrusion Detection System," *ACM Transactions on Autonomous and Adaptive Systems*, Vol. 3, No. 3, 2008, pp. 1-25.

[23] R. Agrawal, T. Imielinski and A. Swami, "Mining Association Rules between Sets of Items in Large Databases," *Proceedings of ACM International Conference on Management of Data (SIGMOD 93)*, Washington DC, 1993, pp. 207-216.

[24] J. Hipp, U. Guntzer and G. Nakhaeizadeh, "Algorithms

for Association Rule Mining—A General Survey and Comparison," *ACM SIGKDD Explorations Newsletter*, Vol. 2 No. 1, 2000, pp. 58-64.

[25] P. H. Sharrod, "TreeBoost: Stochastic Gradient Boosting," 2003. http://www.dtreg.com/treeboost.htm

[26] P. J. Windley "Digital identity," O'Reilly, Sebastopol, 2005.

[27] S. Axelsson, "Combining a Bayesian Classifier with Visualization: Understanding the IDS," *Proceedings of ACM Workshop on Visualization and Data Mining for Computer Security*, New York, 2004, pp. 99-108.

[28] A. H. R. Karim, R. M. Rajatheva and K. M. Ahmed, "An Efficient Collaborative Intrusion Detection System for MANET Using Bayesian Approach," *Proceedings of 9th*

ACM International Symposium on Modeling Analysis and Simulation of Wireless and Mobile Systems (*MSWiM* 06), New York, 2006, pp. 187-190.

[29] P. Mell, V. Hu, R. Lippman, J. Haines and M. Zissman, "An Overview of Issues in Testing Intrusion Detection Systems" 2003. http://csrc.nist.gov/publications/PubsNISTIRs.html

[30] P. Fournier-Viger, "Computer Software Documentation," 2008. http://www.philippe-fournierviger.com/spmf/

[31] United States of America (USA), "US Government Protection Profile: Intrusion Detection System for Basic Robustness Environments," National Security Agency (NSA), Washington DC, 2007.

17

Hadoop Based Defense Solution to Handle Distributed Denial of Service (DDoS) Attacks

Shweta Tripathi[1], Brij Gupta[1*], Ammar Almomani[2], Anupama Mishra[1], Suresh Veluru[3]
[1]School of Computing Science & Engineering, Galgotias Universiy, Greater Noida, India
[2]Faculty of Computing and Information Technology, North Jeddah Branch, King Abdulaziz University, Jeddah, Saudi Arabia
[3]School of Engineering and Mathematical Sciences, City University London, London, UK

ABSTRACT

Distributed denial of service (DDoS) attacks continues to grow as a threat to organizations worldwide. From the first known attack in 1999 to the highly publicized Operation Ababil, the DDoS attacks have a history of flooding the victim network with an enormous number of packets, hence exhausting the resources and preventing the legitimate users to access them. After having standard DDoS defense mechanism, still attackers are able to launch an attack. These inadequate defense mechanisms need to be improved and integrated with other solutions. The purpose of this paper is to study the characteristics of DDoS attacks, various models involved in attacks and to provide a timeline of defense mechanism with their improvements to combat DDoS attacks. In addition to this, a novel scheme is proposed to detect DDoS attack efficiently by using MapReduce programming model.

Keywords: DDoS; DoS; Defense Mechanism; Characteristics; Hadoop; MapReduce

1. Introduction

DDoS attack is a distributed, large scale coordinated attempt of flooding the network with an enormous amount of packets which is difficult for victim network to handle, and hence the victim becomes unable to provide the services to its legitimate user and also the network performance is greatly deteriorated [1]. This attack exhausts the resources of the victim network such as bandwidth, memory, computing power etc. The system which suffers from attacked or whose services are attacked is called as "primary victim" and on other hand "secondary victims" is the system that is used to originate the attack. These secondary victims provide the attacker, the ability to wage a more powerful DDoS attack as it is difficult to track down the real attacker [2].

Denial of Service (DoS) attacks is used to consume all the resources of the target machine (victim's services) and becomes a known issue in 1980's. But, in 1990's these attacks have been noticed as it becomes a serious problem to the Internet society gradually [2-4]. DDoS attack is a distributed, large scale coordinated attempt of exhausting the network with an enormous amount of request, which overload the victim's machine and the victim's machine becomes unable to provide the services to its legitimate user and hence the network performance will be greatly deteriorated.

In DDoS attack, the attacker selects the compromised machine (*i.e.* those machines which have loopholes) and network of the compromised machines are called botnet. These botnets are further instructed to execute commands in order to consume all the resources available on victim's system. Currently attacks are being launched by using two approaches. The first approach is to send malicious packet injected with virus, worms as a running application, is called as vulnerability attack. The other very common method is to debilitate the victim's system, by exhausting the resources such as input-output bandwidth, database bandwidth, CPU, memory, etc. [5].

A group called "Izz ad-Din al-Qassam Cyber Fighters" [6] has launched DDoS attack against many US Banks such as Bank of America, Citi Group, HSBC and Capital One. As a result, these online banking sites have degraded. **Figure 1** shows various attacks over the years. From the figure, we can see that total number of attacks increases gradually every year. **Table 1** shows some serious DDoS attack incidents in past years. It is noted that attacks incidents are increasing gradually specially in financial market.

---

*Corresponding author.

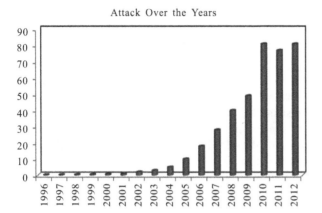

Figure 1. Timeline of attacks over the years.

Rest of the paper is organized as follows: Section 2 describes DDoS attacker's motivation factors, Section 3 contains history of DDoS attacks, Section 4 presents DDoS attack characteristics and models, Section 5 describes DDoS attack toolkit, Section 6 presents how DDoS attacks are preformed using botnet, Section 7 describes various DDoS defense mechanisms, Section 8 contains our proposed model for DDoS attacks detection and finally, Section 9 concludes the paper and discusses some future work.

2. DDoS Attacker's Motivation Factors

Human beings are not born to become an attacker. They are enough motivated due to some reasons to launch the attack. Based on some obvious reasons and facts, the motivation factor can be categorized as [7]:

1) Financial Benefit

The attackers of this category are highly skilled and hard to be detected. They only concern here is to have financial gain.

2) Professional Skills

The attackers target systems for experiment purpose to check their vulnerabilities and strength of security mechanism. The attackers who are very much enthusiastic and ready to face challenges fall into this category.

3) Payback Attitude

In this category, the attackers are usually very much frustrated and low skilled persons, perform attack only to take revenge.

4) Cyber Warfare

In this category, attackers are usually high skilled and intellectual person who generally belong to military or terrorist organizations of a country. They attack to defend their country or their organizations [8].

3. History of DDoS Attacks

3.1. Analytical Study of DDoS Attacks

A long run way which has no end point of attacks can be seen even in advanced technical society. To develop defense mechanism, behavior of attack can be analyzed, which leads to the categorization of DDoS attack.

Practical Unix and Internet Security [14], the "bible" for many system administrators of the early commercial web, offers a chapter on denial of service attacks. Carnegie Mellon's Computer Emergency Response Team[*]

Table 1. DDoS attack statistics.

2013	The Czech financial sector was targeted in cyber attacks on Wednesday, at the same time on the national bank and stock exchange websites which get disrupted by dedicated denial of service (DDoS) attacks—London, 8 March, 2013.
2012	US and UK Government Sites Knocked Down by Anonymous—April 16, 2012. DDoS Attack Impacts Canadian Political Party Elections—March 24, 2012.
2011	A DDoS attack on Sony was used—April 16-20 2011.
2010	PayPal Transaction is suspended over WikiLeaks website after attacked by DDoS—December 3-5, 2010.
2009	The Mydoom virus code was re-used to launch DDoS flooding attacks against major government news media and financial websites in South Korea and the United States in July 2009 [9].
2008	BBC hit by DDoS Attack, two DDoS attacks on Amazon.com and eBuy.
2007	Estonia Cyber Attack [10].
2006	US Banks have been targeted for financial gain.
2004	SCO Group website inaccessible to legitimate users.
2003	Mydoom defiled thousands of victims to attack SCO and Microsoft [11].
2002	13 root servers that provide the Domain Name System (DNS) service to Internet users around the world shut down for an hour because of a DDoS flooding attack [12].
2001	First major attack involving DNS servers as reflectors. The target was Register.com. The Irish Government's Department of Finance server was hit by a denial of service attack carried out as part of a student campaign from NUI Maynooth.
2000	Yahoo! Experienced one of the first major DDoS flooding attacks that kept the company's services off the Internet for about 2 hours incurring a significant loss in advertising revenue [13].

(CERT) [15,16] published its first bulletin on SYN flooding* (a popular technique for overwhelming target system) in September 1996, and a more thorough bulletin on denial of service in October 1997, suggesting that denial of service was beginning to emerge as a priority for network administrators. While CERT and others offered helpful advice for mitigating DDoS attacks, the particular attack documented in 1996—SYN flooding—is still common today, pointing to the wide gap between understanding these attacks and successfully defending against them. Similarly, the US National Information Infrastructure Protection Act of 1996 took steps to criminalize DDoS, redefining computer fraud "damage" as preventing the right to use a computer system. Previous definitions had focused on unauthorized access and damage to systems. But as per Arbor's annual survey reports, many system administrators do not bother to reporting DDoS attacks to the authorities.

Shortly after denial of service emerged as a concern for system administrators, activists began using it as a political technique. Ricardo Dominguez, co-founder of Electronic Disturbance Theatre, was one of the leaders in using denial of service as a tool for activists in 1998. He built FloodNet, a tool designed to allow activists to crash the websites of the Frankfurt Stock Exchange, the Pentagon, and Mexican President Ernesto Zedillo [17]. But as these protests failed to shut down the sites, they were not much discussed outside the art community. Denial of service took on new visibility and importance in February 2000, when it took down several websites like Yahoo, Buy.com, ZDNet.com, eBay, CNN, Amazon.com.

DDoS attacks became more common in 2000 and in 2001, it is used to compromise large numbers of Windows systems. Worms and Trojan horse programs sent via email demonstrated the ability to exploit known vulnerabilities to compromise large numbers of systems [18]. At the same time, attackers began to organize compromised computers into networks centrally controlled by IRC "bots". These "botnets", allows a single controller to manipulate thousands of compromised computers and order them to send spam email and do other mischievous things like stealing credit card information, or mounting DDoS attacks.

Most existing techniques for defending against denial of service attacks were based on identifying the attacking computers by IP address. Botnets invalidated many of these techniques because a single botnet could include thousands of computers with randomly distributed IP addresses, which is very difficult to distinguish by IP address alone.

Despite the rise of botnets, various other forms of DDoS have continued to ask for media coverage and attention. Recently, an organization named "Help Israel Win" invited individuals to install a software package ("Patriot DDoS") on their PCs which would give a remote administrator the capability to harness the machine in an attack on a (Palestinian) target [19].

In 2010, during the Iranian Green Movement protests, protesters used a page refreshing service to manually execute a DDoS attack that was an attempt to bring down President Mahmoud Ahmadinejad's website [20,21]. On the similar lines, "Operation Payback" requires participants to download a software named "Low Orbit Ion Cannon" that allows a computer to become part of a botnet controlled by administrators of the Anonymous group via IRC.

Some (In) famous DDoS Attacks.

The Iranian Cyber Army: It happened on December 17, 2009, when attackers replaced the front page of a famous social networking site, Twitter.com with an image of the Iranian flag along with text including: "This site has been hacked by the Iranian Cyber Army", although they could not succeed in their act, but managed to change the twitter.com domain name to point to a other IP address. The attack causes Twitter to take down its home page and twitter.com remained down for a couple of hours [22,23].

The attacks on the major Web sites began in early February 2000, with the first major attack being on Yahoo! The surprise attack took the Yahoo! Site down for more than three hours. It was based on the Smurf attack, and most likely, the Tribe Flood Network technique. At the peak of the attack, Yahoo! was receiving more than one gigabit per second of data requests.

In February, 2010, a group of people loosely connected through Internet forums calling themselves "Anonymous" executed a DDoS attack against the Australian Parliament's website. The attack not only took down the site for two days but also defaced the Prime Minister's website, by replacing the front page with pornographic images for a brief period of time. The attack was termed "Operation Titstorm" by its organizers [24] referring to a mandatory Internet filtering policy proposed by Australia's ruling party designed in part to counter pornography [25].

3.2. DDoS Observations

1) The ideology of an attacker and the method chosen for attacks is not correlated.

2) It is found that there is specific geographic pattern of DDoS attacks.

3) Easily accessible tools that helps to make successful attacks on small websites, suggests that distressed individuals may use DDoS as a weapon for building score or making a political point.

3.3. Recent Attacks

1) Mt. Gox under largest DDoS attack

The largest bit coin exchange said that on April 4 2013, it is fighting an intense distributed denial-of-service attack and it believes that it is intended at manipulating the price of virtual currency, which has seen unstable price fluctuation in the past few days. According to Facebook, Mt. Gox, which is based in Tokyo, the attacks have caused its worst trading lags ever and caused error pages to be displayed to traders. As per their own estimation, 80 percent of the bit coin trades in US dollars are executed on Mt. Gox's trading platform and a significant amount of trade in other currencies [26-28].

2) American Express under DDoS Attack

American Express confirms it was hit by a distributed-denial-of-service attack that disrupted online-account access for about two hours during the late afternoon on March 28. The attack began at about 3:00 PM ET on March 28, caused intermittent disruptions. It was said that there is no evidence to suggest that customer data or account information was exposed or compromised during the attack. AmEx issued a statement regarding the attack on how their operations were getting affected by DDoS attack [29-31].

3) Attack on Spamhaus

UK and Switzerland-based nonprofit organization, which operates a filtering service, has been strike by distributed denial of service (DDoS) attack, which has proven to be the largest DDoS till today. Security firm Kaspersky Lab confirmed the attack and claimed it to be the largest DDoS cyber-attack. As per Kaspersky Lab the attack was evaluated to at 300 Gigabits per second and supposed to be one of the largest DDoS operations to date [32].

4) Latest attacks on banks of US

In December 14, 2012, the major US banks websites were attacked. The attackers, who call themselves the Izz ad-Din al-Qassam Cyber Fighters, launched attacks on Tuesday against the websites of US Bancorp, JP Morgan Chase & Co., Bank of America, PNC Financial Services-Group and SunTrust Banks. Dan Holden, who is director of security research at Arbor Networks, said "While the DDoS attack could not hamper the online operation of bank but they taught lesson to those who faced the threat" [29].

In Nov. 8 2012, Webster Bank and Zions Bancorp joined the list of banks which experienced the online outages linked to distributed-denial-of-service attacks. Webster, a $20 billion institution based in Connecticut, a DDoS attack hit its website at about 4:30 p.m. Nov. 6 and continued until about 2 a.m. Nov. 7. And Zions, a $53 billion bank based in Utah, an attack caused four hours of intermittent outages for online-banking and website access during the late afternoon and evening of Nov. 8.

5) Go Daddy stopped by DDoS attack

An attacker has claimed responsibility for DoS attack that has knocked out millions of website hosted by world's largest domain registrar GoDaddy [33].

6) iMassage DDoS attack

A group of iOS developers are targeted with a series of rapid-fire texts sent over Apple's iMessage system. The messages which seem to be transmitted via the OS X Messages application used a simple AppleScript which rapidly fill up the Messages app on iOS or the Mac with text and force users to constantly clear both notifications and messages. In some of the cases, the messages were so large that they completely lock up the Messages app on iOS, constituting a "denial of service" (DoS) attack [32].

3.4. Well-Known DoS Attacks Mechanism

This paper would be incomplete without reference to some of the most well-known DDoS attacks. Some of the most famous standard DDoS attacks are summarized as follows:

- Apache 2: This attack is build up against an Apache Web server where the client asks for a service by sending a request with many HTTP headers. Upon receiving the large amount of HTTP request Apache Web server cannot outface the load and it crashes.
- ARP Poison: Address Resolution Protocol (ARP) Poison attacks claims the attacker to have key in to the victim's LAN. The attacker spoof the hosts of a specific LAN by providing them with wrong MAC addresses for hosts with already-known IP addresses. This can be done by the attacker through the following procedure: The network is monitored for "who-has" requests type which is an ARP request. The moment such a request is received; the malevolent attacker tries to respond as fast as feasible to the questioning host so that it can mislead it for the requested address.
- Back: In Back type of attack the requests are send an apache Web server, where the server is flooded with requests containing a large number of front-slash (/) characters in the URL description. When the server tries to process all these requests, it becomes unable to process other legitimate requests and hence it denies service to its legitimate user.
- CrashIIS: The CrashIIS attack is commonly a projected towards Microsoft Windows NT IIS Web server. The attacker sends the victim a malicious GET request, which causes the Web server to crash.
- Land: In this type of attack the attacker sends TCP SYN packet to the victim that contains the same IP address as the source and destination addresses. Such a packet completely blocks the victim's system.
- DoS Nuke: This kind of attack is launched against the Microsoft Windows NT victim is inundated with

"out-of-band" data (MSG_OOB). The packets that are sent by the attacking machines are flagged "urg" because of the MSG_OOB flag. This causes the target to get down, and this leads to displays a "blue screen of death" on the victim machine.

- Mail bomb: In this type of attack, the victim's mail queue is flooded by a huge amount of messages, causing system failure.
- SYN Flood: A SYN flood attack take place during the three-way handshake that marks the onset of a TCP connection. In the three-way handshake, a client sends a TCP SYN packet to a server requesting for a new connection. Thereby, the server sends a SYN/ACK packet back to the client and places the connection request in a queue. As a final point, the client acknowledges the SYN/ACK packet. When an attack takes place, however, the attacker sends an abundance of TCP SYN packets to the victim, forcing it for both: 1) to open a lot of TCP connections and 2) to respond to them. Then the attacker does not execute the final step of the three-way handshake that follows, exposing the victim that is not capable to accept any new incoming connections, since its queue is full of half-open TCP connections.
- Ping of Death: In Ping of Death attacks, the attacker creates a packet that contains more than 65,536 bytes, which is out of the limit of the IP protocol. This packet can produce different kinds of damage to the machine that receives it, that results in crashing and rebooting.
- Process Table: This attack use the feature of some network services to generate a new process each time a new TCP/IP connection is set up. The attacker considers making as many uncompleted connections to the victim as possible in order to force the victim's system to generate as many as processes. For this reason, as the number of processes that are running on the system cannot be very much large, the attack renders the victim unable to serve any other request.
- Smurf Attack: In a "smurf" attack, the victim is thronged with Internet Control Message Protocol (ICMP) "echo-reply" packets. The attacker sends voluminous ICMP "echo-request" packets to the broadcast address of numerous subnets. These packets have the source IP address field updated with victims address. Every machine that is associated with any of these subnets responds by sending ICMP "echo-reply" packets to the victim. Smurf attacks are very alarming, because they are intensely distributed attacks.
- SSH Process Table: This attack makes large amount of connections to the victim with the Secure Shell (SSH) Protocol without carrying out the login process. In this way, the zombie contacted by the SSH on the victim's system is indulged to start so many SSH

processes that it is fatigued.
- Syslogd: In this type of attack the Solaris 2.5 server is banged by sending large amount of messages with illegal source IP address.
- TCP Reset: In TCP Reset attacks, the network is scrutinized for "tcp connection" requests which are send to the victim. The moment such a request is found; the malicious attacker sends a spoofed TCP RESET packet to the victim and obliges it to lay off the TCP connection.
- Teardrop: A Teardrop attack causes a stream of IP fragments with their offset field overloaded. As a packet travels from the source machine to the destination machine, it is broken up into smaller sections or fragments, through the process of fragmentation. The destination host that tries to reassemble these abnormal fragments in the long run clangs or reboots.
- UDP Storm: In a User Datagram Protocol (UDP) connection, when it receive a UDP packet, a character generation ("chargen") service generates a series of characters, while an echo service echoes any character it receives. Manipulating the above two services, the attacker sends a packet to another machine with the source misleading to be that of the victim. Then, the echo service of the anterior machine echoes the data of that packet back to the victim's machine and the victim's machine, consecutively, responds in the similar fashion. Hence, a constant stream of unserviceable load is created that problems the network [32].

4. DDoS Attack: Characteristics and Models

4.1. Characteristics of DDoS Attack

Following are the different ways to characterize the distributed denial of service attack:

1) Disruptive/Degrade Impact

After being a part of attack, the victim either to stop providing services to the client or the services are degraded that means some of the services are still being provided to the client even the victim's system is under the attack.

2) Exploiting Vulnerability

Network of machines which follows the instructions of master attacker to send request for a service on a victim's machine to consume its all the resources.

3) Dynamic Attack Rate

Sometime attacker make down the websites very quickly by sending large no of request more than its capacity, is known as constant attack rate. While sometimes attacker takes time to make it down by sending packets in variable length of request that is not constant, known as variable attack rate.

4) Automated Tools

Attackers can be classified by automated tools also and their skills. Attack can be performed manually; semi automated or fully automated tools

4.2. DDoS Attacks Components

Figure 2 describes the component of DDoS attack, who initiates the attack by selecting vulnerable system as agents and further the agents use botnet to exhaust the victim's system.

1) Master Mind/Planner: The Original Attacker, who creates reasons and answers for, why, when, how and by whom the attack will be performed.

2) Controller/Handler: Co-ordinator of original attacker, who may be one or more than one machine, is used to exploit other machines to process DDoS attack

3) Agents/Zombies/Botnets: Agents, also known as slaves or attack daemons, sub ordinates are programs that actually conduct the attack on the victim. These programs are usually deployed on host computers. These daemons influence both the machines: target and the host computers. It facilitates the attacker to gain access and infiltrate the host computers.

4) Victim/Target: A victim is a target host that has been selected to receive the impact of the attack.

4.3. DDoS Architecture Models

Two types of DDoS attack networks have emerged: the Agent-Handler model and the Internet Relay Chat (IRC)-based model [1,5,35].

1) The Agent-Handler model of a DDoS attack consists of agents, handlers and client. **Figure 3** shows the Agent-Handler Model, in which the Agent and handler knows each-others identity. The client is the interface where the attacker/mastermind communicates with the rest of the DDoS Components. The handlers are software

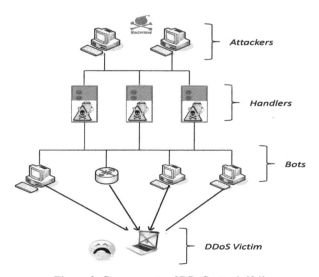

Figure 2. Components of DDoS attack [34].

packages distributed all over the Internet so that it helps to client to convey its command to the agents. The agent software's are vulnerable systems, compromised by the handlers and actually launch the attack on victim's machine. The agent's status and schedule for launching attack can be upgraded by the handler when it is required. Communication relation between agent and handler is either one to one or one to many. Most Common way to attack is by installing handler instructions either on compromised route on network layer or on network server. This makes it difficult to identify messages exchanged by the client-handler and between the handler-agents.

2) The IRC-based DDoS attack: IRC *i.e.* Internet Relay Chat, **Figure 4** shows the architecture of this model where attacker and agent does not know their identity. It is a communication channel to connect the clients to the agents, which provides some additional benefits to the attacker such as use of IRC ports to send the commands to the agents. Because of this, tracking the DDoS command packets becomes difficult. In addition to that, because of heavy traffic going through IRC servers attacker can easily hide its presence. As the attacker has direct access of IRC server, the attacker has access to a list of all available agents [36]. The attacker does not need to have a list of the agents. The agent software that installed in the IRC network which communicates to the IRC channel, notifies the attacker on when the agent is up and running.

5. DDoS Attack Toolkit

With time the attackers are using sophisticated tools to materialize the attacks, this sections lists the tool kits used in some of the attacks discussed in this paper.

1) Trinoo: It uses TCP to communicate between attacker and control master program. The communication between the trinoo master and daemon is held using UDP packets. It implements UDP flood attack against victim. The master and daemons are password protected and prevent system administrators to take control of the trinoo network [5].

2) WIN TRINOO: This is a variant trinoo that works on Windows platform. It sends large amount of UDP packets to the victim as an action of attack.

3) MStream: The mstream program which is based on the "stream.c" attack, includes a "master controller" and a "zombie". As the name indicates master controller controls all of the zombie agents. There is no encryption in the communications between the client, master, and zombie. An attacker connects to the master controller using Telnet to control the zombies. The zombie can slow a computer down by using up CPU cycles via a modified version of stream's attack .The attack consumes network bandwidth when the target host tries to send

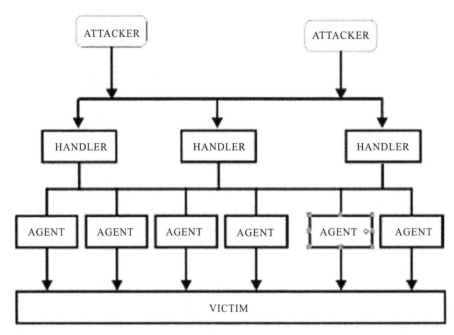

Figure 3. Agent-handler model.

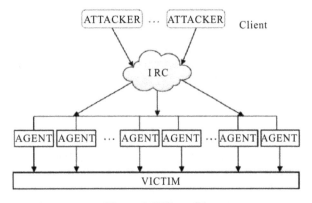

Figure 4. IRC model.

TCP RST packets to non-existent IP addresses in addition to the incoming ACK packets which cause Routers to return ICMP host/network unreachable packets to the victim, consequential the starvation of bandwidth. This consumes large amount of network bandwidth and at the same time distributed method of attack multiplies the effect on the CPU.

4) Tribe Flood Network (TFN): In this technique, a command line interface is used to communicate between attacker and control master program. The communication between the two is done through ICMP Echo reply packets. Following attacks are implemented through TFN's attack daemons: Smurf attack, SYN flooding, UDP flood and ICMP flood attack [37,38].

5) Stacheldraht: Stacheldraht is another master/slave DDoS attack toolkit based on TFN attack. But unlike TFN, it uses an encrypted TCP connection to communicate between attacker and master control program. Communication between master and daemon is held using TCP and ICMP and it involves an automatic update technique for attack daemons. Following attacks are implemented through stacheldraht attack daemons: smurf, UDP flood, ICMP flood attacks, SYN flood [39].

5) Shaft: It is modeled after trinoo. But unlike trinoo, the communication between control master program and attack daemons is achieved using UDP packets and they communicate via a simple TCP Telnet connection. An important feature of shaft is its ability to switch control master servers and ports in real time and hence making detection by intrusion detection tools difficult. Hence, attacks implemented through Shaft are difficult to detect [40].

6) TFN2K: Uses TCP, UDP, ICMP or all three to communicate between control master and program and the attack daemons. Communication between the real attacker and control master is encrypted using key based CAST-256 algorithm.

6. DDoS Attack Using Botnet

Botnets implement under a command and control (C & C) management infrastructure and compromise a network of machines with programs referred as bot, zombie, or drones [41]. The Botnets affects a series of systems using various tools and by installing a bot that can remotely control the victim using IRC. Present botnets are most frequently used to spread DDoS attacks on the Web [34]. Moreover, the attackers can change their communication approach during the creation of the bots. Majority of bots varied its potentials to participate in such attacks. The most classic and generally implemented Botnet attack on application layer is the HTTP/S flooding attack, which launches bots created by the HTTP server. Such bots are thus called, Web-based bots [42].

The goal of a Botnet based DDoS attack is to entail damage at the victim side. In general, the mysterious intention behind this attack is personal which means block the available resources or degrade the performance of the service which is required by the target machine. Therefore, DDoS attack is committed for the revenge purpose. Another aim to perform these attacks can be to gain popularity in the hacker community. In addition to this, these attacks can also perform for the material gain, which means to break the confidentiality and use data for their use.

7. Defense Mechanisms against Attacks

With the passage of time, DDoS attack techniques have become technically more advanced and hence difficult to detect .There are a number of safety measures that can be performed to make network and neighbor network more secure and reliable to use. The classifications are:

7.1. Prevention Techniques

There are some prevention techniques to prevent the attack. **Table 2** shows not only the various prevention techniques but also focuses on their limitations.

1) Filtering routers: It involves filtering all the packets that either enter or leave the network. This defense mechanism protects the network from malicious attacks and prevents itself from unaware attacker. Even this method can be implemented to defense the DDOS in cloud environment also [43]. This measure requires installation of ingress and egress packet filter on all routers.

2) Disabling unused services: If UDP echo or other unused services exist then services should be disabled to prevent tampering and attacks [44].

3) Applying security patches: To prevent denial of service attacks, host computers must be reorganized with the most recent security patches and techniques. For example, in the case of the SYN Flood attack [29], following measures are taken: increase the size of the connection queue, decrease the time-out waiting for the three-way handshake, and employ vendor software patches to detect and circumvent the problem.

4) IP hopping: DDoS attacks can be prevented by changing the victim computer's IP address with a pre-specified set of IP address ranges, thereby invalidating the old address [44].

5) Disabling IP broadcast: The malicious part of this attack is that the attacker can use a low-bandwidth connection to destroy high-bandwidth connections. The amount of packets that are sent by the attacker is multiplied by a factor equal to the number of hosts behind the router that reply to the ICMP echo packets. So, disabling IP broadcast can be used to defend against the DDoS attack.

So prevention schemes are not reliable because they prevent only IP spoofing which is an outdated way of attacking the host. According to the Internet Architecture Working Group (2005), the percentage of spoofed attacks is declining. Only 4 out of 1127 customer impacting DDoS attacks on a large network used spoofed sources in 2004 [3,44].

7.2. Detection Techniques

DDoS detection mechanism can be classified based on two primary criterions.

1) Detection Timing—Passive detection is a form of detection which is done by analyzing the logs, after the attacker has finished this mission, the detection can be on time if the attack can be detected during the time of attack proactive detection is the detection of attack before it approaches the target machine or before the ruin of the service.

2) Detection activity—Here we are presenting some of the existing detection approaches [45-51]. **Table 3** briefly describes those approaches and their limitations. Based on detection activity the categorization is as follows.

a) Signature based—It involves priori knowledge of attack signatures [52]. SNORT are the two widely used signature-based detection approaches.

b) Anomaly based—It treats any incoming traffic that is violating the normal profile as an anomaly. For detecting DDoS attacks it is first require to know the normal behavior of the host and then finding deviations from that behavior.

Limitation: The common challenge for all anomaly-based intrusion detection systems is that it is difficult to take into account the data that provide all types of normal traffic behaviour. As a result, legitimate traffic can be classified as attack traffic which will result in a false positive. In order to reduce the false positive rate, a many parameters are used to provide more accurate normal profiles, which may increase the computational overhead to detect attack.

c) Hybrid attack detection: Hybrid attack detection has the optimistic features of both: 1) pattern-and 2) anomaly-based attack detection models to achieve high detection accuracy, low false positives and negatives, and increased level of cyber conviction. Even though hybrid attack detection approach decreases false positive rate, it also increases complexity and cost of implementation [52].

d) Third party detection: Mechanisms that deploy third-party detection do not handle the detection process themselves but rely on an external third-party that signals the occurrence of the attack [53]. Examples of mechanisms

Table 2. Prevention techniques-limitations.

Prevention Technique	Limitation
Filtering routers	New signatures cannot be detected.
Disabling unused services	By default the installations of operating systems often include many applications not needed by a user.
Applying security patches	New security patches are launched every day
IP hopping	The attacker can launch the attack at the new IP address.
Disabling IP broadcast	Defense against attacks that use intermediate broadcasting nodes e.g. Smurf attacks, ICMP flood attacks etc. will be successful only if host computers and all the neighboring networks disable IP broadcast.

Table 3. Detection and response techniques-limitations.

Detection Technique	Limitation
Signature based	It cannot warn firsthand attack signature or signature that to some extent varies from old attacks.
Anomaly based	The common defy for all anomaly-based intrusion detection systems is that it is difficult to take into account the data that provide all types of normal traffic behavior. As a result, genuine traffic can be classified as attack traffic which will cause a false positive. In order to bring down the false positive rate, a larger set of parameters is used to provide more accurate normal profiles, which may cause an increase in the computational overhead to detect attack.
Hybrid attack detection	Complexity and cost of implementation is very high to deploy in practice.
Third party detection	Economic factor, security related issues may occur.
Attack source/Path identification	It is not stress-free to trajectory IP traffic to its source as IP protocol is stateless in nature. The attacker can easily satire the source IP address field in the packets and send the packets to the victim without notice.
Filtering	These techniques cause a large number of false positives as it is always challenging to distinguish malicious packets from legitimate packets.

that use third-party detection are easily found among traceback mechanisms [54-57].

7.3. Response Techniques

The aim of appalling response techniques is to reduce the impact of the attack and let the attack causes the minimal damage to the victim. We have classified the response techniques as follows:

1) Attack Source/Path Identification: After detecting an attack ideally the attack traffic should be blocked at its source. Unfortunately, it is not easy to track IP traffic to its source as IP protocol is stateless in nature. The attacker can easily spoof the source IP address field in the packets and send the packets to the victim without notice. To address this limitation, several ideas have been proposed to support IP traceability [58]. Attack source identification mechanisms provide the victim with information about the identity and path taken by the machines that are responsible for performing the attack [59].

2) Filtering: Filtering techniques are used to filter out incoming traffic that has been characterized as malicious by the detection mechanism only. Though, it is difficult to distinguish rouge packets from the legitimate packets; therefore, thus techniques cause a high number of false positive.

3) Rate Throttling: Rate-throttling is a moderate response technique that imposes a rate throttle on the incoming traffic that has been characterized as malicious by the detection mechanism. It is usually deployed when

the detection mechanism has a high level of false positives or cannot precisely characterize the malicious traffic [60-62].

4) Reconfiguration: Reconfiguration mechanisms [63] modify the topology of the victim or the intermediate network by either adding more resources to the victim or to isolate the attack machines.

7.4. DDoS Attack Tolerance and Mitigation Techniques

Attack tolerance and mitigation technique assumes that it is impossible to prevent or abort DDoS attack completely. Therefore, this technique try to minimizing the attack impact and focuses on providing optimal level of service as per quality of its service requirement to legitimate users while the service provider is still under attack.

This is not a comprehensive solution in any way; parallel and achieve their goals by providing sufficient assurance and gentle heal in terms of time to providers that the legitimate clients are being served. **Table 4** shows a comparative study of mitigation approaches. Attack tolerance and mitigation classifications are as following:

1) Over Provisioning of Resources

An abundance of resources, for example, high bandwidth link between victim machine, a pool of servers with load balancer and upstream routers are used to tolerate these attacks [64,65]

2) Router's Queue Management

Router's queue management techniques aim to reduce

Table 4. Mitigation approaches [35].

Mitigation Approach	Benefits	Limitations
IntServ	It provides service classes, which closely match the different application types described earlier and their requirements.	How to authorize and prioritize reservation requests, and what happens when signaling is not deployed end-to-end.
DiffServ	Scalability and flexibility is much better then IntServ.	DiffServ does not keep per flow state information. This makes it more difficult to support end-to-end QoS.
Class Based Queuing (CBQ)	Avoid bandwidth starvation problem.	Does not perform fair allocation of bandwidth, if the packet size is not same (variable size).
Proactive Server Roaming	Provide good response time in case of attack.	It has insignificant overhead in case of attack free situation.
Resource Accounting	Each flow gets a fair amount of resources.	Needed client puzzle software.
Resource Pricing	By employing different price and purchase function, architecture can achieve QoS.	System can be populated with fake request by the malicious user at low cost.
Pushback Approach	Upstream routers are not needed. Incremental deployment approach.	Great storage requirement.
Throttling	Helps to define an accurate and efficient packet filter.	At the time of implementation it is still hard to differentiate between legitimate traffic and malicious traffic.

the impact of attack or congestion simply without providing fairness between the traffic flows. Therefore, NPSR for these schemes is very low [66,67].

3) Router's Traffic Scheduling

Router's traffic scheduling algorithm reduces the congestion or attack impact and manages the flow of traffic along with it but they are too expensive in terms of delays and state monitoring [68-70].

4) Target Roaming

Active servers change their location within distributed homogeneous servers proactively to eliminate or chop DDoS attacks impact [71].

7.5. Detection of DDoS Using Hadoop

Hadoop [72], which was created by Doug Cutting, is the Apache Software Foundation open source and Java-based implementation of the MapReduce framework.

Hadoop provides the tools for processing vast amounts of data using the MapReduce framework and, implements the Hadoop Distributed File System (HDFS) [73,74]. It can be used to process vast amounts of data in parallel on large clusters in a reliable and fault-tolerant fashion. Yeonhee Lee and Youngseok Lee [75] presented two algorithm using MapReduce that detect the DDoS attack. There are two distinct algorithms that have been proposed:

1) Counter based method: This method relies on three key parameters: time interval which is the duration during which packets are to be analyzed, threshold which indicates frequency of requests and unbalance ratio which denotes the anomaly ratio of response per page requested between specific client and server.

The number of requests from a specific client to the specific URL within the same time duration is counted using the masked timestamp. The reduce function aggregates the number of URL requests, number of page requests, and total server responses between a client and a server. Finally values per server are aggregated by the algorithm. When the threshold is crossed and the unbalance ratio is higher than normal ratio from h, the clients are marked as attackers.

The key advantage of utilizing this algorithm is its low complexity. However the authors have indicated that the threshold value determination could be a key deciding factor in the implementation but do not offer any further information on how to determinate the value.

2) Access pattern based method: This method is based on a pattern which differentiates the normal traffic from DDoS traffic. This method requires more than two MapReduce jobs:

- First job gets the access sequence to the web page between a client and a web server and computes the spending time and the bytes count for each request of the URL;
- Second job finds infected hosts by comparing the access sequence and the spending time among clients trying to access the same server.

Limitation: This method used First In Fist Out scheduling in which ad-hoc queries are delayed.

3) Triangle Exception defense mechanism: This method is based on the fact that attacker machines uses Command and Control server to send the attacking command to Zombie Systems, which they use to attack the target web server. In triangle expectation defense mechanism network connection information from many routers is collected to analyze the triangle expectations. Once the Triangle expectations are computed, the zombie systems are identified and blocked. The sampling method used in this approach is called DOULION and is implemented with Map reduce.

8. Proposed Model

8.1. Scheduling in Hadoop

8.1.1. FIFO Scheduling

By default Hadoop uses First-in First-out (FIFO) scheduling. It can be implemented on a single node as well as cluster nodes. Its job can be assigned by sharing cluster resources. It uses the concept of Master-Slave. Job scheduling in Hadoop is performed by Job Tracker (master node). A Job tracker splits the job into number of chunks with some target and assigns these tasks to the Slave nodes (Map nodes). Map nodes compute the assigned task and resultant to be reported to Master node. Then master sorts the results and gives the output to the client. Hadoop monitors the progress of the task by using a progress score. Progress score of a task lies between 0 - 1.

Progress score is calculated by using the following formula:

$$PS = \begin{cases} M/N & \text{For Map Task} \\ 1/3 \times (K + M/N) & \text{For Reduce Task} \end{cases} \quad (1)$$

$$PS_{avg} = \sum_{i=1}^{R} PS[i] \Big/ T \quad (2)$$

$$\text{For task } T_i : PS[i] < PS_{avg} - 20\% \quad (3)$$

where M—Number of key/value pairs computed

N—Number of key/value pairs to be computed

K—Phase number of the reducer (possible K values are 0, 1, and 2)

T—Number of Tasks

PS—Progress Score

PS_{avg}—Progress Score Average

If the above inequality-(3) holds, then the task is considered as slow task and Job tracker copies the task and find the empty slave node and starts executing the task in that slave node. This process is called speculative execution. If the new task executes first then it kills the old slow task else the new task is killed.

The reducer computation has three phases: copy phase, sort phase and reduce phase. Copy phase is to copy results from the map nodes. Sort phase is to sort the results. Reduce phase is to reduce the results based on user specified key. In Hadoop each phase in reducer was given progress score of 0.33 (Hadoop assumes that all the phases in reducer take same amount of time) [75,76]. Now observed Loop Holes in default scheduling:

1) In Hadoop, the values of R1, R2, R3, M1, M2 are 0.33, 0.33. 0.34, 1 and 0 respectively. However in case of heterogeneous environment, R1, R2, R3, M1 and M2 should be dynamic as tasks running on different nodes.

2) Hadoop may launch backup tasks for wrong tasks as it always executes backup tasks for those tasks those PSs are less than $PS_{avg} - 20\%$.

3) Sometimes Hadoop may launch backup tasks for fast tasks [75].

8.1.2. SAMR Scheduling

To overcome the shortcoming of Hadoop scheduling SAMR scheduling was proposed. **Figure 5** shows the working of SAMR for counter based algorithm. After a job is committed, SAMR splits the job into map and reduce tasks, and assigns them to a series of nodes. In the interim, it reads historical information which stored on every node and updated it after every execution. In that case, SAMR adjusts time weight of each stage of map and reduce tasks according to the historical information respectively.

As a result, it gets the progress of each task accurately and finds which tasks need backup tasks. It identifies slow nodes and classfies them into the sets of slow nodes dynamically. SAMR launches the backup tasks on the basis of information of these slow nodes and ensures that the backup tasks are not slow tasks. It gets the final results of the tasks when either slow tasks or backup tasks finish first. Tentative results show that SAMR significantly decreases the time of execution up to 25% compared with Hadoop's scheduler [72,77].

8.2. Proposed Model

Even though there are many DDoS solutions proposed by different researchers, literature shows that there has been no effective way proposed to defend against DDoS attacks. To Detect DDoS, Counter based and Pattern Based Algorithm are quietly famous approach in Hadoop but still the major challenges are that they still have a lot of orientation towards batch processing and because of this ad hoc query jobs are delayed [77].

Hadoop is open source software based on scalability, distributed and reliability concept. It is best suited for large scale *i.e.* big data, provides optimum analyzed data by distributing big data into multiple chunks. It uses scheduling algorithms for MapReduce.

We already discuss the loopholes available in the existing scheme. Our aim is to proposed a model that uses SAMR Counter based algorithm that improve the efficiency as it reads historical information which stored on every node and updated it after every execution. This give more accurate Progress score and finds which task needs backup task.

This model inputs three parameters: time interval, threshold and unbalance ratio, which are stored in HDFS through packet loader. The packet collector receives IP packets from trace files on the disk, and writes them to HDFS. IP packets are stored in the binary format of libpcap. The threshold and unbalanced ratios for server are passed as parameters along with the timestamp. Job starts at the client and Job Tracker running SAMR scheduler splits the job into map and reduces tasks and

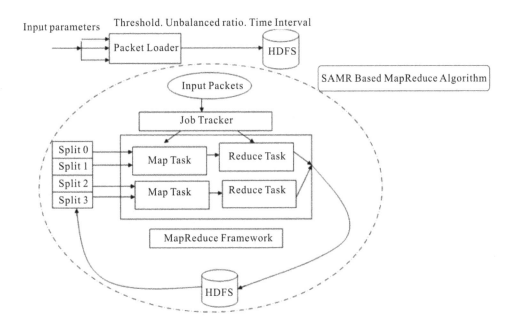

Figure 5. SAMR scheduling based map-reduce algorithm for counter-based DDOS detection.

assigns them to a series of nodes while doing thus it also reads historical information which is stored on every node and is updated after every execution. SAMR then adjusts time weight of each stage of map and reduce tasks as per the historical information respectively. Thus, it gets the progress scores of each task accurately and finds which of the tasks need backup tasks to run and also identifies the slow nodes and classifies them into the sets of slow nodes dynamically.

It gets the final results of the fine-grained tasks when either slow tasks or backup tasks finish first. The map task generates keys to classify the requests and response HTTP messages. Then, the reduce task summarizes the HTTP request messages and marks the abnormal traffic load by comparing it with the threshold. The map task generates keys to classify the requests and response HTTP messages. Then, the reduce task summarizes the HTTP request messages and marks the abnormal traffic load by comparing it with the threshold. The results are saved back to HDFS.

9. Conclusions and Future Work

This paper discusses the history the of DDoS attacks along with some major incidents to provide a better understanding and gravity of the problem. The paper includes latest techniques such as Hadoop along with other available techniques for prevention and detection of distributed denial of service attacks so that a comprehensive solution can be developed with several detection layers to trap the intrusion keeping in mind the limitations of these prevention and detection techniques.

The paper also discusses some of the recent development happened in the sphere of DDoS using Hadoop. Though this technique sounds promising, it can be further optimized. At last a proposed model is given which replace default scheduling via fair scheduler in Hadoop based algorithm to detect DDoS attack.

REFERENCES

[1]   B. M. Leiner, V. G. Cerf, D. D. Clark, R. E. Kahn, L. Kleinrock, D. C. Lynch, J. Postel, L. G. Roberts and S. Wolff, "A Brief History of the Internet," 2000. http://www.isoc.org/internet/history/brief.shtml

[2]   B. B. Gupta, R. C. Joshi and M. Misra, "Defending against Distributed Denial of Service Attacks: Issues and Challenges," *Information Security Journal: A Global Perspective*, Vol. 18, No. 5, 2009, pp. 224-247.

[3]   C. Douligeris and A. Mitrokotsa "DDoS Attacks and Defense Mechanisms: Classification and State of the Art," *Elsevier Science Direct Computer Networks*, Vol. 44, No. 5, 2004, pp. 643-666.

[4]   S. M. Specht and R. B. Lee, "Distributed Denial of Service: Taxonomies of Attacks, Tools, and Countermeasures," *Proceedings of the International Workshop on Security in Parallel and Distributed Systems*, San Francisco, 15-17 September 2004, pp. 543-550.

[5]   A. Mishra, B. B. Gupta and R. C. Joshi, "A Comparative Study of Distributed Denial of Service Attacks, Intrusion Tolerance and Mitigation Techniques," *European Intelligence and Security Informatics Conference, EISIC* 2011, 12-14 September 2011, pp. 286, 289.

[6]   T. Kitten, "DDoS: Lessons from Phase 2 Attacks," 2013.

http://www.bankinfosecurity.com/ddos-attacks-lessons-from-phase-2-a-5420/op-1

[7]   A. ALmomani, T.-C. Wan, B. B. Gupta, A. Altaher, E. A. Lmomani and S. Ramadass, "A Survey of Phishing Email Filtering Techniques," *IEEE Communications Surveys & Tutorials*, Vol. PP, No. 99, 2013, pp. 1-21.

[8]   S. Zargar, J. Joshi and D. Tipper, "A Survey of Defense Mechanisms against Distributed Denial of Service (DDoS) Flooding Attacks," *Communications Surveys & Tutorials, IEEE*, Vol. PP, No. 99, 2013, pp. 1-24.

[9]   K. Zetter, "Lazy Hacker and Little Worm Set off Cyberwar Frenzy," 2009. http://www.wired.com/threatlevel/2009/07/mydoom/

[10]   L. Greenemeier, "Estonian Attacks Raise Concern over Cyber "Nuclear Winter"," Information Week, 2007. http://www.informationweek.com/estonian-attacks-raise-concern-over-cybe/199701774

[11]   J. Vijayan, "Mydoom Lesson: Take Proactive Steps to Prevent DDoS Attacks," 2004. http://www.computerworld.com/s/article/89932/Mydoom_lesson_Take_proactive_steps_to_prevent_DDoS_attacks?%20taxonomyId=017

[12]   "Powerful Attack Cripples Internet," 2002. http://www.greenspun.com/bboard/q-and-a-fetch-msg.tcl msgid=00A7G7

[13]   Yahoo on Trail of Site Hackers," Wired.com, 2000. http://www.wired.com/techbiz/media/news/2000/02/34221

[14]   S. Garfinkel and G. Spafford, "Practical Internet and UNIX Security," O'Reilly Media, 1996

[15]   "CERT Advisory: SYN Flooding and IP Spoofing Attacks," CERT® Coordination Center Software Engineering Institute, Carnegie Mellon, 2010. http://www.cert.org/advisories/CA-1996-21.html

[16]   CERT, "Tech Tips: Denial of Service Attacks," CERT® Coordination Center Software Engineering Institute, Carnegie Mellon, 2010. http://www.cert.org/tech_tips/denial_of_service.html

[17]   "Notable Hacks," PBS Frontline, 2010. http://www.pbs.org/wgbh/pages/frontline/shows/hackers/whoare/notable.html

[18]   K. J. Houle, G. M. Weaver, N. Long and R. Thomas, "Trends in Denial of Service Attack Technology," CERT® Coordination Center, 2001.

[19]   N. Schactman, "Wage Cyberwar against Hamas, Surrender Your PC," Wired: Danger Room Blog, 2009.

[20]   P. Wilkinson, "Briton's Software a Surprise Weapon in Iran Cyberwar," Cable News Network, Atlanta, 2009.

[21]   B. Martin, "Have Script, Will Destroy (Lessons in DoS)," 2000. http://attrition.org/~jericho/works/security/dos.html

[22]   X. Wang and M. Reiter, "WRAPS: Denial-of-Service Defense through Web Referrals," *Proceedings of the 25th IEEE Symposium on Reliable Distributed Systems, (SRDS'06)*, Leeds, 2-4 October 2006, pp. 51-60.

[23]   R. Mackey, "'Iranian Cyber Army' Strikes Chinese Website," New York Times Lede Blog, 2011.

[24]   D. Kravetz, "Anonymous Unfurls 'Operation Titstorm'," Wired Threat Level Blog, 2010.

[25]   J. Nazario, "Politically Motivated Denial of Service Attacks," Arbor Networks, 2009.

[26]   DDoS-for-Hire Service Is Legal and Even Lets FBI Peek in, Says a Guy with an Attorney," 2012. http://www.ddosdefense.net

[27]   "Internet Creaks Following Cyber Attack on Spamhaus," 2013. http://www.cbronline.com/news/security/internet-slows-down-following-ddos-attack-on-spamhaus-280313

[28]   T. Kitten, "2 More Banks Are DDoS Victims," 2012. http://www.bankinfosecurity.com/2-more-banks-are-ddos-victims-a-5298

[29]   T. Kitten, "DDoS Strikes American Express," 2013. http://www.bankinfosecurity.com/american-express-a-5645

[30]   "iMessage DDoS Attacks Foreshadow a Bigger Threat," 2013. http://soshitech.com/2013/04/01/imessage-ddos-attacks-foreshadow-a-bigger-threat/

[31]   J. Kirk, "Mt. Gox under Largest DDoS Attack as Bitcoin Price Surges," 2013. http://www.computerworld.com/s/article/9238118/Mt._Gox_under_largest_DDoS_attack_as_bitcoin_price_surges

[32]   "Mstream Distributed Denial of Service Tool (Zombie Detected) (DdosMstreamZombie)," 2013. http://www.iss.net/security_center/reference/vuln/ddos-mstream-zombie.htm

[33]   N. McAllister, "GoDaddy Stopped by Massive DDoS Attack," 2012. http://www.theregister.co.uk/2012/09/10/godaddy_ddos_attack/

[34]   E. Alomari, S. Manickam, B. B. Gupta, S. Karuppayah and R. Alfaris, "Botnet-Based Distributed Denial of Service (DDoS) Attacks on Web Servers: Classification and Art," *International Journal of Computer Applications*, Vol. 49, No. 7, 2012, pp. 24-32.

[35]   B. B. Gupta, M. Misra and R. C. Joshi, "FVBA: A Combined Statistical Approach for Low Rate Degrading and High Bandwidth Disruptive DDoS Attacks Detection in ISP Domain," *16th IEEE International Conference on Networks*, 12-14 December 2008, New Delhi, pp. 1-4.

[36]   J. Lo, *et al.*, "An IRC Tutorial," 1997. http://www.irchelp.org/irchelp/irctutorial.html#part1

[37]   D. Dittrich, "The Tribe Flood Network Distributed Denial of Service Attack Tool," University of Washington, Seattle, 1999. http://staff.washington.edu/dittrich/misc/tfn.analysis.txt

[38]   J. Barlow and W. Thrower, "TFN2K—An Analysis," Axent Security Team, 2000. http://security.royans.net/info/posts/bugtraq_ddos2.shtml

[39]   D. Dittrich, "The Stacheldraht Distributed Denial of Service Attack Tool," University of Washington, Seattle, 1999. http://staff.washington.edu/dittrich/misc/stacheldraht.analysis.txt

[40] D. Dittrich, S. Dietrich and N. Long, "An Analysis of the 'Shaft' Distributed Denial of Device Tool," *USENIX Systems Administration Conference*, March 2000. http://www.soscholar.net/detail?paper_id=2bb7f2f9-2ed7-3422-78d2-e938aaaf44af

[41] F. Freiling, *et al.*, "Botnet Tracking: Exploring a Root-Cause Methodology to Prevent Distributed Denial-of-Service Attacks," *Computer Security-ESORICS* 2005, Milan, 12-14 September 2005, pp. 319-335.

[42] Z. S. Zhu, G. H. Lu, Y. Chen, Z. Fu, P. Roberts and K. Han, "Botnet Research Survey," *32nd Annual IEEE International Conference on Computer Software and Applications, COMPSAC'08*, Turku, 28 July-1 August 2008, pp. 967, 972.

[43] P. Negi, A. Mishra and B. B. Gupta, "Enhanced CBF Packet Filtering Method to Detect DDoS Attack in Cloud Computing Environment," *International Journal of Computer Science Issues*, Vol. 10, No. 1, 2013, pp 142-146.

[44] X. Geng and A. B. Whinston, "Defeating distributed denial of Service Attacks," *IEEE IT Professional*, Vol. 2, No. 4, 2000, pp. 36-42.

[45] T. M. Gil and M. Poletto, "Multops: A Data-Structure for Bandwidth Attack Detection," *Proceedings of the 10th USENIX Security Symposium*, Washington DC, 2001, pp. 23-38.

[46] J. Li, J. Mirkovic, M. Wang, P. Reiher and L. Zhang, "SAVE: Source Address Validity Enforcement Protocol," *21st Annual Joint Conference of the IEEE Computer and Communications Societies*, New York, 23-27 June 2002, pp. 1557-1566.

[47] B. Bencsath and I. Vajda, "Protection against DDoS Attacks Based on Traffic Level Measurements," *Proceedings of the Western Simulation Multi Conference*, San Diego, 2004, pp. 22-28.

[48] B. B. Gupta, M. Misra and R. C. Joshi, "An ISP Level Solution to Combat DDoS Attacks Using Combined Statistical Based Approach," *International Journal of Information Assurance and Security*, Vol. 3, No. 2, 2008, pp. 102-110.

[49] Y. Chen, K. Hwang and W. Ku, "Collaborative Detection of DDoS Attacks over Multiple Network Domains," *IEEE Transaction on Parallel and Distributed Systems*, Vol. 18, No. 12, 2007, pp. 1649-1662.

[50] L. Feinstein, D. Schnackenberg, R. Balupari and D. Kindred, "Statistical Approaches to DDoS Attack Detection and Response," *Proceedings of DARPA Information Survivability Conference and Exposition*, Washington DC, 22-24 April 2003, pp. 303-314.

[51] A. Lakhina, M. Crovella and C. Diot, "Mining Anomalies Using Traffic Feature Distributions," ACM SIGCOMM Computer Communication Review, Vol. 35, No. 4, 2005, pp. 217-228.

[52] K. Hwang, M. Cai, Y. Chen and M. Qin, "Hybrid Intrusion Detection with Weighted Signature Generation over Anomalous Internet Episodes," *IEEE Transaction on Dependable and Secure Computing*, Vol. 4, No. 1, 2007, 41-55.

[53] J. Mirkovic and P. Reiher, "A Taxonomy of DDoS Attack and DDoS Defense Mechanisms," *ACM SIGCOMM Computer Communications Review*, Vol. 34, No. 2, 2004, pp. 39-53.

[54] S. Savage, D. Wetherall, A. Karlin and T. Anderson, "Practical Network Support for IP Traceback," *Proceedings of ACM SIGCOMM*, Stockholm, 2000, pp. 295-306.

[55] A. C. Snoeren, C. Partridge, L. A. Sanchez, C. E. Jones, F. Tchakountio, S. T. Kent and W. T. Strayer, "Hash-Based IP Traceback," *Proceedings of ACM SIGCOMM*, San Diego, 2001, pp. 3-14.

[56] S. Bellovin, M. Leech and T. Taylor, "ICMP Traceback Messages," 2001. Internet draft: draft-ietf-itrace-01.txt

[57] D. Dean, M. Franklin and A. Stubblefield, "An Algebraic Approach to IP Traceback," *ACM Transactions on Information and System Security*, Vol. 5, No. 2, 2002, pp. 119-137.

[58] Y. Manzano, "Tracing the Development of Denial of Service Attacks: A Corporate Analogy," 2003. http://www.acm.org/crossroads/xrds10-1/tracingDOS.html

[59] A. Belenky and N. Ansari, "IP Traceback with Deterministic Packet Marking," *IEEE Communication Letter*, Vol. 7, No. 4, 2003, pp. 162-164.

[60] C. Papadopoulos, R. Lindell, J. Mehringer, A. Hussain, and R. Govindan, "COSSACK: Coordinated Suppression of Simultaneous Attacks," *Proceedings of the DARPA Information Survivability Conference and Exposition*, Vol. 2, Washington DC, 22-24 April 2003, pp. 2-13.

[61] J. Mirkovic, G. Prier and P. Reiher, "Attacking DDoS at the Source," 10th *IEEE International Conference on Network Protocols*, Paris, 12-15 November 2002, pp. 312-321.

[62] S. Floyd, S. Bellovin, J. Loannidis, K. Kompella, R. Mahajan and V. Paxson, "Pushback Messages for Controlling Aggregates in the Network," 2001. draft-floyd-pushback-messages-00.txt

[63] D. G. Andersen, H. Balakrishnan, M. F. Kaashoek and R. Morris, "Resilient Overlay Networks," In Proceedings of 18th ACM SOSP, Banff, Canada, 2001, pp. 131-145.

[64] R. B. Lee, "Taxonomies of Distributed Denial of Service Networks, Attacks, Tools and Countermeasures," Princeton University, Princeton, 2003. http://www.princeton.edu/ee/

[65] R. Bush, D. Karrenberg, M. Kosters and R. Plzak, "Root Name Server Operational Requirements," RFC Editor, United States, BCP 40, RFC 2870, June 2000.

[66] S. Floyd and V. Jacobon, "Random Early Detection Gateways for Congestion Avoidance," *IEEE/ACM Transactions on Networking*, Vol. 1, No. 4, 1993, pp. 397-413.

[67] S. Floyd and K. Fall, "Promoting the Use of End-to-End Congestion Control in the Internet," *IEEE/ACM Transactions on Networking*, Vol. 7, No. 4, 1999, pp. 458-472.

[68] A. Demers, S. Keshav and S. Shenker, "Analysis and Simulation of a Fair Queuing Algorithm," *Journal of Internetworking Research and Experience*, Vol. 1, No. 1,

1990, pp. 3-26.

[69] P. Mckenny, "Stochastic Fairness Queuing," *9th Annual Joint Conference of the IEEE Computer and Communication Societies, the Multiple Facets of Integration*, Piscataway, 3-7 June 1990, pp. 733-740.

[70] A. Mankin and K. Ramakrishnan, "Gateway Congestion Control Survey," 1991.
http://www.rfc-editor.org/rfc.html

[71] S. M. Khattab, C. Sangpachatanaruk, R. Melhem, D. Mosse and T. Znati, "Proactive Server Roaming for Mitigating Denial of Service Attacks," *1st International Conference on International Technology: Research and Education*, Newark, 2003, pp. 500-504.

[72] Apache Hadoop. http://hadoop.apache.org/

[73] S. Ghemawat, H. Gobio and S.-T. Leung, The Google File System," *ACM SIGOPS Operating Systems Review*, Vol. 37, No. 5, 2003, pp. 29-43.

[74] K. V. Shvachko, "HDFS Scalability: The Limits to Growth," *USENIX*, Vol. 35, No. 2, 2010, pp. 6-16.

[75] Y. Lee, W. Kang and Y. Lee, "A Hadoop-Based Packet Trace Processing Tool," *3rd International Conference on Traffic Monitoring and Analysis*, Vienna, 27 April 2011, pp. 51-63.

[76] T. White, "Hadoop: The Definitive Guide," O'Reilly Media, Yahoo! Press, New York, 2009.

[77] Q. Chen, D. Q. Zhang, M. Y. Guo, Q. N. Deng and S. Guo, "Samr: A Self-Adaptive Mapreduce Scheduling Algorithm in Heterogeneous Environment," *International Conference on Computer and Information Technology*, Bradford, 29 June-1 July 2010, pp. 2736-2743.

18

Analysis of Malware Families on Android Mobiles: Detection Characteristics Recognizable by Ordinary Phone Users and How to Fix It

Hieu Le Thanh[1,2]

[1]School of Computer Science and Technology, Huazhong University of Science and Technology, Wuhan, China
[2]Hue University's College of Education, Hue, Vietnam

ABSTRACT

The sale of products using the android Operation System (OS) phone is increasing in rate: the fact is that its price is cheaper but its configured hardware is higher, users easily buy it and the approach to this product increases the risk of the spread of mobile malware. The understanding of majority of the users of this mobile malware is still limited. While they are growing at a faster speed in the number and level of sophistication, especially their variations have created confusion for users; therefore worrying about the safety of its users is required. In this paper, the author discussed the identification and analysis of malware families on Android Mobiles. The author selected the recognizable characteristics from ordinary users with their families collected from 58 malware families and 1485 malware samples and proposed solutions as recommendations to users before installing it with the ultimate desire to mitigate the damage in the community that is on the android phone, especially the ordinary users with limited understanding about potential hazards. It would be helpful for the ordinary users to identify the mobile malware in order to mitigate the information security risk.

Keywords: Mobile Security; Android Malware Families

1. Introduction

In recent years, Sales of products using Android phones have continued to accelerate. Specifically in 2012, phones which use the android operating system rose from 52.5% to 72.4% compared to 2011, while the IOS operating system fells from 15% to 13.9% compared to 2011, according to Gartner [1]. Some applications of the android operating system from Android Market are growing to compete with the largest application. Now Apps store is developed by third—party market, not to mention the thousands of everyday applications. According to Xyologic: "Android to overtake Apple soon", Apple's App store has now reached 25 billion downloads, Android's App store has now reached 10 billion downloads, but both tracked at 1 billion downloads a month [2].

This increases the amount of malicious software on the Android operating system. According to security Kaspersky Labs, in the second quarter of 2012 the mobile malware increased in three folds. In 2012, 99% of all the mobile malware they detected every month was designed for Android. The most widespread malicious objects detected on Android smartphones can be divided into three main groups: SMS Trojans, advertising modules and exploits to gain root access to smartphones [3]. Specifically, 40% of modern smartphone owners do not use antivirus software [4].

Whilst malware is growing rapidly, a number of ordinary users that have easy access to the smartphone device do not have basic understanding of the potential danger. So we need to have the classification of samples according to similar characteristics, as well as collect more new malware to create malware families. Then, we can analyze it fully to make recognizable signs from ordinary users and guard solutions to mitigate the threats of the impact and risk of malwares before installing it from official android market or third-party market.

In this paper, the author first discussed the feature to select a sample of malware families and method to analysis them. Next, in Section 2, the author presented methods and tools to analyse malware samples. In section 3, the author presented some selected results of the features that ordinary users can easily recognize. From the analysis on the samples, the author collected the list from the project, blog and threat reports of antivirus companies [5,6] (including existing malware families and add them every day) and the threats that malicious applications can do. Section 4 shows the detection results with ten representatives of mobile phone antivirus software. In Section 5, the author discussed six (6) steps to security android phones. Finally, Section six (6) is the summary.

2. Methods and Tools to Analyze Malware Samples

In this section, the author first discussed the feature to select a sample of malware families and methods to analyses them.

2.1. Malware Family

Malware family feature that comes to notice is that of closeness which certain traits are preserved, including: similar activation, facial features, hereditary diseases and a host of other commonalities.

One of the variations which is most harmful is KungFu malware family. There are variations with different names KungFuA (KungFu1), KungFuB (KungFu2), KungFuC (KungFu3), KungFuD (KungFu4), KungFuE (KungFu Sapp) or KungFu Lena (Legacy Native) with properties which are analysed as follows:

All KungFu malwares are packaged and downloaded from third markets and fora. It adds into applications a new service and a new receiver. With privilege root exploits, it automatically launches the service so that it doesn't interact with the user. KungFu can collect information on the infected mobile phone, including IMEI number, phone model, version of Android OS. The first variant, KungFuA exploits Dalvik codes based on Java and a single C&C server and payload is encrypted with AES. Differently, KungFuB exploits native code and three C&C servers. KungFuC inherits from KungFuB, it exploits vulnerability to allow local users to gain privilege by sending a NETLINK message (CVE-2009-1185) [7]. KungFuD inherits from KungFuA and encrypted its native binaries. KungFuE inherits from KungFuD and encrypting a few strings to obfuscate its code and use a custom certificate in official market [8-10]. "DroidKungFu" variants structure mentioned in **Figure 1**.

Its purpose is to evade the detection of mobile antivirus software. So the virus software is difficult to effectively detect variants with a rate of 100%.

2.2. Methods and Tools to Analyze Android Mobile Malware Sample

Common method for analysing malware in android OS is reverse engineering. Reverse engineering is the process of discovering the technological principles of a device, object, or system through analysis of its structure, function, and operation [10]. Android OS was developed by

Google and is based upon the Linux kernel and GNU software in which the malware application package files use the apk extension. They include all of the application's code (.dex files), resources, assets, and manifest file. Dex file (Dalvik Executable) is compiled Android application code file. Tools that focus three groups on examining inner-workings of Android mobile applications:

1) Command line:
- Tool to unpack the .apk file: Winzip, Rar
- Tool to get the bytecode from the .dex file: *for example*, smali to compile and baksmali to decompile (or dex2jar and jd-gui), dexdump...

The author analysed a sample (RU .apk) below:

Step 1: The malware is an apk package extract of its content, show example **Figure 2**.

Step 2: Use *smali .rar* to compile smali file: extracted the byte code from classes .dex file, show example **Figure 3**.

Step 3: Open code contained in the MoviePlayer.smali file. You can discover the purpose of it, show example **Figure 4**.

2) Software to compile and decompile:
- Compile: Java code, smalicode and .dex: for example APKtoJava.

We analysed a sample (RU .apk) below:

Step 1: open APKtoJava (show **Figure 5**).

Step 2: open class java to read program file (show example **Figure 6**).

3) Using website: for example http://anubis.iseclab.org *He analysed a sample (RU .apk) below*:

Choose file apk website to analyse, show example **Figure 7**.

Figure 1. "DroidKungFu" variants structure.

Figure 2. Classes is dex file to analyze.

Figure 3. Movie player. Smali is main code of malware.

Analysis of Malware Families on Android Mobiles: Detection Characteristics Recognizable by Ordinary Phone Users
and How to Fix It

177

```
82    invoke-virtual/range {v0 .. v5}, Landroid/telephony/SmsManager;->sendTextMessage
83    :try_end_2d
84    .catch Ljava/lang/Exception; {:try_start_2a .. :try_end_2d} :catch_44
85
86    .line 63
87    :goto_2d
88    const-string v1, "3354"
```

Figure 4. Malware send a message to phone number 3354.

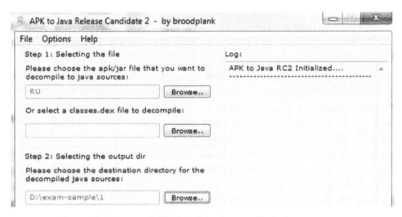

Figure 5. Screen of APK tool to decompile to java sources.

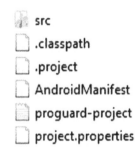

Figure 6. A Class java sources after decompile by APK tool.

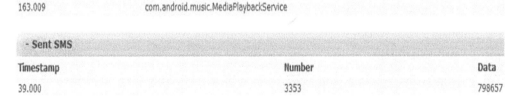

Figure 7. An analysis result for file RU .apk from website.

3. Results of the Features That Ordinary Users Easily Recognize

In the process of analysing the samples the author collected, the author had encountered difficulties with different names of the first authors found it. So his statistics record all the different names for easy sorting into their malware families. In addition to describing the visible symptoms, the author used illustrations or icons in **Table 1**.

Besides, Symptoms of malware which exploits the device to gain root privilege are not easily visible. So we propose to use mobile Security software solutions in the next chapter, with some assessment test results with our samples set.

Statistical results below with reference from the first detection of the authors in manufacturer's anti—virus software: Symantec, NQMobile, F-secure, Lookout, Kaspersky, AVG, … and projects related links, Blog: http://www.csc.ncsu.edu/faculty/jiang, http://www.fortiguard.com,http://androguard.blogspot.com, http://blog.fortinet.com/... [10-52].

In the first column of **Table 4**, the author collected the different names of the same malware families [5,52] by different anti-virus companies, based on installation methods, activation mechanisms or the name of the mali-

Table 1. Describes characterization and area of the effects of malware families.

Area (**)	Malware Familes	Description (*)											
		1	2	3	4	5	6	7	8	9	10	11	12
CN	AnserverBot	x						x					
CN	BaseBridge (AdSMS)	x		x				x					
	BeanBot	x						x					
	Pjapps	x	x	x				x					
	BGSERV	x	x	x				x					
	CruseWin (CruseWind)							x		x			
CN	DroidCoupon	x						x					
	DroidDeluxe			x							x		
	DroidDream (DORDRAE)			x				x					
	DreamLight	x						x					
	DroidKungFu (LeNa)	x			x	x		x					
	Smssend (fakeplayer)							x		x			
CN	gamblersms	x						x					
	Geinimi	x		x				x					
USA, CN, RU	GGTracker	x		x				x		x			
CN	GingerMaster (GingerBreaker)								x		x		
	GoldDream	x		x				x					
	Gone 60 (gonein 60)	x		x				x					
	GPSSMSSpy (mobinauten, SmsHowU, smsspy)						x						
CN	HippoSMS							x		x			
	Jifake					x				x			x
	jSMSHider (smshider, Xsider)							x	x				
CN	KMin (ozotshielder)	x	x					x					
	LoveTrap (cosha, Luvrtrap)	x					x	x		x			
	Nickyspy (Nickispy)			x			x	x					
	Plankton				x	x	x	x					
	RogueLemon						x	x					
	RogueSPPush						x	x					
	SMSReplicator			x				x					
	SndApps	x		x				x					
	Spitmo	x						x				x	
	Tapsnake						x	x					
	Walkinwat	x		x			x	x					
	YZHC							x		x			
	zsone							x		x			

Continued

	Battery Doctor (fakedoc)					x	x		
	CI4					x	x		
	Counterclank		x				x		
JN	Dougalek	x		x			x		
E. EU	DropDialer			x			x	x	
CN, CAN	FakeAngry (AnZhu)	x			x		x		
	Faketimer (oneclickfraud)	x					x		
Spain	FakeToken	x					x	x	
RU	FindAndCall			x			x		
	Gamex (muldrop)					x			
RU, EU	Logastrod	x				x	x	x	
	Luckycat	x	x				x		
	Moghava				x				
ME. EU	Notcompatible	x					x		
RU	Opfake						x	x	
CN	Rootsmart (Bmaster)	x					x		x
	Steek (fakelottery, atakr)	x				x	x		
	VDloader	x	x				x	x	

(*): Details **Table 1** are described in **Table 2**. (**): Details **Table 1** are described in **Table 3**.

Table 2. Gives detailed explanation of stolen information activities of malware.

Num	Description
1	Steal personal information: IMEI, IMSI and phone number
2	Steal Net information: history and bookmarks, APN, IP, Mac
3	Steal phone's state: calls log, SMS, contacts, account
4	Steal file information: change or copy file in external storage
5	Steal apps information: download and install apps
6	Stolen location information: GPS, Google, Country code
7	Send information to A C&C server (SMS messenger)
8	Send information to URL (by connecting internet.)
9	Send to premium-rate SMS messages
10	Exploits root
11	Steal banking codes: mTAN
12	Steal QR code

Table 3. Abbreviated name of areas.

Area: High risk Of infection	Description
CN	China
USA	America
Ru	Russia
JN	Japan
EU	Europe
CAN	Canada
E	Eastern
ME	Middle East

cious packaged applications added. This solved problem of naming schemes of malware families such as [5]: "Last but not least, during the process of collecting malware samples into our current dataset, we felt confusions from disorganized or confusing naming schemes".

From visible symptoms malware families in **Table 5**, the author proposes some specific criterion for identifying the mobile malware:

Ordinary phone users can recognize several features such as: premium-rate services and phone bill abnormal increase, display of a black screen, automatically install a software in which its users has not requested, or without a launcher icon after installation in applications list, warning requirements applica ion not licensed and crack

Table 4. Description about visible symptoms of malware.

Families	Visible Symptoms	Manually Checked by user	Illustrations
AnserverBot	It makes a new dialog to request and upgrade a new apps but does not show any icon.	You remember new apps name and check show icon on your home screen (request upgrade)	
BaseBridge (AdSMS)	Abnormally, high bill to connect internet from data connect or GPRS. 360 Safeguard is installed additional.	Check the regular phone bill. Error message from 360 Safeguard or show 360 Safeguard icon	
BeanBot	The device booting up or hanging up on a phone call.	Check the regular phone bill.	
Pjapps	Request read/write Browse's history and bookmarks and receive SMS when you install it.	View Request read/write Browse's history and bookmarks and receive	
BGSERV	Android market security is running by BgService.	View BgService is running when you don't request	
CruseWin (CruseWind)	Display of a black screen.	Check the regular phone bill. Can view: Flash MMS icon or Flash icon	
DroidCoupon	It uses a popular root exploit—" Rage against the Cage" in Android 2.2 and earlier, hide Platform so we are difficult to detect it.	Phone upgrade to a higher version	
DroidDeluxe	Install password recovery tool. It will not work on android 2.3, with message: "This application has stopped unexpectedly. Please try again".	You can detect it when your phone using version 2.3. View Recovery Deluxe tool	
DroidDream (DORDRAE)	It also disguises itself as apps like battery-monitoring tool, a task-listing tool, and an app listing the permissions used by installed apps.	View my Batter Life	
DreamLight	Service named "CoreService" running. Getting a phone call.	View Illustrations	
DroidKungFu (LeNa)	Install Google search or Google Ssearch.	View Icon 2 apps: Google search or Google Ssearch	
Smssend (fakeplayer)	Running media player application.	Check the regular phone bill. Auto run media player	
gamblersms	Request provide a phone number and an email address.	View: Phone number and email	
Geinimi	Create a shortcut, Change wall paper Appear a popups message about Google map.	check for abnormal appearance on the background	
GGTracker	Website analyzing the phone's battery or request download APK solution battery.	View solution battery	
GingerMaster (GingerBreaker)	Requires add apps list.	Your phone using Android 2.3/2.3 Requires add apps list	
GoldDream	Difficult to identify. You should use anti-virus software. If detects it, you should uninstall apps.		
Gone60 (gonein60)	Pay money from web gi60s.com	Self-uninstallation as figure beside: Enter this code (5-digit code) to gi60s.com (send a website)	
GPSSMSSpy (mobinauten, SmsHowU, smsspy)	The message the spy sends (How are you) is an error or spam.		
HippoSMS	Costs bill from the beginning of 1066.	Check the regular phone bill.	
Jifake	Open link to download file apk, rar, but don't see is that files.	Check the regular phone bill.	
jSMSHider (smshider, Xsider)	"InstallService" service named appeared in Application Manager but don't install.	View Illustrations: "InstallService"	
KMin (ozotshielder)	Changes the Live Wallpape.	View two icons	
LoveTrap (cosha, Luvrtrap)		Check the regular phone bill.	
Nickyspy (Nickispy)	Install Google + application	View Google + application	
Plankton	Removal of installed mobile security software.	Check security software in the system tray or the main screen	

Continued

RogueLemon	Request subscribed value-added service.	Check your phone bill	
RogueSPPush	Request subscribed value-added service.	disagree registration value-added services. Check Your phone bill Show RogueSPPush love app.	
SMSReplicator	Ask a question your interested issues through messages to other phone.	View Alert: Phone Number(s) to answer o another phone number	
SndApps	Built-in: the user clicks this icon with "FREE" and "No Ads" in their descriptions download and install.	View built-in	
Spitmo	See a pop up "Certificate update" or "security" apps.	View Settings: 1 process and popup number	
Tapsnake	If you click Menu button then appear prompted to registrate your information.	Stop SnakeService: Settings/Applications/Running Service, choose SnakeService to Stop.	
Walkinwat	Application Not Licensed Cracking...	You should not choose a crack for apps suggestions (Alert).	
YZHC	Abnormally high bill from SMS sending and connection Internet.	Check regularly phone bill and your account	
zsone	Abnormally high bill from SMS sending .	Check regularly phone bill and your account	
Battery Doctor (fakedoc)	pop-up ads about improve your battery life.	You should not install scare or trick app that you don't need. (Battery Doctor)	
CI4	Without a launcher icon after installation.		
Counterclank	Restrict the use of ad networks.		
Dougalek	An error has occurred and the video has not loaded.		
DropDialer	Uninstall itself after sending.	Check regularly phone bill and your account. Check icon apps after installed a app.	
FakeAngry (AnZhu)	Pop-ups displayed Bookmark Name/Bookmark URL.	Appear Screen Off And Lock apps	
Faketimer (oneclickfraud)	Opens unhealthy content websites.	Remove its	
FakeToken	uses the logo and colours of the bank in the icon of the application when the user don't enter the first factor of authentication then shows an error	Icon of Bank: Santander, BBVA, Banesto,..	
FindAndCall	the app sends SMS spam	View icon apps (Find & call). Remove it	
Gamex (muldrop)	Appear new icon apps and Message in Android 8.2.3 patch	View Android 8.2.3 patch	
Logastrod	Abnormally high bill	Check regularly phone bill	
Luckycat	an "empty" icon or a standard Android icon		
Moghava	JPG images increasing in size: full sdcard	uninstalling the app delete jpg	
Notcompatible	Request open "Unknown sources"	Download from Android market	
Opfake	Its variant have the Opera icon	strange charges to your phone bill	
Rootsmart (Bmaster)	"Settings" icon with Chinese name	"Settings" icon Chinese name	
SteeK (Fatakr, fakelottery)	money the user needs to pay if he wants to participate for applications or gaming	Check regularly phone bill	
VDloader	no corresponding icon in the phone's app	A 3D waterfall wallpaper	

them, …

However, malicious software is not a software bug so when installing or running the software, you should consider bug occurrence with above several features.

4. Detection Results of Malware Families

The author installed four mobile security software from Lenovo Store on a Lenovo phone P70 (version 2.3.5) to

Table 5. Detection results from top anti-virus software 2012.

Malware Families	Num	Dr. Web			Kaspersky			NQ/NetQin			Zoner		
		Num	time	%	Num	time	%	Num	timer	%	Num	time	%
AnserverBot	190	190	128	100	169	93	88.9	2	36	1.1	190	9	100
BaseBridgeA.B.C	126	121	86	96.0	124	134	98.4	61	6	48.4	126	11	100
BeanBot	8	0	1	0.0	0	12	0.0	0	1	0.0	8	3	100
Bgserv	10	10	2	100	10	12	100	1	2	10.0	10	1	100
CruseWin (CruseWind)	2	2	1	100	2	1	100	0	1	0.0	2	1	100
DroidCoupon	1	0	1	0.0	1	0	100	0	1	0.0	0	1	0.0
DroidDeluxe	3	1	1	33.3	2	1	66.7	3	2	100	2	1	66.7
DroidDream (DORDRAE)	26	26	7	100	26	5	100	22	4	84.6	26	2	100
DroidDreamLight	47	47	9	100	17	16	36.2	12	5	25.5	47	4	100
DroidKungFu1 (KungFuA, fokonge, gongfu)	34	34	18	100	34	14	100	33	7	97.1	34	5	100
DroidKungFu2 (KungFuB)	32	32	9	100	32	12	100	5	7	15.6	32	3	100
DroidKungFu3 (KungFuC)	310	309	178	99.7	205	338	66.1	0	74	0.0	310	40	100
DroidKungFu4 (KungFuD)	96	96	54	100	44	274	45.8	96	0	100	96	12	100
DroidKungFuSapp (KungFuE)	3	3	1	100	0	7	0.0	0	2	0.0	3	1	100
FakePlayer (SMSSend)	7	7	1	100	7	2	100	3	1	42.9	7	1	100
GamblerSMS	1	0	1	0.0	0	0	0.0	0	1	0.0	1	1	100
Geinimi	109	97	63	89.0	79	133	72.5	109	41	100	109	15	100
GGTracker	3	3	1	100	3	183	100	0	1	0.0	3	1	100
GingerMaster	4	4	1	100	4	2	100	0	1	0.0	4	1	100
GoldDream (spygold)	49	49	35	100	29	140	59.2	12	12	24.5	49	4	100
Gone60 (gonein60)	14	13	1	92.9	14	8	100	0	2	0.0	14	1	100
GPSSMSSpy (mobinautn, SmsHowU, smsspy)	6	6	2	100	4	1	66.7	0	1	0.0	6	1	100
HippoSMS	4	3	1	75.0	1	1	25.0	2	1	50.0	4	1	100
Jifake	1	1	1	100	1	0	100	0	1	0.0	1	1	100
jSMSHider (smshider)	16	16	5	100	16	16	100	11	3	68.8	16	2	100
KMin (ozotshielder)	100	52	39	52.0	93	124	93.0	0	35	0.0	100	9	100
LoveTrap (cosha)	1	1	1	100	1	2	100	1	1	100	1	1	100
NickySpyABC	3	3	1	100	3	2	100	0	1	0.0	3	1	100
Pjapps	81	60	42	74.1	67	98	82.7	80	21	98.8	81	13	100
Plankton (tonclank)	61	29	12	47.5	11	156	18.0	6	29	9.8	61	10	100
RogueLemon	2	0	1	0.0	0	5	0.0	0	2	0.0	2	1	100
RogueSPPush (autospsubscribe)	9	9	2	100	6	23	66.7	0	4	0.0	9	1	100
SMSReplicator	1	1	1	100	1	0	100	0	1	0.0	1	1	100
SndApps	10	10	3	100	8	6	80.0	1	1	10.0	10	1	100

Continued

Spitmo (zitmo)	1	1	1	100	1	2	100	0	1	0.0	1	1	100
Tapsnake	2	2	1	100	2	2	100	0	1	0.0	2	1	100
Walkinwat	1	1	1	100	1	4	100	0	1	0.0	1	1	100
YZHC (uxipp, wukong)	24	21	6	87.5	13	29	54.2	5	4	20.8	24	2	100
Zsone	12	12	3	100	12	9	100	11	3	91.7	12	1	100
.Battery Doctor (fakedoc)	1	1	1	100	1	2	100	0	1	0.0	1	1	100
CI4 SMS Bot	1	0	1	0.0	0	1	0.0	0	1	0.0	1	1	100
Counterclank	6	6	2	100	0	27	0.0	0	5	0.0	6	2	100
Dougalek (dougaleaker)	6	0	1	0.0	0	1	0.0	0	1	0.0	6	1	100
DropDialer	2	0	1	0.0	0	5	0.0	0	1	0.0	2	1	100
FakeAngry (AnZhu)	1	1	1	100	0	1	0.0	0	1	0.0	1	1	100
Faketimer (oneclickfraud)	4	3	1	75.0	0	1	0.0	0	1	0.0	3	1	75.0
FakeToken	1	1	1	100	0	1	0.0	0	1	0.0	1	1	100
FindAndCall	1	0	1	0.0	0	1	0.0	0	1	0.0	1	1	100
Gamex (muldrop)	1	1	1	100	0	1	0.0	0	1	0.0	1	1	100
Logastrod	4	4	1	100	0	1	0.0	0	1	0.0	4	1	100
LUCKYCAT	1	0	1	0.0	0	1	0.0	0	1	0.0	0	1	0.0
Moghava	1	1	1	100	0	12	0.0	0	3	0.0	0	1	0.0
notcompatible	1	1	1	100	0	1	0.0	0	1	0.0	1	1	100
opfake	7	2	1	28.6	0	6	0.0	0	2	0.0	4	1	57.1
ROOTSMART	13	2	0	15.4	1	27	7.7	3	5	23.1	13	1	100
SMSZombie	8	8	2	100	0	11	0.0	0	2	0.0	7	2	87.5
Steek (fakelottery)	14	0	1	0.0	0	49	0.0	0	8	0.0	14	3	100
VDloader	2	0	1	0.0	0	9	0.0	0	2	0.0	2	1	100
Total samples	1485	1303	742	87.7	1045	2025	70.4	479	357	32.3	1476	190	99.4

assess the effectiveness test on the same configuration and the same phone, the same samples set. (Dr. Web Anti-virus v7.00.3 (Dr. Web), Kaspersky Mobile Security. 9.10.139 (Kaspersky), NQmobile antivirus v5.2 (NQ or NetQin) and Zoner Mobile Security v1.0.0 (Zoner).

From the testing results, we are shown that some software like Zoner detection rate to 99.4% (**Tables 5** and **6**, **Figure 8**).

5. Discussion

From the analysis of malware families and samples, the author saw that the ability to detect malware from the users is usually limited. The rapid development of new applications and variations to immune with mobile security software requires overall solution from the analysis of new variants and detect new viruses to alert the com-

Table 6. Result detect malware families (total).

Name \ Detect	Dr. Web	Kaspersky	NetQin	Zoner
Num	1303	1045	479	1476
Time	742	2025	357	190

munity, and then users should also take preventive measures:

1) Users carefully read and understand permissions, an application and compare it with the real features of this app. In particular, users should not install or update software not necessary for the unknown effects of this app.

2) When an app is installed, users should check that the extraordinary can happen: no icon appears corresponding with this app (without, more one icon), Check

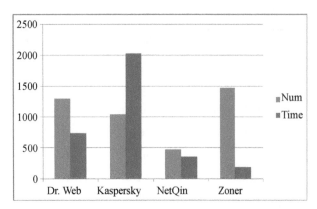

Figure 8. Result detect malware families (Chart).

regularly phone bill or account.

3) Users should invest a mobile security software copyright and install all apps from the official Android Market instead of third—party market.

4) Users should download an app with thousands of downloads and mostly positive comments.

5) Turn off unused features such as: GPS, GPRS, WIFI (Settings > Wireless & networks > Wi-Fi), extend memory (Settings -> Applications -> Development -> USB debugging), ... Especially, Android OS allows users to install file. APK in unknown sources directly and the malware easily penetrate the user's phone. (Settings -> Applications -> unknown sources).

6) Keep your phone patched up to date.

6. Conclusions

From the analysis of the characteristics of the collected malware samples, the author classified them into their existing families or their addition of a new family for their collection with 58 malware families and 1485 malware samples. And the author introduced three different techniques to analyze the sample introduced in Section 1.

The author selected the recognizable characteristics from ordinary users with their families that had collected (**Table 1**), and proposed solutions as recommendations to users before installing it with the ultimate desire to mitigate the damage in the community that is on the android phone, especially the ordinary users with limited understanding about potential hazards. The visible Symptoms of malware which exploit the device to gain root privilege are difficult to see and detect because they silently execute malicious code in the platform OS. Mostly, they steal information and send to remote server or URL by SMS messages (premium rate number or not).

The author presented evaluation results of the test 04 mobile security software of top ten software from AV-TEST in 2012 [51] with each family in order for the users to have the appropriate choice to proceed with fixing them and prevent them in the future, especially with

malwares using root exploits when detecting the infection.

Beside, ordinary phone users recognize malwares by visible symptoms in order to fix it (**Table 4**) and they are careful when downloading and installing apps from official Android Market with security advisories (Section 5). If users are really concerned with the potential risks, they should consider investing in an effective mobile security app because it is still the best bet to stay protected anywhere, anytime. Also, when we are installing software of unknown source, the phones are also infected with malicious software before it can protect the phones.

REFERENCES

[1] UK, "Worldwide Mobile Device Sales to End Users by Operating System in third Quarter of 2012,"2012. http://www.gartner.com/it/page.jsp?id=2237315

[2] R. Thurner, "A Breakdown by Country of the Most Popular App Download Services to Help Make the Business Case," 2012. http://www.smartinsights.com/mobile-marketing/app-marketing/app-download-statistics/

[3] Kaspersky Lab, "The overall statistics for 2012," 2012. http://www.securelist.com/en/analysis/204792255/Kaspersky_Security_Bulletin_2012_The_overall_statistics_for_2012#1

[4] "Number of the Week: 40% of Modern Smartphones Owners Do Not Use Antivirus Software," 2012. http://www.kaspersky.com/about/news/press/2012/number-of-the-week-40-percent-of-modern-smartphones-owners-do-not-use-antivirus-software

[5] Y. J. Zhou and X. X. Jiang, "Dissecting Android Malware: Characterization and Evolution," *Proceedings of the 33rd IEEE Symposium on Security and Privacy (Oakland 2012)*, San Francisco, 20-23 May 2012, pp. 95-109.

[6] Contagio Mobile, "Download Malware Categories". http://contagiominidump.blogspot.com/

[7] US-CERT/NIST, "Vulnerability Summary for CVE-2009-1185," 2009. http://web.nvd.nist.gov/view/vuln/detail?   vulnId=CVE-2009-1185

[8] X. X. Jiang, "Security Alert: New Sophisticated Android Malware DroidKungFu Found in Alternative Chinese App Markets," 2011. http://www.cs.ncsu.edu/faculty/jiang/DroidKungFu/

[9] X. X. Jiang, "Security Alert: New DroidKungFu Variants Found in Alternative Chinese Android Markets," 2011. http://www.cs.ncsu.edu/faculty/jiang/DroidKungFu2/

[10] X. X. Jiang, "Security Alert: New DroidKungFu Variant AGAIN! Found in Alternative Android Markets," 2011. http://www.csc.ncsu.edu/faculty/jiang/Droid KungFu3/

[11] Wikipedia, "Reverse_Engineering". http://en.wikipedia.org/wiki/ Reverse_engineering

[12] X. X. Jiang, "Security Alert: AnserverBot, New Sophisticated Android Bot Found in Alternative Android Markets," 2011.

http://www.csc.ncsu.edu/faculty/jiang/AnserverBot/

[13] Symantec, "Android.Basebridge," 2011.
http://www.symantec.com/   secu-
rity_response/writeup.jsp?docid=2011-060915-4938-99
&tabid=2

[14] X. X. Jiang, "Security Alert: New BeanBot SMS Trojan
Discovered," 2011.
http://www.csc.ncsu.edu/faculty/ jiang/BeanBot/

[15] Trendmicro, "ANDROIDOS_BGSERV.A," 2011.
http://about-threats.
trendmicro.com/us/malware/AndroidOS_BGSERV.A

[16] Symantec, "Android.Pjapps," 2011.
http://www.symantec.com/securit   yre-
sponse/writeup.jsp?docid=2011-022303-3344-99&tabid=
2

[17] M. Balanza, "Android Malware Acts as an SMS Relay,"
Trend Labs, 2011.
http://blog.trendmicro.com/trendlabs-security-intellige
nce /android-malware-acts-as-an-sms-relay/

[18] NQMobile, "DroidCoupon".
http://labs.netqin.com/us/?p=112

[19] Kindsight Lab, Malware Analysis Report, "AndroidOS/
DroidDeluxe," 2011.
https://www.kindsight.net/
sites/default/files/Kindsight_Malware_Analysis-Android-
Trojan-DroidDeluxe-final.pdf

[20] Lookout, "Technical Analysis DroidDream Malware,"
2011. https:// blog.lookout.com/droiddream/

[21] Trendmicro, "ANDROIDOS_DORDRAE.N," 2011.
http://about-
threats.trendmicro.com/us/malware/ANDROIDOS_DOR
DRAE.N

[22] AVGbobilation, "Malware Information: DroidDreamLight,"
2011.
http://cms.avg-hrd.appspot.com/securitycenter/securitypo
st_20110601.html

[23] X. X. Jiang, "Security Alert: New Sophisticated Android
Malware Droid KungFu Found in Alternative Chinese
App Markets," 2011.
http://www.cs.ncsu.edu/faculty/jiang/DroidKung Fu/

[24] X. X. Jiang, "Security Alert: Be Cautious with Android
Spyware—GamblerSMS," 2011.
http://www.cs.ncsu.edu/ faculty/jiang/GamblerSMS/

[25] Symantec, "Android.Ggtracker," 2011.
http://www.symantec.com/
security_response/writeup.jsp?docid=2011-062208-5013-
99&tabid= 2

[26] Symantec, "Android.Geinimi," 2011.
http://www.symantec.com/   secu-
rity_response/writeup.jsp?docid=2011-010111-5403-99&
tabid=-9

[27] AVGbobilation, "Malware information: GingerMaster".
http://cms.avg-hrd.appspot.com/securitycenter/securitypo
st_20110825.html#tabs-2

[28] Symantec, "Android.Golddream," 2011.
http://www.symantec.com/
security_response/writeup.jsp?docid=2011-070608-4139-
99& tabid=2

[29] AVGbobilation, "Malware Information: Gone60," 2011.
http://cms.avg-hrd.appspot.com/securitycenter/securitypo
st_20110927.html#tabs-2

[30] Y. Takash, "Beta Version of Spytool App for Android
Steals SMS Messages," i, TrenLabs, 2012.
http://blog.trend   mi-
cro.com/trendlabs-security-intelligence/beta-version-of-sp
ytool-app-for-android-steals-sms-messages/

[31] A. Apvrille, "QR Code and Mobile Malware: It Happened!"
FortiBlog, 2011.
http://blog.fortinet.com/qr-code-and-mobile-   mal-
ware-it-happened/

[32] Mcafee, "Virus Profile: Android/J.SMSHider.A," 2011.
http://home.
mcafee.com/VirusInfo/VirusProfile.aspx?key=527859#no
ne

[33] Symantec, "LoveTrap" 2011.
http://www.symantec.com/security_res
ponse/writeup.jsp?docid=2011-072806-2905-99&tabid=2

[34] Symantec, "Android.Ozotshielder," 2011.
http://www.symantec.com
/security_response/writeup.jsp?docid=2011-091505-3230
-99

[35] AVGbobilation, "Malware Information: NickiSpy".
http://cms.avg-hrd.appspot.com/securitycenter/securitypo
st_20110804.htm#tabs-2

[36] M. Ballano, "Android Threats Getting Steamy," 2011.
http://www.symantec.com/connect/blogs/android-threats-
getting-steamy

[37] X. Jiang, "Security Alert: New Stealthy Android Spyware—
Plankton—Found in Official Android Market," 2011.
http://www.csc.ncsu.edu/faculty/jiang/Plankton/

[38] X. Jiang, "Security Alert: New Rogue App RogueLemon
Found in Alternative Chinese Android Markets," 2011.
http://www.csc.ncsu.edu/faculty/jiang/RogueLemon/

[39] X. Jiang, "New Rogue Android App—Ro-gueSPPush—
Found in Alternative Android Markets," 2011
http://www.cs.ncsu.edu/faculty/jiang/RogueSPPush/

[40] Zimry, Irene, Raulf and Leong-F-Secure, "On Android
threats Spyware: Android/SndApps.A and Trojan: An-
droid/SmsSpy.D," 2011.
http://www.f-secure.com/weblog/archives/00002202.html

[41] Forensic Blog, "Detailed Analysis of Android.Spitmo,"
2011,
http://forensics.spreitzenbarth.de/2011/12/06/detailed-ana
lysis-of-android-spitmo/

[42] Symantec, "Walkinwat," 2011.
http://www.symantec.com/security_response/writeup.jsp?
docid=2011-033008-4831-99&tabid=2

[43] Symantec, "Tapsnake," 2010.
http://www.symantec.com/security_response/writeup.jsp?
docid=2010-081214-2657-99

[44] T. Strazzere, "Security Alert: Zsone Trojan Found in
Android Market," 2011.
https://blog.lookout.com/blog/2011/05/11/security-alert-z
sone-trojan-found-in-android-market

[45] Symantec, "Android.Counterclank," 2012.

http://www.symantec.com/security_response/writeup.jsp?docid=2012-012709-4046-99&tabid=2

[46] Symantec, "Android.Dougalek," 2012.
http://www.symantec.com/security_response/writeup.jsp?docid=2012-041601-3400-99

[47] L. Arsene, "Android SMS Bot Uses Twitter to Hide C&C Server," 2012.
http://www.hotforsecurity.com/blog/android-sms-bot-uses-twitter-to-hide-cc-server-2602.html

[48] I. Asrar, "Android.Dropdialer Identified on Google Play," 2012.
http://www.symantec.com/connect/blogs/androiddrodialer-identified-google-play

[49] B. Botezatu, "From China with Love: New Android Backdoor Spreading through Hacked Apps," 2012.
http://www.hotforsecurity.com/blog/from-china-with-lov

e-new-android-backdoor-spreading-through-hacked-apps-1317.html

[50] I. Asrar, "Scam Proves Privacy Concerns on Mobile Devices," 2012.
http://www.symantec.com/connect/blogs/scam-proves-privacy-concerns-mobile-devices-0

[51] AV-TEST, "Test Report: Anti-Malware solutions for Android," 2012.
http://www.av-test.org/en/tests/mobile-devices/android/

[52] Open Source Database of Android Malware (links + signatures), 2012
https://code.google.com/p/androguard/wiki/DatabaseAndroMawares#Open_Source_database_of_android_malwares

19

RFID Applications: Prospects and Challenges in Bangladesh

Abdul Kadar Muhammad Masum, Faruk Bhuiyan, Kazi Golam Azam

Department of Business Administration, International Islamic University, Chittagong, Bangladesh

ABSTRACT

Radio frequency identification (RFID) is an emerging technology, radio wave communication between a microchip and an electronic reader, consisting of data gathering, distribution, and management systems that has the ability to identify or scan information for remoting recognition of objects with increased speed and accuracy. An attempt has been made to know how using of RFID technology helps to improve services and business process efficiency in public and private sectors of Bangladesh. With this aim, we have conducted extensive literature survey. At the end of this attempt, we have come to the conclusion that the potential use of this technology includes RFID chipped passports, human implants, item-level tagging, inventory tracking and access control systems. RFID technology is at its early stage of adoption in Bangladesh with a few business applications and pilot studies. However, when tags begin to be associated with individuals, privacy is threatened. RFID is a new type of threat to personal information and must be treated as such; indeed, it must be recognized that existing privacy legislation is not adequate. This paper also explores some current and emerging applications of RFID in Bangladesh and examines the challenges including privacy and ethical issues arising from its use, as well as addressing potential means of handling those issues.

Keywords: RFID (Radio Frequency Identification); Potential Applications; Challenges; Bangladesh

1. Introduction

RFID is not a new technology despite rapidly growing interest in RFID technology in recent years. The concept of the technology dates to the mid to late 1940s, following on from technological developments in the 1930s and the development of radar during World War II [1]. In the 1950s, several technologies related to RFID technology were developed. Technological innovations and their consequences are becoming indispensable parts of our daily lives. RFID, as one of these innovations, is a system that provides easy, secure and quick data entry, storage and transmission. It is used in many places such as shops, stores, hospitals, pharmaceuticals companies, logistic services etc. where real time data should be used. It is important in improving efficiency and visibility, cutting costs, delivering better asset utilization, producing higher quality goods, reducing shrinkage and counterfeiting, and increasing sales by reducing out-of-stocks [2]. Most of developed and developing countries are using RFID technology in their private and public sectors.

Although implementing RFID technology is a com-

plicated process, the right planning and development of an RFID strategy can offer important advantages to business systems and public sectors. While RFID technology has received a fair amount of attention in media recently [3], many are still unfamiliar with RFID and the benefits it can offer. In the face of the need for clear, extensive information about RFID and its benefits, this paper presents the opportunities offered by the technology for any organization or any agency of Bangladesh government involved in the production, management, and sale of goods or services.

In this paper, we motivate our work in Section 2, and the methodology of the research is mentioned in Section 3. Related previous study of RFID Technology is described in Section 4. Furthermore, we have briefly described the working mechanism of RFID technology and its characteristics in Sections 5 and 6. Besides, Section 7 includes RFID applications in present world. Implication of RFID Technology and its possible applications for Bangladesh are explored in Sections 8 and 9. Moreover, Considerable issues and some suggestions to implementation of RFID technology in Bangladesh are given Sections 10 and 11.

2. Objectives of the Study

In this study, an attempt has been made to know how using of RFID technology helps to improve services and business process efficiency in public and private sectors of Bangladesh. However, the specific objectives of the study are set forth as below:

a) To delineate the concise essentials of RFID technology;

b) To explore its current and emerging applications in present world with especial reference of Bangladesh;

c) To evaluate the challenges to implement RFID technology in Bangladesh;

d) To provide some recommendation for prevail over those challenges.

3. Methodology of the Study

In light of the objectives of the study, the paper has been designed to investigate how using of RFID technology enhance the efficiency of services and business processes in public and private sector of Bangladesh. To this end an extensive literature survey has been conducted. The study is based largely on secondary data. Data and information from secondary sources were collected by reviewing different published articles, online journals, working papers, existing case studies and websites.

4. Literature Review

Radio frequency identification (RFID) technology is currently one of the technological most promising and discussed auto-identification and data capture (AIDC) technologies [4]. It is not actually a new technology, but it is being applied in new ways, spurred by technological advances and decreased costs. Once used during World War II to identify friendly aircraft, RFID is now being used in a variety of public and private sectors setting from hospital to the highway [5]. A number of studies show that it can be used in many different ways to create value. That is why, several world largest companies use RFID technology to boost up the business performance with great care of consumers and environmental concerns. Chao-Che Lin and Teh-Hsing Ku demonstrates how participating employees with a systemic view can adopt a better methodology to solve problems in RFID and how performance can be enhanced through Systems Thinking [6]. A workshop report was presented from the staff of US federal commission in March, 2005. The workshop brought together RFID proponents, privacy experts, and other interested parties to discuss RFID's various current and potential applications and their implications for con-

sumer privacy. It also highlighted proposals to address these implications and generated discussion about the merits of these different approaches [7]. Another study conducted by Mehmet Barut, Bobert Brown, Nicole Freund, Jonathan may, and Elizabeth Reinhart proposed to add comprehensive ethical and investment deliberation as a means to explore the true value of RFID and its applications [8]. The first exhaustive empirical analysis of performance measurement behavior in the RFID field conducted by to measure the economic performance of their applications and how is the success of RFID applications affected by performance measurement. Nemeth *et al.* [9] present a state-of-the-art on RFID systems and the challenges and possibilities of the integration to supply chains. Chao *et al.* [10] review the literature on trends and forecast of RFID technologies from 1991 to 2005 by a historical review method and bibliometric analyze. They focus on the RFID innovation, deployment by enterprises and market diffusion in supply chain management. Recently, Delaunay *et al.* [11] present a survey on the causes of inventory inaccuracy in supply chain management. Dolgui and Proth [12] also present a literature review on RFID technology in supply chain. They focus on the advantages of RFID technologies in inventory management. They also analyze some problems and present perspectives dealing with privacy and authentication properties of RFID technologies. In Bangladesh, Apollo Hospitals, Dhaka and Bangladesh Army are the early adopters of RFID technology.

5. RFID (Radio Frequency Identification Device)

RFID has come to signify system solutions for tracking and tracing objects both globally and locally using RFID tags. RFID is one of several technologies collectively known as auto-ID procedures—procedures for identifying objects automatically [13]. RFID by itself is not a location-tracking technology. At sites where readers are installed, RFID may be used to track tagged objects, but this static readability differs from technology such as global positioning systems, or GPS, which uses a network of satellites to pinpoint the location of a receiver [14]. The effectiveness of an RFID application in addressing desired functionality depends on several important factors:

Contactless: An RFID tag can be read without any physical contact between the tag and the reader.

Writable Data: The data of a read-write (RW) RFID tag can be rewritten several times.

Absence of Line-of-Sight: A line of sight is generally not required for an RFID reader to read a tag.

Variety of Reading Ranges: An RFID tag can have a reading range from as small as a few inches to as large as more than 100 feet.

Wide Data-Capacity Range: A tag can store from a few bytes of data to virtually any amount of data.

Support for Multiple Tag Readings: It is possible to use an RFID reader to automatically read several RFID tags in its reading zone within a short period of time.

Durable: RFID tags and readers can easily operate under difficult conditions.

Perform Smart Tasks: In addition to the tasks of carrying and transmitting of data, an RFID system can be designed to perform some other tasks (e.g., acculturation to environmental conditions, operating at high or low temperature and pressure).

Extreme Reading Accuracy: Tanks to extreme reading accuracy advantage, RFID is an accurate and secure technology for data gathering and management.

The advantages listed above are generic for any type of RFID systems. Some additional factors such as privacy and security concerns, data mining, and the integration of the RFID with other technologies such as biometric systems, Global Positioning Systems (GPS) and wireless communication technologies are needed to be considered for applications [15].

6. How Does RFID Work?

RFID devices have three primary elements: a chip, an antenna, and a reader. A fourth important part of any RFID system is the database where information about tagged objects is stored. The chip contains information about the item to which it is attached. Chips used by retailers and manufacturers to identify consumer goods may contain an Electronic Product Code ("EPC") [16]. EPC chips are encrypted with a unique product code that identifies the individual product to which it is attached, and can be read using radio frequency. The antenna attached to the chip is responsible for transmitting information from the chip to the reader, using radio waves. The chip and antenna combination is referred to as a transponder or, more commonly, as a tag. The reader, or scanning device, also has its own antenna, which it uses to communicate with the tag [17]. RFID systems can employ authentication and encryption to prevent unauthorized reading of data [18]. "Reading" tags refers to the communication between the tag and reader via radio waves operating at a certain frequency. A stationary reader that could be used to track tagged cases of goods entering a warehouse a mobile reader used to monitor inventory on a retail store floor and a prototype of a glove embedded with a scanner used to track daily domestic living activities, a reader communicates with a tag in order to capture the data stored in the tag. The reader usually sends a low-power radio signal to activate the tag and the tag then sends data back to the reader. Most

readers are—as their names suggest—only capable of reading data, although some also have the capability to write to certain tags. Normally, readers forward the data to other systems (such as PCs) for subsequent processing. In comparison to tags, readers consume more power, are larger and more expensive. RFID systems use radiosignals to communicate, but only certain frequency bands are available for license-free use. There is international variation in the frequencies and power levels available for RFID systems. Due to different national regulations, an RFID system produced in one country may not work in another country. The database, or other back-end logistics system, stores information about RFID-tagged objects. Access to both a reader and its corresponding database are necessary before information stored on an RFID tag can be obtained and understood.

There are two types of tags, namely active and passive tags. Active tags are larger, heavier and more expensive than passive ones as they contain their own power source (battery). Nevertheless, they emit stronger signal, operating normally at higher frequencies (455 MHz - 950 MHz or 2.45 - 5.8 GHz) capable of being captured by the reader over a longer distance measuring 20 - 100 meters. The tags are more suitable for tracking valuable items. On the hand, passive tags are much smaller, lighter and cheaper than active tags. Typically it is operating at lower frequencies (30 kHz - 134 KHz or 13.6 MHz) with a capture range of between several centimeters and 10 meters. They are commonly used for asset tracking and security applications.

7. Present Scenario of RFID Applications in World

According to the European e-Business Watch large-scale survey [19] of RFID adoption strategies and impacts in four broad economic sectors, 14% of the European companies interviewed were piloting, using or implementing RFID technology in 2007. Companies that were using RFID or planning to use RFID expected major effects on: a) inventory management (49% of companies using or planning to use RFID), b) control and efficiency of inbound logistics (46%), and c) merchandise management and reduced out-of-stocks (44%). The major costs for those using or planning to use the technology were seen to be the costs of project implementation and system integration (39% of all companies using or planning to use RFID). Interestingly, for those companies not using or planning to use RFID technology, 64% stated that a relevant reason for not using it was the insufficient evidence of a strong return on investment (ROI). Wal-Mart and the Department of Defense (DOD) of US told their top suppliers to begin tagging cases and pallets with RFID tags by January of 2005. Indeed, Gartner anticipates that by 2012 most "enterprises will be forced to redesign their value chain processes as a result of RFID changing the storage, collection, and use of data concerning goods in the supply chain". If predictions are true, then the RFID market will approach $4 billion by 2012 [15]. Selected RFID applications in the public sector in some countries are given below:

Health Sector: Austria tests by the municipal administration of Vienna on the applicability of RFID in the health care system. Mexico has Health insurance card: RFID technology is integrated in the "popular insurance" card where the username, information on doctors as well as prescribed drugs are stored. Korea uses RFID technology in hospitals.

e-Passport: In Denmark, e-passport is available since mid-2006; biometric passport relying on RFID embedded fingerprint technology is introduced mid-2009. Germany has introduced e-passport since the end of 2005 and electronic ID card since the end of 2009. Biometric passport is relying on RFID technology in Netherlands, USA and UK. Portugal has e-passport and e-passport control systems at Portuguese airports.

Public Services: Austria tests in the Viennese parking facility management. Germany uses Waste management in different communities. Korea has implemented Pilot projects in the fields of procurement, baggage handling, container management, ammunition management, tracking hazardous waste, museums etc. RFID tags replace paper season parking tickets at car parks in public housing estates in Singapore.

Education Sector: RFID technology is used in Denmark, Germany, Singapore, Netherlands and United States of America implementing for lending systems in libraries.

Logistics/Transport Sector: Japan has set-up of the "Free Mobility Assistance System" based on ubiquitous network technology including RFID tags, to provide information for seamless movement (e.g. transfer routes and transport modes). Netherlands has introduced payment cards for public transport. Singapore establishes Nationwide Electronic Road Pricing (ERP) system to control and manage traffic volume; payment of road usage charges. The ERP is applied to all of Singapore's 840,000 vehicles.

8. Implication of RFID Technology for Bangladesh

A little area of both the private and public sectors are driving the RFID market in Bangladesh. Deltech Ltd., a global RFID solution provider has already helped several organizations implement RFID [20]. According to Mr. Delwar Hossain, founder of the Deltech, hands-free access control and employee-tracking systems, as well as asset management are the most popular applications

businesses are asking for. Appollo Hospital, Dhaka has completed the first phase of an RFID project to track employee attendance as well as assets [20]. The Bangladesh Army also plans to employ this technology to track soldiers and visitors entering its Dhaka Cantonment as well as track retail purchases. In many export sectors of Bangladesh ranging from garments to household and office furniture, large international buyers can get rid of the age old barcode-based product identification systems for RFID tags to reduce product tracking and inventory management costs of the items which will ultimately help the country to be competitive in the world market. US retailers like Target, Wal-Mart, etc. are major buyers of Bangladesh's garment products. Since Wal-Mart has already announced its plans to require majority of their suppliers to implement RFID based tracking systems, the Bangladeshi exporters have no choice rather to implement RFID technology to survive in the world market. Besides Wal-Mart and Target, German retailer Metro and furniture maker IKEA (recently commenced operations in Bangladesh on a limited basis), to name a few among the large number of companies, have already started experimenting with RFID integrated supply chain management systems. This sea change in global integrated supply chain management necessitates a rapid mobilization of our government, IT and export industry leaders and experts to devise a uniform RFID strategy for Bangladesh.

9. Potential RFID Applications for Bangladesh

Radio frequency identification can be used in many different ways to create value and the number is growing at the fast pace. To structure this range of application, some fields of application, which may be suitable for Bangladesh, are given below:

Assets Tracking: RFID can play a vital role to track valuable assets. Companies can put RFID tags on assets that are lost or stolen often, that are underutilized or that are just hard to locate at the time they are needed.

Assets Monitoring and Maintenance: High-value assets can be tagged to store information for maintenance purposes. The tagged machines where the maintenance history and information on replaced parts will be stored on the tag. When data will be stored directly on the tag and not on the companies' network, tags with high data capacity will be needed.

Manufacturing: There is an emphasis on using RFID for applications that can track items from the manufacturing point all the way through to the store shelf. This process entails tagging pallets, cartons, reusable containers and individual items to track the movement of goods throughout the supply chain straight through to the sale of the item to the customer. RFID may be used to help automate the processing the incoming shipments of pistachios from grower partners.

Theft Control: Item level RFID tags may be used to prevent theft along the supply chain or at the point of sale. A simple form is electronic article surveillance (EAS) which can be RFID-based. In this case, low-end RFID systems (e.g. 1-bit tags) will be used which communicate when consumers leave the shop if they have not been deactivated. Applications for theft control in mail order for high-value products such as mobile phones use more sophisticated tags.

Authentication: For authentication purposes, RFID may be used to provide secure identification mechanisms for persons and objects. e-passports combine the traditional paper document with an RFID tag where the critical information is stored. The RFID tag often contains biometric data such as data for facial recognition and fingerprints.

Security and Access Control: RFID may be used as an electronic key to control who has access to office buildings or areas within office buildings. It is convenient (an employee can hold up a badge to unlock a door, rather than looking for a key or swiping a magnetic stripe card) because there is no contact between the card and reader, there is less wear and tear, and therefore less maintenance.

Public Services: Public services include services such as the management of parking facilities and waste management. In waste management RFID may be used for two main purposes: for tracking (hazardous) waste to protect the environment and to allocate costs according to the amount of waste.

Health Service: RFID may be used to track assets such as beds or containers, to identify patients for medication control and to track babies and dementia patients to increase their security. Information such as user name and prescribed drugs are stored on the embedded RFID chip. Hospitals can also plan to deploy RFID to identify patients, call up records, reduce medical errors and improve overall productivity.

Document Administration/Postal Services: RFID technology may be used for the administration of documents. In this field, RFID tags will be attached to documents to improve the location of documents and thus to increase process efficiency and quality. RFID may also be used for postal services in distribution centers to facilitate the sorting of mail items.

Public Transport: RFID may be used by the public sector in the fields of logistics and public transports. One of the most popular uses of RFID may be pay for road tolls without stopping vehicles. RFID is also catching on as a convenient way to pay for bus, subway and train rides. Newer applications are access cards for public transport, RFID-based bus schedules as well as particular location-based services.

10. Challenges to Implementation RFID Technology in both Public and Private Sectors of Bangladesh

Utilization of RFID for widespread mass commercial applications has been limited primarily due to challenges arising from several key factors. To assess the overall challenge presented to the organization we propose the use of a simple, "Challenge Assessment Matrix" (CAM) based on Likert-like approach.

Management Commitment: The most significant challenge to implementation is the commitment of management to adopting new technology and having appropriate expectations of RFID capabilities.

Selection of Tag and Tag Reader: Several key factors need to be considered, namely the tag type and size, read distance and other tag reader requirements. Active tags are thicker than the passive ones. Another important feature that should be provided is anti-collision since it allows multiple tags to be read in a single pass.

Cost: Even though the RFID tags are getting cheaper, tag costs are obviously the major variable cost component for RFID, but what about other related cost components? Software, systems integration, process redesign and organizational impacts will be significant and must be part of the business case as well. With the anticipated scale and scope of RFID deployment, tag costs are expected to continue their decline. For RFID implementation, organizations have to analyze Return-on-Investment (ROI) according to their business processes.

Data Management: Most ERP systems and WMS systems are not designed for RFID data capture. The Electronic Product Code occupies a larger data field than the Universal Product Code now in place. New structures for data management should be considered prior to any RFID investment.

International Standards: A key challenge is the continually evolving standards in technology, application, data, conformance, firmware changes, and tracking methods. In addition, different companies often use different standards making cooperation between suppliers and manufacturers difficult.

Availability of Resources: The shortage of existing skilled resources and lack of comprehensive, accessible information has cost implications for training and presents potential implementation problems.

Security: For certain implementations, illicit tracking of RFID tags presents problems. This is particularly relevant for military installations but security challenges are relevant also for corporations and individuals. For example, scanning and cloning of RFID tags can potentially provide undesired access to important facilities or use for payment in commercial transactions.

Business Process Changes: Process automation through RFID will require new work methods and performance measurements for the supply chain. The design of any RFID strategy must consider new processes and procedures to automate tasks and decision making where possible, as well as consider organizational changes.

Ethical Problems: The privacy concern of Bangladeshi consumers is information. The concern of information privacy is the tracking the purchasing habits and other information regarding a particular consumer. This information may be used for targeted advertising or possibly used in evaluating a consumer for various programs such as credit worthiness.

Government Regulations: Implementations are complicated by varying specifications and regulatory requirements, for example operational frequencies and power specifications vary from country to country.

11. Recommendations for Prevail over Those Challenges

Bangladesh is always among the last few countries to start using any technology that is already in use for several years in the other developed countries. The primary reasons are the lack of know-how and risk of investment in a new technology. Here, we have provided some suggestions to implement RFID in public and private sectors of Bangladesh.

a) Invest in pilot tests to determine the capabilities and limitations of the software and hardware, as well as the true costs and benefits of RFID. Update the business case based upon the findings.

b) Do not underestimate the need to change business processes to achieve the automation and asset visibility that RFID can provide.

c) At this moment the RFID initiative is discrete in Bangladesh and do not have any long-term strategy leading into implementation-to-diffusion process. Without having a clear strategy to achieve large scale diffusion discrete RFID adoption may not inspire the process in reaching the full potential of RFID.

d) Begin an RFID education effort with a dedicated team that is chartered to recommend and follow a course of action. Research the standards development underway to ensure that the technologies under consideration will meet both domestic and global standards.

e) Businesses must be candid with consumers about the how RFID technology is used in the products which consumers purchase.

f) Consumers should be informed of the existence and location of RFID tag in any product sold. Optimally under these guidelines consumers would have the option of having the devices deactivated at the time of purchase.

g) Ensure that the RFID technology does not interfere

with the privacy concerns of consumers is for stores to automatically deactivate RFID tags at point of purchase. RFID tags can be killed in a number of ways; tags designed with a kill switch built in so that upon receiving an instruction they deactivate themselves permanently.

h) Consumer education is a vital part of protecting consumer privacy. Industry members, privacy advocates, and government should develop education tools that inform consumers about RFID technology, how they can expect to encounter it, and what choices they have with respect to its usage in particular situations.

i) Many of the potential privacy issues associated with RFID are inextricably linked to database security. As in other contexts in which personal information is collected from consumers, a company that uses RFID to collect such information must implement reasonable and appropriate measures to protect that data.

j) Government should regulate the use of RFID tags in consumer goods. Optimally a law would require that RFID tags be permanently disabled at the time of purchase. The state would have in the usefulness of RFID tags in public activates such as law enforcement, it is unlikely that the government will be quick to set controls on how these devices are used.

k) Govern should design of an Auto-ID strategy for Bangladesh with a focus upon how business processes and the customer experience can be improved.

12. Conclusion

Despite the hype, the promise of RFID technology is real, and can provide increased asset visibility, enhanced information content and velocity. Equally as real are the pitfalls of RFID including cost, competing standards, technology limitations and privacy concerns. The transition to RFID may not occur overnight, but this technology has been given a jump start by leading industries in Europe. Bangladesh can adopt any suitable model for its overall automation in public and private sectors. Anticipate that return on investment for RFID will be low or non-existent initially, but that future gains are possible by redesigning business processes. We recommend RFID education for Bangladeshi consumers and development of the business case and pilot to size the potential benefits and adoption efforts. Finally, we recommend the design of an Auto-ID strategy for Bangladesh with a focus upon how business processes and the customer experience can be improved.

REFERENCES

[1]   Danish Board of Technology, "RFID from Production to Consumption—Risks and Opportunities from RFID Technology in the Value Chain," 2006.
www.tekno.dk/pdf/projekter/p06_rapport_RFID.pdf

[2] C. C. Chao, J. M. Yang and W. Y. Jen, "Determining Technology Trends and Forecasts of RFID by a Historical Review and Bibliometric Analysis from 1991 to 2005," *Technovation*, Vol. 27, No. 5, 2007, pp. 268-279.

[3] OECD, "RFID Implementation in Germany: Challenges and Benefits," 2007.
www.oecd.org/dataoecd/19/23/39693586.pdf

[4] M. Martin, "The History of RFID Technology," *RFID Journal*, 2007.
http://www.rfidjournal.com/article/articleview/1338/1/12 9/

[5] C. Delaunay, E. Sahin and Y. Dallery, "A Literature Review on Investigations Dealing with Inventory Management with Data Inaccuracies in RFID Eurasia, 1st Annual," 2007, pp. 1-7.

[6] W. Minli, W. Gang and H. Dajun, "Device Management in RFID Public Service Platform," *3rd International Conference on Convergence and Hybrid Information Technology*, Busan, Vol. 1, 2008, pp. 1133-1136.

[7] Y. Choi, D. Kang, H. Chae and K. Kim, "An Enterprise Architecture Framework for Collaboration of Virtual Enterprise Chains," *The International Journal of Advanced Manufacturing Technology*, Vol. 35, No. 11-12, 2008, pp. 1065-1078.

[8] T. Phillips, T. Karygiannis and R. Kuhn, "Security Standards for the RFID Market," *IEEE Security and Privacy*, 2005, pp. 85-88.

[9] A. Dolgui and J. M. Proth, "RFID Technology in Supply Chain Managment: State of the Art and Perspectives," *17th World Congress the International Federation of Automatic Control*, Seoul, 2008, pp. 4465-4475.

[10] A. Sarac, N. Absi and S. Dauzere-Peres, "A Literature Review on the Impact of RFID Technologies on Supply Chain Management," *International Journal of Production Economics*, Vol. 128, No. 1, 2010, pp. 77-95.

[11] S. Veronneau and J. Roy, "RFID Benefits, Costs, and Possibilities: The Economical Analysis of RFID Deployment in a Cruise Corporation Global Service Supply Chain," *International Journal of Production Economics*, Vol. 122, No. 2, 2009, pp. 692-702.

[12] V. D. Hunt, A. Puglia and M. Puglia, "RFID: A Guide to Radio Frequency Identification," John Wiley & Sons Inc., New Jersey, 2007.

[13] Y. Xiao, S. Yu, K. Wu, Q. Ni, C. Janecek and J. Nordstad, "Radio Frequency Identification: Technologies, Applications," *Wireless Communications and Mobile Computing*, Vol. 7, No. 4, 2007, pp. 45-472.

[14] B. Bacheldor, "RFID Takes Root in Bangladesh," *RFID Journal*, 2008.

[15] P. Nmeth, L. Toth and T. Hartvanyi, "Adapting RFID in Supply Chains," *3rd International Conference on Mechatronics*, 2006, pp. 263-266.

[16] M. A. Khan, M. Sharma and R. B. Prabhu, "A Survey of RFID Tags," *International Journal of Recent Trends in Engineering*, Vol. 1, No. 4, 2007, pp. 68-71.

[17] Y. Choi, D. Kang, H. Chae and K. Kim, "An Enterprise Architecture Framework for Collaboration of Virtual Enterprise Chains," *The International Journal of Advanced Manufacturing Technology*, Vol. 35, No. 11-12, 2008, pp. 1065-1078.

[18] M. Ohkubo, K. Suzuki and S. Kinoshita, "RFID Privacy Issues and Technical Challenges," *Communications of the ACM*, Vol. 48, No. 9, 2005, pp. 66-71.

[19] M. L. Chuang and W. H. Shaw, "RFID: Integration Stages in Supply Chain Management," *IEEE Engineering Management Review*, Vol. 35, No. 2, 2007, pp. 80-87.

[20] S. B. Miles, S. E. Sarma and J. R. Williams, "RFID Technology and Applications," Cambridge University Press, Cambridge, 2008.

20

All-Optical EXOR for Cryptographic Application Based on Spatial Solitons

Mario Marco Corbelli[1], Fabio Garzia[1,2], Roberto Cusani[1]
[1]Department of Information, Electronics and Telecommunication Engineering,
LA SAPIENZA, University of Rome, Rome, Italy
[2]Wessex Institute of Technology, Ashurst Lodge, Ashurst, Southampton, England

ABSTRACT

The purpose of this paper is to present an all-optical EXOR for cryptographic application based on spatial soliton beams. The device is based on the propagation and interactions properties of spatial soliton in a Kerr nonlinear material. The interaction force between parallel soliton beam is analyzed from the analytical point of view and an exact solution is presented.

Keywords: All-Optical EXOR; Cryptography; Spatial Solitons; All-Optical Device

1. Introduction

Spatial solitons are optical beams that propagate without changing their shape, thanks to the balance between nonlinear effect (self-focusing) and diffraction [1]. This balance effect has demonstrated to be stable in two-dimensional waveguides.

Propagation and interaction properties of spatial solitons are extremely interesting and useful in order to allow and realize all-optical devices, thanks to their robustness to the external disturbs. A plenty of all-optical devices have been proposed, such as filter [2], multiplexer and demultiplexer, arithmetic and logical unit [3, 4], high velocity router [5].

In this paper an all-optical EXOR for cryptographic application is proposed. The device is based on two peculiar properties of spatial soliton: swing effect [6,7] and interaction between parallel soliton beams.

Swing effect represents an oscillating behavior of soliton beams that propagate in a non-constant transversal refractive index [6]. It has been demonstrated that soliton oscillations depends on the intensity of the soliton itself and on the shape of the transversal refractive index.

Another interesting property of spatial soliton is represented by the interaction force between two parallel propagating soliton due to the non-linear effects of the material. This force is an exponential function of the relative distance between solitons and a sinusoidal function of their relative phase [8,9].

Unfortunately, nothing can be said about the coefficients necessary to derive this force in an analytical way.

Nevertheless an empirical method has been recently proposed [9] to derive a proper equation that could quantify the interaction force necessary to design all-optical devices.

Thanks to the numerical solution of this empirical formula it has been possible to propose different all-optical devices [5,9,10] whose correct behavior has been confirmed by numerical simulations. In the present paper this empirical formula is used and a proper analytical solution has been found.

The proposed device can be used in cryptographic application since it represents a stream cipher that can be exploited either in ciphering or deciphering phase. The ciphered message is obtained by sending the message to be ciphered as a string of bits to the input to the device, together with the key string. The same key string can be used, on the same device in the receiving phase, together with the ciphered string, to obtain the original message (plaintext). Soliton beams represent the information medium and the processing activities (EXOR) is obtained thanks to the properties of soliton propagation and interaction.

The great advantage of the proposed device is represented by the operative velocity that is limited, from the theoretical point of view, only by the response time of the used material.

2. Structure of the Device

The device is composed by two inputs and one output, since it has to execute a logical EXOR operation. The complete scheme is shown in **Figure 1**.

It is composed by two input waveguides, a main waveguide, two drain waveguides and two parabolic waveguides. The waveguides are characterized by different geometries and different transversal refractive index profiles: main waveguide is chosen to have a constant transversal refractive index profile whereas input waveguides and parabolic waveguides are characterized by a triangular transversal refractive index profile.

The two inputs are labeled with letters A and B. If the device must be integrated, two proper laser diodes can be used to generate input pulses whose intensity is capable of generating spatial solitons in the material.

Input A is used to send the bit related to the message to be ciphered whereas input B is used to send the bit related to the cryptographic key. For simplicity, the two input pulses are supposed to be characterized by the same phase, without any loss of generality.

In the following it is illustrated how the proposed device performs the EXOR logical operation.

Since we deal with a passive device, if the two inputs are equal to a logical zero (no input pulses are present), the output is equal to zero.

If input A is equal to a logical 1 (a pulse is present) and input B is equal to a logical 0 (no pulse is present), the pulse A generates a soliton that propagates in the input waveguide 1 following an oscillating path due to inclination and to the triangular transversal refractive index profile of waveguide 1 [2]. It enters the main waveguide with a certain transversal velocity (inclination) where it follows a linear trajectory, due to the absence of transversal refractive index profile, reaching the input of parabolic waveguide 2. Then it propagates inside this last waveguide, reaching the output of the device. The properties of input waveguides and parabolic waveguides are illustrated in the following. At the moment, it is sufficient to know that, if the geometry and the transversal refractive index profile are correctly designed, the soliton beam is capable of reaching the output, performing an EXOR operation.

If input A is equal to a logical 0 (no pulse is present) and input B is equal to a logical 1 (a pulse is present), pulse B generates a soliton that propagates in the input waveguide 2 following an oscillating path due to inclination and to the triangular transversal refractive index profile of waveguide 2. The situation is similar to the previ-

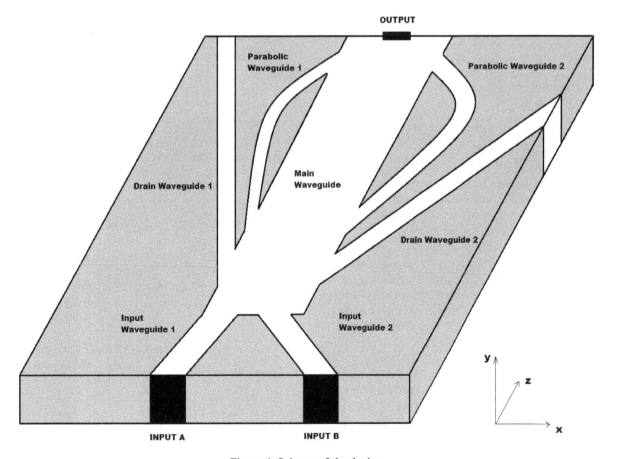

Figure 1. Scheme of the device.

ous one with the difference that the dissimilar inclination of waveguide 2, with respect to waveguide 1, induces a different phase variation on soliton B, with respect to soliton A, when it enters the main waveguide, This phase variations is properly controlled in the design phase, thanks to the different inclination of the input waveguides, to allow a controlled interaction when two soliton beams are present, at the same time, in the main waveguide. This controlled interaction is illustrated in the following and allows to reaching the desired goal. After propagation in input waveguide 2, the soliton enters the main waveguide with a certain transversal velocity (inclination) where it follows a linear trajectory, due to the absence of transversal refractive index profile, reaching the input of parabolic waveguide 1 where it propagates reaching, at the end of propagation, the output of the device.

The last situation verifies when both inputs are equal to a logical 1. In this case solitons A and B propagates inside the related input waveguides, reaching the main waveguide with a converging trajectory. When they start to approach, they can experience an interaction force, and therefore acceleration, that can be attractive or repulsive. It is well known [8,9] that they attract if their relative phase is variable between 0 and $\pi/2$ and they repulse if their relative phase is variable between $3\pi/2$ and 2π. If the geometry of input waveguides is designed on purpose, the two solitons experience a proper repulsive behavior that pushes them towards the inputs of lateral drain waveguides, where they are expelled by the device, without reaching the output. In this case a logical 0 in present at the output.

In this way it has been shown, from the qualitative point of view, the EXOR performance of the proposed device.

It has been said that soliton A could reach the output with a different relative phase with respect to soliton B. Since a cryptographic device is considered, this different phase between the two solitons could be detected by an eavesdropper in order to acquire significant information about the ciphering device, breaking its security. For this reason properly designed parabolic waveguides are used. These waveguides are characterized by different lengths so that solitons that propagate inside them are characterized by the same phase when they reach their end, being undistinguishable when they approach the output.

It is now necessary to describe the device from the quantitative point of view.

3. Study of the Interaction Force between Solitons

To correctly design the device, it is necessary to know exactly what happens when two parallel and close soliton beam propagate, influencing each other as in the main waveguide of the device. It has already been said that they can experience a transversal attractive or repulsive force as a function of their relative phase. Until now it was not possible to have an analytical expression of this force. It is only possible to know that it is a cosinusoidal function of the relative phase and an exponential function of the relative distance [8,9].

In the present work an empirical formula [9] derived from Gordon theory and from numerical simulations is used to derive an analytical expression of the interaction force between parallel solitons. The derived formula allows to calculate the transversal acceleration as a function of the relative phase and of the relative distance between two parallel solitons.

Let's consider two soliton beams that propagate along Z direction. It is well known [11] that the expression of a fundamental soliton in a Kerr material is given by:

$$E(X,Z) = \frac{1}{\beta a}\sqrt{\frac{n_0}{n_2}}\exp\left(\frac{iZ}{2\beta a_0^2}\right)\mathrm{sech}\left(\frac{X}{a_0}\right) \tag{1}$$

where n_0 is the linear refractive index, n_2 the nonlinear refractive index, β the wavenumber of the guided mode, X the transversal coordinate, Z the longitudinal coordinate and a_0 a parameter that is a function of the transversal dimension of the beam.

If we set $\beta X = x$, $\beta Z = z$, $A\sqrt{n_2/n_0} = Q$, $1/\beta a_0 = C$ and substitute in Equation (1) we obtain the normalized formula of the fundamental soliton, whose modulus is equal to:

$$Q(x) = C\,\mathrm{sech}(Cx) \tag{2}$$

In **Figure 2** the schematization of the considered situation of interaction between parallel solitons is shown.

Using this expression, the transversal acceleration between two parallel solitons, whose relative phase is equal to ϕ, is given by [9]:

$$\frac{d^2x(z)}{dz^2} = -\frac{C^2}{5}\exp\left(2x_{HHHW} - x(z)\right)\cos\phi \tag{3}$$

that is valid under the condition $x \geq 2x_{HHHW}$.

The parameter x_{HHHW} (half height half width) represents the distance from the center of the beam where the amplitude reduces to one half. It is possible to demonstrate that [9]:

$$x_{HHHW} = \frac{1}{C}\log\left(2+\sqrt{3}\right) \tag{4}$$

both x_{HHHW} and C are real positive.

Since a dynamic analysis is used, the second derivative of x with respect to z is considered as a transversal acceleration whereas the first derivative of x with respect to z is considered as a transversal velocity.

From this point of view, z is considered as a sort of

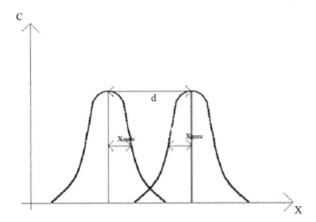

Figure 2. Schematization of the considered situation of interaction between two parallel solitons.

time variable.

Equation (3) has already been used to design all-optical device [9,10] even if from the numerical point of view.

In the present work, a proper analytical solution of Equation (3) is derived and the obtained solution is used to design part of the device whose correct behavior is demonstrated by the numerical simulations.

If we set $-c^2/5\cos(\phi) \equiv T$ and $2x_{HHHW} \equiv k$, Equation (3) can be written as:

$$\frac{d^2x}{dz^2} = T\exp\left(C(k-x)\right) \tag{5}$$

Equation (5) represents a proper form of second order differential equation where the variable is represented by x.

This equation can be transformed in a first order differential equation since it is of the form $x'' = f(x)$.

We can therefore write:

$$x'' = f(x) \rightarrow \frac{(x')^2}{2} - F(x) = c_1 \tag{6}$$

where $F(x)$ is a primitive function of $f(x)$ and c_1 a proper constant that depends of initial conditions.

In our situation $f(x) = T\exp(k-x)$ and therefore $F(x) = -T/C\exp\left[C(k-x)\right]$.

Substituting in Equation (6) and separating the variables we have:

$$\frac{dx}{\sqrt{c_1 - \frac{T}{C}e^{c(k-x)}}} = \sqrt{2}dz \tag{7}$$

that is an integrable expression whose solution is:

$$x(z) = 2x_{HHHW}$$
$$-\frac{1}{C}\ln\left[\frac{5c_1}{-2\cos\phi}\text{sech}^2\left(\frac{1}{2}C\sqrt{c_1}(z+c_2)\right)\right] \tag{8}$$

the integration constants c_1 and c_2 depend on the initial conditions, represented by the relative velocity and relative distance of the two solitons.

In particular c_1 and c_2 represents the solution of the following system:

$$x'(0) = \sqrt{c_1}\tanh\left(\frac{1}{2}C\sqrt{c_1}c_2\right) \tag{9}$$

$$x(0) = 2x_{HHHW} - \frac{1}{C}\ln\left[\frac{5c_1}{-2\cos\phi}\text{sech}^2\left(\frac{1}{2}C\sqrt{c_1}c_2\right)\right] \tag{10}$$

It is evident that c_1 must be real positive.

The argument of logarithm is positive since we are interested in the situation where $\cos(\phi) < 0$.

Let's analyze now Equation (8) to verify if it correctly represents the considered situation. Since we are interested at repulsive interaction $\pi/2 < \phi < 3\pi/2$, two different situations can verify:

1) If the initial transversal velocity is equal to zero $(x'(0)=0)$ and if the initial distance is quite short, the two solitons start to detach under the effect of the repulsive force. The more they detach and the more the transversal acceleration decreases, as demonstrated by the exponential term of Equation (3), until reaching a limit value equal to zero. If we set $x'(0)=0$ in Equation (9) we obtain $c_2 = 0$ and Equation (9) can be solved giving:

$$c_1 = 2\frac{T}{C}\exp\left(C(k-x_0)\right) \tag{11}$$

that is a real positive.

A graphical example is shown in **Figure 3** where coherent values for C, k, x_0 e ϕ, without taking care of their physical meaning, have been used. The behavior of the obtained curve is coherent with what one could expect.

2) If the initial velocity is negative (that is the two solitons are characterized by a convergent trajectory, as in the situation considered in our device), the relative distance decreases until the exponential term of Equation (8) becomes significant. In this situation the repulsive force

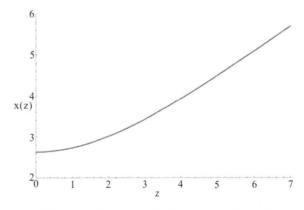

Figure 3. $x(z)$ vs z for $C = 1$, $\phi = \pi$, $x_0 = k$, $v_0 = 0$.

decreases the approaching velocity until reducing it to zero and inverting it until reaching a value that is opposite with respect to the initial value.

In this situation, it is necessary to impose that both velocity and initial position are different from zero: in this case the system represented by Equations (9) and (10) is not solvable in an analytical way. It is possible to demonstrate that the condition $x'(0) < 0$ implies $c_2 < 0$. This is evident from Equation (9), since both C and c_1 must be real positive.

A graphical example is shown in **Figure 4** where coherent values for C, k, x_0 e ϕ without taking care of their physical meaning have been used. The behavior of obtained curve is coherent with what one could expect.

The obtained analytical solution has been compared with the numerical result, confirming the correctness of the found theoretical solution found.

4. Design of the Device

4.1. Choice of the Material and Normalization

After illustrating the theory necessary to understand the interaction of solitons in the main waveguide, it is possible to start to design and dimension the device.

We first design the device in normalized units and successively in real units.

In the design all the physical restrictions are considered. In this way the real device is immediately derivable from the normalized device.

The used normalization has already been shown previously. It is very useful since it allows to transform path difference of solitons directly into phase difference between the two solitons.

Given a certain material and a certain source characterized by a given wavelength, the minimum value of intensity necessary to generate a fundamental soliton is [11]:

$$I_s^{(1)} = \frac{2n_0}{d_0^2 n_2 \beta^2} \tag{12}$$

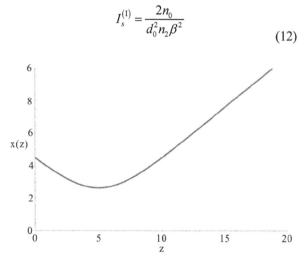

Figure 4. $x(z)$ vs z for $C = 1$, $\phi = \pi$, $x_0 = k$, $c_2 = -5$.

where d_0 is the spot size of the beam whereas all the other parameters have already been illustrated previously.

It is also well known that the minimum value of intensity $I_s^{(II)}$ necessary to generate a second order soliton is equal to twice $I_s^{(I)}$ [11].

It is also possible to express the intensity of the soliton as a function of the normalized amplitude C [2]:

$$I_s^{(1)} = \frac{1}{\log(2 + \sqrt{3})} \frac{n_0}{2n_2} C^2 \tag{13}$$

We choose, as material, a Schott Glass B270, whose optical parameters, at a wavelength $\lambda_0 = 620$ nm, are $n_0 = 1.53$ and $n_2 = 3.4 \times 10^{-20}$ m^2/W [12].

Further, we choose a spot size of laser beam equal to 10 μm.

Using Equation (12) it is possible to calculate the values $I_s^{(I)}$ e $I_s^{(II)}$.

Using Equation (13) it is possible to calculate the related values of $I_s^{(I)}$ e $I_s^{(II)}$ expressed in normalized amplitude that are $C^{(I)} = 0.017$ e $C^{(II)} = 0.034$: the normalized amplitude of the soliton beams used in the device must be variable between these two values to be sure to generate a fundamental soliton.

We chose, for our design, $C = 0.03$.

It is now possible, from Equation (4), to calculate the half height half maximum width, that is equal to:

$$x_{HHHW} = \frac{1}{C} \log(2 + \sqrt{3}) = 43.8986 \tag{14}$$

It is now necessary to define the maximum variation Δn_0 of the linear refractive index that characterizes the transversal index profile of input waveguides and parabolic waveguide. We choose, for our purpose, $\Delta n_0 = 10^{-2}$.

For practical realization reasons, it is necessary both the input waveguides and parabolic waveguides to be characterized by the same value of Δn_0.

4.2. Design of Input Waveguides

The two inputs waveguides are directly interfaced with input laser sources. They represent two oblique waveguides, whose width is equal to $2b$, characterized by different longitudinal inclinations and by a transversal triangular refractive index profile, as shown in **Figure 5**.

The input waveguides must be designed such that the solitons inside them exit:

1) with a relative phase equal to π;

2) equal and opposite transversal velocities directed towards the center of the main waveguide where they interact in a controlled way, repelling each other.

The propagation of a soliton beam in such waveguide has already been studied [2]. It is possible to demonstrate that swing effect takes place inside the waveguide, so that the soliton propagates following an oscillating path,

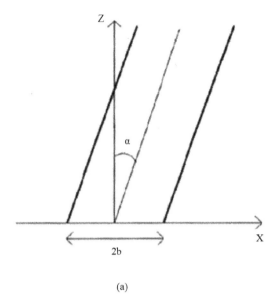

(a)

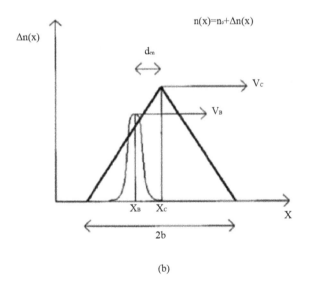

(b)

Figure 5. Upper view of inclined input waveguides (a) and transversal view of the same waveguide together with a soliton beam, where position and transversal velocity of both waveguide and soliton are shown (b).

if a proper lock-in condition is respected:

$$C > \frac{v_G}{2\sqrt{\Delta n_0}}$$

(15)

where v_G represents the tangent of the inclination angle α between the longitudinal axes and waveguide axes, as shown in **Figure 5**.

Since C has already been defined, it imposes a restriction on v_G. It is also necessary to remember that all the considered theory is valid under paraxial approximation

that imposes a certain limit ($8°$ - $10°$) to the longitudinal propagation inclination of solitons.

Let x_G be the position of the center of the waveguide. The local inclination of the waveguide with respect to z axes can be regarded as the relative transversal velocity between the waveguide itself and the soliton that propagates inside it:

$$v_G = \frac{dx_G(z)}{dz} = \tan(\alpha)$$

(16)

It has been demonstrated that a soliton that propagates in a waveguide characterized by a triangular refractive index profile experience a transversal acceleration equal to [5,12]:

$$a_T = \frac{2\Delta n_0}{b}C^2$$

(17)

that remains constant until the soliton beam moves inside one of the lateral zone of the waveguide.

At the beginning of propagation the soliton beam is positioned in the centre of the waveguide. Since the waveguide seems to move transversally with respect to the soliton, the soliton itself enters the constant acceleration zone of the waveguide where its velocity grows linearly with z. If the lock-in condition is respected, the soliton is capable of reaching the center of the waveguide, crossing it and reaching the other zone of the waveguide where the negative acceleration decreases its transversal velocity until stopping it, reversing again its trajectory. It is clear that, if the lock-in condition is respected, the soliton propagates inside the waveguide following an oscillating path.

Let's design now the waveguides.

If $C = 0.003$ then $x_{HHHM} = 43.8986$. Equation (17) is valid only if $b \gg x_{HHHM}$. To respect this last condition we choose $b = 200$. Since have chosen $\Delta n_0 = 10^{-2}$, from Equation (15) we can calculate the lock-in condition:

$$v_G < 2C\sqrt{\Delta n_0} = 0.006$$

(18)

If v_{G1} e v_{G2} are, respectively, the inclination of the first and of the second waveguide with respect to z direction, we choose $v_{G1} = 0.0025$ e $v_{G2} = 0.005$. This choice satisfies the paraxial approximation. As it is possible to see, we have chosen an inclination of the second waveguide equal to twice the inclination of the first waveguide: this greatly simplifies the design of the device, as it is shown in the following.

We want now to describe the motion of the soliton inside waveguide 1, where $v_{G1} = 0.0025$.

First of all, we want to calculate the longitudinal distance Z_{01} that the soliton must propagate before reaching the center of the waveguide. To calculate Z_{01} we have to impose that $x_B(z) = x_G(z)$, that is:

$$v_{G1}Z_{01} = \frac{1}{2}a_T Z_{01}^2 \rightarrow Z_{01} = \frac{2v_{G1}}{a_T} = 55555.\bar{5}$$

$$(19)$$

To reach a longitudinal distance Z_{01} the soliton has propagated along a parabolic path whose it is necessary to calculate the distance. Considering the first derivative of $x_B(z)$ with respect to z, we have:

$$x_B = \frac{1}{2}a_T z^2 \rightarrow dx = a_T z dz$$

$$(20)$$

and the elementary distance along the parabolic path with respect to x is equal to:

$$dl = \sqrt{dx^2 + dz^2} = dz\sqrt{1 + a_T^2 z^2}$$

$$(21)$$

Integrating Equation (21) we have:

$$L_{01} = \int_{L_{01}} dl = \int_0^{Z_{01}} \sqrt{1 + a_T^2 z^2}\,dz = 55555.7869$$

$$(22)$$

It is clear that it is necessary to design together the input waveguides such that the path difference (and therefore the phase difference) of the two solitons that propagate inside them can reach the desired value which induces a repulsive action when the two solitons reach the center of the main waveguide.

In a similar way, we have for input waveguide 2:

$$v_{G2}Z_{02} = \frac{1}{2}a_T Z_{02}^2 \rightarrow Z_{02} = \frac{2v_{G2}}{a_T} = 111111.\bar{1}$$

$$(23)$$

$$L_{02} = \int_{L_{01}} dl = \int_0^{Z_{02}} \sqrt{1 + a_T^2 z^2}\,dz = 111112.9628$$

$$(24)$$

Let $Z_0 = Z_{02} = 2Z_{01}$. After this longitudinal distance the soliton inside input waveguide 1 has made a complete oscillation, reaching again the center of the waveguide while the soliton inside waveguide 2 has made half oscillation.

In **Figure 6** the trajectory followed by a soliton in an oblique waveguide characterized by a triangular transversal refractive index profile is shown.

Due to the difference path followed, a relative phase difference Δ_0 has generated. This phase difference can be calculated by means of the difference of path, since the wavenumber β_0 has been assumed to be equal to one in the normalization operation.

We therefore have:

$$\Delta_0 = L_{02} - 2L_{01} = 1.388 \text{ rad}$$

$$(25)$$

Since a repulsive interaction in the center of the main waveguide is desired, the relative phase difference must be variable between $\pi/2$ e $3/2\pi$. It is therefore necessary a longitudinal length of the two waveguides almost equal to twice Z_0. Further, it is necessary the two solitons enter the main waveguide with opposite transversal velocities directed towards the center of the main waveguide. The choice made about the inclination of the two input

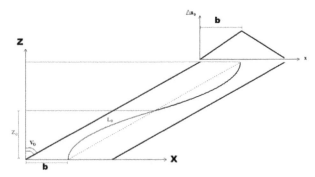

Figure 6. Trajectory followed by a soliton in an oblique waveguide characterized by a triangular transversal refractive index profile.

waveguides ($v_{G2} = 2v_{G1}$) allows to reach this goal if $Z_{TOT} = 5Z_{01} = 277777.7$.

The trajectories followed by the solitons inside input waveguides are shown in **Figure 7**.

The obtained phase difference is equal to $\Delta = 2\Delta_0 = 2.777$ rad.

When the two solitons reach $z = Z_{TOT}$ they are characterized by the same opposite velocity equal, in modulus, to $v_{G2} = 2v_{G1} = 0.005$. This behavior is due to the choice of proper inclination (one twice the other) of the two input waveguides.

At the entrance of the main waveguide, soliton 1 is positioned in the center of waveguide whereas soliton 2 is shifted of a distance d' with respect to the axes of the waveguide.

Due to the periodicity of motion, it is possible to calculate d' as the transversal distance between the center of the waveguide and the beam at $z = Z_{01}$ since it is the same distance at $z = 5Z_{01}$:

$$d' = |x_G(Z_{01}) - x_B(Z_{01})|$$
$$= \left| v_{G2}Z_{01} - \frac{1}{2}a_T Z_{01}^2 \right| = 138.889$$

$$(26)$$

4.3. Design of the Main Waveguide

The design of the main waveguide is aimed at finding its width X_G and the distances Z_D and Z_P where to position, respectively, the drain waveguides and the parabolic waveguides.

The width X_G must be obviously greater than the width of the two input waveguides. For this reason, it has been chosen $X_G = 1138.889$ that guarantees a distance between the outputs of the two input waveguides (whose width is equal to 400 normalized units) equal to 200 normalized units plus a distance $d' = 138.889$ necessary to make symmetric the path of the two solitons. This choice allows to position the left and the right drain and parabolic waveguides at the same longitudinal distance Z_D e Z_P respectively.

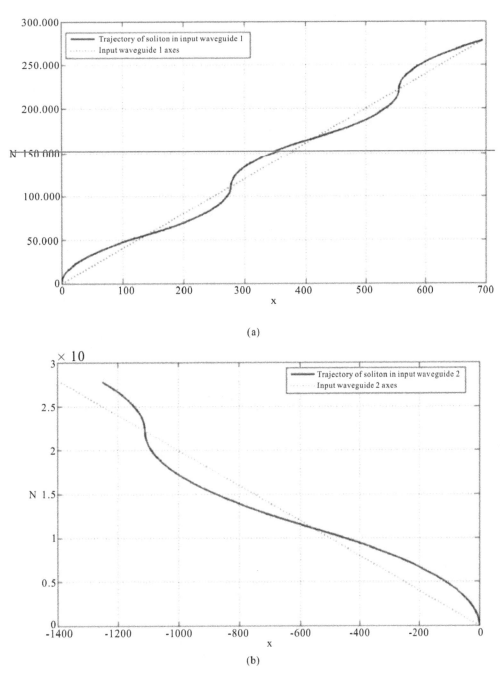

Figure 7. (a) Trajectory of soliton A inside *input waveguide* 1. (b) Trajectory of soliton B inside *input waveguide* 2.

It is now possible to calculate Z_P. Both the solitons enter the main waveguide with an inclination with respect to the longitudinal distance equal to 0.005 and they must propagate along a distance equal to 938.889. Therefore we have:

$$Z_P = \frac{938.889}{0.005} = 187777.78 \qquad (27)$$

To calculate Z_D it is necessary to study, from the analytical point of view, Equation (3) related to the interaction force between two different solitons. We have de-

monstrated that this equation is solvable and we found the transversal distance x as a function of the longitudinal coordinate z. Since we have already designed the two input waveguides, we know the initial distance x_0 and the relative velocity v_0 of the two solitons entering the main waveguide.

This allows to calculating the two constant c_1 e c_2 of Equation (8), solving the system composed by Equations (9) and (10).

Substituting the values $x_0 = 738.889$ and $v_0 = -0.01$ we have:

$$c_1 = 0.0001000000368712 \qquad (28)$$

$$c_2 = -53998.4715691338 \qquad (29)$$

The behavior of $x_G(z)$ is shown in **Figure 8**.

The obtained behavior is coherent with what one could expect. It is possible to see that the relative distance between the two solitons decreases linearly with z until the repulsive force becomes more intense due to the reduced relative distance. At this point they invert their motion and they start to detach with a velocity equal and opposite with respect to the initial velocity. Using Equation (3) we can solve the following (30) with respect to Z_D:

$$x(Z_D) = 1138.889 \qquad (30)$$

Thus we have the propagation distance Z_D necessary to reach the side of mainwaveguide where it is possible to position the parabolic waveguides:

$$Z_D = 147996.936 \qquad (31)$$

For brevity, further details about drain waveguides are not given since they design is similar to the design of input waveguides. Their purpose is to take the single solitons away from the device, to avoid them to reach the output of the device, realizing the desired EXOR logical operation.

4.4. Design of Parabolic Waveguides

It is now necessary to design the parabolic waveguides.

It has been shown that the input waveguides generate a relative phase difference between solitons equal to $\Delta = 2.777$ rad. This phase difference is necessary to generate a repulsive reciprocal action when both solitons propagate inside the main waveguide, pushing them towards the drain waveguide and generating a logical 0 when both inputs are equal to 1.

This phase difference is very critical when only single solitons propagate inside the main waveguide since it represents information about the input that generates

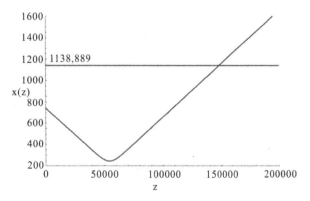

Figure 8. Behavior of relative distance between the two solitons in the main waveguide as a function of z.

the output which could be used by an eavesdropper to attack the device and discover the original enciphered message.

It is therefore necessary to use two different waveguides that compensate the relative phase difference induced by the two input waveguides to let the single solitons coming from the inputs to reach the output of the device with the same phase, becoming indistinguishable from the phase point of view.

To reach this scope, two parabolic waveguides are used that must be correctly designed.

A parabolic waveguide has been chosen since it represents the simpler curve that takes a soliton from an inclination that respects the paraxial approximation to an inclination with respect to the longitudinal axes equal to zero and vice versa. Further, parabolic trajectory is the one followed by a soliton that propagates inside a triangular refractive index profile waveguide.

The longitudinal parabolic waveguide has already been studied [13]. In the following we report only the significant parameters necessary to design the parabolic waveguide of the considered device.

In a longitudinal parabolic waveguide the position $x_G(z)$ of the central part of the waveguide as a function of z coordinates is:

$$x_G(z) = \frac{z^2}{a} - \frac{2\sqrt{d}}{a}z \qquad (32)$$

where a is a real constant responsible for the curvature of the waveguide and d a real constant responsible for the position of the curve.

In a similar way to the oblique waveguide, a lock-in condition exists. This lock-in value is [13]:

$$C_D = \frac{1}{a}\left(\frac{d-b}{\Delta n_0}\right)^{\frac{1}{2}} \qquad (33)$$

where b represents the half width of the triangular transversal refractive index profile. It is possible to demonstrate that the length of the curve expressed by Equation (32) (that is half of the total length of the whole waveguide) is equal to:

$$\frac{L_G}{2} = \frac{d}{2}\sqrt{\frac{4d+a^2}{d}}$$
$$+ \frac{a^2}{8}\log\left(8d + a^2 + 4d\sqrt{\frac{4d+a^2}{d}}\right) \qquad (34)$$
$$- \frac{a^2}{4}\log a$$

The paraxial condition must be respected also for this curve. Since the curvature reaches its maximum value at the begin, it is sufficient to check the respect of the paraxial condition only in this last point:

$$|v_G(0)| = \frac{2\sqrt{d}}{a} \le \tanh 8° = 0.14 \quad (35)$$

It is also well known that in this kind of waveguide the half of its longitudinal length can be calculated from its parameters a and d:

$$a\sqrt{d} = \frac{\hat{Z}}{2} \quad (36)$$

It is now possible to design both the parabolic waveguides.

Let L_1 and L_2 be the length of parabolic waveguides 1 and 2 respectively. If Δ is the relative phase difference (and therefore the path difference since we are working with normalized units), if a compensation of the phase difference between the two solitons is desired (relative phase difference equal to zero), it is necessary that:

$$L_2 = L_1 + \Delta \quad (37)$$

In our design process we decide to design the parabolic waveguide 1 in an independent way with respect to the parabolic waveguide 2, choosing realistic values of the parameters and respecting Equation (33) and Equation (35). After this choice it is possible to determine the length L_1. Once determined L_1 we impose the same value $\hat{Z}$ for waveguide 2 and we express the parameters a_2 and d_2 as a function of d_1 by means of a proper parameter k:

$$d_2 = kd_1 \quad (38)$$

$$a_2 = \frac{\hat{Z}/2}{\sqrt{kd_1}} \quad (39)$$

At this point it is possible to calculate L_2 as a function of k and to solve the following equation:

$$L_2(k) = L_1 + \Delta \quad (40)$$

with respect to k. Once found the value k that satisfies Equation (40), it is possible to calculate the parameters a_2 and d_2 from Equations (38) and (39).

Finally it is necessary to verify that lock-in condition and paraxial approximation are respected in the calculated waveguide 2.

The used process is heuristic and different attempts can be necessary before finding the optimal solution, since the respect of the paraxial condition can be verified only at the end of the calculation. It is anyway evident that if $\hat{Z}$ increases (and therefore the parameters a of the waveguides increase), Equation (35) can be satisfied in an easier way.

Let's apply the proposed method to the design of the longitudinal parabolic waveguides.

A proper value is $\hat{Z} = 700000$ that allows to write:

$$a_1\sqrt{d_1} = a_2\sqrt{d_2} = 350000 \quad (41)$$

The width of the waveguides is equal to $2b^*$, being b^* equal to one half the width of the triangular transversal refractive index profile. In this case it has been chosen $b^* = 150$, that is a different value with respect to the relative value of input waveguides and drain waveguides. Since it must be $2b^* < d_1$, we choose $d_1 = 500$, obtaining, from Equation (36), $a_1 = 15652.47584$.

The length of the first parabolic waveguide can be calculated from Equation (34) obtaining $L_1 = 700000.952$. Given this value, using Equations (37)-(39) and the condition $\Delta = 2.77$, it is possible to calculate the parameters of the second parabolic waveguide that are:

$$a_2 = 11126.54; d_2 = 989.5; L_2 = 700003.711 \quad (42)$$

Once calculated all the parameters, it is necessary to verify that the two parabolic waveguides respect the condition expressed by Equation (33) and Equation (35). Substituting the numerical values obtained for the two waveguides, with $C = 0.03$, $\Delta n_0 = 0.01$ and $b^* = 150$, we have:

$$\frac{1}{a_1}\left(\frac{d_1 - b'}{\Delta n_0}\right)^{\frac{1}{2}} = 0.012 < 0.03 \quad (43)$$

$$\frac{1}{a_2}\left(\frac{d_2 - b'}{\Delta n_0}\right)^{\frac{1}{2}} = 0.026 < 0.03 \quad (44)$$

which demonstrate that the lock-in condition is satisfied. We also have:

$$\frac{\sqrt{d_1}}{a_1} = 0.014 < 0.07 \quad (45)$$

$$\frac{\sqrt{d_2}}{a_2} = 0.028 < 0.07 \quad (46)$$

which demonstrates that the paraxial approximation is satisfied.

To complete the design of the device it is necessary to calculate the distance from the end of the parabolic waveguides where it is necessary to position the output of the device itself. The two solitons, due to the feature of the parabolic waveguides, exit the waveguides themselves with the same entrance inclination equal to $v = 0.005$. Since they have to cross a transversal distance equal to $X_G/2$ to reach the center of the main waveguide, the related longitudinal distance where to position the output of the device is equal to:

$$Z_{OUT} = \frac{X_G/2}{v} = 113888.889 \quad (47)$$

5. Numerical Simulations

To verify the correctness of the designed device, the different operative conditions have been simulated using a FD-BPM algorithm and the results are compared with what one could expect from the developed theory.

In **Figure 9** the numerical simulation when A = 1 and B = 0 is shown. It is possible to see that the soliton A, at the beginning remains confined into the input waveguide 1, where it propagates oscillating according to the theory. Once reached the exit of the input waveguide, the soliton enters the main waveguide. It propagates through it reaching the entrance of the parabolic waveguide where it propagates, changing its phase, until reaching again the main waveguide where it propagates reaching the output. The soliton experiences some slight refractive index profile variations when it leaves one waveguide and enter the next one, as it is possible to see in the numerical simulation. This refractive index variation has not been considered in the theory, for brevity, but they do not influence in a significant way the functionality of the device that behaves according to the theory.

In **Figure 10** the numerical simulation when A = 0 and B = 1 is shown. Also in this situation the numerical simulation confirms the correctness of the design theory.

In this case both solitons are present. It is possible to see that they interact in a repulsive way when they meet at the center of the main waveguide, pushing each other towards the drain waveguides. In this situation the output of the device is equal to a logical 0 since the two solitons are not capable of reaching the output itself. Also this numerical simulation confirms what one could expect

from the developed theory.

It has therefore been shown that all the numerical simulations confirm the developed theory. The slight variation obtained with respect to the theory is due to other effects, such as the interface refractive index variation between waveguides, and that have not been considered in this paper for brevity.

The last simulation (A = 1, B = 1) is shown in **Figure 11**.

Numerical simulations were performed in normalized units.

6. Practical Considerations

To design the device from a physical point of view it is sufficient remember the normalization: $\beta X = x$, $\beta Z = z$. Inverting them properly and applying them to the values obtained in the normalized design phase, it is possible to have a real device.

Using the physical parameters related to the considered material (Schott Glass B270), it is possible, by means of Equation (13), to calculate the intensity of the laser beam necessary to induce a soliton in the device:

$$I_s^{(1)} = \frac{1}{\log\left(2+\sqrt{3}\right)}\frac{n_0}{2n_2}C^2 = 1.167565 \times 10^{16}\frac{W}{m^2}$$
(48)

This value ensures the generation of a fundamental soliton that follows the trajectories imposed by the design phase since all the effects depended on the normalized amplitude C and therefore on its real intensity expressed by Equation (48).

We want now to do some considerations about the op-

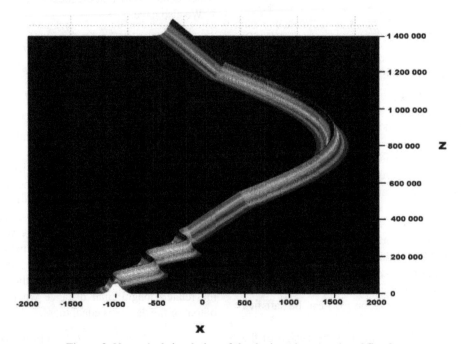

Figure 9. Numerical simulation of the device when A = 1 and B = 0.

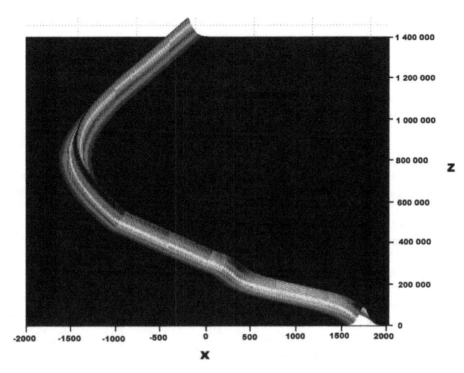

Figure 10. Numerical simulation of the device when A = 0 and B = 1.

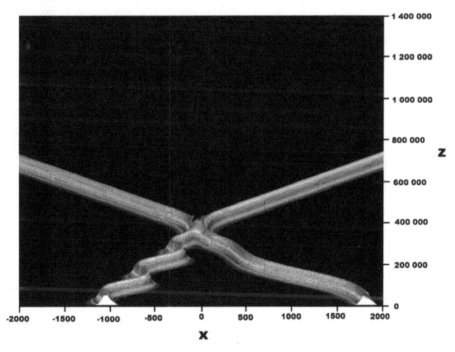

Figure 11. Numerical simulation of the device when A = 1 and B = 1.

erative velocity of the device. The main parameter that characterizes the computing time of the device is represented by the response time of third order nonlinearities of the used material. The origin of these kinds of nonlinearities, at the atomic level, is not quite clear [14]. In borosilicate glass, such as the considered Schott B270, the response time of Kerr effect is lesser than 10 ps [15].

This extremely low value shows that the temporal performances of the considered device are mainly limited by the repetition rate of the laser source. Due to the structure of the device, it is possible to operate on train of solitons, provided that their temporal distance is greater than the nonlinear response time of the material. Further consideration about the temporal behavior of the device are out of the scope of the paper.

7. Conclusions

An all-optical EXOR for cryptographic application has been studied. Its working principle is based on the propagation and interaction properties of spatial soliton beams.

The proposed device is composed by different kind of waveguides characterized by particular transversal refractive index profiles. The property of these waveguides was already known and they have been applied to our specific situation.

The novelty is represented by the study of interaction force between parallel propagating solitons where an analytical solution was found. This solution was applied to the interaction phase between two solitons in the main waveguide, allowing to correctly positioning the drain waveguides necessary to avoid the solitons to reaching the output of the device when both input are logical 1.

The proposed device can be used both in the ciphering and in dechipering phase. The computing time is limited, from the theoretical point of view, only by the response time of the third order nonlinearities of the material that, in our case is lesser that 10 ps.

The problem of the different relative phase of the two solitons that reach the output has been analyzed and solved, ensuring the two different solitons to reach the output with the same relative phase, becoming undistinguishable to an eventual eavesdropper and guaranteeing a high level of security of the device.

REFERENCES

[1]   R. Y. Ciao, E. Garmire and C. H. Townes, "Self-Trapping of Optical Beams," *Physical Review Letters*, Vol. 13, No. 15, 1964, pp. 479-482.

[2]   F. Garzia, C. Sibilia and M. Bertolotti, "High Pass Intensity Controlled Soliton Filter," *Optics Communications*, Vol. 152, No. 1-3, 1998, pp. 153-160.

[3]   C. S. Garzia and M. Bertolotti, "All-Optical Arithmetic Operations by Means of Spatial Soliton Interactions Properties," *Institute of Physics Conference Series on Optical Computing*, No. 139, Part IV, 1995, pp. 649-652.

[4]   Q. Wang, P. K. A. Wai, C. J. Chen and C. R. Menyuk, "Numerical Modeling of Soliton-Dragging Logic Gates," *Journal of the Optical Society of America B*, Vol. 10, No. 11, 1993, pp. 2006-2029.

[5]   F. Garzia, C. Sibilia and M. Bertolotti, "All-Optical Soliton Based Router," *Optics Communications*, Vol. 168, No. 1, 1999, pp. 277-285.

[6]   F. Garzia, C. Sibilia and M. Bertolotti, "Swing Effect on Spatial Soliton," *Optics Communications*, Vol. 139, No. 4, 1997, pp. 193-198.

[7]   F. Garzia , A. Di Vito, C. Sibilia and M. Bertolotti, "Swing Effect of Spatial Soliton in Second Order Material," *Optical and Quantum Electronics*, Vol. 31, No. 9-10, 1999, pp. 1085-1092.

[8]   J. P. Gordon, "Interaction Forces Among Solitons in Optical Fibers," *Optics Letters*, Vol. 8, No. 11, 1983, pp. 596-598.

[9]   F. Garzia, C. Sibilia and M. Bertolotti, "All-Optical Serial Switcher," *Optical and Quantum Electronics*, Vol. 32, No. 6-8, 2000, pp. 781-798.

[10]   F. Garzia and M. Bertolotti, "All Optical Security Coded Key," *Optical and Quantum Electronics*, Vol. 33, No. 4-5, 2001, pp. 527-540.

[11]   J. S. Aitchison, A. M. Weiner, Y. Silverberg, M. K. Oliver, J. L. Jackel , D. E. Leaird, E. M. Vogel and P. W. E. Smith, "Observation of Spatial Optical Solitons in a Nonlinear Glass Waveguide," *Optics Letters*, Vol. 15, No. 9, 1990, pp. 471-473.

[12]   H. W. Chen and T. Liu, "Nonlinear Wave and Soliton Propagation in Media with Arbitrary Inhomogeneities," *Physics of Fluids*, Vol. 21, No. 3, 1978, pp. 471-478.

[13]   F. Garzia, C. Sibilia and M. Bertolotti, "New Phase Modulation Technique Based on Spatial Soliton Switching," *IEEE Journal of Lightwave Technology*, Vol. 19, No. 7, 2001, pp. 1036-1050.

[14]   J. E. Aber, M. C. Newstein and B. A. Garetz, "Femtosecond Optical Kerr Effect Measurements in Silicate Glasses," *Journal of the Optical Society of America B*, Vol. 17, No. 1, 2000, pp. 210-127.

[15]   I. Kang, T. D. Krauss, F. W. Wise, B. G. Aitken and N. F. Borrelli, "Femtosecond Measurement of Enhanced Optical Nonlinearities of Sulfide Glasses and Heavy-Metal-Doped Oxide Glasses," *Journal of the Optical Society of America B*, Vol. 12, No. 11, 1995, pp. 2053-2059.

Permissions

The contributors of this book come from diverse backgrounds, making this book a truly international effort. This book will bring forth new frontiers with its revolutionizing research information and detailed analysis of the nascent developments around the world.

We would like to thank all the contributing authors for lending their expertise to make the book truly unique. They have played a crucial role in the development of this book. Without their invaluable contributions this book wouldn't have been possible. They have made vital efforts to compile up to date information on the varied aspects of this subject to make this book a valuable addition to the collection of many professionals and students.

This book was conceptualized with the vision of imparting up-to-date information and advanced data in this field. To ensure the same, a matchless editorial board was set up. Every individual on the board went through rigorous rounds of assessment to prove their worth. After which they invested a large part of their time researching and compiling the most relevant data for our readers. Conferences and sessions were held from time to time between the editorial board and the contributing authors to present the data in the most comprehensible form. The editorial team has worked tirelessly to provide valuable and valid information to help people across the globe.

Every chapter published in this book has been scrutinized by our experts. Their significance has been extensively debated. The topics covered herein carry significant findings which will fuel the growth of the discipline. They may even be implemented as practical applications or may be referred to as a beginning point for another development. Chapters in this book were first published by Scientific Research Publishing Inc.; hereby published with permission under the Creative Commons Attribution License or equivalent.

The editorial board has been involved in producing this book since its inception. They have spent rigorous hours researching and exploring the diverse topics which have resulted in the successful publishing of this book. They have passed on their knowledge of decades through this book. To expedite this challenging task, the publisher supported the team at every step. A small team of assistant editors was also appointed to further simplify the editing procedure and attain best results for the readers.

Our editorial team has been hand-picked from every corner of the world. Their multi-ethnicity adds dynamic inputs to the discussions which result in innovative outcomes. These outcomes are then further discussed with the researchers and contributors who give their valuable feedback and opinion regarding the same. The feedback is then collaborated with the researches and they are edited in a comprehensive manner to aid the understanding of the subject.

Apart from the editorial board, the designing team has also invested a significant amount of their time in understanding the subject and creating the most relevant covers. They scrutinized every image to scout for the most suitable representation of the subject and create an appropriate cover for the book.

The publishing team has been involved in this book since its early stages. They were actively engaged in every process, be it collecting the data, connecting with the contributors or procuring relevant information. The team has been an ardent support to the editorial, designing and production team. Their endless efforts to recruit the best for this project, has resulted in the accomplishment of this book. They are a veteran in the field of academics and their pool of knowledge is as vast as their experience in printing. Their expertise and guidance has proved useful at every step. Their uncompromising quality standards have made this book an exceptional effort. Their encouragement from time to time has been an inspiration for everyone.

The publisher and the editorial board hope that this book will prove to be a valuable piece of knowledge for researchers, students, practitioners and scholars across the globe.

List of Contributors

Georg Disterer
Department of Business Administration and Computer Science, University of Applied Sciences and Arts, Hannover, Germany

Norziana Jamil
College of Information Technology, Universiti Tenaga Nasional, Kajang, Malaysia
Faculty of Computer Science and Information Technology, Universiti Putra Malaysia, Seri Kembangan, Malaysia

Ramlan Mahmod, Nur Izura Udzir and Zuriati Ahmad Zukarnain
Faculty of Computer Science and Information Technology, Universiti Putra Malaysia, Seri Kembangan, Malaysia

Muhammad Reza Z'aba
Cryptography Lab, MIMOS Berhad, Technology Park Malaysia, Bukit Jalil, Malaysia

Walid I. Khedr
Faculty of Computers and Informatics, Zagazig University, Zagazig, Egypt

Konstantinia Charitoudi and Andrew Blyth
Information Security Research Group, University of Glamorgan, Trefforest, UK

Amirhossein Ebrahimzadeh and Abolfazl Falahati
Digital Cryptography and Coding Laboratory (DCCS Lab), Department of Electrical Engineering, Iran University of Science and Technology, Tehran, Iran

Patricia Ghann, Changda Wang and Conghua Zhou
School of Computer Science and Telecommunication Engineering, Jiangsu University, Jiangsu, China

Raffaele Pinardi and Roberto Cusani
Department of Information, Electronics and Telecommunications Engineering Sapienza University of Rome, Rome, Italy

Fabio Garzia
Department of Information, Electronics and Telecommunications Engineering Sapienza University of Rome, Rome, Italy
Wessex Institute of Technology, Southampton, UK

Maria Chroni, Angelos Fylakis and Stavros D. Nikolopoulos
Department of Computer Science, University of Ioannina, Ioannina, Greece

Kuljeet Kaur and Geetha Ganesan
School of Computer Applications, Lovely Professional University, Phagwara, India

Jörg Uffen, Nico Kaemmerer and Michael H. Breitner
Information Systems Institute, Leibniz Universität, Hannover, Germany

Khalid Benlhachmi and Mohammed Benattou
Laboratory of Research in Computer Science and Telecommunications, Faculty of Science, Ibn Tofail University, Kenitra, Morocco

Ahmed Tallat, Hiroshi Yasuda and Kilho Shin
Applied Information Engineering, Tokyo Denki University, Tokyo, Japan

Abou-el-ela Abdou Hussien
Department of Computer Science, Faculty of Science and Humanities, Shaqra University, Shaqra, KSA

Nermin Hamza and Hesham A. Hefny
Department of Computer and Information Sciences, Institute of Statistical Studies and Research, Cairo University, Giza, Egypt

Siti Rahayu Selamat, Shahrin Sahib, Nor Hafeizah, Robiah Yusof and Mohd Faizal Abdollah
Faculty of Information and Communication Technology, Universiti Teknikal Malaysia Melaka, Melaka City, Malaysia

Meghna Chhabra and Brij Gupta
School of Computing Science & Engineering, Galgotias Universiy, Greater Noida, India

Ammar Almomani
Faculty of Computing and Information Technology, North Jeddah Branch, King Abdulaziz University, Jeddah, Saudi Arabia

Rita M. Barrios
Computer Information Systems, Cyber Security, University of Detroit Mercy Detroit, Detroit, USA

Shweta Tripathi, Brij Gupta and Anupama Mishra
School of Computing Science & Engineering, Galgotias Universiy, Greater Noida, India

Ammar Almomani
Faculty of Computing and Information Technology, North Jeddah Branch, King Abdulaziz University, Jeddah, Saudi Arabia

Suresh Veluru
School of Engineering and Mathematical Sciences, City University London, London, UK

Hieu Le Thanh
School of Computer Science and Technology, Huazhong University of Science and Technology, Wuhan, China
Hue University's College of Education, Hue, Vietnam

Abdul Kadar Muhammad Masum, Faruk Bhuiyan and Kazi Golam Azam
Department of Business Administration, International Islamic University, Chittagong, Bangladesh

Fabio Garzia
Department of Information, Electronics and Telecommunication Engineering, LA SAPIENZA, University of Rome, Rome, Italy
Wessex Institute of Technology, Ashurst Lodge, Ashurst, Southampton, England

Mario Marco Corbelli and Roberto Cusani
Department of Information, Electronics and Telecommunication Engineering, LA SAPIENZA, University of Rome, Rome, Italy

Printed in the USA
CPSIA information can be obtained
at www.ICGtesting.com
JSHW051439221024
72173JS00006B/1515

9 781632 403063